AMERICAN
MEN AND WOMEN

AMERICAN MEN AND WOMEN

Demographics of the Sexes

BY THE NEW STRATEGIST EDITORS

New Strategist Publications, Inc.
Ithaca, New York

01-634

New Strategist Publications, Inc.
P.O. Box 242, Ithaca, New York 14851
800-848-0842
www.newstrategist.com

ISBN 1-885070-29-2

Printed in the United States of America

Table of Contents

List of Tables

Chapter 2. Education

Chapter 3. Health

Chapter 4. Income

Chapter 5. Labor Force

Chapter 6. Living Arrangements

Chapter 7. Population

Chapter 8. Spending

Chapter 9. Wealth

List of Charts

Chapter 5. Labor Force

Chapter 6. Living Arrangements

Chapter 7. Population

Chapter 8. Spending

Chapter 9. Wealth

Introduction

The lives of men and women have changed during the past few decades. As the manufacturing economy of the mid-twentieth century gave way to one of services and high-tech, both men and women had the opportunity to expand their roles in society. Men added the role of nurturer to that of breadwinner, while women added the role of breadwinner to that of nurturer. These changes have been nothing short of revolutionary, affecting every institution in our society—from the family to the workplace, from politics to the consumer marketplace.

The sex role revolution is now nearing completion and the egalitarian model has become the norm. The baby-boom generation was the first to welcome egalitarian sex roles. Today, the oldest boomers are in their mid-fifties. Their children, raised with the egalitarian model, have accepted men's and women's expanded roles without hesitation. Today, the egalitarian model is deeply entrenched among Americans under age 55. As boomers age into their sixties, the attitudes and behavior of the older population will be equally transformed.

The new attitudes and lifestyles of men and women have reshaped the American marketplace. For many businesses, no longer is there a distinct men's or women's market. The grocery store is now the domain of both sexes, as is the auto repair shop. Both men and women are far more sophisticated, demanding, and pressed for time than their mothers and fathers were. The many businesses struggling to boost their bottom line in today's competitive economy must leave behind their traditional notions about the sexes—which are no more than a quaint relic from the past—and appeal to the new consumer, the fusion of male and female.

American Men and Women: Demographics of the Sexes describes these powerful new consumers, their lifestyles, how much they earn, and what they think. It examines the lives of men and women in rich detail, from the proportion of the self-employed to the number of Americans sharing their home with grown children, from the earnings of those with professional degrees to what men and women think about egalitarian sex roles. It also looks into the future, with projections of key data such as males and females by race and age, educational degrees earned, and labor force participation.

As we publish *American Men and Women,* dramatic technological change has reshaped the demographic reference industry. The government's detailed demographic data, once widely available in printed reports, is now accessible only to Internet users or in unpublished tables obtained by calling the appropriate government agency with a specific request. The government's web sites, which house enormous spreadsheets of data, are of great value to researchers with the time and skills to first download and then extract the needed nuggets of information. The shift from printed reports to web sites—while convenient for number-crunchers—has made demographic analysis a bigger chore. For many, it is more time-consuming than ever to get no-nonsense answers to questions about the demographic characteristics of Americans.

American Men and Women has the answers. It has the numbers and the stories behind them. Thumbing through its pages, you can gain more insight into the marketplace than you could by spending an afternoon surfing databases on the Internet. By having it on your bookshelf, you can get answers to your questions faster than you could with a high-speed Internet connection.

How to Use This Book

We designed *American Men and Women* for easy use. It consists of nine chapters, organized alphabetically: Attitudes and Behavior, Education, Health, Income, Labor Force, Living Arrangements, Population, Spending, and Wealth.

Most of the tables in the book are based on data collected and published by the federal government, in particular the Census Bureau, the Bureau of Labor Statistics, the National Center for Education Statistics, and the National Center for Health Statistics. The federal government continues to be the best source of up-to-date, reliable information on the changing characteristics of Americans. If government data were not available about an important topic, we have included data from other surveys and studies. To explore the attitudes of men and women, New Strategist extracted data from the nationally representative General Social Survey of the University of Chicago's National Opinion Research Center. The GSS is a biennial survey NORC conducts through face-to-face interviews with an independently drawn, representative sample of 1,500 to 3,000 noninstitutionalized English-speaking people aged 18 or older who live in the United States. The GSS is the premier source of attitudinal data on Americans available today.

While the government produced most of the data in the book, we do not simply reprint government spreadsheets—as many reference books do. New Strategist individually compiled and created each of the tables in the book after our statisticians performed calculations to reveal the stories behind the statistics. A page of text accompanies most of the tables, analyzing the data and highlighting the trends. Researchers who want even more information than the tables and text provide can use the source listed at the bottom of each table to locate the original data.

The book contains a list of all tables to help readers locate the information they need. For a more detailed search, use the index in the back of the book. Also in the back of the book is the glossary, with terms commonly used in tables and text. A contact list also appears in the back of the book as a handy reference allowing researchers to contact government specialists and web sites.

American Men and Women will help you understand the wants and needs of today's consumers. Explore, reflect, imagine.

1

Attitudes and Behavior

❖ **Men are more likely than women to find life exciting.**

Among people aged 25 to 34, the majority of men but only 39 percent of women say life is exciting.

❖ **Most women are afraid to walk alone at night in their neighborhood.**

Only 26 percent of men are afraid to walk alone at night anywhere within a mile of their home compared with the 52 percent majority of women.

❖ **The majority of men and women believe in God without any doubts.**

Sixty-eight percent of women believe in God without a doubt, as do 57 percent of men.

❖ **Men are more likely to read a daily newspaper than women.**

Women are more likely than men to read novels and other fiction. Seventy-four percent of women have read fiction during the past 12 months.

❖ **Most say their standard of living is better than their parents' was.**

Men and women also believe their children's standard of living will be better than theirs is now.

❖ **Few men or women would stop working if rich.**

The majority of Americans say they enjoy work for its own sake, although few believe work is a person's most important activity.

❖ **Men are more likely to work in dangerous or physically demanding jobs.**

Nearly equal proportions of men and women find their work stressful, however.

Most Men and Women Are Pretty Happy

Nearly half the men say life is exciting.

Men and women have similar levels of happiness. The majorities of both sexes say they are "pretty happy," while about one-third are "very happy." The proportion of people who are "not too happy" is greatest among men under age 25 (18 percent) and among women aged 55 or older (15 percent).

Evidently, excitement does not necessarily create happiness. Men aged 18 to 24, who are most likely to be not too happy, are also the ones who find life most exciting—56 percent said it was so. At the same time, the happiest men—those aged 65 or older—are the ones least likely to find life exciting.

Men find life more exciting than women at almost every age. The gap is biggest in the younger age groups. Among people aged 25 to 34, the majority of men, but only 39 percent of women, say life is exciting. In the 45-to-54 age group, women are slightly more likely than men to find life exciting, 47 versus 45 percent.

❖ Family and work responsibilities account for the differing perspectives of men and women regarding life's excitement. Many younger women are at home raising children while younger men are out climbing the career ladder. By middle age, men have tired of the career climb while women are exploring new opportunities now that their children are grown.

Men are more likely than women to find life exciting

(percent of people who say life is exciting, by sex, 1998)

48%

42%

men   *women*

Are You Happy? 1998

"Taken all together, how would you say things are these days? Would you say that you are very happy, pretty happy, or not too happy?"

(percent of people aged 18 or older responding by sex and age, 1998)

	very happy	pretty happy	not too happy
Total men	**30.6%**	**58.4%**	**10.9%**
Aged 18 to 24	20.4	62.0	17.6
Aged 25 to 34	34.3	55.0	10.7
Aged 35 to 44	24.2	64.7	10.8
Aged 45 to 54	29.0	60.6	10.4
Aged 55 to 64	35.8	56.7	7.5
Aged 65 or older	40.2	49.2	10.6
Total women	**32.6**	**54.3**	**13.0**
Aged 18 to 24	24.6	61.9	13.4
Aged 25 to 34	31.4	56.5	12.1
Aged 35 to 44	35.7	52.0	12.0
Aged 45 to 54	31.2	56.9	11.9
Aged 55 to 64	35.3	49.5	15.2
Aged 65 or older	33.3	51.9	14.8

Note: Figures may not sum to 100 percent because "don't know" is not shown.
Source: 1998 General Social Survey, National Opinion Research Center, University of Chicago; calculations by New Strategist

Is Life Exciting? 1998

"In general, do you find life exciting, pretty routine, or dull?"

(percent of people aged 18 or older responding by sex and age, 1998)

	exciting	pretty routine	dull
Total men	**48.2%**	**47.0%**	**4.4%**
Aged 18 to 24	55.6	34.7	8.3
Aged 25 to 34	52.5	43.8	3.1
Aged 35 to 44	50.2	46.9	2.9
Aged 45 to 54	45.4	49.6	5.0
Aged 55 to 64	49.5	47.3	3.2
Aged 65 or older	36.8	55.6	6.8
Total women	**42.1**	**50.5**	**6.3**
Aged 18 to 24	46.8	45.7	7.4
Aged 25 to 34	39.3	54.5	5.4
Aged 35 to 44	48.4	45.9	4.9
Aged 45 to 54	46.6	49.4	2.9
Aged 55 to 64	38.2	53.4	6.1
Aged 65 or older	34.2	52.3	11.6

Note: Figures may not sum to 100 percent because "don't know" is not shown.
Source: 1998 General Social Survey, National Opinion Research Center, University of Chicago; calculations by New Strategist

While Many People Are Wary, the American Dream Lives On

Young men and women are the most cynical.

Most men and women regard themselves as trusting despite their lack of faith in the motives of others. Fifty-five percent of women and 51 percent of men think of themselves as a trusting person. But 38 percent of women and 48 percent of men do not trust other people. Young adults are especially likely to think others are looking out only for themselves. The majorities of men under age 35 and women under age 25 believe others are just looking out for themselves rather than trying to be helpful. Trust in others rises with age among both men and women.

Despite their lack of faith in the motives of others, most men and women believe they can improve their standard of living and achieve the good life. Their cynicism has not robbed them of their belief in the American Dream. More than 70 percent of men and women think a better standard of living is within their reach, with the figures highest among the youngest adults.

❖ The growing cynicism of Americans is an obstacle for politicians and businesses alike. Yet both can circumvent the cynicism by tapping into the deeply held belief in the American Dream.

How Trusting Are You? 1998

"Do you think of yourself as a trusting person?"

(percent of people aged 18 or older responding by sex and age, 1998)

	very trusting	somewhat trusting	somewhat, very distrusting
Total men	**51.2%**	**41.3%**	**6.9%**
Aged 18 to 24	39.3	50.0	10.7
Aged 25 to 34	54.6	36.2	8.5
Aged 35 to 44	48.3	47.0	4.7
Aged 45 to 54	53.5	39.4	5.1
Aged 55 to 64	48.3	44.8	6.9
Aged 65 or older	58.1	33.7	8.1
Total women	**54.6**	**37.3**	**8.2**
Aged 18 to 24	56.1	36.4	7.6
Aged 25 to 34	50.6	42.6	6.8
Aged 35 to 44	55.3	36.5	8.1
Aged 45 to 54	48.5	40.2	11.4
Aged 55 to 64	51.1	38.9	10.0
Aged 65 or older	65.3	28.6	6.1

Note: Figures may not sum to 100 percent because "don't know" is not shown.
Source: 1998 General Social Survey, National Opinion Research Center, University of Chicago; calculations by New Strategist

Helpfulness of Others, 1998

**"Would you say that most of the time people try to be helpful,
or that they are mostly just looking out for themselves?"**

(percent of people aged 18 or older responding by sex and age, 1998)

	trying to be helpful	looking out for themselves	depends
Total men	**42.5%**	**48.1%**	**9.1%**
Aged 18 to 24	36.6	57.7	4.2
Aged 25 to 34	33.0	57.7	9.3
Aged 35 to 44	41.5	49.3	9.2
Aged 45 to 54	47.1	45.8	6.5
Aged 55 to 64	42.1	47.4	10.5
Aged 65 or older	56.6	29.5	13.2
Total women	**52.0**	**38.3**	**9.3**
Aged 18 to 24	32.3	59.1	8.6
Aged 25 to 34	43.2	44.4	11.5
Aged 35 to 44	53.8	36.3	9.6
Aged 45 to 54	53.3	41.9	4.8
Aged 55 to 64	61.3	30.2	7.5
Aged 65 or older	62.9	25.7	11.4

Note: Figures may not sum to 100 percent because "don't know" is not shown.
Source: 1998 General Social Survey, National Opinion Research Center, University of Chicago; calculations by New Strategist

Can You Achieve the Good Life? 1998

"The way things are in America, people like me and my family have a good chance of improving our standard of living. Do you agree or disagree?"

(percent of people aged 18 or older responding by sex and age, 1998)

	agree	*neither*	*disagree*
Total men	**74.5%**	**10.2%**	**14.2%**
Aged 18 to 24	77.5	8.5	14.1
Aged 25 to 34	75.3	13.9	9.3
Aged 35 to 44	77.4	8.8	13.8
Aged 45 to 54	74.5	11.1	13.7
Aged 55 to 64	74.7	6.3	17.9
Aged 65 or older	66.7	10.1	20.2
Total women	**71.4**	**11.7**	**14.9**
Aged 18 to 24	76.3	12.9	8.6
Aged 25 to 34	75.2	11.1	11.5
Aged 35 to 44	74.6	12.1	12.5
Aged 45 to 54	67.1	10.8	21.0
Aged 55 to 64	70.1	11.2	18.7
Aged 65 or older	65.2	12.4	17.6

Note: Figures may not sum to 100 percent because "don't know" is not shown.
Source: 1998 General Social Survey, National Opinion Research Center, University of Chicago; calculations by New Strategist

Women Are More Fearful Than Men

The majority of women are afraid to walk alone at night.

Not surprisingly, men and women feel very differently about personal safety. While few men say they are afraid to walk alone at night in their neighborhood, most women are.

Among both men and women, the proportion of those who are afraid to walk alone at night is highest in the oldest age group. Among people aged 65 or older, 35 percent of men and 58 percent of women are afraid to walk alone at night in their neighborhood. The proportion of those who are afraid to walk alone at night is lowest among middle-aged men and women. In fact, among women aged 45 to 54, the 53 percent majority say they are not afraid to walk alone at night in their neighborhood.

Middle-aged men and women are least afraid of walking alone at night because they are in their peak-earning years and tend to live in neighborhoods where crime is uncommon. Younger adults, in contrast, are more likely to live in higher-crime areas. Feelings of vulnerability to crime increase with age.

❖ As the population ages, fear of crime will boost demand for security systems and other crime-fighting products and services.

Most women are afraid to walk alone at night

(percent of people who are afraid to walk alone at night within a mile of their home, by sex, 1998)

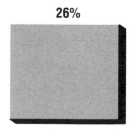

52%

26%

women

Are You Afraid to Walk Alone at Night? 1998

"Is there any area right around here—that is, within a mile— where you would be afraid to walk alone at night?"

(percent of people aged 18 or older responding by sex and age, 1998)

	yes	no
Total men	**25.6%**	**73.6%**
Aged 18 to 24	23.6	76.4
Aged 25 to 34	32.1	67.3
Aged 35 to 44	22.7	77.3
Aged 45 to 54	20.7	78.6
Aged 55 to 64	18.1	79.8
Aged 65 or older	35.0	63.2
Total women	**52.3**	**45.6**
Aged 18 to 24	51.1	45.7
Aged 25 to 34	51.4	46.9
Aged 35 to 44	52.0	47.2
Aged 45 to 54	45.4	53.4
Aged 55 to 64	55.7	42.7
Aged 65 or older	58.3	37.2

Note: Figures may not sum to 100 percent because "don't know" is not shown.
Source: 1998 General Social Survey, National Opinion Research Center, University of Chicago; calculations by New Strategist

Majorities of Men and Women Believe in God

Religious faith and participation is greater among women than men.

In nearly every age group, most men and women believe in God and have no doubts about it. Only among men aged 25 to 34 do fewer than half believe in God without a doubt. Women have more faith than men. Sixty-eight percent of women and a smaller 57 percent of men believe in God without any doubts. For both men and women, religious faith is most common in the oldest age groups. Overall, only 5 percent of men and 2 percent of women do not believe in God.

Fifty percent of men and 58 percent of women identify themselves as Protestants. Young adults are least likely to be Protestants. Only 44 percent of women aged 18 to 24 are Protestants versus 72 percent of women aged 65 or older. Among men, only 42 percent of those aged 18 to 24 are Protestants versus 60 percent of men aged 65 or older. Many young adults have no religious affiliation, including 29 percent of men and 22 percent of women aged 18 to 24.

Women are much more likely than men to attend religious services each week. While slightly fewer than 20 percent of men attend services weekly, the figure is a much higher 30 percent among women. At every age, women are more likely than men to go to church.

❖ While younger men and women are less likely to be involved with organized religion than older Americans, religious faith is strong even among the young.

Belief in God, 1998

"Which statement comes closest to expressing what you believe about God?
I don't believe in God.
I don't know whether there is a God and I don't believe there is any way to find out.
I don't believe in a personal God, but I do believe in a Higher Power of some kind.
I find myself believing in God some of the time, but not at others.
While I have doubts, I feel that I do believe in God.
I know God really exists and I have no doubts about it."

(percent of people aged 18 or older responding by sex and age, 1998)

	no doubts	believe, but have doubts	believe sometimes	Higher Power	don't know, no way to find out	don't believe
Total men	**56.5%**	**15.5%**	**4.1%**	**12.6%**	**6.5%**	**4.9%**
Aged 18 to 24	53.2	12.8	4.3	17.0	8.5	4.3
Aged 25 to 34	46.0	24.6	0.8	16.7	6.3	5.6
Aged 35 to 44	57.2	10.9	6.5	12.3	7.2	5.8
Aged 45 to 54	57.5	16.0	4.7	10.4	6.6	4.7
Aged 55 to 64	65.2	15.2	1.5	9.1	7.6	1.5
Aged 65 or older	65.8	9.6	6.8	9.6	2.7	5.5
Total women	**67.8**	**14.0**	**5.1**	**7.5**	**3.5**	**1.9**
Aged 18 to 24	55.2	20.7	1.7	13.8	6.9	1.7
Aged 25 to 34	64.1	18.6	2.6	7.1	3.2	4.5
Aged 35 to 44	70.6	13.1	4.4	6.9	3.1	1.3
Aged 45 to 54	67.3	14.9	4.0	8.9	4.0	1.0
Aged 55 to 64	68.4	10.1	10.1	8.9	1.3	1.3
Aged 65 or older	74.6	7.9	8.7	4.0	4.0	0.8

Note: Figures may not sum to 100 percent because "don't know" is not shown.
Source: 1998 General Social Survey, National Opinion Research Center, University of Chicago; calculations by New Strategist

Religious Preference, 1998

"What is your religious preference?"

(percent of people aged 18 or older responding by sex and age, 1998)

	Protestant	Catholic	Jewish	other	none
Total men	**50.2%**	**24.7%**	**2.1%**	**4.8%**	**18.2%**
Aged 18 to 24	41.7	19.4	0.9	9.3	28.7
Aged 25 to 34	38.9	28.7	1.8	6.5	24.0
Aged 35 to 44	49.7	25.5	1.0	4.6	18.9
Aged 45 to 54	58.0	21.5	2.7	4.1	13.7
Aged 55 to 64	55.6	25.6	3.0	3.0	12.8
Aged 65 or older	59.7	23.8	3.3	1.7	11.6
Total women	**57.6**	**25.5**	**1.6**	**4.0**	**11.0**
Aged 18 to 24	44.0	28.4	1.5	3.0	21.6
Aged 25 to 34	50.4	26.2	0.6	6.9	15.9
Aged 35 to 44	53.4	27.0	1.6	5.7	12.3
Aged 45 to 54	61.6	22.1	2.3	4.7	9.3
Aged 55 to 64	61.7	28.4	2.2	1.1	6.6
Aged 65 or older	71.5	22.7	1.7	0.3	3.1

Note: Figures may not sum to 100 percent because "don't know" is not shown.
Source: 1998 General Social Survey, National Opinion Research Center, University of Chicago; calculations by New Strategist

Religious Attendance, 1998

"How often do you attend religious services?"

(percent of people aged 18 or older responding by sex and age, 1998)

	at least weekly	at least monthly but less than once a week	several times a year	less than once a year or never
Total men	**19.5%**	**21.7%**	**23.0%**	**35.8%**
Aged 18 to 24	8.5	24.5	26.4	40.6
Aged 25 to 34	14.5	18.6	31.6	35.3
Aged 35 to 44	18.3	21.9	22.5	37.3
Aged 45 to 54	20.6	23.9	21.6	33.9
Aged 55 to 64	23.5	19.7	19.7	37.1
Aged 65 or older	31.6	23.2	13.0	32.2
Total women	**29.8**	**23.8**	**20.6**	**25.8**
Aged 18 to 24	12.3	24.6	26.2	36.9
Aged 25 to 34	19.7	26.6	25.4	28.3
Aged 35 to 44	31.0	23.6	20.7	24.7
Aged 45 to 54	33.7	22.9	20.2	23.3
Aged 55 to 64	31.9	18.7	22.5	26.9
Aged 65 or older	43.2	24.3	11.5	20.9

Source: 1998 General Social Survey, National Opinion Research Center, University of Chicago; calculations by New Strategist

More Women See a Doctor

In a typical week, women are more likely to seek medical treatment than men.

While only 12.5 percent of men aged 18 or older have been to a doctor or sought medical treatment in the past seven days, the proportion is a much higher 22 percent among women. Two factors account for this difference: the fact that women bear children, and the fact that the average woman is older than the average man.

The proportion of men who have been to the doctor in the past week rises with age to a high of 22 percent among men aged 65 or older. For women, the proportion peaks in two age groups: among women aged 25 to 34 because of childbearing, and among those aged 55 or older because of the health problems that accompany aging. The biggest gap between the sexes occurs in the 25-to-34 age group, where one in five women has sought medical treatment in the past week versus only 9 percent of men.

❖ For the health care industry, most customers are women. Women's dominance of the industry will grow as the enormous baby-boom generation ages over the next few decades.

Medical Care in Past Week, 1998

"During the last seven days did you go to see a doctor or receive medical treatment at a clinic or hospital?"

(percent of people aged 18 or older responding by sex and age, 1998)

	yes	no
Total men	**12.5%**	**87.5%**
Aged 18 to 24	7.7	92.3
Aged 25 to 34	8.9	91.1
Aged 35 to 44	8.8	91.3
Aged 45 to 54	13.9	86.1
Aged 55 to 64	16.7	83.3
Aged 65 or older	21.9	78.1
Total women	**22.1**	**77.9**
Aged 18 to 24	17.6	82.4
Aged 25 to 34	21.3	78.7
Aged 35 to 44	19.2	80.8
Aged 45 to 54	17.2	82.8
Aged 55 to 64	24.5	75.5
Aged 65 or older	31.1	68.9

Source: 1998 General Social Survey, National Opinion Research Center, University of Chicago; calculations by New Strategist

Older Americans Are Much More Likely to Read a Daily Newspaper

When it comes to reading fiction, however, young and middle-aged adults are somewhat more likely to do so than older people.

The habit of reading a daily newspaper is disappearing among younger generations. While most older men and women read a newspaper daily, the figure falls to about one in four among men and women under age 35. Most women under age 35 read a newspaper no more than once a week.

The pattern changes when it comes to fiction—novels, shorts stories, poems, or plays. Young and middle-aged adults are slightly more likely to have read a work of fiction in the past 12 months than older adults, but the differences are small. Among men, those most likely to have read fiction in the past year are aged 25 to 44, with 64 percent having done so. Among women, the biggest readers are those aged 35 to 54, with 78 to 79 percent having read a work of fiction in the past year.

❖ Young and middle-aged adults are turning away from print as a source of information, but they still enjoy reading as a leisure pursuit.

Men are more likely to read a daily newspaper, while women are more likely to read fiction

(percentages of people reading a newspaper daily and fiction within the past 12 months, by sex, 1998)

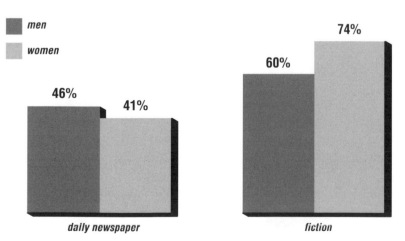

men
women

46%   41%

74%

60%

daily newspaper   fiction

Newspaper Reading, 1998

"How often do you read the newspaper?"

(percent of people aged 18 or older responding by sex and age, 1998)

	daily	few times a week	once a week	less than once a week or never
Total men	**46.2%**	**22.4%**	**14.9%**	**16.4%**
Aged 18 to 24	20.5	39.7	16.4	23.3
Aged 25 to 34	28.6	31.1	19.9	20.4
Aged 35 to 44	43.3	22.7	15.5	18.6
Aged 45 to 54	56.5	13.6	17.7	12.2
Aged 55 to 64	62.7	16.9	7.2	13.3
Aged 65 or older	72.0	11.9	6.8	9.3
Total women	**40.6**	**22.5**	**16.3**	**20.6**
Aged 18 to 24	23.5	29.6	17.3	29.6
Aged 25 to 34	21.9	23.2	27.2	27.7
Aged 35 to 44	31.6	32.0	16.6	19.8
Aged 45 to 54	44.1	22.9	15.6	17.3
Aged 55 to 64	55.8	17.8	10.1	16.3
Aged 65 or older	67.9	8.8	7.8	15.5

Source: 1998 General Social Survey, National Opinion Research Center, University of Chicago; calculations by New Strategist

Reading Fiction, 1998

"Have you read novels, short stories, poems, or plays, other than those required by work or school, during the past 12 months?"

(percent of people aged 18 or older responding by sex and age, 1998)

	yes	no
Total men	**59.8%**	**40.2%**
Aged 18 to 24	61.5	38.5
Aged 25 to 34	63.7	36.3
Aged 35 to 44	64.2	35.8
Aged 45 to 54	54.9	45.1
Aged 55 to 64	53.8	46.2
Aged 65 or older	56.8	43.2
Total women	**73.9**	**26.1**
Aged 18 to 24	66.2	33.8
Aged 25 to 34	75.9	24.1
Aged 35 to 44	77.8	22.2
Aged 45 to 54	78.7	21.3
Aged 55 to 64	76.3	23.7
Aged 65 or older	65.1	34.9

Source: 1998 General Social Survey, National Opinion Research Center, University of Chicago; calculations by New Strategist

Men and Women Are Equally Likely to Go to a Movie

Movie attendance is highest among young adults of both sexes.

About 13 percent of men and women have been to a movie in the past seven days, while two out of three have been to a movie in the past year. The rate of movie attendance is about the same for men and women; the frequency of attendance falls with age.

One in four 18-to-24-year-olds has been to a movie in the past week, a figure that falls to a low of 8 percent among women aged 65 or older and 6 percent among the oldest men. In the past year, more than 85 percent of men and women aged 18 to 24 have been to a movie. That figure falls to 45 percent among men aged 65 or older and 37 percent among the oldest women.

Although many movies are designed for teens and young adults, the majority of men under age 55 and women under age 65 have been lured to a theater at least once in the past year. If more movies were created for older Americans, and more theaters designed to appeal to older customers, attendance among older age groups could rise.

❖ Movies continue to be a popular form of entertainment despite the rapid growth of the video rental industry. Movies' success depends partly on the fact that theaters provide people with a place to gather with friends. More attention by theater owners to this motivation could boost ticket sales.

Movie Attendance, 1998

(percent of people aged 18 or older who have seen a movie in the past seven days or in the past 12 months, by sex and age, 1998)

	past seven days	past 12 months
Total men	**13.2%**	**66.4%**
Aged 18 to 24	25.0	84.6
Aged 25 to 34	17.8	80.8
Aged 35 to 44	13.1	69.0
Aged 45 to 54	12.3	67.2
Aged 55 to 64	6.4	46.2
Aged 65 or older	6.3	45.3
Total women	**13.6**	**66.5**
Aged 18 to 24	25.0	88.2
Aged 25 to 34	16.2	77.6
Aged 35 to 44	13.9	77.1
Aged 45 to 54	13.3	70.1
Aged 55 to 64	9.6	52.7
Aged 65 or older	7.9	37.3

Source: 1998 General Social Survey, National Opinion Research Center, University of Chicago; calculations by New Strategist; calculations by New Strategist

Women Are More Likely to Participate in Arts and Crafts

Women are also more likely to attend dance performances.

Fully 44 percent of women have participated in an arts and crafts activity in the past year. Arts and crafts activities include needlework, which many women enjoy. Participation in arts and crafts peaks among women aged 35 to 44 at 50 percent. Among men, only 31 percent took part in arts and crafts activities (including woodworking) in the past year. The youngest men were most likely to do so

Many people attend arts events, and popular-music concerts and art museums attract the largest crowds. The majority of 18-to-24-year-old men and women have been to a popular-music concert in the past year. Attendance at art museums peaks among women aged 35 to 54 at about 48 percent.

Men and women are equally likely to attend classical-music or opera performances, while women are more likely than men to attend ballet or dance performances. Attendance at nonmusical stage plays is highest among women aged 35 to 64, at more than 30 percent in the past year.

❖ Among arts events, popular-music concerts hold the most allure for young adults. Art museums appeal to middle-aged and older Americans, which explains the growing crowds at major arts exhibits across the nation over the past few years.

Attendance at Arts Events, 1998

(percent of people aged 18 or older who have attended selected arts events, not including school performances, or visited an art museum or gallery in the past 12 months, by sex and age, 1998)

	classical-music or opera performance	ballet or dance performance	nonmusical stage play	popular-music concert	visited art museum or gallery
Total men	**16.7%**	**16.1%**	**21.6%**	**40.2%**	**36.5%**
Aged 18 to 24	15.4	23.1	21.2	53.8	32.7
Aged 25 to 34	19.9	13.0	21.2	46.6	35.6
Aged 35 to 44	13.2	17.6	20.8	45.3	37.1
Aged 45 to 54	18.0	15.6	23.8	43.4	37.7
Aged 55 to 64	16.7	15.4	21.8	25.6	46.2
Aged 65 or older	16.8	15.8	21.1	22.1	29.5
Total women	**17.1**	**22.8**	**25.3**	**36.9**	**36.9**
Aged 18 to 24	16.2	10.3	20.6	51.5	30.9
Aged 25 to 34	14.4	21.3	20.1	46.0	31.0
Aged 35 to 44	16.4	29.8	30.4	40.9	48.5
Aged 45 to 54	23.6	27.0	33.1	37.8	48.0
Aged 55 to 64	23.7	26.9	30.1	34.4	39.8
Aged 65 or older	12.0	16.0	18.0	16.0	22.0

Source: 1998 General Social Survey, National Opinion Research Center, University of Chicago; calculations by New Strategist

Arts Participation, 1998

(percent of people aged 18 or older who have participated in selected arts activities in the past 12 months, by sex and age, 1998)

	arts and crafts such as pottery, woodworking, quilts, painting	music, dance, or theatrical performance	play a musical instrument such as piano
Total men	**31.0%**	**12.1%**	**22.4%**
Aged 18 to 24	42.3	15.4	38.5
Aged 25 to 34	36.3	18.6	26.0
Aged 35 to 44	34.6	12.6	23.9
Aged 45 to 54	30.3	10.7	22.1
Aged 55 to 64	17.9	9.0	15.4
Aged 65 or older	22.3	4.2	11.6
Total women	**43.7**	**9.3**	**24.5**
Aged 18 to 24	42.6	8.8	22.4
Aged 25 to 34	47.7	11.5	28.3
Aged 35 to 44	50.3	7.6	23.5
Aged 45 to 54	45.7	12.7	29.9
Aged 55 to 64	36.6	6.5	23.7
Aged 65 or older	34.7	8.0	18.0

Source: 1998 General Social Survey, National Opinion Research Center, University of Chicago; calculations by New Strategist

Most Men and Women Want More Time with Their Family

Few would spend extra time at work.

When asked to name what they wished they could spend more time doing, 79 percent of both men and women said they wanted more time with their family. This longing is greatest among women under age 55 and men aged 25 to 54, but the majorities of men and women in every age group want more family time.

Leisure activities rank second as something both men and women would like to spend more time doing. Between 71 and 72 percent of people aged 18 or older long to have more time for fun. Third on the list is time with friends. Women aged 18 to 24 are especially hungry for time with friends, with 78 percent wishing they could spend more time with them.

Few men or women want to spend more time doing household chores or working, but some do. Young adults are particularly desirous of spending more time at work, with 41 percent of men and 47 percent of women wishing they had more time on the job. Young adults are working their way up the career ladder, and many want to devote more hours to their progress.

❖ The greatest longing of Americans is for more family time. Consumers will relish products and services that clear the way for family time or provide venues for family togetherness.

Time Preferences, 1998

"Suppose you could change the way you spend your time, spending more on some things and less on others. Which of these things would you like to spend more time on?"

(percent of people aged 18 or older responding by sex and age, 1998)

	family	leisure activities	friends	household work	paid job
Total men	**78.6%**	**71.4%**	**61.8%**	**25.2%**	**26.6%**
Aged 18 to 24	68.0	74.0	68.0	40.0	41.3
Aged 25 to 34	85.5	74.3	64.2	31.2	34.3
Aged 35 to 44	84.7	76.2	66.9	23.9	25.4
Aged 45 to 54	83.9	79.6	62.5	19.8	17.4
Aged 55 to 64	73.9	68.1	63.0	10.9	22.7
Aged 65 or older	60.6	48.6	43.1	23.9	20.9
Total women	**78.8**	**72.0**	**66.7**	**24.0**	**20.0**
Aged 18 to 24	84.5	70.7	77.6	30.5	46.6
Aged 25 to 34	77.5	72.2	67.3	24.7	22.6
Aged 35 to 44	84.8	86.0	70.8	27.1	19.3
Aged 45 to 54	84.1	81.5	69.8	24.3	22.3
Aged 55 to 64	75.3	67.1	64.0	21.1	13.9
Aged 65 or older	66.9	46.7	53.7	17.2	6.1

Source: 1998 General Social Survey, National Opinion Research Center, University of Chicago; calculations by New Strategist

Smaller Families for Baby-Boom Men and Women

Most older men and women have three or more children.

The shrinking size of the American family is evident in statistics on the number of children people have. Overall, one in four women and one in three men are childless. The childlessproportion falls sharply with age to a low of 15 percent among men aged 55 to 64 and to 8 percent among their female counterparts.

The smaller families of the baby-boom generation are apparent in the proportions of women with three or more children. The majority of women aged 55 or older have had three, four, or even more children. In contrast, only 28 percent of women aged 35 to 54 have had three or more children. While some of these women will bear additional children, the number will not be enough to change these proportions significantly. Most women aged 35 to 54 have had only one or two children.

❖ Baby boomers will be able to share the work of caring for aging parents with their many siblings. The children of boomers won't have as much help, making caregiving a growing burden as boomers age.

Number of Children, 1998

"How many children have you ever had? Please count all that were born alive at any time."

(percent of people aged 18 or older responding by sex and age, 1998)

	none	one	two	three	four or more
Total men	**33.9%**	**16.1%**	**25.5%**	**12.4%**	**12.1%**
Aged 18 to 24	85.0	11.2	2.8	0.9	0.0
Aged 25 to 34	53.6	20.3	15.6	6.9	3.6
Aged 35 to 44	30.4	21.7	28.2	12.3	7.4
Aged 45 to 54	15.5	15.0	38.2	17.3	14.1
Aged 55 to 64	14.8	9.6	36.3	20.7	18.5
Aged 65 or older	16.5	9.3	25.8	15.4	33.0
Total women	**24.1**	**17.3**	**26.9**	**16.2**	**15.4**
Aged 18 to 24	68.7	22.4	7.5	0.7	0.7
Aged 25 to 34	33.3	23.3	25.0	11.2	7.2
Aged 35 to 44	19.7	18.1	33.5	16.8	11.9
Aged 45 to 54	18.8	18.8	34.2	16.5	11.5
Aged 55 to 64	8.2	8.7	30.1	24.6	28.4
Aged 65 or older	13.3	11.0	21.6	22.9	31.2

Source: 1998 General Social Survey, National Opinion Research Center, University of Chicago; calculations by New Strategist

For Most Americans, Mom Is Still Alive

But for the majority, Dad is no longer living.

Overall, 68 percent of men and 59 percent of women have living mothers. The substantial difference in the proportions of men and women with living mothers is due to the fact that the average woman is older than the average man. Forty-nine percent of men and 44 percent of women have living fathers.

The proportion of people with living mothers does not fall below 50 percent until the 55-to-64 age group. Those with living fathers become a minority in the 45-to-54 age group because men typically die at a younger age than women.

❖ As the population ages, the proportion of adults with living parents is growing, and so is the proportion of children with living grandparents. This happy fact provides expanding opportunities for companies that service family get-togethers such as reunions and travel.

Most men and woman have living mothers

(percent of people with living mothers and fathers, by sex, 1998)

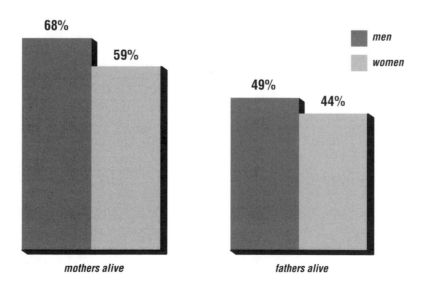

men

women

68%

59%

49%

44%

mothers alive

fathers alive

People with Living Parents, 1994

"Is your mother/father still living?"

(percent of people aged 18 or older with living mothers and fathers, by sex and age, 1994)

	mother alive	father alive
Total men	**67.6%**	**49.4%**
Aged 18 to 24	96.2	92.3
Aged 25 to 34	92.0	83.9
Aged 35 to 44	84.5	60.0
Aged 45 to 54	71.3	33.9
Aged 55 to 64	39.3	5.4
Aged 65 or older	3.9	2.9
Total women	**58.9**	**43.5**
Aged 18 to 24	98.4	93.8
Aged 25 to 34	90.0	76.8
Aged 35 to 44	78.0	57.6
Aged 45 to 54	60.4	34.0
Aged 55 to 64	33.3	11.7
Aged 65 or older	2.9	0.0

Source: 1994 General Social Survey, National Opinion Research Center, University of Chicago; calculations by New Strategist

One-Fourth of Americans Have Been Married More Than Once

Most describe their current marriage as "very happy."

The proportion of people who have been married more than once peaks in the 45-to-54 age group at one in three. This age group is filled with the oldest boomers, whose first marriages were disrupted by changes in women's roles and the turmoil surrounding the Vietnam war.

Among the currently married, nearly two out of three husbands and wives describe their marriage as "very happy." Another one-third say it is "pretty happy." Only 2 percent of husbands and 3 percent of wives say they are "not too happy."

Marital happiness varies by age. Men tend to become happier in their marriages with advancing age, while women's marital happiness is highest among the youngest adults.

Slight majorities of men and women want it to be more difficult to divorce in this country. Older women are most in favor of making it harder, and 67 percent of those aged 65 or older support tougher divorce laws. Those least in favor of making divorce more difficult are the youngest women. Thirty-six percent of women aged 18 to 24 want it to be easier to divorce.

❖ Men and women today have mixed feelings about marriage. While many have been married more than once, most want divorce to be harder to obtain.

Have You Been Married Before? 1994

"Have you been married more than once?"

(percent of people aged 18 or older responding by sex and age, 1994)

	yes	no
Total men	**26.7%**	**73.3%**
Aged 18 to 24	0.0	100.0
Aged 25 to 34	14.4	85.6
Aged 35 to 44	27.2	72.8
Aged 45 to 54	34.3	65.7
Aged 55 to 64	27.3	72.7
Aged 65 or older	30.1	69.9
Total women	**25.2**	**74.3**
Aged 18 to 24	0.0	100.0
Aged 25 to 34	21.5	78.5
Aged 35 to 44	23.9	75.6
Aged 45 to 54	33.3	66.7
Aged 55 to 64	28.6	69.5
Aged 65 or older	23.0	76.4

Source: 1994 General Social Survey, National Opinion Research Center, University of Chicago; calculations by New Strategist

Marital Happiness, 1998

"Taking things all together, how would you describe your marriage? Would you say that your marriage is very happy, pretty happy, or not too happy?"

(percent of people aged 18 or older responding by sex and age, 1998)

	very happy	*pretty happy*	*not too happy*
Total men	**64.2%**	**33.2%**	**2.4%**
Aged 18 to 24	61.5	23.1	15.4
Aged 25 to 34	63.1	35.9	1.0
Aged 35 to 44	59.3	36.5	3.6
Aged 45 to 54	60.4	37.3	2.2
Aged 55 to 64	74.2	24.7	1.1
Aged 65 or older	69.4	28.8	1.8
Total women	**63.7**	**33.3**	**3.1**
Aged 18 to 24	75.0	25.0	0.0
Aged 25 to 34	67.9	31.5	0.6
Aged 35 to 44	63.0	33.6	3.3
Aged 45 to 54	57.6	38.8	3.6
Aged 55 to 64	63.2	30.5	6.3
Aged 65 or older	64.4	32.2	3.4

Note: Percentages are based on respondents who were married or living as married.
Source: 1998 General Social Survey, National Opinion Research Center, University of Chicago; calculations by New Strategist

Should It Be Easier to Divorce? 1998

"Should divorce in this country be easier or more difficult to obtain than it is now?"

(percent of people aged 18 or older responding by sex and age, 1998)

	easier	stay as is	more difficult
Total men	**23.2%**	**21.8%**	**50.3%**
Aged 18 to 24	24.7	19.2	50.7
Aged 25 to 34	28.1	18.9	48.5
Aged 35 to 44	25.8	18.6	51.5
Aged 45 to 54	21.8	23.1	48.3
Aged 55 to 64	15.7	31.3	49.4
Aged 65 or older	16.9	25.4	54.2
Total women	**22.7**	**16.5**	**52.9**
Aged 18 to 24	35.8	11.1	44.4
Aged 25 to 34	28.3	16.6	46.2
Aged 35 to 44	23.0	19.4	50.0
Aged 45 to 54	24.6	17.9	52.5
Aged 55 to 64	16.3	21.7	55.0
Aged 65 or older	13.0	9.8	66.8

Note: "Stay as is" was a volunteered response; numbers will not add to total because "don't know" is not shown.
Source: 1998 General Social Survey, National Opinion Research Center, University of Chicago; calculations by New Strategist

Most Believe Their Standard of Living Is Better Than Their Parents'

Their children's standard of living will be even higher, say most men and women.

Nearly two out of three men and women believe their standard of living is higher than their parents' standard of living was at the age they are now. The proportion of people who think this way is highest in the oldest age groups. Three out of four men aged 55 or older say their standard of living is higher than their parents' was. Sixty-nine percent of their female counterparts agree.

The opposite pattern emerges when people speculate whether their children's standard of living will be better than theirs. Younger adults are most likely to believe it will be better, while older adults are somewhat more dubious. Nevertheless, the majorities of men and women in all but one age group believe their children's standard of living will be higher than their own. The lone exception is men aged 45 to 54, only 49 percent of whom believe their children's standard of living will be better than theirs. Even among these men, however, only 20 percent believe their children's standard of living will be worse.

❖ The belief in economic progress is a fundamental part of the American Dream. Despite today's widespread cynicism, most men and women still believe in economic progress.

Standard of Living Compared to Parents', 1998

"Compared to your parents when they were the age you are now, do you think your own standard of living now is better, about the same, or worse than theirs was?"

(percent of people aged 18 or older responding by sex and age, 1998)

	better	same	worse
Total men	**62.9%**	**21.1%**	**14.8%**
Aged 18 to 24	62.0	15.5	16.9
Aged 25 to 34	59.3	21.6	17.5
Aged 35 to 44	55.8	27.2	16.6
Aged 45 to 54	61.4	19.6	18.3
Aged 55 to 64	74.7	17.9	6.3
Aged 65 or older	73.6	17.1	8.5
Total women	**64.2**	**21.6**	**12.3**
Aged 18 to 24	58.1	34.4	5.4
Aged 25 to 34	57.7	22.6	16.7
Aged 35 to 44	65.8	18.8	15.0
Aged 45 to 54	65.9	18.6	15.0
Aged 55 to 64	69.2	16.8	14.0
Aged 65 or older	68.6	22.9	4.3

Note: Figures may not sum to 100 percent because "don't know" is not shown.
Source: 1998 General Social Survey, National Opinion Research Center, University of Chicago; calculations by New Strategist

Future Standard of Living for Children, 1998

"When your children are at the age you are now, do you think their standard of living will be better, about the same, or worse than yours is now?"

(percent of people aged 18 or older responding by sex and age, 1998)

	better	*same*	*worse*
Total men	**57.6%**	**22.6%**	**14.9%**
Aged 18 to 24	66.7	22.2	7.9
Aged 25 to 34	63.6	17.9	15.0
Aged 35 to 44	56.8	21.9	16.1
Aged 45 to 54	48.9	25.5	20.4
Aged 55 to 64	54.9	25.6	14.6
Aged 65 or older	57.5	25.7	9.7
Total women	**62.1**	**20.7**	**12.6**
Aged 18 to 24	69.8	17.4	8.1
Aged 25 to 34	64.2	20.9	11.2
Aged 35 to 44	67.3	18.9	11.1
Aged 45 to 54	53.7	22.8	19.1
Aged 55 to 64	58.4	22.8	14.9
Aged 65 or older	58.3	21.4	12.3

Note: Figures may not sum to 100 percent because "don't know" is not shown.
Source: 1998 General Social Survey, National Opinion Research Center, University of Chicago; calculations by New Strategist

Working Mothers Do Not Harm Families

Women are especially likely to believe working mothers are OK.

Does family life suffer if a woman has a full-time job? The 52 percent majority of women do not believe so. Only 44 percent of men agree with them, however.

In all but one age group (the oldest), the majority of women see no harm when women have full-time jobs. Men are much more hesitant to support working women. Only among those aged 25 to 34 does the majority agree that women with full-time jobs do not harm their families.

Men are even more wary of working mothers if they have preschoolers. Fully 48 percent of men believe preschoolers suffer if their mother works. Among women, only 36 percent believe preschoolers suffer. The proportion of men and women who believe preschoolers are harmed by working mothers rises with age, from a low of 23 percent among women aged 18 to 24 (41 percent among their male counterparts) to a high of 53 percent among women aged 65 or older (64 percent among the oldest men).

❖ As younger generations of career-oriented women have replaced older generations of housewives, tolerance towards working mothers has grown—especially among women themselves.

Most women do not believe families suffer if mother works full-time

*(percent of people who believe that family life does not suffer
if the woman has a full-time job, by sex, 1998)*

44% men

52% women

Do Families Suffer If Mother Works? 1998

"All in all, family life suffers when the woman has a full-time job— do you agree or disagree?"

(percent of people aged 18 or older responding by sex and age, 1998)

	agree	neither	disagree
Total men	**32.6%**	**20.8%**	**44.1%**
Aged 18 to 24	26.5	30.6	40.8
Aged 25 to 34	23.1	18.5	57.7
Aged 35 to 44	28.3	22.5	47.8
Aged 45 to 54	34.0	19.8	41.5
Aged 55 to 64	51.6	10.9	37.5
Aged 65 or older	42.7	25.3	25.3
Total women	**28.4**	**17.7**	**52.2**
Aged 18 to 24	14.8	23.0	55.7
Aged 25 to 34	25.9	16.0	56.8
Aged 35 to 44	25.2	11.7	62.0
Aged 45 to 54	36.9	9.7	53.4
Aged 55 to 64	24.1	22.8	50.6
Aged 65 or older	37.8	28.3	32.3

Note: Figures may not sum to 100 percent because "don't know" is not shown.
Source: 1998 General Social Survey, National Opinion Research Center, University of Chicago; calculations by New Strategist

Do Preschoolers Suffer If Mother Works? 1998

"A preschool child is likely to suffer if his or her mother works—do you agree or disagree?"

(percent of people aged 18 or older responding by sex and age, 1998)

	agree	*disagree*
Total men	**47.6%**	**49.1%**
Aged 18 to 24	41.1	56.2
Aged 25 to 34	40.0	56.4
Aged 35 to 44	44.6	53.9
Aged 45 to 54	46.3	49.0
Aged 55 to 64	56.8	38.3
Aged 65 or older	64.4	32.2
Total women	**36.2**	**61.3**
Aged 18 to 24	22.5	76.3
Aged 25 to 34	26.0	71.3
Aged 35 to 44	35.6	62.8
Aged 45 to 54	36.5	61.2
Aged 55 to 64	38.5	58.5
Aged 65 or older	52.9	43.5

Note: Figures may not sum to 100 percent because "don't know" is not shown.
Source: 1998 General Social Survey, National Opinion Research Center, University of Chicago; calculations by New Strategist

Older Men and Women Back Traditional Roles

Young adults embrace equality between the sexes.

Only 22 percent of men and women believe the man should be the achiever outside the home while the woman takes care of the family. By age, however, there are significant differences in the degree of support for traditional sex roles. The youngest men and women are least interested in traditional roles, as only 15 to 20 percent of men and women under age 55 support separate roles for men and women. In contrast, fully 41 percent of men and women aged 65 or older support traditional roles.

A much larger proportion of older people believe that a wife should help her husband's career rather than have a career herself. Forty-one percent of men and 46 percent of women aged 65 or older think women should support their husband. The majority of younger adults believe the careers of husband and wife are equally important.

❖ As the career-oriented baby-boom generation enters its sixties in the next decade, the traditional attitudes of older Americans will disappear, to be replaced by the more egalitarian outlook of younger generations.

Should the Man Be the Achiever Outside the Home? 1998

"It is much better for everyone involved if the man is the achiever outside the home and the woman takes care of the home and family—do you agree or disagree?"

(percent of people aged 18 or older responding by sex and age, 1998)

	agree	neither agree nor disagree	disagree
Total men	**21.9%**	**18.5%**	**57.5%**
Aged 18 to 24	14.6	14.6	68.8
Aged 25 to 34	14.5	18.3	67.2
Aged 35 to 44	20.3	20.3	58.7
Aged 45 to 54	16.2	18.1	62.9
Aged 55 to 64	32.8	18.8	45.3
Aged 65 or older	40.8	18.4	34.2
Total women	**21.7**	**19.1**	**57.7**
Aged 18 to 24	18.0	11.5	68.9
Aged 25 to 34	17.3	15.4	66.0
Aged 35 to 44	15.2	15.2	68.3
Aged 45 to 54	17.5	20.4	60.2
Aged 55 to 64	20.3	26.6	49.4
Aged 65 or older	41.4	26.6	31.3

Note: Figures may not sum to 100 percent because "don't know" is not shown.
Source: 1998 General Social Survey, National Opinion Research Center, University of Chicago; calculations by New Strategist

Is a Husband's Career More Important? 1998

"It is more important for a wife to help her husband's career than to have one herself—do you agree or disagree?"

(percent of people aged 18 or older responding by sex and age, 1998)

	agree	disagree
Total men	**18.3%**	**77.9%**
Aged 18 to 24	19.2	79.5
Aged 25 to 34	11.3	83.6
Aged 35 to 44	15.6	81.8
Aged 45 to 54	12.9	82.3
Aged 55 to 64	17.5	80.0
Aged 65 or older	40.7	54.2
Total women	**19.0**	**78.8**
Aged 18 to 24	7.4	91.4
Aged 25 to 34	10.9	88.2
Aged 35 to 44	11.9	87.0
Aged 45 to 54	13.6	85.3
Aged 55 to 64	21.5	75.4
Aged 65 or older	45.8	48.4

Note: Figures may not sum to 100 percent because "don't know" is not shown.
Source: 1998 General Social Survey, National Opinion Research Center, University of Chicago; calculations by New Strategist

For Most, Work Is More Than a Paycheck

Even if they were rich, the majority would keep working.

More than two out of three men and women who are currently working would continue to work even if they had enough money to live comfortably for the rest of their lives. Just 29 percent of men and 31 percent of women would stop working.

Behind this commitment to work is the enjoyment people get out of the routine of going to work, the interactions with colleagues, and the feelings of competence they get from their job. Fifty-eight percent of men and women say they would enjoy having a paying job even if they did not need the money. Only among people aged 65 or older does the proportion fall below the majority.

Despite the pleasure people get out of working, most do not believe work is a person's most important activity. Forty-five percent of men and 54 percent of women do not agree that work is the most important thing. Men aged 55 or older are the only ones among whom the majority or near-majority believe work is the defining element of a person's life.

❖ While most men and women regard work as important for a variety of reasons, few put their jobs at the center of their lives. For most, family holds that position.

Would You Work If You Were Rich? 1998

"If you were to get enough money to live as comfortably as you would like for the rest of your life, would you continue to work or would you stop working?"

(percent of people aged 18 or older responding by sex and age, 1998)

	continue to work	stop working
Total men	**69.7%**	**28.7%**
Aged 18 to 24	67.3	30.9
Aged 25 to 34	80.5	18.8
Aged 35 to 44	68.6	28.4
Aged 45 to 54	64.9	33.6
Aged 55 to 64	63.1	36.9
Aged 65 or older	63.0	37.0
Total women	**67.6**	**31.2**
Aged 18 to 24	84.4	15.6
Aged 25 to 34	67.0	32.4
Aged 35 to 44	66.2	31.3
Aged 45 to 54	66.0	33.3
Aged 55 to 64	61.5	36.9
Aged 65 or older	65.5	34.5

Note: Asked only of those currently working or unemployed but looking for work. Figures may not sum to 100 percent because "don't know" is not shown.
Source: 1998 General Social Survey, National Opinion Research Center, University of Chicago; calculations by New Strategist

Enjoy Work for Its Own Sake, 1998

"Thinking of work in general, do you agree or disagree with this statement: I would enjoy having a paying job even if I did not need the money?"

(percent of people aged 18 or older responding by sex and age, 1998)

	agree	neither	disagree
Total men	**57.7%**	**16.6%**	**23.0%**
Aged 18 to 24	64.0	18.0	18.0
Aged 25 to 34	56.8	17.1	23.4
Aged 35 to 44	59.8	12.9	25.8
Aged 45 to 54	58.4	19.1	20.2
Aged 55 to 64	59.6	19.1	17.0
Aged 65 or older	48.6	17.1	28.6
Total women	**58.4**	**14.8**	**23.8**
Aged 18 to 24	67.8	15.3	16.9
Aged 25 to 34	64.9	13.2	20.5
Aged 35 to 44	63.5	15.2	20.2
Aged 45 to 54	66.4	12.1	19.6
Aged 55 to 64	55.1	14.1	28.2
Aged 65 or older	33.9	18.5	37.1

Note: Figures may not sum to 100 percent because "don't know" is not shown.
Source: 1998 General Social Survey, National Opinion Research Center, University of Chicago; calculations by New Strategist

Work Is Most Important, 1998

"Thinking of work in general, do you agree or disagree with this statement: Work is a person's most important activity?"

(percent of people aged 18 or older responding by sex and age, 1998)

	agree	neither	disagree
Total men	31.8%	22.1%	44.9%
Aged 18 to 24	30.0	20.0	50.0
Aged 25 to 34	23.6	20.0	54.5
Aged 35 to 44	28.0	23.5	48.5
Aged 45 to 54	25.0	29.5	43.2
Aged 55 to 64	50.0	17.4	32.6
Aged 65 or older	49.3	18.3	29.6
Total women	28.2	16.4	54.2
Aged 18 to 24	33.9	11.9	54.2
Aged 25 to 34	27.2	19.9	51.7
Aged 35 to 44	20.7	17.3	61.5
Aged 45 to 54	27.8	14.8	57.4
Aged 55 to 64	25.6	16.7	57.7
Aged 65 or older	39.1	14.1	42.2

Note: Figures may not sum to 100 percent because "don't know" is not shown.
Source: 1998 General Social Survey, National Opinion Research Center, University of Chicago; calculations by New Strategist

Most Men and Women Have Worked for Many Employers

Women are more likely to have worked for only one employer.

More than half the working men and women have worked for at least three employers during their careers. Twenty-eight percent of men have worked for six or more employers, while a substantial 11 percent have worked for more than 10. Only 5 percent of women have worked for more than 10 employers. Not surprisingly, the proportion of workers who have worked for only one or two employers falls with age, while the proportion having worked for six or more rises.

Sixty-five percent of working men and 81 percent of working women go to work at one location away from home—such as an office or factory. Fewer than 4 percent work at home, while another 4 to 5 percent work partly at home. Twenty-eight percent of men work at various locations, such as salesmen who travel from company to company selling their goods.

❖ Contrary to public opinion, job hopping is not a new phenomenon introduced by younger generations of workers. The oldest workers have the longest resumes.

More than one in four men and one in five women have worked full-time for six or more employers during their work life

(percent of working people who have worked full-time for six or more employers during their work life, by sex, 1998)

28%

men

21%

women

Number of Employers, 1998

"For how many employers have you ever worked full time?"

(percent of people aged 18 or older responding by sex and age, 1998)

	one	two	three to five	six to ten	more than ten
Total men	**13.4%**	**14.6%**	**43.5%**	**17.2%**	**11.1%**
Aged 18 to 24	48.5	21.2	28.8	1.5	0.0
Aged 25 to 34	11.4	17.1	46.8	17.1	7.0
Aged 35 to 44	9.1	12.8	44.4	19.8	13.9
Aged 45 to 54	10.3	15.4	46.3	15.4	12.5
Aged 55 to 64	3.2	8.1	48.4	24.2	16.1
Aged 65 or older	8.7	4.3	26.1	34.8	26.1
Total women	**13.9**	**17.1**	**47.6**	**16.4**	**4.9**
Aged 18 to 24	27.7	27.7	36.2	6.4	2.1
Aged 25 to 34	16.3	25.0	42.9	11.4	3.8
Aged 35 to 44	11.2	10.7	53.0	20.9	4.2
Aged 45 to 54	10.4	14.3	50.6	18.2	6.5
Aged 55 to 64	12.7	15.5	46.5	18.3	7.0
Aged 65 or older	20.0	16.0	40.0	16.0	8.0

Note: Asked only of people working full-time or part-time in the week prior to the survey.
Source: 1998 General Social Survey, National Opinion Research Center, University of Chicago; calculations by New Strategist

Place of Work, 1998

"Which of the following best describes where you work?"

(percent of people aged 18 to 64 responding by sex and age, 1998)

	work one place away from home, such as an office or factory	work at home	work part of week at home, part away from home	work various places
Total men	**65.1%**	**3.5%**	**3.8%**	**27.6%**
Aged 18 to 24	77.1	2.9	0.0	20.0
Aged 25 to 34	67.8	2.2	3.3	26.7
Aged 35 to 44	62.3	6.6	0.0	31.1
Aged 45 to 54	73.5	1.2	4.8	20.5
Aged 55 to 64	41.2	2.9	20.6	35.3
Total women	**81.4**	**3.9**	**5.2**	**9.4**
Aged 18 to 24	83.7	4.7	4.7	7.0
Aged 25 to 34	81.9	4.3	3.4	10.3
Aged 35 to 44	82.6	1.4	6.9	9.0
Aged 45 to 54	78.2	4.6	5.7	11.5
Aged 55 to 64	83.3	6.3	6.3	4.2

Note: Asked only of people who were currently working.
Source: 1998 General Social Survey, National Opinion Research Center, University of Chicago; calculations by New Strategist

Men Are More Likely to Have Dangerous Jobs

Their work is also more likely to be physically demanding.

The pay gap between men and women is often blamed on discrimination, but another reason for the gap are the different employment choices the sexes make. Men are more likely than women to accept dangerous or physically demanding jobs. Twenty-one percent of working men say they always or often work in dangerous conditions, compared with only 6 percent of working women. Twenty-six percent of men say they always or often have to do hard physical work versus 18 percent of women. Dangerous, physically demanding jobs often pay a premium, creating some of the pay gap between men and women.

While women are less likely to work in dangerous or physically demanding jobs than men, they are more likely to come home from work exhausted. Forty-four percent of working women always or often feel exhausted after work compared with 38 percent of men. Workplace stress is about equal for men and women: 40 percent of men and 37 percent of women say they always or often find their work stressful.

❖ Men and women are about equally likely to find their work mentally demanding. Exhausted and stressed-out workers get relief from products and services that make their home lives easier.

Dangerous Working Conditions, 1998

"How often do you work in dangerous conditions?"

(percent of people aged 18 to 64 responding by sex and age, 1998)

	always or often	sometimes	hardly ever or never
Total men	**20.9%**	**22.3%**	**56.3%**
Aged 18 to 24	28.6	14.3	57.1
Aged 25 to 34	27.5	22.0	50.5
Aged 35 to 44	20.5	26.2	51.6
Aged 45 to 54	16.9	22.9	60.2
Aged 55 to 64	9.4	21.9	68.8
Total women	**6.2**	**13.2**	**80.4**
Aged 18 to 24	11.6	14.0	74.4
Aged 25 to 34	5.3	14.0	80.7
Aged 35 to 44	6.9	17.9	75.2
Aged 45 to 54	4.7	8.1	86.0
Aged 55 to 64	4.2	8.3	87.5

Note: Asked only of people working 10 or more hours per week.
Source: 1998 General Social Survey, National Opinion Research Center, University of Chicago; calculations by New Strategist

Physically Demanding Work, 1998

"How often do you have to do hard physical work?"

(percent of people aged 18 to 64 responding by sex and age, 1998)

	always or often	sometimes	hardly ever or never
Total men	**26.3%**	**30.0%**	**43.4%**
Aged 18 to 24	48.6	22.9	28.6
Aged 25 to 34	35.2	27.5	37.4
Aged 35 to 44	27.0	32.0	40.2
Aged 45 to 54	15.7	34.9	49.4
Aged 55 to 64	9.4	21.9	68.8
Total women	**17.8**	**20.4**	**61.6**
Aged 18 to 24	16.3	39.5	44.2
Aged 25 to 34	16.7	21.9	61.4
Aged 35 to 44	21.4	17.9	60.0
Aged 45 to 54	17.2	17.2	65.5
Aged 55 to 64	16.7	16.7	66.7

Note: Asked only of people working 10 or more hours per week.
Source: 1998 General Social Survey, National Opinion Research Center, University of Chicago; calculations by New Strategist

Exhausted after Work, 1998

"How often do you come home from work exhausted?"

(percent of people aged 18 to 64 responding by sex and age, 1998)

	always or often	sometimes	hardly ever or never
Total men	**37.9%**	**49.9%**	**11.7%**
Aged 18 to 24	42.9	42.9	14.3
Aged 25 to 34	40.7	50.5	8.8
Aged 35 to 44	35.0	51.2	12.2
Aged 45 to 54	37.3	54.2	8.4
Aged 55 to 64	36.4	39.4	24.2
Total women	**43.9**	**46.3**	**9.6**
Aged 18 to 24	46.5	39.5	14.0
Aged 25 to 34	39.1	53.0	7.8
Aged 35 to 44	45.5	48.3	6.2
Aged 45 to 54	47.7	39.5	11.6
Aged 55 to 64	52.1	37.5	10.4

Note: Asked only of people working 10 or more hours per week.
Source: 1998 General Social Survey, National Opinion Research Center, University of Chicago; calculations by New Strategist

Is Your Work Stressful? 1998

"How often do you find your work stressful?"

(percent of people aged 18 to 64 responding by sex and age, 1998)

	always or often	sometimes	hardly ever or never
Total men	**39.6%**	**43.9%**	**16.3%**
Aged 18 to 24	34.3	42.9	22.9
Aged 25 to 34	39.6	46.2	14.3
Aged 35 to 44	46.7	37.7	14.8
Aged 45 to 54	37.3	45.8	16.9
Aged 55 to 64	27.3	51.5	21.2
Total women	**37.3**	**46.9**	**15.8**
Aged 18 to 24	27.9	51.2	20.9
Aged 25 to 34	36.0	51.8	12.3
Aged 35 to 44	37.9	52.4	9.7
Aged 45 to 54	48.8	30.2	20.9
Aged 55 to 64	37.5	45.8	16.7

Note: Asked only of people working 10 or more hours per week.
Source: 1998 General Social Survey, National Opinion Research Center, University of Chicago; calculations by New Strategist

2

Education

❖ **Both men and women are better educated than ever.**

Between 1940 and 1998, the proportion of men with a high school diploma climbed from 23 to 83 percent. Among women, the figure grew from 26 to 83 percent.

❖ **There are sharp generational differences in educational attainment.**

Among women, the youngest are the best educated. Among men, the middle-aged have the highest level of educational attainment.

❖ **Among young adults, women are better educated than men.**

In the 25-to-34 age group, women are more likely than men to be college graduates. They are also more likely to have a high school diploma.

❖ **Most college students are women.**

In 1960, there were two men for every woman enrolled in college. Today, women account for the 56 percent majority of college students.

❖ **Among college students, women are older than men.**

Twenty percent of female students are aged 35 or older, versus only 14 percent of the men enrolled in college.

❖ **Male and female college students have similar objectives.**

Among college freshmen, 72 percent of women and 76 percent of men say financial well-being is very important to them.

❖ **Women earn the majority of college degrees.**

Women earned 56 percent of bachelor's degrees in 1996–97.

Men and Women Are Nearly Equal in Educational Attainment

Men are still more likely than women to have a college diploma.

The educational attainment of the U.S. population has soared as baby boomers and younger generations entered adulthood, replacing older, less-educated generations. In 1940, few people had even graduated from high school—only 26 percent of women and 23 percent of men had a high school diploma. By 1970, the majority of men and women were high school graduates. Today, 83 percent of men and women have a high school degree.

The proportion of men and women with a college degree has climbed sharply over the past half-century. In 1940, just 4 percent of women and 6 percent of men were college graduates. By 1998, 22 percent of women and 27 percent of men had completed college. While men have been more likely than women to have a college degree, this is no longer true among people under age 35. Consequently, the proportion of women with a college degree will continue to approach that of men.

❖ The rapid rise in educational attainment of men and women has contributed to the economic boom of today. With women's educational attainment now almost equal to that of men, the number of affluent, two-earner couples will continue to rise—boosting economic growth in the 21st century.

Women are catching up to men

(percent of people who are high school or college graduates, by sex, 1998)

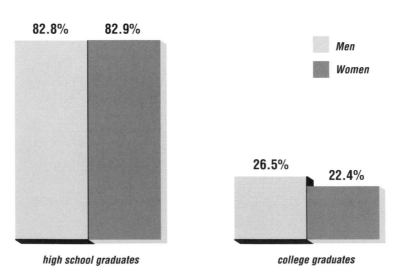

Men
Women

82.8%   82.9%

26.5%   22.4%

high school graduates   college graduates

Educational Attainment by Sex, 1940 to 1998

(percent of people aged 25 or older who are high school or college graduates by sex, and percentage point difference between men and women, 1940–98)

	high school graduates			college graduates		
	men	women	percentage point difference	men	women	percentage point difference
1998	82.8%	82.9%	–0.1	26.5%	22.4%	4.1
1995	81.7	81.6	0.1	26.0	20.2	5.8
1990	77.7	77.5	0.2	24.4	18.4	6.0
1985	74.4	73.5	0.9	23.1	16.0	7.1
1980	69.2	68.1	1.1	20.9	13.6	7.3
1975	63.1	62.1	1.0	17.6	10.6	7.0
1970	55.0	55.4	–0.4	14.1	8.2	5.9
1965	48.0	49.9	–1.9	12.0	7.1	4.9
1959	42.2	45.2	–3.0	10.3	6.0	4.3
1950	32.6	36.0	–3.4	7.3	5.2	2.1
1940	22.7	26.3	–3.6	5.5	3.8	1.7

Source: Bureau of the Census, Educational Attainment in the United States: March 1998 (Update), detailed tables for Current Population Report P20-513, 1998; Internet web site <http://www.census.gov/population/www/socdemo/edu-attn.html>; calculations by New Strategist

Young Women Are Better Educated Than Young Men

Among people under age 35, women are more likely to be college graduates.

Men and women are equally likely to be high school graduates, with 83 percent of each sex having a high school diploma. The proportion ranges from a low of 62 to 63 percent among the oldest Americans to a high of 87 to 90 percent for the youngest adults. Among 25-to-29-year-olds, women are more likely than men to have a high school diploma.

Men are more likely than women to have a college degree, but this is not the case among young adults. Women under age 35 are more likely to be college graduates. Fully 29 percent of women aged 25 to 29 have a college diploma, versus 26 percent of their male counterparts. The gap reverses in the older age groups, and among people aged 65 to 69, the proportion of men with a college degree is nearly double that of women—24.5 versus 12.6 percent.

Among whites, the same pattern holds true. Older men are better educated than older women, while young women are better educated than young men. Fully 30 percent of white women aged 25 to 29 have a college degree, nearly 4 percentage points more than their male counterparts. Among blacks, women in most age groups are better educated than men. Among Hispanics, there is no consistent difference in the educational attainment of men and women by age.

❖ Women are pursuing higher education in record numbers. As their college graduation rate overtakes that of men, the earnings gap between men and women will continue to narrow.

High School and College Graduates by Age and Sex, 1998

(percent of people aged 25 or older who are high school or college graduates by age and sex, and percentage point difference between men and women by age, 1998)

	men	women	percentage point difference
High school graduates			
Total people	**82.8%**	**82.9%**	**−0.1**
Aged 25 to 29	86.6	89.6	−3.0
Aged 30 to 34	87.0	88.5	−1.5
Aged 35 to 39	86.1	88.6	−2.5
Aged 40 to 44	87.9	89.5	−1.6
Aged 45 to 49	88.3	89.0	−0.7
Aged 50 to 54	84.5	86.7	−2.2
Aged 55 to 59	82.3	81.9	0.4
Aged 60 to 64	77.7	75.1	2.6
Aged 65 or older	67.6	66.6	1.0
Aged 65 to 69	73.8	72.7	1.1
Aged 70 to 74	67.6	69.6	−2.0
Aged 75 or older	62.7	61.5	1.2
College graduates			
Total people	**26.5**	**22.4**	**4.1**
Aged 25 to 29	25.6	29.0	−3.4
Aged 30 to 34	26.8	28.4	−1.6
Aged 35 to 39	26.3	25.0	1.3
Aged 40 to 44	27.5	26.6	0.9
Aged 45 to 49	31.4	26.8	4.6
Aged 50 to 54	32.4	24.8	7.6
Aged 55 to 59	27.5	20.5	7.0
Aged 60 to 64	25.1	14.8	10.3
Aged 65 or older	19.8	11.2	8.6
Aged 65 to 69	24.5	12.6	11.9
Aged 70 to 74	20.5	11.0	9.5
Aged 75 or older	15.6	10.5	5.1

Source: Bureau of the Census, Educational Attainment in the United States: March 1998 (Update), *detailed tables for Current Population Report P20-513, 1998; Internet web site <http://www.census.gov/population/www/socdemo/edu-attn.html>; calculations by New Strategist*

High School and College Graduates by Race, Hispanic Origin, Age, and Sex, 1998

(percent of people aged 25 or older who are high school or college graduates by race and Hispanic origin, age, and sex; percentage point difference between men and women, 1998)

	high school graduates			college graduates		
	men	*women*	*percentage point difference*	*men*	*women*	*percentage point difference*
Total blacks	**75.2%**	**76.7%**	**–1.5**	**13.9%**	**15.4%**	**–1.5**
Aged 25 to 29	87.6	87.6	0	14.2	17.0	–2.8
Aged 30 to 34	86.6	86.3	0.3	15.7	14.2	1.5
Aged 35 to 39	82.2	84.1	–1.9	13.7	12.5	1.2
Aged 40 to 44	80.7	87.8	–7.1	14.5	20.9	–6.4
Aged 45 to 49	81.4	83.2	–1.8	18.9	22.4	–3.5
Aged 50 to 54	70.5	80.4	–9.9	17.2	15.5	1.7
Aged 55 to 59	67.5	71.2	–3.7	14.4	16.5	–2.1
Aged 60 to 64	57.5	56.8	0.7	10.0	14.4	–4.4
Aged 65 or older	41.9	44.4	–2.5	6.0	7.7	–1.7
Aged 65 to 69	57.8	55.1	2.7	8.6	10.6	–2.0
Aged 70 to 74	38.8	40.3	–1.5	4.9	6.6	–1.7
Aged 75 or older	29.5	39.2	–9.7	4.4	6.2	–1.8
Total Hispanics	**55.7**	**55.3**	**0.4**	**11.1**	**10.9**	**0.2**
Aged 25 to 29	59.9	66.3	–6.4	9.5	11.3	–1.8
Aged 30 to 34	60.0	61.1	–1.1	10.2	13.3	–3.1
Aged 35 to 39	59.0	59.0	0	13.8	12.8	1.0
Aged 40 to 44	61.6	61.9	–0.3	12.0	12.2	–0.2
Aged 45 to 49	56.8	56.2	0.6	13.2	11.0	2.2
Aged 50 to 54	51.3	54.6	–3.3	11.6	12.5	–0.9
Aged 55 to 59	49.0	50.1	–1.1	10.8	11.5	–0.7
Aged 60 to 64	49.5	40.6	8.9	12.6	3.3	9.3
Aged 65 or older	32.0	27.7	4.3	6.8	4.5	2.3
Aged 65 to 69	37.8	27.1	10.7	9.7	3.1	6.6
Aged 70 to 74	30.2	30.6	–0.4	6.5	6.4	0.1
Aged 75 or older	28.2	26.3	1.9	4.5	4.6	–0.1

(continued)

(continued from previous page)

	high school graduates			college graduates		
	men	women	percentage point difference	men	women	percentage point difference
Total whites	**83.6%**	**83.8%**	**–0.2**	**27.3%**	**22.8%**	**4.5**
Aged 25 to 29	86.3	90.0	–3.7	26.5	30.4	–3.9
Aged 30 to 34	86.7	89.1	–2.4	27.0	29.8	–2.8
Aged 35 to 39	86.5	89.3	–2.8	27.2	26.6	0.6
Aged 40 to 44	88.8	90.0	–1.2	28.4	26.9	1.5
Aged 45 to 49	89.2	90.1	–0.9	32.4	26.7	5.7
Aged 50 to 54	85.7	87.9	–2.2	33.4	25.5	7.9
Aged 55 to 59	83.8	83.5	0.3	28.0	20.2	7.8
Aged 60 to 64	79.6	78.2	1.4	26.0	14.6	11.4
Aged 65 or older	69.8	69.0	0.8	20.8	11.5	9.3
Aged 65 to 69	75.4	74.7	0.7	25.8	12.6	13.2
Aged 70 to 74	69.8	73.0	–3.2	21.7	11.6	10.1
Aged 75 or older	65.6	63.6	2.0	16.4	10.8	5.6

Source: Bureau of the Census, Educational Attainment in the United States: March 1998 (Update), *detailed tables for Current Population Report P20-513, 1998; Internet web site <http://www.census.gov/population/ www/socdemo/edu-attn.html>; calculations by New Strategist*

Young Women Are Better Educated Than Older Women

Among men, educational attainment peaks in the 50-to-54 age group.

Among women aged 65 or older, only two out of three are high school graduates. But among women under age 50, nearly 90 percent have completed high school. The same pattern is true among men.

College graduation rates, however, show different patterns for men and women. Younger women are more likely than older women to have a college degree. In contrast, the percentage of men with a bachelor's degree peaks in middle age—at 32 percent among those aged 50 to 54. Men in this age group are most likely to have a college degree because many went to college to avoid the Vietnam War. Without such an incentive, younger men have been less likely to graduate from college.

❖ Differences in educational attainment help explain the generation gap in attitudes and lifestyles between older and younger Americans. Because of their college experience, boomers and younger generations have different wants and needs than their mothers and fathers did at the same age.

Educational Attainment of Men by Age, 1998

(number and percent distribution of men aged 25 or older by age and educational attainment, 1998; numbers in thousands)

	total	not a high school graduate	high school graduate or more				bachelor's degree or more				
			total	high school graduate only	some college	associate's degree	total	bachelor's degree only	master's degree	professional degree	doctoral degree
Total men	**82,3776**	**14,173**	**68,199**	**26,575**	**14,122**	**5,670**	**21,832**	**14,090**	**4,640**	**1,740**	**1,353**
Aged 25 to 29	9,450	1,266	8,184	3,024	1,967	768	2,425	1,960	359	75	31
Aged 30 to 34	10,076	1,310	8,766	3,568	1,690	808	2,700	1,971	462	167	100
Aged 35 to 39	11,299	1,572	9,727	4,003	1,855	893	2,976	2,014	596	227	139
Aged 40 to 44	10,756	1,300	9,456	3,535	2,040	927	2,954	1,957	578	247	172
Aged 45 to 49	9,116	1,068	8,048	2,600	1,728	859	2,861	1,719	695	257	190
Aged 50 to 54	7,483	1,163	6,320	2,101	1,267	529	2,423	1,372	646	194	211
Aged 55 to 59	5,869	1,040	4,829	2,022	919	275	1,613	883	445	143	142
Aged 60 to 64	4,804	1,070	3,734	1,639	670	218	1,207	667	299	123	118
Aged 65 or older	13,524	4,384	9,139	4,084	1,986	393	2,676	1,549	560	317	250
Aged 65 to 69	4,286	1,123	3,163	1,286	678	147	1,052	577	253	123	94
Aged 70 to 74	3,706	1,200	2,506	1,112	538	97	759	458	165	65	70
Aged 75 or older	5,532	2,061	3,471	1,687	771	148	865	514	142	124	85

(continued)

(continued from previous page)

	total	not a high school graduate	high school graduate or more								
			total	high school graduate only	some college	associate's degree	bachelor's degree or more				
							total	bachelor's degree only	master's degree	professional degree	doctoral degree
Total men	**100.0%**	**17.2%**	**82.8%**	**32.3%**	**17.1%**	**6.9%**	**26.5%**	**17.1%**	**5.6%**	**2.1%**	**1.6%**
Aged 25 to 29	100.0	13.4	86.6	32.0	20.8	8.1	25.7	20.7	3.8	0.8	0.3
Aged 30 to 34	100.0	13.0	87.0	35.4	16.8	8.0	26.8	19.6	4.6	1.7	1.0
Aged 35 to 39	100.0	13.9	86.1	35.4	16.4	7.9	26.3	17.8	5.3	2.0	1.2
Aged 40 to 44	100.0	12.1	87.9	32.9	19.0	8.6	27.5	18.2	5.4	2.3	1.6
Aged 45 to 49	100.0	11.7	88.3	28.5	19.0	9.4	31.4	18.9	7.6	2.8	2.1
Aged 50 to 54	100.0	15.5	84.5	28.1	16.9	7.1	32.4	18.3	8.6	2.6	2.8
Aged 55 to 59	100.0	17.7	82.3	34.5	15.7	4.7	27.5	15.0	7.6	2.4	2.4
Aged 60 to 64	100.0	22.3	77.7	34.1	13.9	4.5	25.1	13.9	6.2	2.6	2.5
Aged 65 or older	100.0	32.4	67.6	30.2	14.7	2.9	19.8	11.5	4.1	2.4	1.8
Aged 65 to 69	100.0	26.2	73.8	30.0	15.8	3.4	24.5	13.5	5.9	3.0	2.2
Aged 70 to 74	100.0	32.4	67.6	30.0	14.5	2.6	20.5	12.4	4.5	1.8	1.9
Aged 75 or older	100.0	37.3	62.7	30.5	13.9	2.7	15.6	9.3	2.6	2.2	1.5

Source: Bureau of the Census, Educational Attainment in the United States: March 1998 (Update), detailed tables for Current Population Report P20-513, 1998; Internet web site <http://www.census.gov/population/www/socdemo/edu-attn.html>; calculations by New Strategist

Educational Attainment of Women by Age, 1998

(number and percent distribution of women aged 25 or older by age and educational attainment, 1998; numbers in thousands)

| | total | not a high school graduate | total | high school graduate only | some college | associate's degree | high school graduate or more | | | | |
| | | | | | | | bachelor's degree or more | | | | |
							total	bachelor's degree only	master's degree	professional degree	doctoral degree
Total women	**89,835**	**15,382**	**74,455**	**31,599**	**15,516**	**7,198**	**20,142**	**14,215**	**4,592**	**822**	**515**
Aged 25 to 29	9,546	990	8,556	2,730	2,189	869	2,768	2,236	412	87	33
Aged 30 to 34	10,282	1,187	9,095	3,247	1,939	989	2,920	2,200	531	147	42
Aged 35 to 39	11,392	1,300	10,092	3,906	2,171	1,165	2,850	2,084	581	83	97
Aged 40 to 44	11,015	1,155	9,860	3,693	2,081	1,161	2,925	2,101	623	133	63
Aged 45 to 49	9,518	1,049	8,469	3,299	1,691	928	2,551	1,618	737	110	86
Aged 50 to 54	7,941	1,060	6,881	2,943	1,379	592	1,967	1,240	563	75	89
Aged 55 to 59	6,321	1,142	5,179	2,462	989	431	1,297	844	381	40	32
Aged 60 to 64	5,261	1,307	3,954	2,187	748	239	780	496	220	38	26
Aged 65 or older	18,558	6,192	12,366	7,130	2,328	825	2,083	1,396	544	95	47
Aged 65 to 69	5,075	1,385	3,690	2,174	606	270	640	406	176	34	24
Aged 70 to 74	4,807	1,463	3,344	1,926	643	245	530	352	150	22	6
Aged 75 or older	8,677	3,344	5,333	3,030	1,079	311	913	638	218	40	17

(continued)

(continued from previous page)

	total	not a high school graduate	high school graduate or more				bachelor's degree or more				
			total	high school graduate only	some college	associate's degree	total	bachelor's degree only	master's degree	professional degree	doctoral degree
Total women	**100.0%**	**17.1%**	**82.9%**	**35.2%**	**17.3%**	**8.0%**	**22.4%**	**15.8%**	**5.1%**	**0.6%**	**0.9%**
Aged 25 to 29	100.0	10.4	89.6	28.6	22.9	9.1	29.0	23.4	4.3	0.3	0.9
Aged 30 to 34	100.0	11.5	88.5	31.6	18.9	9.6	28.4	21.4	5.2	0.4	1.4
Aged 35 to 39	100.0	11.4	88.6	34.3	19.1	10.2	25.0	18.3	5.1	0.9	0.8
Aged 40 to 44	100.0	10.5	89.5	33.5	18.9	10.5	26.6	19.1	5.7	0.6	1.3
Aged 45 to 49	100.0	11.0	89.0	34.7	17.8	9.7	26.8	17.0	7.7	0.9	1.2
Aged 50 to 54	100.0	13.3	86.7	37.1	17.4	7.5	24.8	15.6	7.1	1.1	0.9
Aged 55 to 59	100.0	18.1	81.9	38.9	15.6	6.8	20.5	13.4	6.0	0.5	0.6
Aged 60 to 64	100.0	24.8	75.2	41.6	14.2	4.5	14.8	9.4	4.2	0.5	0.7
Aged 65 or older	100.0	33.4	66.6	38.4	12.5	4.5	11.2	7.5	2.9	0.3	0.5
Aged 65 to 69	100.0	27.3	72.7	42.8	11.9	5.3	12.6	8.0	3.5	0.5	0.7
Aged 70 to 74	100.0	30.4	69.6	40.1	13.4	5.1	11.0	7.3	3.1	0.1	0.5
Aged 75 or older	100.0	38.5	61.5	34.9	12.4	3.6	10.5	7.4	2.5	0.2	0.5

Source: Bureau of the Census, Educational Attainment in the United States: March 1998 (Update), detailed tables for Current Population Report P20-513, 1998; Internet web site <http://www.census.gov/population/www/socdemo/edu-attn.html>; calculations by New Strategist

Women Are More Likely to Attend School

Among students aged 30 or older, women greatly outnumber men.

The value Americans place on education is apparent in school enrollment statistics. Virtually all children aged 5 to 17 are enrolled in school. And although it was once rare for children to attend preschool, today more than half the 3- and 4-year-olds go to school.

Beginning at age 18, women are more likely than men to attend school. The gender gap is largest in the 18-to-21 age group. Among 18- and 19-year-olds, 64 percent of women and 60 percent of men are enrolled in school. In the 20-to-21 age group, 47 percent of women and 43 percent of men are in school. The gap between the genders narrows in older age groups, but remains significant nonetheless. Among people aged 30 or older, there are 1 million more women than men enrolled in school—2.6 million women versus 1.6 million men.

❖ Increasingly, education is viewed as a lifelong pursuit rather than something reserved for the young. Whether it's for career advancement or self-fulfillment, women appear more willing or able than men to return to school as adults.

School Enrollment by Age and Sex, 1998

(number and percent of people aged 3 or older enrolled in school, by age and sex, 1998; numbers in thousands)

	males		females	
	number	*percent*	*number*	*percent*
Total people	**35,979**	**28.6%**	**36,130**	**27.3%**
Aged 3 to 4	2,157	53.3	2,007	50.9
Aged 5 to 6	4,064	95.2	3,838	95.9
Aged 7 to 9	6,221	98.7	5,882	98.8
Aged 10 to 13	8,017	99.0	7,728	99.1
Aged 14 to 15	3,896	98.3	3,757	98.5
Aged 16 to 17	3,825	93.5	3,631	94.3
Aged 18 to 19	2,399	60.1	2,515	64.4
Aged 20 to 21	1,600	42.7	1,597	47.2
Aged 22 to 24	1,235	24.6	1,372	25.2
Aged 25 to 29	997	10.9	1,219	12.9
Aged 30 to 34	547	5.5	775	7.7
Aged 35 to 44	642	2.9	1,123	5.0
Aged 45 to 54	300	1.8	531	3.0
Aged 55 or older	82	0.3	154	0.5

Source: Bureau of the Census, School Enrollment: Social and Economic Characteristics of Students: October 1998, *detailed tables for Current Population Report P20-521, 1999; Internet web site <http://www.censu.gov/ population/www/socdemo/school.html>*

Women's College Enrollment Rate Has Soared

Women are now more likely to go to college than men.

In 1960, only 38 percent of women entered college within 12 months of graduating from high school. Today, 70 percent of women go from high school into college. The college enrollment rate of men has also increased, rising from 54 percent in 1960 to 64 percent in 1997.

The gap between the college enrollment rates of men and women was a full 16 percentage points in favor of men in 1960. It narrowed in the 1960s and 1970s as the women of the baby-boom generation went to college. In 1988, women's college enrollment rate surpassed that of men for the first time. It has continued to do so in most years since.

❖ Outreach programs designed to increase the number of men in higher education would not only help colleges and universities boost their enrollment, but also help men earn the educational credentials they need to achieve financial security.

Most high school graduates go to college

(percent of high school graduates who were enrolled in college within 12 months of graduating from high school, by sex, 1960 to 1997)

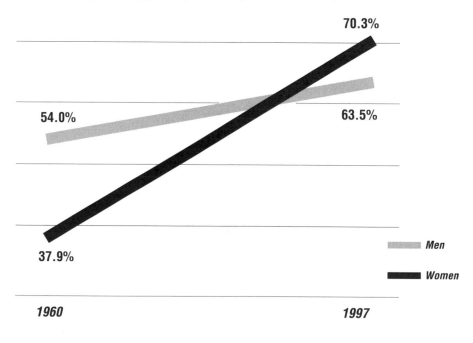

70.3%

54.0% 63.5%

37.9%

Men

Women

1960   1997

College Enrollment Rates by Sex, 1960 to 1997

(percent of people aged 16 to 24 who graduated from high school in the 12 months preceding the survey and were enrolled in college as of October, by sex; percentage point difference between enrollment rates of men and women, 1960–97)

	men	women	percentage point difference
1997	63.5%	70.3%	–6.8
1996	60.1	69.7	–9.6
1995	62.6	61.4	1.2
1994	60.6	63.2	–2.6
1993	59.7	65.4	–5.7
1992	59.6	63.8	–4.2
1991	57.6	67.1	–9.5
1990	57.8	62.0	–4.2
1989	57.6	61.6	–4.0
1988	57.0	60.8	–3.8
1987	58.4	55.3	3.1
1986	55.9	51.9	4.0
1985	58.6	56.9	1.7
1980	46.7	51.8	–5.1
1975	52.6	49.0	3.6
1970	55.2	48.5	6.7
1965	57.3	45.3	12.0
1960	54.0	37.9	16.1

Source: National Center for Education Statistics, Digest of Education Statistics 1998, *Internet web site <http://nces.ed.gov/pubsearch/pubsinfo.asp?pubid=1999036>; calculations by New Strategist*

Most College Students Are Women

Before 1980, men accounted for the majority of college students.

In 1960, there were two men for every woman enrolled in college. Today, women account for the 56 percent majority of students. Of the 15.5 million people enrolled in college in 1998, 8.6 million were women.

Women's growing share of the college population reflects the changing roles of women in society. Women are earning the educational credentials that will further their career opportunities. Among young adults, women are the educational equals of men. As they embark on careers, their earnings will reflect their high levels of education.

Women are the majority of college students among blacks, Hispanics, and whites. Among black college students, women account for the 62 percent majority. They have been in the majority since the mid-1960s. Among Hispanics, women account for 60 percent of college students, while among whites they account for 55 percent.

❖ Colleges and universities have prospered as women surged into the market for higher education. This trend is projected to continue, to the benefit of the higher education industry.

Women are the majority of students among blacks, Hispanics, and whites

(percent of college students who are women, by race and Hispanic origin, 1998)

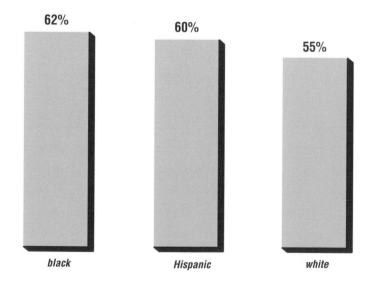

62% black

60% Hispanic

55% white

College Enrollment by Sex, 1960 to 1998

(number of people aged 15 or older enrolled in college by sex, and female share of total, 1960–98; numbers in thousands)

	total	men	women number	women percent
1998	15,546	6,905	8,641	55.6%
1997	15,436	6,843	8,593	55.7
1996	15,226	6,820	8,406	55.2
1995	14,715	6,703	8,013	54.5
1994	15,022	6,764	8,258	55.0
1993	14,394	6,599	7,795	54.2
1992	14,035	6,192	7,844	55.9
1991	14,057	6,439	7,618	54.2
1990	13,621	6,192	7,429	54.5
1985	12,524	5,906	6,618	52.8
1980	11,387	5,430	5,957	52.3
1975	10,880	5,911	4,969	45.7
1970	7,413	4,401	3,013	40.6
1965	5,675	3,503	2,172	38.3
1960	3,570	2,339	1,231	34.5

Source: Bureau of the Census, Internet web site <http://www.census.gov/population/socdemo/school/taba-6 .txt>; calculations by New Strategist

College Enrollment by Race, Hispanic Origin, and Sex, 1960 to 1998

(number of people aged 15 or older enrolled in college by race, Hispanic origin, and sex, and female share of total, 1960–98; numbers in thousands)

	total	men	women number	women percent
Black				
1998	2,016	770	1,247	61.9%
1997	1,903	723	1,180	62.0
1996	1,901	764	1,136	59.8
1995	1,772	710	1,062	59.9
1990	1,393	587	807	57.9
1985	1,263	552	712	56.4
1980	1,163	476	686	59.0
1975	1,099	523	577	52.5
1970	522	253	269	51.5
1965	274	126	148	54.0
1960	227	125	102	44.9
Hispanic				
1998	1,363	550	814	59.7
1997	1,260	555	704	55.9
1996	1,223	529	693	56.7
1995	1,207	568	639	52.9
1990	748	364	384	51.3
1985	580	279	299	51.6
1980	443	222	221	49.9
1975	411	218	193	47.0

(continued)

(continued from previous page)

	total	men	women number	women percent
White				
1998	12,401	5,602	6,799	54.8%
1997	12,442	5,552	6,890	55.4
1996	12,189	5,453	6,735	55.3
1995	12,021	5,535	6,486	54.0
1990	11,488	5,235	6,253	54.4
1985	10,781	5,103	5,679	52.7
1980	9,925	4,804	5,121	51.6
1975	9,546	5,263	4,284	44.9
1970	6,759	4,066	2,693	39.8
1965	5,317	3,326	1,991	37.4
1960	3,342	2,214	1,128	33.8

Note: Data for Hispanics not available prior to 1975.
Source: Bureau of the Census, Internet web site <http://www.census.gov/population/socdemo/school/taba-6 .txt>; calculations by New Strategist

Among Students, Women Are Older Than Men

One in five women enrolled in college is aged 35 or older.

Women account for two out of three college students in the 35-or-older age group. Among college students in the traditional 18-to-21 age group, women are a smaller 53 percent majority.

The age distribution of female students has changed much more than that of male students over the past few decades. Since 1970, the percentage of male students aged 18 to 21 has fallen from 55 to 46 percent of all male students. Among women, the proportion of students in that age group has plummeted from 67 to 41 percent of all female students. Behind the declining share of students aged 18 to 21 is the entry of the small baby-bust generation into the age group. The percentage of college students in the 18-to-21 age group will rise during the next few years as the large millennial generation goes to school.

The growing share of college students aged 22 or older is the consequence of the aging of the large baby-boom generation. Furthermore, today's students spend more time earning a bachelor's degree than students in the past did. It takes today's average student about six years to earn a bachelor's degree as higher college costs force more students to go to school part-time.

❖ Women will continue to dominate the student population in the years ahead. Not only are they more likely than men to enroll in college after graduating from high school, but they are also more likely to return to college as adults.

Men in College by Age, 1950 to 1998

(number and percent distribution of men aged 15 or older enrolled in college by age; 1950–98; numbers in thousands)

	total	15 to 17	18 to 19	20 to 21	22 to 24	25 to 29	30 to 34	35+
1998	6,905	48	1,667	1,517	1,219	979	521	953
1997	6,843	59	1,561	1,521	1,292	1,052	457	899
1996	6,820	97	1,489	1,379	1,319	1,038	485	1,013
1995	6,703	68	1,431	1,423	1,235	1,008	553	985
1990	6,192	86	1,443	1,364	1,115	910	502	772
1985	5,906	131	1,349	1,313	1,087	942	522	561
1980	5,430	96	1,369	1,246	989	853	472	405
1975	5,911	128	1,426	1,256	1,011	1,025	496	569
1970	4,401	130	1,346	1,083	902	684	256	–
1965	3,503	113	1,218	804	699	458	211	–
1960	2,339	99	734	503	411	399	193	–
1955	1,579	57	432	647*		337	107	–
1950	1,474	74	395	692*		314	–	–
1998	100.0%	0.7%	24.1%	22.0%	17.7%	14.2%	7.5%	13.8%
1997	100.0	0.9	22.8	22.2	18.9	15.4	6.7	13.1
1996	100.0	1.4	21.8	20.2	19.3	15.2	7.1	14.9
1995	100.0	1.0	21.3	21.2	18.4	15.0	8.3	14.7
1990	100.0	1.4	23.3	22.0	18.0	14.7	8.1	12.5
1985	100.0	2.2	22.8	22.2	18.4	15.9	8.8	9.5
1980	100.0	1.8	25.2	22.9	18.2	15.7	8.7	7.5
1975	100.0	2.2	24.1	21.2	17.1	17.3	8.4	9.6
1970	100.0	3.0	30.6	24.6	20.5	15.5	5.8	–
1965	100.0	3.2	34.8	23.0	20.0	13.1	6.0	–
1960	100.0	4.2	31.4	21.5	17.6	17.1	8.3	–
1955	100.0	3.6	27.4	41.0*		21.3	6.8	–
1950	100.0	5.0	26.8	46.9*		21.3	–	–

* Data are for 20-to-24 age group.
Note: (–) means data not available.
Source: Bureau of the Census, Internet web site <http://www.census.gov/population/socdemo/school/taba-6 .txt>; calculations by New Strategist

Women in College by Age, 1950 to 1998

(number and percent distribution of women aged 15 or older enrolled in college by age; 1950–98; numbers in thousands)

	total	15 to 17	18 to 19	20 to 21	22 to 24	25 to 29	30 to 34	35+
1998	8,641	74	2,003	1,574	1,342	1,170	745	1,732
1997	8,593	112	1,801	1,622	1,406	1,102	658	1,892
1996	8,406	140	1,821	1,528	1,233	1,177	743	1,765
1995	8,013	90	1,671	1,518	1,263	1,135	653	1,684
1990	7,429	91	1,576	1,403	1,063	1,017	732	1,546
1985	6,618	129	1,559	1,303	926	941	658	1,100
1980	5,957	153	1,565	1,178	882	788	590	802
1975	4,969	164	1,517	1,058	668	590	357	614
1970	3,013	130	1,248	774	452	255	154	–
1965	2,172	151	997	522	241	156	105	–
1960	1,231	123	565	287	98	92	66	–
1955	800	90	313	285*		69	43	–
1950	701	106	338	247*		10	–	–
1998	100.0%	0.9%	23.2%	18.2%	15.5%	13.5%	8.6%	20.0%
1997	100.0	1.3	21.0	18.9	16.4	12.8	7.7	22.0
1996	100.0	1.7	21.7	18.2	14.7	14.0	8.8	21.0
1995	100.0	1.1	20.9	18.9	15.8	14.2	8.1	21.0
1990	100.0	1.2	21.2	18.9	14.3	13.7	9.9	20.8
1985	100.0	1.9	23.6	19.7	14.0	14.2	9.9	16.6
1980	100.0	2.6	26.3	19.8	14.8	13.2	9.9	13.5
1975	100.0	3.3	30.5	21.3	13.4	11.9	7.2	12.4
1970	100.0	4.3	41.4	25.7	15.0	8.5	5.1	–
1965	100.0	7.0	45.9	24.0	11.1	7.2	4.8	–
1960	100.0	10.0	45.9	23.3	8.0	7.5	5.4	–
1955	100.0	11.3	39.1	35.6*		8.6	5.4	–
1950	100.0	15.1	48.2	35.2*		1.4	–	–

* Data are for 20-to-24 age group.
Note: (–) means data not available.
Source: Bureau of the Census, Internet web site <http://www.census.gov/population/socdemo/school/taba-6 .txt>; calculations by New Strategist

Women Dominate Enrollment in Higher Education

Most graduate students, as well as undergraduates, are women.

Overall, women account for 56 percent of the nation's college students. This proportion does not vary much by type of school. Women account for 56 percent of students at two-year colleges, 54 percent of those attending four-year schools, and 58 percent of graduate students. Among students aged 35 or older enrolled full-time at four-year schools, fully 79 percent are women.

Men account for the majority of students only in certain age groups. The slight majority of students aged 20 to 21 attending two-year colleges are men. Men are also the majority of students aged 22 to 24 at four-year schools, and men account for the majority of graduate students aged 30 to 34.

Among black college students, women account for at least 60 percent of students at two-year, four-year, and graduate schools. The proportion reaches 68 percent among full-time graduate students. Among Hispanics, women account for at least 60 percent of students at two-year and graduate schools, and for 56 percent of those at four-year schools. The proportions are only slightly lower among whites.

❖ If these trends continue for another few decades, American women will be better educated than American men. This will boost the incomes of women, giving them greater economic power and further transforming relations between the sexes.

College Students by Sex, Age, and Attendance Status, 1998

(number of people aged 15 or older enrolled in college by sex, age, and attendance status, 1998; numbers in thousands)

	total	undergraduate						graduate		
		two-year college			four-year college					
		total	full-time	part-time	total	full-time	part-time	total	full-time	part-time
Total men in college	**6,906**	**1,845**	**1,049**	**796**	**3,777**	**3,002**	**775**	**1,284**	**615**	**669**
Aged 15 to 17	48	–	–	–	23	23	–	–	–	–
Aged 18 to 19	1,668	597	462	135	1,060	987	73	–	–	–
Aged 20 to 21	1,517	393	287	106	1,101	1028	73	23	23	–
Aged 22 to 24	1,219	285	157	128	711	589	122	223	180	43
Aged 25 to 29	978	188	45	143	428	259	169	362	205	157
Aged 30 to 34	521	101	29	72	158	49	109	262	90	172
Aged 35 or older	948	219	42	177	272	51	221	375	93	282
Total women in college	**8,642**	**2,389**	**1,286**	**1,103**	**4,499**	**3,478**	**1021**	**1,754**	**758**	**996**
Aged 15 to 17	73	22	22	–	39	39	–	–	–	–
Aged 18 to 19	2,003	647	519	128	1,323	1254	69	33	33	–
Aged 20 to 21	1,574	309	209	100	1,216	1095	121	49	34	15
Aged 22 to 24	1,342	334	174	160	695	542	153	313	249	64
Aged 25 to 29	1,171	291	119	172	442	255	187	438	209	229
Aged 30 to 34	744	258	109	149	235	91	144	251	74	177
Aged 35 or older	1,731	475	121	354	537	193	344	666	156	510

(continued)

(continued from previous page)

Female share of college students	total	undergraduate						graduate		
		two-year college			four-year college					
		total	*full-time*	*part-time*	*total*	*full-time*	*part-time*	*total*	*full-time*	*part-time*
total	**55.6%**	**56.4%**	**55.1%**	**58.1%**	**54.4%**	**53.7%**	**56.8%**	**57.7%**	**55.2%**	**59.8%**
Aged 15 to 17	60.3	–	–	–	62.9	62.9	–	–	–	–
Aged 18 to 19	54.6	52.0	52.9	48.7	55.5	56.0	48.6	–	–	–
Aged 20 to 21	50.9	44.0	42.1	48.5	52.5	51.6	62.4	68.1	59.6	–
Aged 22 to 24	52.4	54.0	52.6	55.6	49.4	47.9	55.6	58.4	58.0	59.8
Aged 25 to 29	54.5	60.8	72.6	54.6	50.8	49.6	52.5	54.8	50.5	59.3
Aged 30 to 34	58.8	71.9	79.0	67.4	59.8	65.0	56.9	48.9	45.1	50.7
Aged 35 or older	64.6	68.4	74.2	66.7	66.4	79.1	60.9	64.0	62.7	64.4

Note: (–) means sample is too small to make a reliable estimate.

Source: Bureau of the Census, School Enrollment: Social and Economic Characteristics of Students: October 1998, detailed tables for Current Population Report P20-521, 1999; Internet web site <http://www.census.gov/population/www/socdemo/school.html>; calculations by New Strategist

College Students by Race, Hispanic Origin, Sex, and Attendance Status, 1998

(number of people aged 15 or older enrolled in college by race, Hispanic origin, and attendance status, and percent distribution by sex, 1998; numbers in thousands)

	total	undergraduate						graduate		
		two-year college			four-year college					
		total	full-time	part-time	total	full-time	part-time	total	full-time	part-time
Total enrolled in college	**15,546**	**4,234**	**2,336**	**1,898**	**8,275**	**6,480**	**1,795**	**3,037**	**1,372**	**1,655**
Percent male	44.4%	43.6%	44.9%	41.9%	45.6%	46.3%	43.2%	42.3%	44.8%	40.2%
Percent female	55.6	56.4	55.1	58.1	54.4	53.7	56.9	57.8	55.2	59.8
Blacks enrolled in college	**2,017**	**628**	**321**	**307**	**1,063**	**838**	**225**	**326**	**126**	**200**
Percent male	38.2%	38.7%	43.9%	33.2%	38.6%	38.5%	38.7%	36.2%	31.7%	39.0%
Percent female	61.8	61.3	56.1	66.8	61.4	61.5	61.3	63.8	68.3	61.0
Hispanics enrolled in college	**1,364**	**640**	**362**	**278**	**560**	**375**	**185**	**164**	**65**	**99**
Percent male	40.3%	38.4%	34.8%	43.2%	43.6%	44.5%	41.6%	36.6%	40.0%	34.3%
Percent female	59.7	61.6	65.5	56.5	56.4	55.5	58.4	63.4	60.0	65.7
Whites enrolled in college	**12,400**	**3,389**	**1,870**	**1,519**	**6,632**	**5,150**	**1,482**	**2,379**	**991**	**1,388**
Percent male	45.2%	44.3%	44.5%	43.9%	46.6%	47.4%	43.9%	42.5%	44.5%	41.1%
Percent female	54.8	55.8	55.5	56.1	53.4	52.6	56.1	57.5	55.6	58.9

Source: Bureau of the Census, School Enrollment: Social and Economic Characteristics of Students: October 1998, detailed tables for Current Population Report P20-521, 1999; Internet web site <http://www.census.gov/population/www/socdemo/school.html>; calculations by New Strategist

Objectives of Male and Female College Students Are Similar

Making money is the top priority for both.

Seventy-six percent of male college freshmen say being "very well off financially" is a priority for them. Among women, a nearly equal 72 percent say this is an essential or very important objective. The goals of male and female college freshmen are mostly similar, and only a few objectives show signficant gaps between the sexes.

Men are more likely than women to want to "be successful in my own business." Forty-five percent of men cite this as an essential or very important objective compared with only 33 percent of women. At the other extreme, 68 percent of women say helping others in difficulty is an essential or very important objective, 18 percentage points more than the 50 percent of male college freshmen for whom this is a top priority.

Men are slightly more likely than women to want to "make a theoretical contribution to science" and to "become an authority in my field." Women are slightly more likely than men to want to "develop a meaningful philosophy of life."

❖ Today's young men and women are seeking financial security above all else. Both want to succeed in their careers and achieve recognition for their efforts.

Important Objectives of College Freshmen by Sex, 1998

(percent of college freshmen citing objective as essential or very important by sex, and percentage point difference between men and women, 1998; ranked by percentage point difference between men and women)

	men	women	percentage point difference
Be successful in my own business	45.4%	33.4%	12.0
Keep up to date with politics	29.1	23.3	5.8
Make theoretical contribution to science	17.8	13.2	4.6
Be very well off financially	76.0	72.4	3.6
Be an authority in my field	61.8	58.8	3.0
Obtain recognition from colleagues	50.8	49.0	1.8
Write original works	14.0	13.1	0.9
Be a community leader	30.2	29.6	0.6
Create artistic work	14.0	13.6	0.4
Achieve in performing art	12.8	12.7	0.1
Develop philosophy of life	40.2	41.5	−1.3
Help others in difficulty	49.9	68.3	−18.4

Source: Higher Education Research Institute, UCLA, The American Freshman: National Norms for Fall 1998; calculations by New Strategist

Among College Freshmen, Men Are More Confident Than Women

College women may underestimate their abilities, while men overestimate theirs.

Among college freshmen, men are far more likely than women to believe they are above average or in the top 10 percent on a wide range of characteristics including athletic ability, competitiveness, physical health, intellectual self-confidence, popularity, mathematical ability, and emotional health, according to a survey by UCLA's Higher Education Research Institute. Women are more confident than men in only a handful of areas, including drive to achieve, spirituality, writing ability, and understanding of others.

The majority of both men and women say they are above average or in the top 10 percent in their leadership ability, self-understanding, academic ability, drive to achieve, and understanding of others. A minority of both sexes feel confident in their popularity, mathematical ability, public speaking ability, spirituality, and writing ability.

❖ Building self-esteem is an important part of today's elementary and high school curriculum. It appears to be working—especially for boys.

Self-Confidence of College Freshmen by Sex, 1998

(percent of college freshmen rating themselves above average or in the top 10 percent in selected characteristics by sex, 1998; percentage point difference between men and women; ranked by percentage point difference between men and women)

	men	women	percentage point difference
Athletic ability	55.8%	27.9%	27.9
Competitiveness	67.5	41.7	25.8
Physical health	64.9	45.7	19.2
Self-confidence (intellectual)	61.7	47.5	14.2
Popularity	44.9	31.2	13.7
Mathematical ability	46.2	32.9	13.3
Emotional health	58.2	47.5	10.7
Self-confidence (social)	53.4	44.4	9.0
Leadership ability	58.4	51.3	7.1
Self-understanding	56.9	50.4	6.5
Academic ability	58.4	55.0	3.4
Public speaking ability	32.6	29.6	3.0
Drive to achieve	64.1	66.3	–2.2
Spirituality	41.1	44.7	–3.6
Writing ability	38.8	43.0	–4.2
Understanding of others	58.1	64.8	–6.7

Source: Higher Education Research Institute, UCLA, The American Freshman: National Norms for Fall 1998; *calculations by New Strategist*

Women Earn 61 Percent of Associate's Degrees

They earn a minority of doctoral and first-professional degrees.

Of the 2.3 million degrees awarded by institutions of higher education in 1996–97, women earned the 56 percent majority. Among blacks, women earned fully 65 percent of all degrees awarded that year, while among Native Americans the figure was 62 percent. Among foreign students (called nonresident aliens) who earned degrees in 1996–97, women accounted for only 41 percent.

Women earned fully 61 percent of associate's degrees awarded in 1996–97. They also earned the majority of bachelor's and master's degrees granted that year. But women accounted for only 41 percent of doctoral degrees and 42 percent of first-professional degrees awarded in 1996–97. Among blacks, however, women earned the majority of doctoral and first-professional degrees.

❖ As today's highly educated young women enter the workforce and replace less-educated older women, the earnings gap between men and women will shrink substantially.

Degrees Conferred by Level of Degree, Sex, Race, and Hispanic Origin, 1996–97

(number of degrees earned by level of degree, sex, race, and Hispanic origin, and percent of degrees awarded to women, 1996–97)

	total	non-Hispanic white	non-Hispanic black	Hispanic	Asian	Native American	non-resident alien
Total degrees	**2,288,112**	**1,673,161**	**180,911**	**122,641**	**119,324**	**15,610**	**112,343**
Men	998,120	725,507	62,972	51,502	56,331	5,999	66,268
Women	1,289,992	947,654	117,939	71,139	62,993	9,611	46,075
Percent earned by women	56.4%	56.6%	65.2%	58.0%	52.8%	61.6%	41.0%
Associate's degrees	**571,226**	**419,994**	**55,054**	**42,568**	**24,586**	**5,852**	**10,764**
Men	223,948	164,795	18,906	17,545	10,665	2,018	4,677
Women	347,278	255,199	36,148	25,023	13,921	3,834	6,087
Percent earned by women	60.8%	60.8%	65.7%	58.8%	56.6%	65.5%	56.5%
Bachelor's degrees	**1,172,879**	**878,460**	**91,986**	**60,902**	**67,086**	**7,242**	**38,928**
Men	520,515	392,794	32,724	25,616	31,654	2,916	21,698
Women	652,364	485,666	59,262	35,286	35,432	4,326	17,230
Percent earned by women	55.6%	55.3%	64.4%	57.9%	52.8%	59.7%	44.3%
Master's degrees	**419,401**	**288,552**	**26,901**	**14,574**	**17,898**	**1,844**	**49,552**
Men	180,947	118,023	8,431	5,848	8,578	697	30,237
Women	238,454	170,529	18,470	8,726	9,320	1,147	19,315
Percent earned by women	56.9%	59.1%	68.7%	59.9%	52.1%	62.2%	39.0%
Doctoral degrees	**45,876**	**27,183**	**1,786**	**1,068**	**2,528**	**169**	**11,453**
Men	27,146	14,683	760	557	1,554	84	8,535
Women	18,730	12,500	1,026	511	974	85	2,918
Percent earned by women	40.8%	46.0%	57.4%	47.8%	38.5%	50.3%	25.5%
First-professional degrees	**78,730**	**58,972**	**5,184**	**3,529**	**7,226**	**503**	**1,646**
Men	45,564	35,212	2,151	1,936	3,880	284	1,121
Women	33,166	23,760	3,033	1,593	3,346	219	525
Percent earned by women	42.1%	40.3%	58.5%	45.1%	46.3%	43.5%	31.9%

Note: Numbers will not add to total because degrees awarded to people whose race/ethnicity is unknown are not shown.
Source: National Center for Education Statistics, Degrees and Other Awards Conferred by Title IV Eligible, Degree-granting Institutions: 1996–97, *NCES 2000-174, 1999; calculations by New Strategist*

Men Earn Most Degrees in Engineering, Women in Education

The percentage of degrees awarded to women varies greatly by field.

Women earned most of the associate's, bachelor's, and master's degrees awarded in 1996–97. Men earned the majority of doctoral and first-professional degrees.

The share of associate's degrees awarded to women ranged from a low of 5 percent in the construction trades to a high of 93 percent in home economics. Women earned more than 80 percent of bachelor's degrees awarded in 1996–97 in the health professions and library science, while men earned most of those in architecture, protective services, and theological studies. Although women earn most master's degrees, men earn the majority of degrees in fields such as computer and information sciences, engineering, and mathematics.

Women earned the majority of doctorates awarded in education, English language and literature, foreign languages, and psychology. Men dominate many doctoral fields including business management, communications, and social sciences.

❖ Professions traditionally dominated by women typically pay less than those dominated by men. Until women break into the hard sciences—such as engineering—they will have difficulty narrowing the pay gap with men.

Associate's Degrees Conferred by Field of Study and Sex, 1996–97

(number of associate's degrees conferred by field of study and sex, and percent awarded to women, 1996–97)

	total	men	women number	women percent
Total degrees	**571,226**	**223,948**	**347,278**	**60.8%**
Agricultural business and production	4,176	2,756	1,420	34.0
Agricultural sciences	845	431	414	49.0
Architecture and related programs	316	56	260	82.3
Area, ethnic, and cultural studies	84	32	52	61.9
Biological sciences/life sciences	2,116	769	1,347	63.7
Business management and admin. services	95,532	26,301	69,231	72.5
Communications	2,030	985	1,045	51.5
Communications technologies	1,743	1,091	652	37.4
Computer and information sciences	10,990	5,860	5,130	46.7
Conservation and renewable natural resources	1,442	1,142	300	20.8
Construction trades	1,928	1,829	99	5.1
Education	10,526	3,356	7,170	68.1
Engineering	1,952	1,681	271	13.9
Engineering-related technologies	33,810	29,452	4,358	12.9
English language and literature/letters	1,455	528	927	63.7
Foreign languages and literatures	689	231	458	66.5
Health professions and related sciences	98,921	15,970	82,951	83.9
Home economics	986	66	920	93.3
Law and legal studies	8,968	1,105	7,863	87.7
Liberal/general studies and humanities	181,341	69,572	111,769	61.6
Library science	126	17	109	86.5
Marketing operations/marketing and distribution	5,656	1,335	4,321	76.4
Mathematics	792	443	349	44.1
Mechanics and repairers	12,180	11,388	792	6.5
Military technologies	556	521	35	6.3
Multi/interdisciplinary studies	9,182	4,398	4,784	52.1
Parks, recreation, leisure, and fitness	913	554	359	39.3
Personal and miscellaneous services	8,211	5,115	3,096	37.7
Philosophy and religion	89	51	38	42.7
Physical sciences	1,728	856	872	50.5
Precision production trades	10,368	8,033	2,335	22.5

(continued)

(continued from previous page)

	total	men	women number	women percent
Protective services	19,889	13,588	6,301	31.7%
Psychology	1,612	377	1,235	76.6
Public administration and services	4,270	667	3,603	84.4
Science technologies	798	425	373	46.7
Social sciences and history	4,056	1,550	2,506	61.8
Theological studies/religious vocations	574	321	253	44.1
Transportation and material moving	1,612	1,349	263	16.3
Visual and performing arts	13,593	5,872	7,721	56.8
Vocational home economics	7,565	649	6,916	91.4
Undesignated fields	7,606	3,226	4,380	57.6

Source: National Center for Education Statistics, Degrees and Other Awards Conferred by Title IV Eligible, Degree-granting Institutions: 1996–97, *NCES 2000-174, 1999; calculations by New Strategist*

Bachelor's Degrees Conferred by Field of Study and Sex, 1996–97

(number of bachelor's degrees conferred by field of study and sex, and percent awarded to women, 1996–97)

	total	men	women number	women percent
Total degrees	**1,172,879**	**520,515**	**652,364**	**55.6%**
Agricultural business and production	5,027	3,510	1,517	30.2
Agricultural sciences	7,876	4,378	3,498	44.4
Architecture and related programs	7,944	5,090	2,854	35.9
Area, ethnic, and cultural studies	5,839	1,995	3,844	65.8
Biological sciences/life sciences	63,975	29,470	34,505	53.9
Business management and admin. services	221,875	114,500	107,375	48.4
Communications	47,230	19,412	27,818	58.9
Communications technologies	538	276	262	48.7
Computer and information sciences	24,768	18,037	6,731	27.2
Conservation and renewable natural resources	9,699	5,906	3,793	39.1
Construction trades	108	93	15	13.9
Education	105,233	26,271	78,962	75.0
Engineering	61,185	50,058	11,127	18.2
Engineering-related technologies	13,816	12,452	1,364	9.9
English language and literature/letters	49,345	16,531	32,814	66.5
Foreign languages and literatures	13,674	4,138	9,536	69.7
Health professions and related sciences	85,631	15,877	69,754	81.5
Home economics	16,113	1,735	14,378	89.2
Law and legal studies	2,038	603	1,435	70.4
Liberal/general studies and humanities	34,776	13,483	21,293	61.2
Library science	48	6	42	87.5
Marketing operations/marketing and distribution	4,549	1,892	2,657	58.4
Mathematics	12,820	6,908	5,912	46.1
Mechanics and repairers	48	45	3	6.3
Military technologies	4	4	–	0.0
Multi/interdisciplinary studies	26,137	8,901	17,236	65.9
Parks, recreation, leisure, and fitness	15,401	7,858	7,543	49.0
Personal and miscellaneous services	209	127	82	39.2
Philosophy and religion	7,685	4,882	2,803	36.5
Physical sciences	19,417	12,164	7,253	37.4
Precision production trades	326	257	69	21.2

(continued)

(continued from previous page)

	total	men	women number	women percent
Protective services	25,165	15,150	10,015	39.8%
Psychology	74,191	19,379	54,812	73.9
Public administration and services	20,649	4,177	16,472	79.8
Science technologies	114	64	50	43.9
Social sciences and history	124,891	64,115	60,776	48.7
Theological studies/religious vocations	5,591	4,119	1,472	26.3
Transportation and material moving	3,547	3,130	417	11.8
Visual and performing arts	50,083	20,729	29,354	58.6
Vocational home economics	458	179	279	60.9
Undesignated fields	4,856	2,614	2,242	46.2

Source: National Center for Education Statistics, Degrees and Other Awards Conferred by Title IV Eligible, *Degree-granting Institutions: 1996–97, NCES 2000-174, 1999; calculations by New Strategist*

Master's Degrees Conferred by Field of Study and Sex, 1996–97

(number of master's degrees conferred by field of study and sex, and percent awarded to women, 1996–97)

	total	men	women number	women percent
Total degrees	**419,401**	**180,947**	**238,454**	**56.9%**
Agricultural business and production	598	370	228	38.1
Agricultural sciences	1,609	970	639	39.7
Architecture and related programs	4,034	2,336	1,698	42.1
Area, ethnic, and cultural studies	1,651	739	912	55.2
Biological sciences/life sciences	6,466	3,035	3,431	53.1
Business management and admin. services	96,923	59,235	37,688	38.9
Communications	5,227	1,800	3,427	65.6
Communications technologies	374	204	170	45.5
Computer and information sciences	10,098	7,248	2,850	28.2
Conservation and renewable natural resources	2,309	1,268	1,041	45.1
Education	110,087	25,806	84,281	76.6
Engineering	25,787	21,120	4,667	18.1
Engineering-related technologies	1,040	808	232	22.3
English language and literature/letters	7,722	2,733	4,989	64.6
Foreign languages and literatures	3,077	1,004	2,073	67.4
Health professions and related sciences	35,958	7,702	28,256	78.6
Home economics	2,866	439	2,427	84.7
Law and legal studies	2,886	1,817	1,069	37.0
Liberal/general studies and humanities	2,661	892	1,769	66.5
Library science	4,982	1,115	3,867	77.6
Marketing operations/marketing & distribution	673	371	302	44.9
Mathematics	3,783	2,241	1,542	40.8
Military technologies	136	132	4	2.9
Multi/interdisciplinary studies	2,819	1,214	1,605	56.9
Parks, recreation, leisure, and fitness	1,966	965	1,001	50.9
Personal and miscellaneous services	23	5	18	78.3
Philosophy and religion	1,252	745	507	40.5
Physical sciences	5,546	3,739	1,807	32.6
Precision production trades	3	3	–	0.0
Protective services	1,845	1,098	747	40.5
Psychology	14,353	3,852	10,501	73.2

(continued)

(continued from previous page)

	total	men	women number	women percent
Public administration and services	24,781	6,957	17,824	71.9%
Science technologies	17	13	4	23.5
Social sciences and history	14,787	7,830	6,957	47.0
Theological studies/religious vocations	4,975	3,025	1,950	39.2
Transportation and material moving	919	863	56	6.1
Visual and performing arts	10,627	4,470	6,157	57.9
Vocational home economics	22	1	21	95.5
Undesignated fields	4,519	2,782	1,737	38.4

Source: National Center for Education Statistics, Degrees and Other Awards Conferred by Title IV Eligible, Degree-granting Institutions: 1996–97, *NCES 2000-174, 1999; calculations by New Strategist*

Doctoral Degrees Conferred by Field of Study and Sex, 1996–97

(number of doctoral degrees conferred by field of study and sex, and percent awarded to women, 1996–97)

	total	men	women number	percent
Total degrees	**45,876**	**27,146**	**18,730**	**40.8%**
Agricultural business and production	181	132	49	27.1
Agricultural sciences	690	495	195	28.3
Architecture and related programs	135	93	42	31.1
Area, ethnic, and cultural studies	182	95	87	47.8
Biological sciences/life sciences	4,812	2,738	2,074	43.1
Business management and admin. services	1,334	946	388	29.1
Communications	296	152	144	48.6
Communications technologies	4	3	1	25.0
Computer and information sciences	857	721	136	15.9
Conservation and renewable natural resources	346	257	89	25.7
Education	6,751	2,512	4,239	62.8
Engineering	6,201	5,438	763	12.3
Engineering-related technologies	9	8	1	11.1
English language and literature/letters	1,575	670	905	57.5
Foreign languages and literatures	915	385	530	57.9
Health professions and related sciences	2,672	1,176	1,496	56.0
Home economics	382	95	287	75.1
Law and legal studies	81	59	22	27.2
Liberal/general studies and humanities	77	34	43	55.8
Library science	46	16	30	65.2
Marketing operations/marketing and distribution	2	1	1	50.0
Mathematics	1,174	891	283	24.1
Multi/interdisciplinary studies	451	232	219	48.6
Parks, recreation, leisure, and fitness	108	60	48	44.4
Philosophy and religion	593	418	175	29.5
Physical sciences	4,467	3,438	1,029	23.0
Protective services	31	15	16	51.6
Psychology	4,053	1,350	2,703	66.7
Public administration and services	518	243	275	53.1
Science technologies	7	6	1	14.3
Social sciences and history	3,989	2,479	1,510	37.9
Theological studies/religious vocations	1,395	1,143	252	18.1
Visual and performing arts	1,060	525	535	50.5
Undesignated fields	482	320	162	33.6

Source: National Center for Education Statistics, Degrees and Other Awards Conferred by Title IV Eligible, Degree-granting Institutions: 1996–97, *NCES 2000-174, 1999; calculations by New Strategist*

Women Account for Nearly Half of Newly Minted Doctors and Lawyers

Women earn the majority of degrees in pharmacy and veterinary medicine.

Not long ago, it was unusual to find women physicians, lawyers, dentists, or pharmacists. Now, women make up a substantial share of those earning degrees in these and other fields.

As of 1996–97, women earned the majority of degrees in pharmacy (65 percent) and veterinary medicine (67 percent). They also earned most of the degrees awarded in optometry (53 percent). In that year, women earned 41 percent of degrees in medicine and 44 percent of law degrees. Women accounted for 37 percent of graduates earning degrees in dentistry and 36 percent of those in osteopathy. Women earned only 27 percent of degrees in chiropractic medicine. Their representation at the professional level was lowest in rabbinical and Talmudic studies (7 percent).

❖ As recent graduates from professional programs replace older professionals who are overwhelmingly men, women's presence in these high-paying fields will become commonplace.

First-Professional Degrees Conferred by Field of Study, 1996–97

(number of first-professional degrees conferred by field of study and sex, and percent awarded to women, 1996–97)

	total	men	women number	women percent
Total degrees	**78,730**	**45,564**	**33,166**	**42.1%**
Chiropractic (D.C. or D.C.M.)	3,654	2,658	996	27.3
Dentistry (D.D.S. or D.M.D.)	3,784	2,387	1,397	36.9
Medicine (M.D.)	15,571	9,121	6,450	41.4
Optometry (O.D.)	1,264	591	673	53.2
Osteopathic medicine (D.O.)	2,011	1,297	714	35.5
Pharmacy (Pharm.D.)	2,708	961	1,747	64.5
Podiatry (Pod.D., D.P., or D.P.M.)	614	423	191	31.1
Veterinary medicine (D.V.M.)	2,188	731	1,457	66.6
Law (LL.B. or J.D.)	40,079	22,548	17,531	43.7
Divinity/Ministry (B.D. or M.Div.)	5,580	4,063	1,517	27.2
Rabbinical and Talmudic Studies (M.H.L. or Rav)	279	260	19	6.8
Other/undefined field	998	524	474	47.5

Source: National Center for Education Statistics, Degrees and Other Awards Conferred by Title IV Eligible, Degree-granting Institutions: 1996–97, *NCES 2000-174, 1999; calculations by New Strategist*

Women Will Earn More Degrees

The number of men earning graduate degrees is projected to decline.

The number of women earning college degrees is projected to climb at all degree levels between 1998 and 2009, according to projections by the National Center for Education Statistics. In contrast, while the number of men earning associate's and bachelor's degrees will climb, the number of those earning master's or higher degrees is projected to fall.

The proportion of degrees awarded to women will grow across the board during the next decade. Women's share of associate's degrees will climb from 60 to 62 percent between 1998 and 2009. Their share of bachelor's degrees will grow from 55 to 58 percent, and they will earn 59 percent of master's degrees, up from 57 percent in 1998.

The number of men enrolled in graduate degree programs will decline during the next decade as the small, baby-bust generation enters the typical graduate-student age groups. Because women are much more likely than men to go back to school as adults, the National Center for Education Statistics does not foresee a decline in women's graduate-level enrollment. Although men earn the majority of doctoral and first-professional degrees today, their share will shrink during the next decade. By 2009, women will earn 41 percent of doctoral degrees and 46 percent of first-professional degrees.

❖ The rising number of women with college degrees will profoundly affect women's status in American society. Women will demand equality not only in the workforce, but at home as well.

Women's dominance of degrees will grow

(percent of degrees awarded to women by level of degree, 2009)

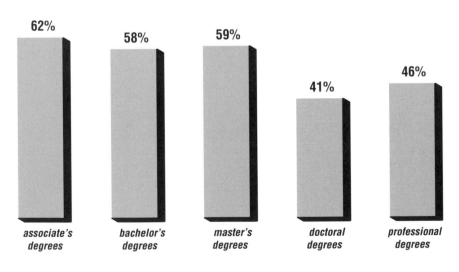

associate's degrees	bachelor's degrees	master's degrees	doctoral degrees	professional degrees
62%	58%	59%	41%	46%

Degrees Conferred by Level of Degree and Sex, 1998 to 2009

(number and percent distribution of degrees conferred by level of degree and sex of degree-holder, 1998 and 2009; percent change in number, 1998–2009)

	1998			2009			percent change, 1998 to 2009		
	total	men	women	total	men	women	total	men	women
Associate's degrees	558,000	224,000	335,000	628,000	236,000	392,000	12.5%	5.4%	17.0%
Bachelor's degrees	1,160,000	517,000	643,000	1,257,000	531,000	725,000	8.4	2.7	12.8
Master's degrees	391,000	171,000	221,000	400,000	164,000	236,000	2.3	-4.1	6.8
Doctoral degrees	44,600	26,900	17,700	44,300	26,100	18,200	-0.7	-3.0	2.8
First-professional degrees	78,100	44,900	33,100	74,300	40,300	34,000	-4.9	-10.2	2.7

	1998			2009			percentage point change, 1998 to 2009	
	total	men	women	total	men	women	men	women
Associate's degrees	100.0%	40.1%	60.0%	100.0%	37.6%	62.4%	-2.6%	2.4%
Bachelor's degrees	100.0	44.6	55.4	100.0	42.2	57.7	-2.3	2.2
Master's degrees	100.0	43.7	56.5	100.0	41.0	59.0	-2.7	2.5
Doctoral degrees	100.0	60.3	39.7	100.0	58.9	41.1	-1.4	1.4
First-professional degrees	100.0	57.5	42.4	100.0	54.2	45.8	-3.3	3.4

Note: (–) means not applicable.
Source: National Center for Education Statistics, Projections of Education Statistics to 2009, Internet web site, http://nces.ed.gov/pubsearch/pubsinfo .asp?pubid=1999038>; calculations by New Strategist

Younger Wives Are Better Educated Than Husbands

Older husbands are better educated than wives.

The influx of young women onto college campuses is evident in the statistics on the education of husbands and wives. Among couples with husbands under age 35, wives are more likely than husbands to have a college degree. Among couples with husbands aged 35 or older, husbands are more likely than wives to be college educated.

Among couples with husbands aged 18 to 24, 13 percent of wives but only 9 percent of husbands have a bachelor's degree. Twenty-nine percent of wives, but only 26 percent of husbands, have at least some college education or an associate's degree.

Among couples with husbands aged 25 to 34, 28 percent of wives and a smaller 27 percent of husbands have a bachelor's degree. Thirty percent of wives have some college education compared with 27 percent of husbands.

For older couples, the reverse is true. Among couples in which the husband is aged 35 to 44, 29 percent of wives and a larger 31 percent of husbands have a bachelor's degree. The gap widens in progressively older age groups. Among couples with a husband aged 65 or older, only 14 percent of wives, but 21 percent of husbands, have a bachelor's degree.

❖ As well-educated younger wives replace older less-educated wives among consumers, businesses will find their markets transformed by women's increased sophistication, self-confidence, and economic clout.

Educational Attainment of Husbands and Wives by Age of Husband, 1998

(percent distribution of married couples aged 18 or older by age of husband and educational attainment of husband and wife, 1998)

Education and age of husband	total wives	education of wife			
		less than high school	high school graduate only	some college or associate's degree	bachelor's degree or more
Total husbands	**100.0%**	**13.6%**	**36.7%**	**25.7%**	**24.1%**
Less than high school	15.9	8.4	5.5	1.6	0.4
High school graduate only	31.7	3.6	18.7	6.7	2.6
Some college or associate's degree	23.9	1.2	8.2	10.1	4.5
Bachelor's degree or more	28.5	0.4	4.3	7.2	16.7
Husbands aged 18 to 24	**100.0**	**21.5**	**36.5**	**29.3**	**12.7**
Less than high school	21.6	12.1	6.5	2.9	0.2
High school graduate only	44.4	8.1	24.9	9.6	1.8
Some college or associate's degree	25.9	1.3	4.8	14.6	5.2
Bachelor's degree or more	8.1	–	0.3	2.2	5.6
Husbands aged 25 to 34	**100.0**	**10.9**	**31.1**	**29.6**	**28.4**
Less than high school	12.1	6.5	4.0	1.5	0.2
High school graduate only	33.7	3.3	17.5	9.2	3.7
Some college or associate's degree	27.1	1.1	7.1	13.4	5.5
Bachelor's degree or more	27.1	0.1	2.5	5.6	18.9
Husbands aged 35 to 44	**100.0**	**9.6**	**33.6**	**28.3**	**28.5**
Less than high school	11.2	5.6	4.0	1.4	0.2
High school graduate only	31.3	2.8	17.9	7.3	3.4
Some college or associate's degree	26.2	0.9	8.0	11.7	5.6
Bachelor's degree or more	31.3	0.3	3.7	7.9	19.4

(continued)

(continued from previous page)

	total wives	education of wife			
		less than high school	high school graduate only	some college or associate's degree	bachelor's degree or more
Husbands aged 45 to 54	**100.0%**	**9.9%**	**35.7%**	**26.8%**	**27.6%**
Less than high school	11.6	5.7	4.3	1.2	0.4
High school graduate only	28.0	2.8	16.8	6.0	2.4
Some college or associate's degree	26.0	1.0	9.4	10.8	4.9
Bachelor's degree or more	34.4	0.4	5.3	8.7	20.0
Husbands aged 55 to 64	**100.0**	**15.0**	**41.9**	**22.8**	**20.3**
Less than high school	17.5	9.0	6.4	1.7	0.3
High school graduate only	34.3	4.4	21.8	6.1	2.1
Some college or associate's degree	19.9	1.1	8.5	6.9	3.5
Bachelor's degree or more	28.3	0.5	5.2	8.1	14.5
Husbands aged 65 or older	**100.0**	**24.1**	**43.6**	**18.5**	**13.9**
Less than high school	29.7	16.5	10.0	2.3	0.9
High school graduate only	30.9	4.9	20.2	4.5	1.4
Some college or associate's degree	18.0	2.0	8.1	6.0	2.0
Bachelor's degree or more	21.4	0.7	5.3	5.7	9.7

Source: Bureau of the Census, Educational Attainment in the United States: March 1998 (Update), *detailed tables for Current Population Report P20-513, 1998; Internet web site <http://www.census.gov/population /www/socdemo/edu-attn.html>; calculations by New Strategist*

Health

❖ **Most older men and women rate their health as good to excellent.**

Among people aged 65 or older, men are much more likely than women to say their health is only fair or poor, 45 to 33 percent.

❖ **The eating habits of men and women differ significantly.**

Men are more likely than women to eat french fries, drink beer, and dine at a fast-food restaurant. Women are more likely to eat yogurt, drink tea, and dine at a friend's house.

❖ **Condoms have become more popular among young women.**

Between 1982 and 1995, the percentage of contracepting women aged 20 to 24 whose partners used a condom rose from 11 to 26 percent.

❖ **Few babies are born to teenagers or women over age 35.**

Mothers aged 20 to 34 accounted for 75 percent of all births in 1998. Only 13 percent of babies were born to women younger than 20, while another 13 percent were born to women aged 35 or older.

❖ **Many young men do not have health insurance coverage.**

Fully 33 percent of men aged 18 to 24 have no health insurance. Among women in the age group, 27 percent lack health insurance.

❖ **Most health care consumers are women.**

Most of those suffering from acute conditions (such as colds and the flu) are women, as are the majority of people suffering from chronic conditions (such as arthritis).

❖ **Men dominate AIDS victims.**

Females account for only 16 percent of Americans diagnosed with AIDS. Among teenagers with the disease, females are a larger 39 percent.

Men and Women Feel Good

Even in old age, most rate their health as good to excellent.

The majority of men and women say their health is good or excellent, with the largest percentage (48 percent) saying it is good. Another 31 percent say they are in excellent health. Between 16 and 17 percent of Americans say their health is fair, while 4 percent of men and 5 percent of women describe their health as poor. Older men are more likely than older women to say they are in poor health.

People aged 18 to 24 are most likely to rate their health as excellent, with 41 percent of women and 43 percent of men in the age group saying so. The percentages fall with age. Among people aged 65 or older, just 14 percent of men and 17 percent of women say they are in excellent health.

The proportion of men who describe their health as only fair or poor rises from 12 percent among those aged 18 to 24 to fully 45 percent among those aged 65 or older. Among women, the figure reaches 33 percent among the elderly, but 67 percent of the oldest women continue to rate their health as good to excellent.

❖ The percentage of older Americans who say their health is good or excellent is rising as people take better care of themselves. As the older population feels better, it is becoming a more important consumer segment.

Men and women rate their health about the same

(percent distribution of people aged 18 or older by health status, by sex, 1998)

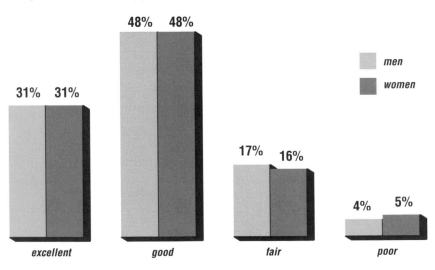

Health Status by Sex and Age, 1998

"Would you say your own health, in general, is excellent, good, fair, or poor?"

(percent of people aged 18 or older responding by sex and age, 1998)

	excellent	good	fair	poor
Total men	**30.6%**	**47.5%**	**17.4%**	**4.5%**
Aged 18 to 24	43.0	44.9	12.1	0.0
Aged 25 to 34	34.9	51.3	12.0	1.8
Aged 35 to 44	33.3	51.1	12.9	2.6
Aged 45 to 54	29.5	44.1	21.8	4.5
Aged 55 to 64	29.6	48.1	15.6	6.7
Aged 65 or older	14.4	40.9	32.0	12.7
Total women	**31.2**	**47.7**	**15.9**	**5.1**
Aged 18 to 24	41.0	42.5	14.9	1.5
Aged 25 to 34	38.4	51.0	9.5	1.1
Aged 35 to 44	34.9	47.8	15.7	1.4
Aged 45 to 54	32.3	46.2	14.6	6.9
Aged 55 to 64	25.0	44.0	20.1	10.9
Aged 65 or older	16.7	49.8	22.4	10.7

Source: 1998 General Social Survey, National Opinion Research Center, University of Chicago; calculations by New Strategist

Women Are More Concerned about Healthy Eating

Men take dietary guidelines less seriously than women.

Women are more likely than men to regard a variety of dietary guidelines as "very important." From "eat a variety of foods" to "maintain a healthy weight," women value each guideline more highly than men.

The gap between the percentages of men and women who regard specific guidelines as very important is greatest for "choose a diet with plenty of fruits and vegtables." Seventy-five percent of women but only 60 percent of men regard that guideline as very important. The gap is smallest—just 6 percentage points— for "choose a diet with plenty of breads, cereals, rice, and pasta."

Overall, the largest percentages of men and women rate "maintain a healthy weight" as most important. Seventy-seven percent of women and 68 percent of men believe this advice is very important.

❖ Women's greater concern with healthy eating makes them the primary audience for health claims in the marketing of food products.

Importance of Dietary Guidelines by Sex, 1994–96

(percent of people saying dietary guidelines are very important by sex, and percentage point difference between men and women, 1994–96; ranked by percentage point difference)

	men	women	percentage point difference
Choose a diet with plenty of fruits and vegetables	59.7%	75.3%	–15.6
Eat at least two servings of dairy products daily	28.2	42.6	–14.4
Choose a diet low in fat	50.6	64.5	–13.9
Choose a diet low in saturated fat	47.1	59.4	–12.3
Eat a variety of foods	54.8	66.1	–11.3
Choose a diet with adequate fiber	44.3	55.5	–11.2
Use sugars only in moderation	45.0	56.0	–11.0
Use salt or sodium only in moderation	45.6	56.1	–10.5
Choose a diet low in cholesterol	50.9	60.4	–9.5
Maintain a healthy weight	68.1	77.0	–8.9
Choose a diet with plenty of breads, cereals, rice, and pasta	28.6	34.3	–5.7

Source: USDA, ARS Food Surveys Research Group, Data Tables: Results from USDA's 1994–96 Continuing Survey of Food Intakes by Individuals *and* 1994–96 Diet and Health Knowledge Survey, *1999; Internet web site <http://www.barc.usda.gov/bhnrc/foodsurvey/home.htm>; calculations by New Strategist*

Men Drink More Beer, Soft Drinks

The eating patterns of men and women sometimes differ significantly.

On an average day, 17 percent of men have a beer compared with fewer than 5 percent of women. While 43 percent of men drink a regular soft drink on an average day, among women the proportion is a much smaller 32 percent. Men are also more likely than women to eat French fries, frankfurters, beef, and potatoes.

Thirty percent of women drink tea on an average day versus a smaller 24 percent of men. Women are also more likely than men to drink diet soft drinks and skim milk, and to eat yogurt.

Overall, women are somewhat more likely than men to consume fruits and vegetables, while men are more likely to eat meat and potatoes. Despite women's slight edge in dietary health, both men and women are more likely to have a soft drink than citrus juice and a larger percentage consume cakes, cookies, pastry, and pie than salad or dark green vegetables.

❖ Most Americans know what it takes to eat a healthy diet. But more often than not, people eat what they want rather than what they should. With age, however, health concerns will prompt many to control their impulses.

Food Consumption by Sex, 1994—96

(percent of people aged 20 or older consuming selected types of foods on an average day, by sex; percentage point difference between men and women, 1994—96; ranked by percentage point difference)

	men	women	percentage point difference
Beer and ale	17.0%	4.5%	12.5
Carbonated soft drinks, regular	42.8	32.3	10.5
French fries	27.8	20.1	7.7
Frankfurters, sausages, luncheon meats	31.9	24.3	7.6
Beef	24.8	18.3	6.5
Potatoes	46.8	40.5	6.3
Tomatoes	42.2	39.3	2.9
Eggs	21.7	18.8	2.9
Coffee	55.8	54.0	1.8
Low-fat milk	24.1	22.7	1.4
Pork	18.1	16.7	1.4
Fish and shellfish	9.8	8.4	1.4
Yeast breads and rolls	68.8	67.4	1.4
Milk desserts	17.3	16.2	1.1
Rice	12.0	11.0	1.0
Cheese	33.1	32.3	0.8
Quick breads, pancakes, french toast	22.5	21.8	0.7
Nuts and seeds	8.6	7.9	0.7
Whole milk	15.3	14.7	0.6
Pasta	7.7	7.1	0.6
Corn, green peas, lima beans	12.0	11.4	0.6
Fruit drinks and ades	14.7	14.4	0.3
Poultry	22.8	22.7	0.1
Candy	12.1	12.2	−0.1
Legumes	14.7	14.8	−0.1
Noncitrus juices and nectars	4.9	5.1	−0.2
Wine	4.7	5.1	−0.4
Citrus juices	20.2	20.9	−0.7
Salad dressings	31.8	32.5	−0.7
Cakes, cookies, pastries, pies	38.8	39.8	−1.0
Lettuce, lettuce-based salads	27.8	28.8	−1.0
Bananas	14.6	15.6	−1.0

(continued)

(continued from previous page)

	men	women	percentage point difference
Green beans	7.3%	8.4%	−1.1
Crackers, popcorn, pretzels, corn chips	25.7	26.9	−1.2
Ready-to-eat cereals	22.3	23.8	−1.5
Apples	10.1	11.8	−1.7
Dark-green vegetables	10.6	12.4	−1.8
Table fats	31.7	33.6	−1.9
Sugars	33.7	36.0	−2.3
Melons and berries	7.3	9.7	−2.4
Deep-yellow vegetables	12.4	15.0	−2.6
Yogurt	2.8	5.4	−2.6
Skim milk	10.4	14.4	−4.0
Carbonated soft drinks, low calorie	13.2	18.2	−5.0
Tea	24.3	30.0	−5.7

Source: USDA, ARS Food Surveys Research Group, Data Tables: Results from USDA's 1994-96 Continuing Survey of Food Intakes by Individuals and 1994–96 Diet and Health Knowledge Survey, 1999; Internet web site <http://www.barc.usda.gov/bhnrc/foodsurvey/home.htm>; calculations by New Strategist

Women Are More Likely to Take Vitamins

The gap between the sexes is largest among people under age 60.

Forty-two percent of men and 56 percent of women aged 20 or older take vitamin or mineral supplements. Among men, the share of those who take supplements rises with age to more than 47 percent of those aged 60 or older. Among women, the share of those who take supplements peaks at 63 percent in the 50-to-59 age group.

Women are more likely than men to take supplements at all ages. The biggest difference occurs in the 50-to-59 age group, when women are 19 percentage points more likely to take supplements than men. Among Americans aged 60 or older, the gap between men and women shrinks to less than 10 percentage points.

❖ Americans aged 50 or older are most likely to take vitamins. As the large baby-boom generation enters its fifties and sixties, sales of vitamin and mineral supplements will surge.

Vitamin Use by Age and Sex, 1994–96

(percent of people aged 20 or older using vitamin and mineral supplements by age and sex, and percentage point difference between men and women, 1994–96)

	men	women	percentage point difference
Aged 20 or older	**41.9%**	**55.8%**	**–13.9**
Aged 20 to 29	36.4	52.0	–15.6
Aged 30 to 39	39.7	54.4	–14.7
Aged 40 to 49	43.8	56.7	–12.9
Aged 50 to 59	43.8	62.6	–18.8
Aged 60 to 69	47.6	57.3	–9.7
Aged 70 or older	47.1	53.6	–6.5

Source: USDA, ARS Food Surveys Research Group, Supplementary Data Tables: USDA's 1994–96 Continuing Survey of Food Intakes by Individuals, *Internet web site <http://www.barc.usda.gov/bhnrc/foodsurvey/home .htm>; calculations by New Strategist*

Men Are More Likely to Eat Out

The majorities of men and women eat at least one meal away from home on an average day.

Sixty-one percent of men and 51 percent of women eat away from home on an average day. Women are less likely than men to eat away from home in part because the average woman is older than the average man and less likely to be out and about.

Fast-food restaurants capture the largest percentage of men eating away from home. Thirty-six percent of men aged 20 or older who eat away from home eat at a fast-food restaurant on an average day compared with a smaller 30 percent of women. Sit-down restaurants capture the largest share of women. Thirty-four percent of women who eat away from home eat at a sit-down restaurant on an average day versus 32 percent of men.

Men are more likely than women to eat at a store—such as a microwaved meal from a convenience store—and 28 percent of men who eat away from home do so versus 22 percent of women. Women are more likely than men to eat at someone else's house or to eat food given to them as a gift—24 versus 17 percent.

❖ The primary customers of fast-food restaurants are men, which explains why fast-food fare is mostly meat and potatoes.

Fast food is more popular among men

(percent of people eating away from home who eat in a fast-food restaurant, by sex, 1994–96)

30%

women

36%

men

People Eating away from Home by Location and Sex, 1994–96

(percent of people aged 20 or older eating away from home on an average day by location and sex, and percentage point difference between men and women, 1994–96; ranked by percentage point difference)

	men	women	percentage point difference
Percent eating away from home	**61.2%**	**51.0%**	**10.2**
Total eating away from home	**100.0%**	**100.0%**	–
Store	27.7	22.3	5.4
Fast-food restaurant	35.6	30.3	5.3
School cafeteria	1.7	2.5	–0.8
Cafeteria	8.5	9.9	–1.4
Sit-down restaurant	32.2	34.1	–1.9
Someone else/gift	17.3	23.5	–6.2

Note: Numbers will not add to 100 because food may be eaten at more than one location during the day.
Source: USDA, ARS Food Surveys Research Group, Supplementary Data Tables: USDA's 1994–96 Continuing Survey of Food Intakes by Individuals, *Internet web site <http://www.barc.usda.gov/bhnrc/foodsurvey/home.htm>; calculations by New Strategist*

Women and Men Are Equally Likely to Be Overweight

The middle-aged have the biggest weight problem.

Overall, 32 percent of men and women were overweight in the 1994-to-1996 period, according to surveys by the United States Department of Agriculture.

Young adults are least likely to be overweight, while people aged 40 to 69 are most likely to tip the scales. Among men aged 20 to 29, only 22 percent are overweight. But fully 41 percent of men aged 60 to 69 weigh more than they should. Among women in their twenties, only 22 percent are overweight. The figure peaks at 38 percent among women aged 50 to 69.

Men in their thirties are significantly more likely than their female counterparts to be overweight. The opposite is true among people in their seventies, with 33 percent of women but only 22 percent of men in that age group considered overweight.

❖ The large baby-boom generation is now entering the ages when maintaining an appropriate weight becomes a growing problem. This quandary should fuel the weight loss industry in its many forms—from appetite-suppressing drugs to low-fat foods, from exercise to counseling and other services.

Overweight People by Age and Sex, 1994–96

(percent of people aged 20 or older who are overweight by age and sex, and percentage point difference between men and women, 1994–96)

	men	women	percentage point difference
Total people	**31.8%**	**31.5%**	**0.3**
Aged 20 to 29	21.5	22.1	–0.6
Aged 30 to 39	32.3	27.4	4.9
Aged 40 to 49	37.0	36.1	0.9
Aged 50 to 59	39.9	37.8	2.1
Aged 60 to 69	40.7	37.8	2.9
Aged 70 or older	22.1	33.4	–11.3

Note: For men, overweight is defined as a body mass index (BMI) equal to or greater than 27.8. For women, it is defined as a BMI equal to or greater than 27.3. BMI is calculated by dividing weight in kilograms by the square of height in meters.
Source: USDA, ARS Food Surveys Research Group, Data Tables: Results from USDA's 1994–96 Continuing Survey of Food Intakes by Individuals and 1994–96 Diet and Health Knowledge Survey, 1999; Internet web site <http://www.barc.usda.gov/bhnrc/foodsurvey/home.htm>; calculations by New Strategist

Men Are More Likely to Smoke

Both men and women are smoking less, however.

Public health campaigns against cigarette smoking have had an effect on both men and women. In 1965, 52 percent of men and 34 percent of women smoked cigarettes. By 1995, the proportions had fallen to 27 and 23 percent, respectively.

Americans aged 35 to 44 are most likely to smoke. In this age group, 32 percent of men and 27 percent of women are smokers. Those least likely to smoke are the oldest adults, with only 15 percent of men and 12 percent of women aged 65 or older doing so. One reason why the oldest adults are least likely to smoke is that many have kicked the habit, some of them following doctor's orders. Another reason is that many of the smokers have already died.

The difference in the percentages of men and women who smoke is greatest among young adults. Among people aged 18 to 24, 28 percent of men but only 22 percent of women smoke cigarettes. Apparently, antismoking campaigns are having a bigger impact on women than on men.

❖ Cigarette smoking is likely to continue to decline among both men and women as cigarette prices rise and smoking is increasingly restricted.

Cigarette Smoking by Age and Sex, 1995

(percent of people aged 18 or older who smoke cigarettes by age and sex, and percentage point difference between men and women, 1995)

	men	women	percentage point difference
Total people	**27.0%**	**22.6%**	**4.4**
Aged 18 to 24	27.8	21.8	6.0
Aged 25 to 34	29.5	26.4	3.1
Aged 35 to 44	31.5	27.1	4.4
Aged 45 to 64	27.1	24.0	3.1
Aged 65 or older	14.9	11.5	3.4

Source: National Center for Health Statistics, Health, United States, 1998; *calculations by New Strategist*

Most Americans Drink Alcohol

Men are more likely to drink than women.

Seventy-five percent of men and 64 percent of women say they drink alcoholic beverages at least occasionally. At most ages, men are more likely to drink than women, with two exceptions. Among 18-to-24-year-olds, women are more likely to drink than men, 87 versus 78 percent. And among 55-to-64-year-olds, women also outdrink men—72 to 67 percent.

The proportion of men who drink peaks in the 25-to-34 age group at 86 percent. It falls fairly steadily with age to a low of 60 percent among men aged 65 or older. Among women, drinking peaks in the 18-to-24 age group. It bottoms out at just 36 percent among those aged 65 or older.

❖ Older men and women are less likely to drink than younger adults because health problems and medications often limit alcohol consumption.

Drinking by Age and Sex, 1994

(percent of people aged 18 or older who drink alcohol by age and sex, and percentage point difference between men and women, 1994)

	men	women	percentage point difference
Total people	**75.0%**	**64.3%**	**10.7**
Aged 18 to 24	78.3	86.7	–8.4
Aged 25 to 34	86.2	79.4	6.8
Aged 35 to 44	74.1	69.2	4.8
Aged 45 to 54	77.1	52.9	24.2
Aged 55 to 64	66.7	72.1	–5.4
Aged 65 or older	59.5	36.2	23.3

Source: 1994 General Social Survey, National Opinion Research Center, University of Chicago; calculations by New Strategist

Women Are More Likely to Have High Cholesterol

Among people under age 45, however, the opposite is true.

One in five women aged 20 or older has high cholesterol, according to the National Center for Health Statistics. Among men, the proportion is a smaller 18 percent.

Men under age 45 are more likely to have high cholesterol than women in the age group. The difference is a tiny 0.9 percentage points among 20-to-34-year-olds, rising to 7.1 percentage points among 35-to-44-year-olds.

The percentage of women with high cholesterol leaps upward in the 45-to-54 age group, closing the gap between the sexes. Among people aged 55 or older, women are 13 to 19 percentage points more likely than men to have high cholesterol.

The proportion of men with high cholesterol peaks at 28 percent in the 55-to-64 age group. Among women, the peak is a much higher 41 percent among those aged 65 to 74.

❖ Despite women's greater interest in eating a healthy diet and their greater consumption of fruits and vegetables on a daily basis, high cholesterol is a bigger problem for women than for men.

High cholesterol is a bigger problem for women

(percent of people aged 20 or older who have high serum cholesterol, by sex, 1988–94)

18%

20%

men

women

High Cholesterol by Age and Sex, 1988–94

(percent of people aged 20 or older who have high serum cholesterol by age and sex, and percentage point difference between men and women, 1988–94)

	men	women	percentage point difference
Total people	**17.5%**	**20.0%**	**–2.5**
Aged 20 to 34	8.2	7.3	0.9
Aged 35 to 44	19.4	12.3	7.1
Aged 45 to 54	26.6	26.7	–0.1
Aged 55 to 64	28.0	40.9	–12.9
Aged 65 to 74	21.9	41.3	–19.4
Aged 75 or older	20.4	38.2	–17.8

Source: National Center for Health Statistics, Health, United States, 1998, *calculations by New Strategist*

High Blood Pressure Is Common among Older Men and Women

Older women are most likely to have high blood pressure.

Twenty-five percent of men and 21 percent of women have high blood pressure. Up to age 55, men are more likely than women to have high blood pressure, but among older people, women are more likely than men to suffer from this condition.

The proportions of men and women with hypertension are highest in the oldest age group. Among people aged 75 or older, 64 percent of men and 77 percent of women have the condition. The majority of adults aged 65 or older suffer from high blood pressure.

Among adults aged 45 to 54, a significant one-third of men and one-fourth of women have hypertension. Even among men aged 35 to 44, a substantial 21 percent have a problem with blood pressure.

❖ As the baby-boom generation ages, high blood pressure will become a bigger problem. The medications and lifestyle changes necessary to alleviate high blood pressure will become commonplace in millions of American households.

Men are more likely to have high blood pressure

(percent of people aged 20 or older with hypertension, by sex, 1988–94)

25%

21%

men

women

High Blood Pressure by Age and Sex, 1988–94

(percent of people aged 20 or older with hypertension by age and sex, and percentage point difference between men and women, 1988–94)

	men	women	percentage point difference
Total people	**25.3%**	**20.8%**	**4.5**
Aged 20 to 34	8.6	3.4	5.2
Aged 35 to 44	20.9	12.7	8.2
Aged 45 to 54	34.1	25.1	9.0
Aged 55 to 64	42.9	44.2	−1.3
Aged 65 to 74	57.3	60.8	−3.5
Aged 75 or older	64.2	77.3	−13.1

Source: National Center for Health Statistics, Health, United States, 1998; *calculations by New Strategist*

Majority of Men Exercise Vigorously at Least Twice a Week

Young men are most likely to exercise frequently.

The majority of men under age 70 say they exercise vigorously at least twice a week. Among women, the proportion of those who frequently exercise vigorously never rises to the majority. Overall, 58 percent of men and 41 percent of women say they exercise vigorously at least twice a week.

The percentage of men who engage in vigorous exercise at least twice weekly falls with age from a high of 69 percent among those aged 20 to 29 to a low of 39 percent among those aged 70 or older. Among women, there is no steady decline with age. Between 43 and 46 percent of women under age 60 exercise vigorously at least two times a week. After age 60, the proportion falls with age to a low of 23 percent among women aged 70 or older.

The difference between the percentages of men and women who exercise vigorously at least twice a week is greatest among the youngest adults, at 23 percentage points. It falls with age to just 8.5 percentage points in the 50-to-59 age group before rising again among the oldest Americans.

❖ Women's significantly lower participation in vigorous exercise compared with men suggests an unmet need among women for opportunities to work out.

Vigorous Exercise by Age and Sex, 1994–96

(percent of people aged 20 or older who exercise vigorously at least twice a week by age and sex, and percentage point difference between men and women, 1994–96)

	men	women	percentage point difference
Total people	**57.8%**	**41.1%**	**16.7**
Aged 20 to 29	68.6	45.4	23.2
Aged 30 to 39	62.2	46.1	16.1
Aged 40 to 49	56.8	43.1	13.7
Aged 50 to 59	53.0	44.5	8.5
Aged 60 to 69	51.5	37.1	14.4
Aged 70 or older	38.5	23.3	15.2

Source: USDA, ARS Food Surveys Research Group, Data Tables: Results from USDA's 1994–96 Continuing Survey of Food Intakes by Individuals *and* 1994–96 Diet and Health Knowledge Survey, *1999; Internet web site <http://www.barc.usda.gov/bhnrc/foodsurvey/home.htm>; calculations by New Strategist*

Condom Use Has Increased Substantially

Younger women are abandoning the pill in favor of condoms.

The percentage of women aged 15 to 44 who rely on condoms as their method of birth control grew from 12 to 20 percent between 1982 and 1995, according to the National Center for Health Statistics. At the same time, the percentage of women relying on birth control pills, diaphragms, and intrauterine devices has fallen. Behind this shift is the need for protection from AIDS, making condoms preferable to other forms of birth control.

The biggest shift in contraceptive use has been among young women. In 1982, fully 64 percent of women aged 15 to 19 who used contraceptives relied on the pill. That proportion had fallen to 44 percent by 1995. Conversely, the share of women in that age group who rely on condoms rose from 21 to 37 percent. A similar shift in birth control use occurred among women aged 20 to 24.

Birth control pills are still the most popular method of contraception among women aged 25 to 34, used by 35 percent. Sterilization is the most popular method of contraception among women aged 35 to 44. Fully 45 percent of women in this age group who practice contraception have been sterilized. Another 19 percent rely on male sterilization to prevent pregnancy.

❖ The shift from birth control pills to condoms has placed greater responsibility on males for preventing pregnancy as well as sexually transmitted diseases. This shift has been a boon to condom manufacturers and has changed the courtship practices of young adults.

Contraceptive Use by Age, 1982 and 1995

(percent of women aged 15 to 44 who use contraception by method and age, 1982 and 1995; percentage point change, 1982–95)

	1995	1982	percentage point change, 1982–95
ANY METHOD			
Total, aged 15 to 44	**64.2%**	**55.7%**	**8.5**
Aged 15 to 19	29.8	24.2	5.6
Aged 20 to 24	63.5	55.8	7.7
Aged 25 to 34	71.1	66.7	4.4
Aged 35 to 44	72.3	61.6	10.7
BIRTH CONTROL PILL			
Total, aged 15 to 44	**26.9**	**28.0**	**–1.1**
Aged 15 to 19	43.8	63.9	–20.1
Aged 20 to 24	52.1	55.1	–3.0
Aged 25 to 34	33.3	25.7	7.6
Aged 35 to 44	8.7	3.7	5.0
CONDOM			
Total, aged 15 to 44	**20.4**	**12.0**	**8.4**
Aged 15 to 19	36.7	20.8	15.9
Aged 20 to 24	26.4	10.7	15.7
Aged 25 to 34	21.1	11.4	9.7
Aged 35 to 44	14.7	11.3	3.4
DIAPHRAGM			
Total, aged 15 to 44	**1.9**	**8.1**	**–6.2**
Aged 15 to 19	0.1	6.0	–5.9
Aged 20 to 24	0.6	10.2	–9.6
Aged 25 to 34	1.7	10.3	–8.6
Aged 35 to 44	2.8	4.0	–1.2
INTRAUTERINE DEVICE			
Total, aged 15 to 44	**0.8**	**7.1**	**–6.3**
Aged 15 to 19	0.0	1.3	–1.3
Aged 20 to 24	0.3	4.2	–3.9
Aged 25 to 34	0.8	9.7	–8.9
Aged 35 to 44	1.1	6.9	–5.8

(continued)

(continued from previous page)

	1995	1982	percentage point change, 1982–95
STERILIZATION, FEMALE			
Total, aged 15 to 44	**27.7%**	**23.2%**	**4.5**
Aged 15 to 19	0.3	0.0	0.3
Aged 20 to 24	4.0	4.5	–0.5
Aged 25 to 34	23.8	22.1	1.7
Aged 35 to 44	45.0	43.5	1.5
STERILIZATION, MALE			
Total, aged 15 to 44	**10.9**	**10.9**	**0.0**
Aged 15 to 19	0.0	0.4	–0.4
Aged 20 to 24	1.1	3.6	–2.5
Aged 25 to 34	7.8	10.1	–2.3
Aged 35 to 44	19.4	19.9	–0.5

Note: Method of contraception used in the month of interview.
Source: National Center for Health Statistics, Health, United States, 1998; *calculations by New Strategist*

More Women Are Childless

The biggest increase in childlessness has been in the 25-to-34 age group.

As more women (and men) have gone to college and entered the workforce, many have delayed starting families until established in a career. The percentage of women who have not yet had children has increased in almost every age group since 1970.

Women aged 25 to 34 are far more likely to be childless today than in 1970. Among women aged 25 to 29, fully 44 percent were childless in 1996, up from 24 percent in 1970. Among women aged 30 to 34, 26 percent were childless in 1996, up from only 12 percent in 1970. Only among 15-to-19-year-olds did the childless share decline slightly between 1970 and 1996, falling one-half of a percentage point to 92.5 percent.

The longer women delay having children, the more likely they are to experience fertility problems, which is one factor driving the increase in childlessness among older women. Among women in their late thirties, 19 percent were childless in 1996, more than double the 9 percent of 1970. Among women in their early forties, 17 percent were childless in 1996, up from 11 percent in 1970.

❖ The soaring demand for fertility services in recent years is due to the fertility problems of baby-boom women, many of whom delayed having children until their late thirties and early forties.

Childless Women by Age, 1970 and 1996

(percent of women aged 18 to 44 who are childless by age, 1970 and 1996, and percentage point change, 1970–96)

	1996	*1970*	*percentage point change, 1970–96*
Aged 15 to 19	92.5%	93.0%	–0.5
Aged 20 to 24	65.0	57.0	8.0
Aged 25 to 29	43.8	24.4	19.4
Aged 30 to 34	26.2	11.8	14.4
Aged 35 to 39	18.5	9.4	9.1
Aged 40 to 44	16.6	10.6	6.0

Source: National Center for Health Statistics, Health, United States, 1998; *calculations by New Strategist*

Most New Mothers Are Twentysomething

More than half the women giving birth in 1998 were aged 20 to 29.

Births to teenagers and older women receive much media attention, but they are not the norm. Three-quarters of all births in 1998 were to women aged 20 to 34. The 52 percent majority were to women in their twenties.

Only 13 percent of births in 1998 were to women aged 35 or older, and just 13 percent were to women aged 15 to 19.

Although many women wait until they are in their thirties to begin a family, most of those aged 30 to 39 who gave birth in 1998 already had children. Only 28 percent of babies born to women aged 30 to 34 and 22 percent of those born to women aged 35 to 39 were first births. Most of the babies born to women aged 40 or older in 1998 were a third or higher-order birth.

❖ Businesses marketing to new parents should target women aged 20 to 34, since younger and older women account for a small share of total births.

Births by Age of Mother and Birth Order, 1998

(number and percent distribution of births by age of mother and birth order, 1998)

	total births	first birth	second birth	third birth	fourth birth or more
Total births	**3,944,046**	**1,577,684**	**1,281,848**	**646,816**	**411,245**
Under age 20	494,456	384,481	87,949	15,263	2,252
Aged 20 to 24	965,414	437,886	334,573	133,837	52,281
Aged 25 to 29	1,083,894	394,728	377,012	193,835	111,914
Aged 30 to 34	890,336	249,340	321,885	186,877	126,905
Aged 35 to 39	425,194	93,499	137,330	99,532	92,061
Aged 40 to 44	80,982	16,881	22,237	16,829	24,480
Aged 45 to 54	3,769	869	861	643	1,352
Percent distribution by birth order					
Total births	**100.0%**	**40.0%**	**32.5%**	**16.4%**	**10.4%**
Under age 20	100.0	77.8	17.8	3.1	0.5
Aged 20 to 24	100.0	45.4	34.7	13.9	5.4
Aged 25 to 29	100.0	36.4	34.8	17.9	10.3
Aged 30 to 34	100.0	28.0	36.2	21.0	14.3
Aged 35 to 39	100.0	22.0	32.3	23.4	21.7
Aged 40 to 44	100.0	20.8	27.5	20.8	30.2
Aged 45 to 54	100.0	23.1	22.8	17.1	35.9
Percent distribution by age					
Total births	**100.0%**	**100.0%**	**100.0%**	**100.0%**	**100.0%**
Under age 20	12.5	24.4	6.9	2.4	0.5
Aged 20 to 24	24.5	27.8	26.1	20.7	12.7
Aged 25 to 29	27.5	25.0	29.4	30.0	27.2
Aged 30 to 34	22.6	15.8	25.1	28.9	30.9
Aged 35 to 39	10.8	5.9	10.7	15.4	22.4
Aged 40 to 44	2.1	1.1	1.7	2.6	6.0
Aged 45 to 54	0.1	0.1	0.1	0.1	0.3

Note: Births by birth order will not add to total because not stated is not included.
Source: National Center for Health Statistics, Births and Deaths: Preliminary Data for 1998, *National Vital Statistics Report, Vol. 47, No. 25, 1999; calculations by New Strategist*

Forty Percent of Births Are to Minority Women

The share is even larger among women under age 25.

Of the 3.9 million babies born in 1998, only 60 percent were born to non-Hispanic white women. Nineteen percent were born to Hispanics, 16 percent to blacks, 4 percent to Asians, and 1 percent to Native Americans.

Among births to women under age 20, only 45 percent were to non-Hispanic whites. Hispanic women accounted for 25 percent of births in that age group, while black women accounted for a slightly larger 27 percent. Non-Hispanic white women accounted for 53 percent of births to women aged 20 to 24 and for more than 60 percent of births to women aged 25 or older.

Although blacks are still the largest minority in the United States, births to Hispanics outnumber births to blacks by a considerable margin—735,019 babies were born to Hispanic women in 1998 compared with 610,203 born to black women.

❖ Businesses targeting new parents must take into account the rapidly growing racial and ethnic diversity of this market.

Births by Age, Race, and Hispanic Origin of Mother, 1998

(number and percent distribution of births by age, race, and Hispanic origin of mother, 1998)

	total births	white	black	Asian	Native American	non-Hispanic white	Hispanic
			race			*Hispanic origin*	
Total births	**3,944,046**	**3,122,391**	**610,203**	**171,284**	**40,167**	**2,364,907**	**735,019**
Under age 20	494,456	345,715	131,156	9,217	8,369	221,437	124,176
Aged 20 to 24	965,414	737,137	189,110	26,150	13,017	511,466	223,200
Aged 25 to 29	1,083,894	881,904	139,472	53,007	9,512	679,390	196,109
Aged 30 to 34	890,336	738,882	93,908	51,634	5,913	604,936	125,770
Aged 35 to 39	425,194	350,244	46,694	25,467	2,789	291,669	54,225
Aged 40 to 44	80,982	65,461	9,515	5,457	548	53,494	11,064
Aged 45 to 54	3,769	3,049	349	352	19	2,516	474

Percent distribution by race and Hispanic origin

Total births	**100.0%**	**79.2%**	**15.5%**	**4.3%**	**1.0%**	**60.0%**	**18.6%**
Under age 20	100.0	69.9	26.5	1.9	1.7	44.8	25.1
Aged 20 to 24	100.0	76.4	19.6	2.7	1.3	53.0	23.1
Aged 25 to 29	100.0	81.4	12.9	4.9	0.9	62.7	18.1
Aged 30 to 34	100.0	83.0	10.5	5.8	0.7	67.9	14.1
Aged 35 to 39	100.0	82.4	11.0	6.0	0.7	68.6	12.8
Aged 40 to 44	100.0	80.8	11.7	6.7	0.7	66.1	13.7
Aged 45 to 54	100.0	80.9	9.3	9.3	0.5	66.8	12.6

Percent distribution by age

Total births	**100.0%**	**100.0%**	**100.0%**	**100.0%**	**100.0%**	**100.0%**	**100.0%**
Under age 20	12.5	11.1	21.5	5.4	20.8	9.4	16.9
Aged 20 to 24	24.5	23.6	31.0	15.3	32.4	21.6	30.4
Aged 25 to 29	27.5	28.2	22.9	30.9	23.7	28.7	26.7
Aged 30 to 34	22.6	23.7	15.4	30.1	14.7	25.6	17.1
Aged 35 to 39	10.8	11.2	7.7	14.9	6.9	12.3	7.4
Aged 40 to 44	2.1	2.1	1.6	3.2	1.4	2.3	1.5
Aged 45 to 54	0.1	0.1	0.1	0.2	0.0	0.1	0.1

Note: Births by race and Hispanic origin will not add to total because Hispanics may be of any race and because "not stated" is not included.
Source: National Center for Health Statistics, Births and Deaths: Preliminary Data for 1998, *National Vital Statistics Report, Vol. 47, No. 25, 1999; calculations by New Strategist*

Unmarried Mothers Have Become Common

One-third of women giving birth in 1997 were not married.

The younger the mother, the more likely she is to be unmarried when she gives birth. More than 78 percent of babies born to women under age 20 in 1997 were out-of-wedlock, as were 47 percent of births to 20-to-24-year-olds. Among babies born to women aged 25 or older in 1997, the out-of-wedlock proportion ranged from 14 to 22 percent. Even among women aged 40 or older, fully 17 percent of births are out-of-wedlock. Some of the older unmarried mothers fit the Murphy Brown stereotype—professional women who have chosen to raise a child by themselves.

Black women are much more likely to have children out of wedlock than both white and Hispanic women. Overall, 69 percent of births to black women are out-of-wedlock versus 41 percent of births to Hispanic women and 22 percent of births to non-Hispanic white women.

❖ The sharp rise in out-of-wedlock births appears to have come to a halt—at least temporarily—with the rate stabilizing at the current one-third level.

Births by Marital Status of Mother, 1997

(total number of births and number and percent to unmarried women, by age, race, and Hispanic origin of mother, 1997)

		race		Hispanic origin	
	total	white	black	non-Hispanic white	Hispanic
Total births	**3,880,894**	**3,072,640**	**599,913**	**2,333,363**	**709,767**
Under age 20	493,341	343,293	133,251	222,097	120,955
Aged 20 to 24	942,048	720,546	182,600	500,928	216,152
Aged 25 to 29	1,069,436	871,636	135,529	674,498	188,669
Aged 30 to 34	886,798	735,571	94,123	603,304	121,539
Aged 35 to 39	409,710	337,423	45,069	280,393	51,601
Aged 40 or older	79,561	64,171	9,341	52,143	10,851
Births to					
unmarried women	**1,257,444**	**793,202**	**415,054**	**502,620**	**290,437**
Under age 20	385,802	244,984	127,668	157,891	87,180
Aged 20 to 24	438,632	276,764	145,647	176,696	99,740
Aged 25 to 29	234,762	147,318	76,977	89,976	57,331
Aged 30 to 34	124,831	77,543	41,520	47,756	29,920
Aged 35 to 39	59,870	37,878	19,223	24,637	13,242
Aged 40 or older	13,547	8,715	4,019	5,664	3,024
Percent of births to					
unmarried women	**32.4%**	**25.8%**	**69.2%**	**21.5%**	**40.9%**
Under age 20	78.2	71.4	95.8	71.1	72.1
Aged 20 to 24	46.6	38.4	79.8	35.3	46.1
Aged 25 to 29	22.0	16.9	56.8	13.3	30.4
Aged 30 to 34	14.1	10.5	44.1	7.9	24.6
Aged 35 to 39	14.6	11.2	42.7	8.8	25.7
Aged 40 or older	17.1	13.6	43.0	10.9	27.9

Note: Births by race and Hispanic origin will not add to total because Hispanics may be of any race and because "not stated" is not included.
Source: National Center for Health Statistics, Births: Final Data for 1997, *National Vital Statistics Report, Vol. 47, No. 18, 1999*

Older Mothers Are Well Educated

Women with college degrees postpone childbearing.

There are dramatic differences by education in the age profiles of new mothers. Of the babies born to college-educated women in 1997, 63 percent were born to women aged 30 or older. Of the babies born to high school-educated women in that year, 72 percent were born to women under age 30. Educated women are likely to postpone childbearing while they get their educational credentials and establish themselves in a career. Less educated women have much less reason to postpone childbearing.

Twenty-three percent of all births in 1997 were to college graduates. Among babies born to women aged 30 or older in that year, however, from 39 to 41 percent had mothers who were college graduates.

❖ Marketers targeting new mothers should pay attention to lifestyle differences by age of mother. Older mothers are likely to be highly educated, making them more sophisticated consumers than younger mothers.

Births by Age and Educational Attainment of Mother, 1997

(number and percent distribution of births by age and educational attainment of mother, 1997)

	total	not a high school graduate	high school graduate only	some college	college graduate
Total births	**3,880,894**	**845,497**	**1,257,946**	**848,379**	**872,733**
Under age 20	493,341	310,139	152,407	22,352	–
Aged 20 to 24	942,048	249,158	412,416	218,654	48,205
Aged 25 to 29	1,069,436	152,465	344,535	281,965	276,014
Aged 30 to 34	886,798	85083	229,782	213,767	346,265
Aged 35 to 39	409,710	39,122	100,508	94,325	169,440
Aged 40 to 54	79,561	9,530	18,298	17,316	32,809

Percent distribution by educational attainment

	total	not a high school graduate	high school graduate only	some college	college graduate
Total births	**100.0%**	**21.8%**	**32.4%**	**21.9%**	**22.5%**
Under age 20	100.0	62.9	30.9	4.5	–
Aged 20 to 24	100.0	26.4	43.8	23.2	5.1
Aged 25 to 29	100.0	14.3	32.2	26.4	25.8
Aged 30 to 34	100.0	9.6	25.9	24.1	39.0
Aged 35 to 39	100.0	9.5	24.5	23.0	41.4
Aged 40 to 54	100.0	12.0	23.0	21.8	41.2

Percent distribution by age

	total	not a high school graduate	high school graduate only	some college	college graduate
Total births	**100.0%**	**100.0%**	**100.0%**	**100.0%**	**100.0%**
Under age 20	12.7	36.7	12.1	2.6	–
Aged 20 to 24	24.3	29.5	32.8	25.8	5.5
Aged 25 to 29	27.6	18.0	27.4	33.2	31.6
Aged 30 to 34	22.9	10.1	18.3	25.2	39.7
Aged 35 to 39	10.6	4.6	8.0	11.1	19.4
Aged 40 to 54	2.1	1.1	1.5	2.0	3.8

Note: (–) means sample is too small to make a reliable estimate.
Source: National Center for Health Statistics, Births: Final Data for 1997, *National Vital Statistics Report, Vol. 47, No. 18, 1999; calculations by New Strategist*

Most Births Are in Hospitals

Physicians attend most births, midwives few.

Virtually all babies are born in hospitals today. Fewer than 40,000 newborns arrived elsewhere in 1997. Physicians attended fully 92 percent of births, while midwives attended just 7 percent. Among births outside of a hospital, however, most were attended by someone other than a physician—usually a midwife.

Among women who did not give birth in a hospital, most gave birth at home. Forty-eight percent of home births were attended by midwives. Only 10,000 births in 1997 took place in a free-standing birthing center, and midwives attended 84 percent of those births.

❖ Recognizing trends is a key to success in any business. By developing birthing centers with a home-like decor, many hospitals successfully headed off competition from free-standing birthing centers.

Births by Place of Delivery and Attendant, 1997

(number and percent distribution of births by place of delivery and attendant, 1997)

	total births	attendant		
		physician	midwife	other
Total births	**3,880,894**	**3,584,686**	**272,201**	**22,207**
In hospital	3,843,506	3,579,057	251,758	12,052
Not in hospital	36,521	5,149	20,164	9,911
Free-standing birthing center	10,264	1,484	8,596	177
Clinic or doctor's office	705	385	168	130
Residence	23,236	2,792	11,082	8,545
Other	2,316	758	318	1,059
Total births	**100.0%**	**92.4%**	**7.0%**	**0.6%**
In hospital	100.0	93.1	6.6	0.3
Not in hospital	100.0	14.1	55.2	27.1
Free-standing birthing center	100.0	14.5	83.7	1.7
Clinic or doctor's office	100.0	54.6	23.8	18.4
Residence	100.0	12.0	47.7	36.8
Other	100.0	32.7	13.7	45.7

Note: Numbers will not add to total because unspecified is not shown.
Source: National Center for Health Statistics, Births: Final Data for 1997, *National Vital Statistics Report, Vol. 47, No. 18, 1999; calculations by New Strategist*

Caesarean Rates Rise with Age

One in five babies born in 1997 was delivered by Caesarean section.

As mothers-to-be grow older, it becomes increasingly likely that they will have a Caesarean delivery. Among babies born to women under age 20, only 14 percent were delivered by Caesarean section. The share rises with age to 32 percent for babies born to women aged 40 to 54.

Most women have vaginal deliveries, but among women who already have had a Caesarean, vaginal deliveries are uncommon. Of all births in 1997, only 3 percent were delivered vaginally by women who had a previous Caesarean.

❖ Older mothers are more likely to encounter complications during pregnancy and childbirth, which explains the greater likelihood of them having a Caesarean.

Births by Delivery Method, 1997

(number and percent distribution of births by age of mother and method of delivery, 1997)

		vaginal		Caesarean		
	total births	total	after previous Caesarean	total	first	repeat
Total births	**3,880,894**	**3,046,621**	**112,145**	**799,033**	**502,526**	**296,507**
Under age 20	493,341	419,228	3,813	70,087	62,475	7,612
Aged 20 to 24	942,048	772,126	21,144	161,513	111,725	49,788
Aged 25 to 29	1,069,436	841,432	32,613	218,191	135,972	82,219
Aged 30 to 34	886,798	668,566	34,843	210,052	117,119	92,933
Aged 35 to 39	409,710	292,033	16,964	113,669	60,466	53,203
Aged 40 to 54	79,561	53,236	2,768	25,521	14,769	10,752
Total births	**100.0%**	**78.5%**	**2.9%**	**20.6%**	**12.9%**	**7.6%**
Under age 20	100.0	85.0	0.8	14.2	12.7	1.5
Aged 20 to 24	100.0	82.0	2.2	17.1	11.9	5.3
Aged 25 to 29	100.0	78.7	3.0	20.4	12.7	7.7
Aged 30 to 34	100.0	75.4	3.9	23.7	13.2	10.5
Aged 35 to 39	100.0	71.3	4.1	27.7	14.8	13.0
Aged 40 to 54	100.0	66.9	3.5	32.1	18.6	13.5

Source: National Center for Health Statistics, Births: Final Data for 1997, *National Vital Statistics Report, Vol. 47, No. 18, 1999; calculations by New Strategist*

Abortion Is Up, Adoption Down

During the past two decades, adoption has become less common and abortion more common.

The number of women aged 18 to 44 who have ever adopted a child fell from 654,000 to 487,000 between 1973 and 1995. The percentage of those who have ever adopted fell from 2.1 to 1.3 percent.

During those same years, the number of women obtaining legal abortions nearly doubled, climbing from 616,000 in 1973 to 1,211,000 in 1995. The number of abortions per 100 live births climbed from 19.6 to 31.1—meaning that in 1995 there was about one abortion for every three lives births.

The percentage of women who have ever adopted a child has fallen for all age, education, and parity groups. Non-Hispanic blacks are the only demographic segment to be more likely to have adopted a child in 1995 than in 1973.

The number of legal abortions per 100 live births has fallen for both younger and older women, but has grown among women in their twenties. It has increased slightly among married women but fallen sharply among the unmarried as it became more acceptable to bear a child out of wedlock.

❖ The percentage of women aged 18 to 44 who have ever adopted a child has fallen in part because more women are opting to have an abortion or keep their baby rather than give it up for adoption.

Legal Abortions by Selected Patient Characteristics, 1973 and 1995

(number of legal abortions, and abortions per 100 live births by selected characteristics of patients, 1973 and 1995; percent change 1973–95)

	1995	1973	percent change
Number of legal abortions (in 000s)	1,211	616	96.6%
Abortions per 100 live births	31.1	19.6	58.7
Age			
Under age 15	66.7	123.7	–46.1
Aged 15 to 19	39.9	53.9	–26.0
Aged 20 to 24	34.9	29.4	18.7
Aged 25 to 29	22.1	20.7	6.8
Aged 30 to 34	16.5	28.0	–41.1
Aged 35 to 39	22.4	45.1	–50.3
Aged 40 or older	38.7	68.4	–43.4
Race			
White	20.4	32.6	–37.7
Black	53.4	42.0	27.1
Hispanic origin			
Hispanic	26.5	–	–
Non-Hispanic	28.0	–	–
Marital status			
Married	7.8	7.6	2.6
Unmarried	64.5	139.8	–53.9
Previous live births			
None	28.6	43.7	–34.6
One	22.1	23.5	–6.0
Two	30.9	36.8	–16.0
Three	31.0	46.9	–33.9
Four or more	23.9	44.7	–46.5

Note: (–) means data not available.
Source: National Center for Health Statistics, Health, United States, 1998; *calculations by New Strategist*

Women Adopting Children, 1973 and 1995

(number of ever-married women aged 18 to 44 and percent who have ever adopted a child, by selected characteristics, 1973 and 1995; numbers in thousands)

	1995	1973
Total number of women	**37,448**	**30,701**
Number who have ever adopted	487	645
Percent who have adopted	1.3%	2.1%
Age		
Aged 18 to 24	0.2	0.4
Aged 25 to 34	0.4	1.8
Aged 35 to 39	1.9	3.1
Aged 40 to 44	2.5	4.0
Race and Hispanic origin		
Non-Hispanic white	1.4	2.3
Non-Hispanic black	1.9	1.6
Hispanic	0.6	1.2
Number of births		
None	3.6	5.9
One birth	0.8	2.7
Two births	0.9	1.1
Three or more births	0.5	0.8
Education		
Not a high school graduate	0.8	1.8
High school graduate	1.2	2.4
Some college	1.4	1.6
College graduate	1.7	4.6

Source: National Center for Health Statistics, Adoption, Adoption Seeking, and Relinquishment for Adoption in the United States, *Advance Data, Number 306, 1999*

Young Men Are Most Likely to Be Uninsured

One-third of those aged 18 to 24 do not have health insurance.

Most Americans have health insurance coverage, but a substantial portion of young adults do not. Among women aged 18 to 24, 27 percent do not have health insurance. Among men in the age group, 33 percent are without coverage. Many 25-to-34-year-olds are also without coverage—19 percent of women and 22 percent of men. Among young adults, women are more likely than men to have health insurance because of their greater Medicaid coverage.

Overall, males are slightly more likely than females to lack health insurance. Seventeen percent of males versus 15 percent of females did not have health insurance in 1998. In the 55-to-64 age group, however, the opposite is the case. Fully 17 percent of women aged 55 to 64 do not have health insurance versus 13 percent of their male counterparts. In this age group, men are more likely than women to have health insurance because of their greater employment-based coverage.

❖ An employment-based health insurance system, as prevails in the United States, can be a problem for those without jobs—such as older women—and for those whose companies do not offer health insurance benefits.

Health Insurance Coverage by Age, 1998: Males

(number and percent distribution of males by age and health insurance coverage status, 1998; numbers in thousands)

| | | covered by private or government health insurance | | | | | | | |
| | | private health insurance | | government health insurance | | | | |
	total	total	total	employment based	total	Medicaid	Medicare	military	not covered
Total males	**132,764**	**109,749**	**93,976**	**84,284**	**29,118**	**11,693**	**15,514**	**4,576**	**23,014**
Under 18	36,910	31,198	24,986	23,526	8,247	7,215	184	1,048	5,713
18 to 24	12,937	8,674	7,843	6,458	1,297	810	79	448	4,263
25 to 34	18,923	13,835	13,027	12,252	1,207	643	232	469	5,088
35 to 44	22,156	18,015	16,781	15,761	1,812	956	436	619	4,142
45 to 54	17,144	14,915	13,835	13,024	1,654	614	586	683	2,229
55 to 64	10,967	9,560	8,521	7,744	1,814	537	965	589	1,407
65 or older	13,727	13,554	8,984	5,519	13,087	917	13,033	720	173
Percent distribution by type of coverage									
Total males	**100.0%**	**82.7%**	**70.8%**	**63.5%**	**21.9%**	**8.8%**	**11.7%**	**3.4%**	**17.3%**
Under 18	100.0	84.5	67.7	63.7	22.3	19.5	0.5	2.8	15.5
18 to 24	100.0	67.0	60.6	49.9	10.0	6.3	0.6	3.5	33.0
25 to 34	100.0	73.1	68.8	64.7	6.4	3.4	1.2	2.5	26.9
35 to 44	100.0	81.3	75.7	71.1	8.2	4.3	2.0	2.8	18.7
45 to 54	100.0	87.0	80.7	76.0	9.6	3.6	3.4	4.0	13.0
55 to 64	100.0	87.2	77.7	70.6	16.5	4.9	8.8	5.4	12.8
65 or older	100.0	98.7	65.4	40.2	95.3	6.7	94.9	5.2	1.3
Percent distribution by age									
Total males	**100.0%**	**100.0%**	**100.0%**	**100.0%**	**100.0%**	**100.0%**	**100.0%**	**100.0%**	**100.0%**
Under 18	27.8	28.4	26.6	27.9	28.3	61.7	1.2	22.9	24.8
18 to 24	9.7	7.9	8.3	7.7	4.5	6.9	0.5	9.8	18.5
25 to 34	14.3	12.6	13.9	14.5	4.1	5.5	1.5	10.2	22.1
35 to 44	16.7	16.4	17.9	18.7	6.2	8.2	2.8	13.5	18.0
45 to 54	12.9	13.6	14.7	15.5	5.7	5.3	3.8	14.9	9.7
55 to 64	8.3	8.7	9.1	9.2	6.2	4.6	6.2	12.9	6.1
65 or older	10.3	12.3	9.6	6.5	44.9	7.8	84.0	15.7	0.8

Note: Numbers will not add to total because people may have more than one type of health insurance coverage.
Source: Bureau of the Census, Internet web site <http://www.census.gov/hhes/lthins/historic/hihist2.html>; calculations by New Strategist

Health Insurance Coverage by Age, 1998: Females

(number and percent distribution of females by age and health insurance coverage status, 1998; numbers in thousands)

		covered by private or government health insurance								not covered
			private health insurance			government health insurance				
	total	total	total	employment based	total	Medicaid	Medicare	military	
Total females	**138,979**	**117,713**	**96,885**	**84,291**	**36,969**	**16,161**	**20,373**	**4,171**	**21,266**
Under 18	35,111	29,751	23,641	22,067	8,153	7,059	141	1,193	5,360
18 to 24	13,031	9,517	8,029	6,649	2,050	1,728	70	348	3,513
25 to 34	19,551	15,512	13,699	12,844	2,409	1,833	191	522	4,039
35 to 44	22,588	19,021	17,353	16,258	2,378	1,623	314	613	3,566
45 to 54	18,088	15,512	14,318	13,377	1,868	996	553	542	2,576
55 to 64	11,943	9,916	8,658	7,466	2,031	878	1,051	488	2,027
65 or older	18,667	18,483	11,187	5,631	18,080	2,044	18,053	466	185

Percent distribution by type of coverage

Total females	**100.0%**	**84.7%**	**69.7%**	**60.7%**	**26.6%**	**11.6%**	**14.7%**	**3.0%**	**15.3%**
Under 18	100.0	84.7	67.3	62.8	23.2	20.1	0.4	3.4	15.3
18 to 24	100.0	73.0	61.6	51.0	15.7	13.3	0.5	2.7	27.0
25 to 34	100.0	79.3	70.1	65.7	12.3	9.4	1.0	2.7	20.7
35 to 44	100.0	84.2	76.8	72.0	10.5	7.2	1.4	2.7	15.8
45 to 54	100.0	85.8	79.2	74.0	10.3	5.5	3.1	3.0	14.2
55 to 64	100.0	83.0	72.5	62.5	17.0	7.4	8.8	4.1	17.0
65 or older	100.0	99.0	59.9	30.2	96.9	10.9	96.7	2.5	1.0

Percent distribution by age

Total females	**100.0%**	**100.0%**	**100.0%**	**100.0%**	**100.0%**	**100.0%**	**100.0%**	**100.0%**	**100.0%**
Under 18	25.3	25.3	24.4	26.2	22.1	43.7	0.7	28.6	25.2
18 to 24	9.4	8.1	8.3	7.9	5.5	10.7	0.3	8.3	16.5
25 to 34	14.1	13.2	14.1	15.2	6.5	11.3	0.9	12.5	19.0
35 to 44	16.3	16.2	17.9	19.3	6.4	10.0	1.5	14.7	16.8
45 to 54	13.0	13.2	14.8	15.9	5.1	6.2	2.7	13.0	12.1
55 to 64	8.6	8.4	8.9	8.9	5.5	5.4	5.2	11.7	9.5
65 or older	13.4	15.7	11.5	6.7	48.9	12.6	88.6	11.2	0.9

Note: Numbers will not add to total because people may have more than one type of health insurance coverage.
Source: Bureau of the Census, Internet web site <http://www.census.gov/hhes/lthins/historic/hihist2.html>; calculations by New Strategist

Females Account for the Majority of Acute Illnesses

Males dominate only a few conditions.

Females suffer 55 percent of the acute illnesses that cause people to restrict their activity for at least half a day or to contact a physician. There are several reasons why females account for the majority of those experiencing acute conditions. One, females outnumber males in the U.S. population. Two, the average female is older than the average male and consequently more vulnerable to illness. Three, females are more likely than males to seek medical attention for health problems.

Among acute conditions that can affect either sex, females account for the largest share of acute urinary conditions (75 percent). They account for a minority of those suffering from common childhood diseases, dental conditions, injuries, and acute musculoskeletal conditions.

❖ In the health care industry, most customers are female. As the large baby-boom generation ages, the dominance of women in the health care market will grow.

Females account for most colds and flu

(female share of acute conditions by type of condition, 1996)

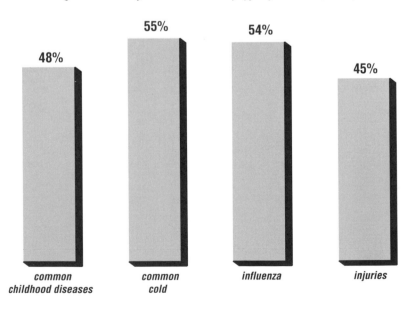

48%	55%	54%	45%
common childhood diseases	common cold	influenza	injuries

Acute Health Conditions by Sex, 1996

(total number of acute conditions by type of condition and sex, and female share of total conditions, 1996; numbers in thousands)

	total conditions	males	females number	females share of total
Total acute conditions	**432,001**	**193,336**	**238,665**	**55.2%**
Infective and parasitic diseases	**54,192**	**23,092**	**31,100**	**57.4**
Common childhood diseases	3,118	1,623	1,495	47.9
Intestinal virus	15,980	6,405	9,576	59.9
Viral infections	15,067	7,770	7,297	48.4
Other	20,027	7,294	12,733	63.6
Respiratory conditions	**208,623**	**90,567**	**118,056**	**56.6**
Common cold	62,251	28,237	34,015	54.6
Other acute upper respiratory infections	29,866	10,107	19,759	66.2
Influenza	95,049	43,868	51,181	53.8
Acute bronchitis	12,116	4,182	7,934	65.5
Pneumonia	4,791	2,337	2,454	51.2
Other respiratory conditions	4,550	1,836	2,713	59.6
Digestive system conditions	**17,646**	**7,648**	**9,998**	**56.7**
Dental conditions	2,970	1,598	1,372	46.2
Indigestion, nausea, and vomiting	7,963	2,548	5,415	68.0
Other digestive conditions	6,713	3,502	3,211	47.8
Injuries	**57,279**	**31,720**	**25,560**	**44.6**
Fractures and dislocations	8,465	4,237	4,228	49.9
Sprains and strains	12,977	6,951	6,026	46.4
Open wounds and lacerations	9,027	6,273	2,754	30.5
Contusions and superficial injuries	9,979	5,986	3,992	40.0
Other current injuries	16,832	8,273	8,559	50.8
Selected other acute conditions	**63,090**	**26,553**	**36,538**	**57.9**
Eye conditions	3,478	1,691	1,788	51.4
Acute ear infections	21,766	11,185	10,580	48.6
Other ear conditions	3,833	1,410	2,423	63.2
Acute urinary conditions	8,405	2,139	6,266	74.6
Disorders of menstruation	839	–	839	100.0

(continued)

(continued from previous page)

	total conditions	males	females number	share of total
Other disorders of female genital tract	1,597	–	1,597	100.0%
Delivery and other conditions of pregnancy	3,279	–	3,279	100.0
Skin conditions	4,986	2,482	2,504	50.2
Acute musculoskeletal conditions	8,461	4,367	4,094	48.4
Headache, excluding migraine	1,738	756	982	56.5
Fever, unspecified	4,708	2,523	2,186	46.4
All other acute conditions	**31,170**	**13,756**	**17,413**	**55.9**

Note: The acute conditions shown here are those that caused people to restrict their activity for at least half a day, or that caused people to contact a physician about the illness or injury. (—) means not applicable or sample is too small to make a reliable estimate.
Source: National Center for Health Statistics, Current Estimates from the National Health Interview Survey, 1996, *Series 10, No. 200, 1999; calculations by New Strategist*

Females Dominate Most Chronic Conditions

For some conditions, women account for more than 80 percent of victims.

Among Americans suffering from arthritis, women account for the 64 percent majority. Similarly with conditions ranging from cataracts to diabetes, high blood pressure to asthma, the majority of those affected are female.

Females dominate chronic conditions even more than acute conditions because there are more females than males in the population and because the average female is older than the average male. Since chronic conditions affect older people more than younger, females account for an even larger majority of chronic conditions than acute conditions.

Males dominate only a few chronic conditions. They are the majority of those with gout, hernias, epilepsy, and emphysema, for example. And men account for most of those suffering from impairments such as color blindness, hearing problems, and absense or paralysis of extremities.

❖ As the women of the baby-boom generation age, chronic conditions affecting older women will surge in importance to the health care industry.

Women account for two out of three Americans with arthritis

(female share of chronic conditions by type of condition, 1996)

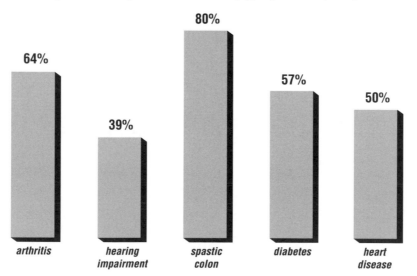

arthritis	hearing impairment	spastic colon	diabetes	heart disease
64%	39%	80%	57%	50%

Chronic Health Conditions by Sex, 1996

(total number of chronic conditions by type of condition and sex, and female share of total conditions, 1996; numbers in thousands)

	total conditions	males	females number	females share of total
Selected skin and musculoskeletal conditions				
Arthritis	33,638	12,774	20,864	64.1%
Gout	2,487	1,780	707	27.8
Intervertebral disc disorders	6,700	3,476	3,224	45.4
Bone spur or tendinitis	2,934	1,221	1,713	61.8
Disorders of bone or cartilage	1,730	405	1,325	72.7
Trouble with bunions	2,360	531	1,829	79.7
Bursitis	5,006	2,038	2,968	61.2
Sebaceous skin cyst	1,190	731	459	45.4
Trouble with acne	4,952	2,332	2,620	55.6
Psoriasis	2,940	1,606	1,334	50.4
Dermatitis	8,249	3,336	4,913	57.7
Trouble with dry (itching) skin	6,627	2,621	4,006	58.8
Trouble with ingrown nails	5,807	3,060	2,747	57.4
Trouble with corns and calluses	3,778	1,481	2,297	71.6
Impairments				
Visual impairment	8,280	4,893	3,387	38.7
Color blindness	2,811	2,538	273	11.9
Cataracts	7,022	2,451	4,571	64.4
Glaucoma	2,595	1,145	1,450	59.6
Hearing impairment	22,044	12,918	9,126	39.4
Tinnitus	7,866	4,524	3,342	42.0
Speech impairment	2,720	1,778	942	28.9
Absence of extremities	1,285	893	392	19.2
Paralysis of extremities	2,138	1,234	904	35.7
Deformity or orthopedic impairment	29,499	14,517	14,982	53.1
Selected digestive conditions				
Ulcer	3,709	1,679	2,030	55.0
Hernia of abdominal cavity	4,470	2,304	2,166	49.4
Gastritis or duodenitis	3,729	1,375	2,354	63.1
Frequent indigestion	6,420	3,288	3,132	47.7

(continued)

(continued from previous page)

	total conditions	males	females number	females share of total
Enteritis or colitis	1,686	512	1,174	59.6%
Spastic colon	2,083	568	1,515	80.3
Diverticula of intestines	2,529	857	1,672	75.2
Frequent constipation	3,149	869	2,280	80.4
Selected conditions of the genitourinary, nervous, endocrine, metabolic, or blood systems				
Goiter or other disorders of the thyroid	4,598	1,008	3,590	83.9
Diabetes	7,627	3,632	3,995	57.1
Anemias	3,457	557	2,900	84.2
Epilepsy	1,335	570	765	36.0
Migraine	11,546	2,447	9,099	75.3
Neuralgia or neuritis	353	140	213	81.2
Kidney trouble	2,553	1,137	1,416	57.8
Bladder disorders	3,139	484	2,655	83.2
Diseases of prostate	2,803	2,802	–	0.0
Diseases of female genital organs	4,420	–	4,420	100.0
Selected circulatory conditions				
Rheumatic fever	1,759	701	1,058	71.3
Heart disease	20,653	10,330	10,323	50.4
Ischemic heart disease	7,672	4,720	2,952	39.0
Heart rhythm disorders	8,716	3,592	5,124	61.0
Other selected diseases of the heart, excl. hypertension	4,265	2,017	2,248	48.9
High blood pressure (hypertension)	28,314	12,177	16,137	55.1
Cerebrovascular disease	2,999	1,785	1,214	52.9
Hardening of the arteries	1,556	880	676	48.7
Varicose veins of lower extremities	7,399	1,411	5,988	81.3
Hemorrhoids	8,531	3,263	5,268	54.2
Selected respiratory conditions				
Chronic bronchitis	14,150	6,049	8,101	61.5
Asthma	14,596	5,751	8,845	55.0
Hay fever	23,721	10,558	13,163	53.6
Chronic sinusitis	33,161	13,461	19,700	58.0
Deviated nasal septum	1,985	901	1,084	46.4
Chronic disease of tonsils or adenoids	2,513	909	1,604	57.1
Emphysema	1,821	956	865	44.5

Note: Chronic conditions are those that last at least three months or belong to a group of conditions that are considered to be chronic regardless of when they began. (–) means not applicable.
Source: National Center for Health Statistics, Current Estimates from the National Health Interview Survey, 1996, *Series 10, No. 200, 1996; calculations by New Strategist*

Females Contact Physicians More Frequently Than Males

The biggest difference between males and females is in the 15-to-44 age group.

Females contact physicians an average of 6.5 times per year, while males do so an average of 5.0 times per year. A physician contact can take place in a doctor's office, at a hospital outpatient department or health clinic, on the phone, or even at home.

Among children under age 14, boys contact physicians more frequently than girls. But among people aged 15 or older, women contact physicians more frequently than men. Women aged 15 to 44 contacted physicians an average of 6.0 times in 1996, while men did so an average of only 3.2 times. Behind this difference is childbearing, and the frequent visits to the doctor common among pregnant women.

Physician contacts peak among the oldest Americans. People aged 75 or older contact physicians more than 13 times a year, on average, with the gap between men and women virtually nonexistent.

The majority of physician contacts take place at a doctor's office. Physician contacts at hospital outpatient departments or at clinics or other nonhospital settings together account for 27 to 29 percent of the total. More than 10 percent of physician contacts take place by phone. Seeing a physician at home—now a rare event—accounts for fewer than 4 percent of contacts. Males are more likely than females to see a physician at a hospital outpatient department, while females are more likely than males to see physicians in their office or talk to them on the phone.

❖ Females account for the majority of health care consumers. Not only do they outnumber males in the population, but they contact physicians more frequently.

Physician Contacts by Age and Sex, 1996

(number of physician contacts per person per year by age and sex, and difference in number by sex; percent distribution of contacts by place of contact and sex, and percentage point difference between men and women; 1996)

	male	female	difference
Contacts per person			
Total people	**5.0**	**6.5**	**−1.5**
Under age 5	7.1	5.9	1.2
Aged 5 to 14	3.6	3.0	0.6
Aged 15 to 44	3.2	6.0	−2.8
Aged 45 to 64	6.0	8.4	−2.4
Aged 65 to 74	9.4	10.9	−1.5
Aged 75 or older	13.5	13.7	−0.2

	male	female	percentage point difference
Place of contact			
Total contacts	**100.0%**	**100.0%**	**0.0**
Doctor's office	54.7	56.5	−1.8
Hospital outpatient department	13.9	11.2	2.7
Telephone	12.1	13.6	−1.5
Home	3.8	2.9	0.9
Clinics, other nonhospital locations	15.4	15.9	−0.5

Source: National Center for Health Statistics, Health, United States, 1999; *calculations by New Strategist*

Men's Hospital Stays Are Longer

The average hospital stay for males is nearly one day longer than that of females.

As insurance companies try to cut costs, hospital stays have shortened. In 1997, the average hospital stay was 4.8 days for females and 5.5 days for males. The biggest difference in length of stay between men and women is found in the 15-to-44 age group. Among men aged 15 to 44 discharged from hospitals in 1997, the average length of stay was 5.0 days compared to just 3.2 days for their female counterparts—most of whom were in the hospital because of childbirth.

Overall, more than 18 million females were discharged from hospitals in 1997 compared with 12 million males. Consequently, females account for 60 percent of all patients discharged from hospitals. The female proportion peaks at 73 percent in the 15-to-44 age group because of childbirth.

❖ Hospitals have made great strides in recent years to market themselves to women, improving birthing rooms, breast care facilities, and other services important to women.

Hospital Stays by Age and Sex, 1997

(number of inpatients discharged from short-stay, nonfederal hospitals by sex and female share of total; average length of stay and difference in number of days by sex; by age, 1997)

	total	male	female number	female share of total
Total discharges (in 000s)	**30,914**	**12,268**	**18,647**	**60.3%**
Under age 15	2,312	1,316	995	43.0
Aged 15 to 44	10,030	2,688	7,341	73.2
Aged 45 to 64	6,377	3,161	3,216	50.4
Aged 65 or older	12,196	5,102	7,094	58.2

	total	male	female	male minus female
Average length of stay (days)				
Total discharges	**5.1**	**5.5**	**4.8**	**0.7**
Under age 15	4.3	4.3	4.2	0.1
Aged 15 to 44	3.7	5.0	3.2	1.8
Aged 45 to 64	5.2	5.3	5.2	0.1
Aged 65 or older	6.3	6.2	6.4	–0.2

Source: National Center for Health Statistics, 1997 Summary: National Hospital Discharge Survey, *Advance Data, Number 308, 1999; calculations by New Strategist*

Most Disabled Americans Are Women

Sixty percent of severely disabled adults are women.

Women account for the majority of the disabled because women outnumber men in the U.S. population, because the average woman is older than the average man, and because the old are more likely to be disabled than the young.

Among people aged 22 or older, 24 percent of men and 27 percent of women have a disability. While sixteen percent of women are severely disabled, the proportion is a smaller 12 percent among men.

Women are more likely than men to suffer from most disabilities including mental disabilities; difficulty lifting, carrying, and climbing; difficulty bathing and dressing; and difficulty keeping track of money and bills. Women account for 62 percent of adults confined to a wheelchair, and they are the 63 percent majority of people who need personal assistance in their daily lives.

The most common disability among women, difficulty climbing stairs without resting, affects 12 percent. The most common disability among men, difficulty walking three city blocks, affects 8 percent.

❖ The aging of the population will mean many more disabled Americans in the years ahead, particularly women.

Disabled People by Sex, 1994–95

(number of people aged 22 or older by disability status, women's share of the disabled, and percent of people with disabilities by sex, 1994–95; numbers in thousands)

	total	percent who are women	percent distribution	
			men	women
Total people	**177,221**	**52.2%**	**100.0%**	**100.0%**
With any disability	**45,433**	**55.6**	**23.8**	**27.3**
Severe	24,496	60.2	11.5	16.0
Not severe	20,937	50.3	12.3	11.4
With a mental disability	8,556	55.1	4.5	5.1
Uses wheelchair	1,672	61.5	0.8	1.1
Used cane/crutch/walker				
for 6 or more months	5,150	60.2	2.4	3.4
Difficulty with or unable to perform				
one or more functional activities	**32,310**	**57.5**	**16.2**	**20.1**
Seeing words and letters	8,144	60.1	3.8	5.3
Hearing normal conversation	9,434	41.2	6.5	4.2
Having speech understood	1,796	48.6	1.1	0.9
Lifting, carrying 10 pounds	15,743	67.0	6.1	11.4
Climbing stairs without resting	17,691	63.3	7.7	12.1
Walking three city blocks	18,076	61.5	8.2	12.0
Difficulty with or unable to perform				
one or more ADLs	**8,042**	**62.2**	**3.6**	**5.4**
Getting around inside the home	3,408	63.6	1.5	2.3
Getting in and out of bed or chair	5,362	61.7	2.4	3.6
Bathing	4,353	66.1	1.7	3.1
Dressing	3,131	60.1	1.5	2.0
Eating	1,014	58.9	0.5	0.6
Getting to, using toilet	1,923	62.8	0.8	1.3
Difficulty with or unable to perform				
one or more IADL's	**11,875**	**61.6**	**5.4**	**7.9**
Going outside alone	7,837	64.4	3.3	5.5
Keeping track of money and bills	3,581	58.4	1.8	2.3
Preparing meals	4,032	64.0	1.7	2.8
Doing light housework	6,642	66.2	2.6	4.8

(continued)

(continued from previous page)

	total	percent who are women	percent distribution	
			men	women
Taking prescribed medicines	2,849	55.7%	1.5%	1.7%
Using the telephone	2,584	47.9	1.6	1.3
Needs personal assistance with an ADL or an IADL	**9,133**	**63.2**	**4.0**	**6.2**

Note: An ADL is an activity of daily living; an IADL is an instrumental activity of daily living.
Source: Bureau of the Census, Internet web site <http://www.census.gov/hhes/www/disabled/sipp/disab9495/ ds9413a.html>; calculations by New Strategist

Women Are More Likely to Be Caregivers

Women account for two out of three caregivers for the ill or disabled.

Among the 9.3 million Americans who regularly provide unpaid care to a family member or friend with a long-term illness or disability, 6.1 million are women. The largest share of caregivers help someone living outside their household, often their own aged parents. On average, caregivers provide 16 hours of care per week, and they have been doing so for four years. The most common tasks they undertake are helping the person with trips outside the home (72 percent) and helping with household chores (56 percent).

More than 4 million caregivers help someone who lives in their own household, often a spouse. These caregivers provide 42 hours of care per week on average, with women putting in 46 hours and men 36. Those who care for someone in their own household have been at the task an average of eight years. The most common chores are helping with trips outside the home (87 percent) and attending to medical needs (70 percent).

❖ As the baby-boom generation ages, the burden of caring for aging parents may ease because the parents of boomers had large families and there will be many siblings to help out. The baby-boom's children will have a greater caregiving burden because the baby-boom generation had few children.

Caregiving by Men and Women, 1996

(selected characteristics of persons aged 15 or older providing regular unpaid care to a family member or friend with a long-term illness or disability, by sex, 1996; numbers in thousands)

	total	men	women
Total number of caregivers	**9,323**	**3,208**	**6,116**
Caregivers as a percent of people aged 15 or older	**4.5%**	**3.3%**	**5.5%**
PROVIDED CARE TO ONE OR MORE PERSONS INSIDE THE HOUSEHOLD			
Number	4,472	1,667	2,805
Average hours of care per week	42	36	46
Average years care has been provided	8.1	7.8	8.3
Type of care provided			
• HELPED WITH ACTIVITIES OF DAILY LIVING			
Number providing care	2,518	939	1,579
Percent providing care	56.3%	56.4%	56.3%
• HELPED WITH MEDICAL NEEDS			
Number providing care	3,131	1,061	2,070
Percent providing care	70.0%	63.7%	73.8%
• HELPED WITH MONEY MANAGEMENT			
Number providing care	3,044	1,065	1,980
Percent providing care	68.1%	63.9%	70.6%
• HELPED WITH TRIPS OUTSIDE THE HOME			
Number providing care	3,910	1,476	2,434
Percent providing care	87.4%	88.5%	86.8%
PROVIDED CARE TO ONE OR MORE PERSONS OUTSIDE THE HOUSEHOLD			
Number	5,027	1,594	3,434
Average hours of care per week	16	12	18
Average years care has been provided	4.1	4.4	4.0
Type of care provided			
• HELPED WITH ACTIVITIES OF DAILY LIVING			
Number providing care	1,596	388	1,208
Percent providing care	31.7%	24.3%	35.2%

(continued)

(continued from previous page)

	total	men	women
• **HELPED WITH MEDICAL NEEDS**			
Number providing care	2,032	521	1,511
Percent providing care	40.4%	32.7%	44.0%
• **HELPED WITH MONEY MANAGEMENT**			
Number providing care	2,523	784	1,739
Percent providing care	50.2%	49.2%	50.6%
• **HELPED WITH HOUSEHOLD CHORES**			
Number providing care	2,814	682	2,133
Percent providing care	56.0%	42.8%	62.1%
• **HELPED WITH TRIPS OUTSIDE THE HOME**			
Number providing care	3,627	1,063	2,564
Percent providing care	72.2%	66.7%	74.7%

Note: If more than one person is cared for, data are for first person cared for.
Source: Bureau of the Census, Preliminary Estimates on Caregiving from Wave 7 of the 1996 Survey of Income and Program Participation, *by John M. McNeil, No. 231, The Survey of Income and Program Participation, 1999*

Men Account for the Great Majority of AIDS Cases

Women's share of AIDS victims is greatest among the young.

Women account for only 16 percent of AIDS cases diagnosed in the U.S. through June 1998. They represent a larger share of cases among the young, however. Females accounted for 39 percent of AIDS cases diagnosed among 13-to-19-year-olds through 1998, versus only 12 percent of those diagnosed among people aged 50 to 59.

More than one-half million men had been diagnosed with AIDS by June 1998, most in the 30-to-39 age group. While most men with AIDS are non-Hispanic whites, non-Hispanic blacks account for a substantial 33 percent. Twenty-five percent of non-Hispanic blacks with AIDS are females, as are 17 percent of Hispanics and 16 percent of American Indians with the disease. Only 8 percent of non-Hispanic whites with AIDS are females.

❖ The threat of AIDS has changed birth control practices among young adults, resulting in greater condom use and a decline in the percentage of women relying on the pill. This could reduce the spread of a variety of sexually transmitted diseases.

More than one-third of teenagers with AIDS are female

(female share of AIDS cases diagnosed in people aged 13 or older through June 1998, by age)

AIDS Cases by Age, Race, Hispanic Origin, and Sex, through June 1998

(cumulative number of AIDS cases diagnosed among people aged 13 or older by age at diagnosis, race, Hispanic origin, and sex, and female share of total; through June 1998)

| | | | female | |
	total	*male*	*number*	*share of total*
Total cases	**635,457**	**536,198**	**99,259**	**15.6%**
Aged 13 to 19	3,154	1,924	1,230	39.0
Aged 20 to 29	110,433	88,475	21,958	19.9
Aged 30 to 39	290,621	245,361	45,260	15.6
Aged 40 to 49	164,277	142,559	21,718	13.2
Aged 50 to 59	48,729	42,793	5,936	12.2
Aged 60 or older	18,243	15,086	3,157	17.3
Race and Hispanic origin				
White, non-Hispanic	294,894	271,446	23,448	8.0
Black, non-Hispanic	235,879	177,356	58,523	24.8
Hispanic	97,286	80,987	16,299	16.8
American Indian	1,821	1,527	294	16.1
Asian or Pacific Islander	4,721	4,184	537	11.4

Source: National Center for Health Statistics, Health, United States, 1999; *calculations by New Strategist*

Heart Disease Is the Leading Killer of Both Sexes

The top three causes of death among men and women are identical.

Heart disease felled nearly one-third of the males and females who died in 1997, killing more than 350,000 people of each sex. The number two cause of death for both sexes was cancer, followed by cerebrovascular disease. Go further down the list, however, and the causes of death diverge between the sexes.

Accidents are the fourth leading cause of death among males, killing 62,000 in 1997, but they rank seventh among females. Males account for 65 percent of all accidental deaths. Suicide and homicide appear on the list of the top 10 causes of death for men, but not for women. Males account for 80 percent of suicide and 78 percent of homicide victims.

Alzheimer's disease is the eighth leading cause of death among females, who account for 68 percent of all Alzheimer deaths. This disease does not rank among the top 10 causes of death for males.

❖ As baby-boom men and women age and their risk of heart disease increases, expect this vocal generation to demand more research into the prevention and treatment of heart disease.

Leading Causes of Death by Sex, 1997

(number and percent distribution of deaths accounted for by the 10 leading causes of death by sex, and share of deaths by sex, 1997)

		deaths among males	
	number of male deaths	percent distribution	male share of total
Leading causes of death among males			
All causes	**1,154,039**	**100.0%**	**49.9%**
1. Diseases of the heart	356,598	30.9	49.1
2. Malignant neoplasms	281,110	24.4	52.1
3. Cerebrovascular diseases	62,564	5.4	39.2
4. Accidents and adverse effects	61,963	5.4	64.8
5. Chronic obstructive pulmonary diseases and allied conditions	55,984	4.9	51.3
6. Pneumonia and influenza	39,284	3.4	45.4
7. Diabetes mellitus	28,187	2.4	45.0
8. Suicide	24,492	2.1	80.2
9. Chronic liver disease and cirrhosis	16,260	1.4	64.6
10. Homicide and legal intervention	15,449	1.3	77.8
All other causes	212,148	18.4	46.8

		deaths among females	
	number of female deaths	percent distribution	female share of total
Leading causes of death among females			
All causes	**1,160,206**	**100.0%**	**50.1%**
1. Diseases of the heart	370,376	31.9	50.9
2. Malignant neoplasms	258,467	22.3	47.9
3. Cerebrovascular diseases	97,227	8.4	60.8
4. Chronic obstructive pulmonary diseases and allied conditions	53,045	4.6	48.6
5. Pneumonia and influenza	47,165	4.1	54.6
6. Diabetes mellitus	34,449	3.0	55.0
7. Accidents and adverse effects	33,681	2.9	35.2
8. Alzheimer's disease	15,347	1.3	68.3
9. Nephritis, nephrotic syndrome, and nephrosis	13,191	1.1	52.1
10. Septicemia	12,741	1.1	56.9
All other causes	224,427	19.3	49.5

Source: National Center for Health Statistics, Deaths: Final Data for 1997, *National Vital Statistics Reports, Vol. 47, No. 19, 1999; calculations by New Strategist*

Females Live Longer Than Males

The gap in life expectancy between males and females shrinks with age.

A girl born in 1998 can expect to live 79.4 years. Her male counterpart can expect to live 73.9 years—or 5.5 years less. The difference between male and female life expectancy remains at or above five years until age 30 and shrinks steadily after that. By age 85, women can expect to live only about one year longer than men. In very old age—age 95 and older—the gap is virtually nonexistent.

If middle age is defined as the age at which you have lived half your life, then men reach middle age sooner than women. At age 40, men have only 36.5 years of life remaining, but 40-year-old women have 41.0 years left. At age 65, the traditional age of retirement, men have 16 years of life left while women have 19.

❖ Because women live longer than men, there are many more elderly women than elderly men. As life expectancy increases and boomers age, the population of elderly women will expand enormously.

Females have a five-year advantage

(years of life remaining for newborns, by sex, 1998)

73.9 years

79.4 years

males

females

Life Expectancy by Age and Sex, 1998

(years of life remaining at selected ages by sex, and difference in male and female life expectancy, 1998)

	total	males	females	difference (male minus female)
Aged 0	76.7	73.9	79.4	–5.5
Aged 1	76.3	73.5	78.9	–5.4
Aged 5	72.4	69.6	75.0	–5.4
Aged 10	67.4	64.6	70.1	–5.5
Aged 15	62.5	59.7	65.2	–5.5
Aged 20	57.7	55.0	60.3	–5.3
Aged 25	53.0	50.4	55.4	–5.0
Aged 30	48.2	45.7	50.6	–4.9
Aged 35	43.5	41.0	45.7	–4.7
Aged 40	38.8	36.5	41.0	–4.5
Aged 45	34.2	32.0	36.3	–4.3
Aged 50	29.8	27.6	31.7	–4.1
Aged 55	25.5	23.5	27.3	–3.8
Aged 60	21.5	19.6	23.1	–3.5
Aged 65	17.7	16.0	19.1	–3.1
Aged 70	14.3	12.8	15.4	–2.6
Aged 75	11.2	10.0	12.1	–2.1
Aged 80	8.5	7.5	9.0	–1.5
Aged 85	6.2	5.5	6.5	–1.0
Aged 90	4.5	4.1	4.6	–0.5
Aged 95	3.3	3.1	3.3	–0.2
Aged 100	2.5	2.4	2.5	–0.1

Source: National Center for Health Statistics, Births and Deaths: Preliminary Data for 1998, *National Vital Statistics Report, Vol. 47, No. 25, 1999; calculations by New Strategist*

4

Income

❖ **Women's incomes have grown while men's have stagnated.**

Between 1970 and 1998, the median income of women grew 63 percent while the median income of men inched up a tiny 0.6 percent, after adjusting for inflation.

❖ **Women's incomes are catching up to men's.**

Among full-time workers in 1998, women's median income was 74 percent as high as men's—$26,855 for women versus $36,252 for men.

❖ **Young men have lost ground, while older women have gained.**

Between 1970 and 1998, the median income of men aged 25 to 34 fell 14 percent, after adjusting for inflation. The median income of women aged 65 or older rose 75 percent during those years.

❖ **Men with professional degrees make the most.**

The median income of men with professional degrees (such as doctors and lawyers) who work full-time stood at $94,737 in 1998. Their female counterparts had a median income of $57,565.

❖ **Dual-income married couples have the highest incomes.**

The median income of married couples in which both husband and wife work full-time stood at $72,930 in 1998.

❖ **Poverty rate is higher for females than for males.**

Females account for the 57 percent majority of the nation's poor, a figure that rises to 76 percent among poor people aged 75 or older.

❖ **Female-headed families have the highest poverty rates.**

Thirty percent of female-headed families lived below poverty level in 1998, versus 12 percent of male-headed families and just 5 percent of married couples.

Women's Incomes Have Grown While Men's Have Stagnated

Women's median income is at a record high, while men's median is below the peak it reached in the early 1970s.

In 1970, the median income of women aged 16 or older was only one-third as high as the median income of their male counterparts, $8,829 versus $26,325 (in 1998 dollars). But over the past three decades, men's income has barely budged while women's has soared. By 1998, the median income of women had grown to 54.5 percent of the median of men—$14,430 versus $26,492. While women's median income climbed 63 percent between 1970 and 1998, men's inched upward only 0.6 percent, after adjusting for inflation.

Women's incomes have grown rapidly because of women's growing attachment to the labor force. Not only does a much larger share of women have incomes from jobs today than in 1970, but more of those jobs are full-time careers. Women's median income remains far below men's, however, because fewer women work and because many of those who work have part-time jobs.

❖ Women's incomes will continue to gain on men's as career-oriented baby boomers and younger generations replace older housewives and "just a job" women in the population.

Women's median income has grown rapidly

(percent change in median income of people aged 15 or older with income, by sex, 1970 to 1998; in 1998 dollars)

63.4%

0.6%

men *women*

Median Income of People by Sex, 1970 to 1998: Total People

(median income of people aged 15 or older with income by sex, and women's income as a percent of men's, 1970 to 1998; percent change for selected years; in 1998 dollars)

	men	women	women's income as a percent of men's
1998	$26,492	$14,430	54.5%
1997	25,605	13,916	54.3
1996	24,761	13,313	53.8
1995	24,131	12,974	53.8
1994	23,889	12,611	52.8
1993	23,804	12,460	52.3
1992	23,765	12,447	52.4
1991	24,497	12,537	51.2
1990	25,308	12,559	49.6
1989	26,150	12,651	48.4
1988	26,052	12,241	47.0
1987	25,520	11,902	46.6
1986	25,452	11,318	44.5
1985	24,709	10,933	44.2
1984	24,474	10,775	44.0
1983	23,944	10,341	43.2
1982	23,785	10,037	42.2
1981	24,374	9,874	40.5
1980	24,816	9,744	39.3
1979	25,946	9,586	36.9
1978	26,406	9,823	37.2
1977	26,108	10,164	38.9
1976	25,866	9,813	37.9
1975	25,677	9,818	38.2
1974	26,545	9,679	36.5
1973	27,821	9,656	34.7
1972	27,350	9,541	34.9
1971	26,106	9,107	34.9
1970	26,325	8,829	33.5
Percent change			
1990 to 1998	4.7%	14.9%	9.8%
1970 to 1998	0.6	63.4	62.4

Source: Bureau of the Census, Money Income in the United States: 1998, *Current Population Reports, P60-206, 1999; calculations by New Strategist*

White Women Have Enjoyed the Biggest Income Gains

Hispanic men have experienced the greatest losses.

Between 1970 and 1998, white women have seen their median income grow 63 percent, after adjusting for inflation. Black women are not far behind, as their median income grew 61 percent between 1970 and 1988. Regardless of race or ethnicity, women's incomes have grown faster than inflation during the past few decades. Hispanic women made the smallest gains, their median income rising 12 percent between 1972 and 1998, after adjusting for inflation.

Men have not been as fortunate as women. Hispanic men saw their median income fall a substantial 19 percent between 1972 and 1998, after adjusting for inflation. The median income of non-Hispanic white men climbed just 3 percent during those years. Among men, blacks made the biggest gains and achieved an 18 percent rise in median income between 1970 and 1998.

❖ Behind the income losses for Hispanic men is the arrival of millions of poorly educated and unskilled immigrants to the United States during the past few decades, pulling down the median for Hispanic men overall.

Median Income of People by Sex, 1988 to 1998: Asians

(median income of Asians aged 15 or older with income by sex, and women's income as a percent of men's, 1988 to 1998; percent change for selected years; in 1998 dollars)

	men	women	women's income as a percent of men's
1998	$25,124	$15,228	60.6%
1997	25,436	14,535	57.1
1996	24,283	15,203	62.6
1995	23,703	13,757	58.0
1994	25,176	13,597	54.0
1993	24,412	13,948	57.1
1992	23,108	13,792	59.7
1991	23,490	13,196	56.2
1990	24,187	13,826	57.2
1989	27,092	14,734	54.4
1988	25,383	12,737	50.2
Percent change			
1990 to 1998	3.9%	10.1%	6.0%
1988 to 1998	−1.0	19.6	20.8

Note: Data prior to 1988 are not available.
Source: Bureau of the Census, Internet web site <http://www.census.gov/hhes/income/histinc/p2.html>; calculations by New Strategist

Median Income of People by Sex, 1970 to 1998: Blacks

(median income of blacks aged 15 or older with income by sex, and women's income as a percent of men's, 1970 to 1998; percent change for selected years; in 1998 dollars)

	men	women	women's income as a percent of men's
1998	$19,321	$13,137	68.0%
1997	18,378	13,251	72.1
1996	17,132	12,230	71.4
1995	17,119	11,723	68.5
1994	16,478	11,597	70.4
1993	16,475	10,725	65.1
1992	15,178	10,325	68.0
1991	15,513	10,551	68.0
1990	16,048	10,386	64.7
1989	16,575	10,352	62.5
1988	16,595	10,126	61.0
1987	16,092	9,971	62.0
1986	16,095	9,765	60.7
1985	16,312	9,509	58.3
1984	14,822	9,670	65.2
1983	14,675	9,071	61.8
1982	15,069	8,974	59.6
1981	15,379	8,870	57.7
1980	15,862	9,071	57.2
1979	16,778	8,806	52.5
1978	16,568	8,952	54.0
1977	16,228	8,911	54.9
1976	16,418	9,324	56.8
1975	16,126	9,011	55.9
1974	17,230	8,838	51.3
1973	17,657	8,799	49.8
1972	17,376	8,972	51.6
1971	16,326	8,112	49.7
1970	16,414	8,142	49.6
Percent change			
1990 to 1998	20.4%	26.5%	5.1%
1970 to 1998	17.7	61.3	37.1

Source: Bureau of the Census, Internet web site <http://www.census.gov/hhes/income/histinc/p2.html>; calculations by New Strategist

Median Income of People by Sex, 1972 to 1998: Hispanics

(median income of Hispanics aged 15 or older with income by sex, and women's income as a percent of men's, 1972 to 1998; percent change for selected years; in 1998 dollars)

	men	women	women's income as a percent of men's
1998	$17,257	$10,862	62.9%
1997	16,469	10,420	63.3
1996	16,037	9,853	61.4
1995	15,872	9,549	60.2
1994	15,948	9,473	59.4
1993	15,442	9,137	59.2
1992	15,577	9,652	62.0
1991	16,537	9,590	58.0
1990	16,799	9,393	55.9
1989	17,615	10,052	57.1
1988	17,953	9,631	53.6
1987	17,548	9,513	54.2
1986	17,151	9,426	55.0
1985	17,321	9,120	52.7
1984	17,415	9,146	52.5
1983	18,457	8,841	47.9
1982	17,853	8,764	49.1
1981	18,458	9,154	49.6
1980	19,130	8,724	45.6
1979	19,540	9,141	46.8
1978	20,236	9,147	45.2
1977	20,109	9,463	47.1
1976	19,346	9,217	47.6
1975	19,656	9,287	47.2
1974	20,235	9,447	46.7
1973	21,411	9,158	42.8
1972	21,241	9,718	45.8
Percent change			
1990 to 1998	2.7%	15.6%	12.6%
1972 to 1998	−18.8	11.8	37.6

Note: Data prior to 1972 are not available.
Source: Bureau of the Census, Internet web site <http://www.census.gov/hhes/income/histinc/p2.html>; calculations by New Strategist

Median Income of People by Sex, 1970 to 1998: Whites

(median income of whites aged 15 or older with income by sex, and women's income as a percent of men's, 1970 to 1998; percent change for selected years; in 1998 dollars)

	men	women	women's income as a percent of men's
1998	$27,646	$14,617	52.9%
1997	26,522	14,007	52.8
1996	25,919	13,465	52.0
1995	25,557	13,173	51.5
1994	24,933	12,791	51.3
1993	24,795	12,708	51.3
1992	24,869	12,737	51.2
1991	25,605	12,831	50.1
1990	26,402	12,867	48.7
1989	27,425	12,898	47.0
1988	27,501	12,543	45.6
1987	27,126	12,206	45.0
1986	26,859	11,541	43.0
1985	25,921	11,145	43.0
1984	25,834	10,902	42.2
1983	25,204	10,508	41.7
1982	25,146	10,174	40.5
1981	25,863	9,984	38.6
1980	26,397	9,798	37.1
1979	27,104	9,676	35.7
1978	27,657	9,942	35.9
1977	27,346	10,319	37.7
1976	27,268	9,895	36.3
1975	26,973	9,919	36.8
1974	27,807	9,789	35.2
1973	29,192	9,749	33.4
1972	28,687	9,604	33.5
1971	27,370	9,258	33.8
1970	27,671	8,943	32.3
Percent change			
1990 to 1998	4.7%	13.6%	8.5%
1970 to 1998	–0.1	63.4	63.6

Source: Bureau of the Census, Internet web site <http://www.census.gov/hhes/income/histinc/p2.html>; calculations by New Strategist

Median Income of People by Sex, 1972 to 1998: Non-Hispanic Whites

(median income of non-Hispanic whites aged 15 or older with income by sex, and women's income as a percent of men's, 1972 to 1998; percent change for selected years; in 1998 dollars)

	men	women	women's income as a percent of men's
1998	$29,862	$15,217	51.0%
1997	27,988	14,613	52.2
1996	27,312	14,039	51.4
1995	27,253	13,698	50.3
1994	26,531	13,138	49.5
1993	26,138	13,084	50.1
1992	26,023	13,073	50.2
1991	26,537	13,166	49.6
1990	27,385	13,196	48.2
1989	28,472	13,162	46.2
1988	28,526	12,836	45.0
1987	28,258	12,480	44.2
1986	28,067	11,736	41.8
1985	26,801	11,268	42.0
1984	26,602	11,076	41.6
1983	–	–	–
1982	25,788	10,477	40.6
1981	26,543	10,164	38.3
1980	27,096	9,863	36.4
1979	27,675	9,928	35.9
1978	27,951	10,381	37.1
1977	27,901	10,791	38.7
1976	27,768	10,573	38.1
1975	27,594	10,488	38.0
1974	28,395	10,279	36.2
1973	29,609	9,956	33.6
1972	29,013	9,692	33.4
Percent change			
1990 to 1998	9.0%	15.3%	5.8%
1972 to 1998	2.9	57.0	52.5

Note: Data prior to 1972 are not available. (–) means data not available.
Source: Bureau of the Census, Internet web site <http://www.census.gov/hhes/income/histinc/p2.html>; calculations by New Strategist

Among Full-Time Workers, Women Are Gaining on Men

Women with full-time jobs make 74 percent as much as their male counterparts.

While the income of the average woman is just 55 percent as high as that of the average man, much of the gap is due to the differing labor force patterns of men and women. Women are less likely to work than men, and many women who have jobs work only part-time. Among full-time workers, women make 74 percent as much as men, up from 57 percent in the early 1970s. In 1998, the median income of women who work full-time stood at $26,855, while men's median was $36,252.

The median income of women who work full-time is approaching that of men because women are enjoying growing incomes while men have seen their incomes stagnate. Between 1970 and 1998, the median income of women who work full-time rose 25 percent. In contrast, the median income of their male counterparts did not increase at all. This trend continued into the 1990s, as women's median income rose 5 percent between 1990 and 1998, after adjusting for inflation, while men's inched up only 0.3 percent.

❖ Among full-time workers, women's incomes will continue to approach those of men, but they will never fully catch up. The gap will persist because women are more likely than men to drop out of the labor force for a few years while their children are young.

Women are closing the income gap

(median income of full-time workers by sex, 1970 and 1998; in 1998 dollars)

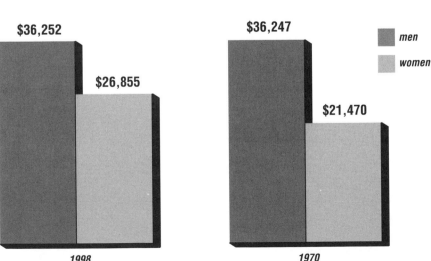

Median Income of Full-Time Workers by Sex, 1970 to 1998

(median income of people aged 15 or older who work full-time, year round, by sex; and women's income as a percent of men's, 1970 to 1998; percent change for selected years; in 1998 dollars)

	men	women	women's income as a percent of men's
1998	$36,252	$26,855	74.1%
1997	35,797	26,434	73.8
1996	34,842	25,904	74.3
1995	34,439	25,431	73.8
1994	34,769	25,588	73.6
1993	35,056	25,346	72.3
1992	35,820	25,668	71.7
1991	36,299	25,425	70.0
1990	36,141	25,680	71.1
1989	37,357	25,814	69.1
1988	37,673	25,552	67.8
1987	38,283	25,202	65.8
1986	38,510	25,049	65.0
1985	37,870	24,620	65.0
1984	37,658	24,194	64.2
1983	36,835	23,696	64.3
1982	36,922	23,296	63.1
1981	37,434	22,536	60.2
1980	37,973	22,957	60.5
1979	38,501	23,197	60.3
1978	38,787	23,281	60.0
1977	38,687	22,732	58.8
1976	38,031	22,809	60.0
1975	37,513	22,388	59.7
1974	38,197	22,531	59.0
1973	39,603	22,406	56.6
1972	38,687	22,222	57.4
1971	36,424	21,561	59.2
1970	36,247	21,470	59.2
Percent change			
1990 to 1998	0.3%	4.6%	4.3%
1970 to 1998	0.0	25.1	25.1

Source: Bureau of the Census, Internet web site <http://www.census.gov/hhes/income/histinc/p36.html>; calculations by New Strategist

Falling Incomes for Men under Age 45

Women aged 65 or older have made biggest gains.

Men's median income climbed just 0.6 percent between 1970 and 1998, with men under age 45 actually losing ground. The median income of men aged 25 to 34 has fallen 14 percent since 1970, after adjusting for inflation. Men aged 35 to 44 saw their median income fall 6 percent. Men in the oldest age group made the biggest gains. Men aged 65 or older experienced a 50 percent increase in median income between 1970 and 1998.

In contrast to men, women of all ages have seen their median income climb sharply since 1970. The median income of women aged 25 to 54 grew more than 40 percent between 1970 and 1998 as baby-boom and younger women entered the labor force. The oldest women have made the biggest income gains, however. The median income of women aged 65 or older rose 75 percent between 1970 and 1998, after adjusting for inflation.

Since 1990, the fortunes of young men have improved, and their incomes are growing significantly. The biggest gains have been among women aged 45 to 64, however, as career-oriented women replace housewives and "just a job" women in the age group.

❖ The rapid income growth for older men and women since 1970 is due to a more educated and affluent generation aging into the 65-or-older age group.

Median Income of Men by Age, 1970 to 1998

(median income of men with income by age, 1970 to 1998; percent change for selected years; in 1998 dollars)

	total	under 25	25 to 34	35 to 44	45 to 54	55 to 64	65 or older
1998	$26,492	$8,190	$28,117	$35,177	$38,922	$32,776	$18,166
1997	25,605	7,584	26,401	33,363	38,210	31,642	18,045
1996	24,761	7,231	26,158	33,418	37,641	30,674	17,333
1995	24,131	7,394	25,251	33,605	38,061	30,996	17,631
1994	23,889	7,752	24,864	33,774	38,422	29,779	16,773
1993	23,804	7,252	24,734	34,227	37,399	28,357	16,901
1992	23,765	7,316	24,975	34,263	37,388	29,759	16,959
1991	24,497	7,517	25,844	35,067	38,032	30,470	17,182
1990	25,308	7,881	26,680	37,131	38,670	30,934	17,688
1989	26,150	8,299	28,087	38,695	40,700	32,110	17,229
1988	26,052	8,051	28,635	39,331	40,754	31,204	17,183
1987	25,520	7,830	28,592	38,801	40,875	31,399	17,114
1986	25,452	7,857	28,498	38,924	41,279	31,282	17,169
1985	24,709	7,567	28,271	38,414	39,152	30,687	16,512
1984	24,474	7,388	28,385	38,540	38,576	30,634	16,394
1983	23,944	7,011	27,502	36,724	37,829	30,594	15,943
1982	23,785	7,548	27,990	36,912	36,731	30,397	15,666
1981	24,374	5,558	29,112	38,203	38,031	31,415	14,722
1980	24,816	9,105	30,857	39,684	39,560	31,519	14,535
1979	25,946	9,375	32,318	40,406	40,122	33,102	14,170
1978	26,406	8,819	32,383	40,018	40,023	32,899	14,407
1977	26,108	8,349	31,880	40,244	39,540	31,576	14,252
1976	25,866	8,153	32,153	39,312	38,675	31,620	14,525
1975	25,677	8,254	32,011	38,665	38,305	30,860	14,383
1974	26,545	8,521	32,923	39,575	38,577	31,322	14,566
1973	27,821	–	34,838	41,544	40,305	32,987	14,180
1972	27,350	–	33,841	40,511	39,542	32,681	13,752
1971	26,106	–	32,381	37,694	36,507	30,006	13,044
1970	26,325	–	32,584	37,356	36,203	30,303	12,140
Percent change							
1990 to 1998	4.7%	3.9%	5.4%	–5.3%	0.7%	6.0%	2.7%
1970 to 1998	0.6	–	–13.7	–5.8	7.5	8.2	49.6

Note: (–) means data not available.
Source: Bureau of the Census, Internet web site <http://www.census.gov/hhes/income/histinc/p8.html>; calculations by New Strategist

Median Income of Women by Age, 1970 to 1998

(median income of women with income by age, 1970 to 1998; percent change for selected years; in 1998 dollars)

	total	under 25	25 to 34	35 to 44	45 to 54	55 to 64	65 or older
1998	$14,430	$6,534	$18,257	$20,285	$21,588	$14,675	$10,504
1997	13,916	6,441	17,922	18,997	20,854	14,600	10,219
1996	13,313	6,110	17,021	19,164	19,786	13,834	10,000
1995	12,974	5,679	16,639	18,607	18,956	13,242	10,006
1994	12,611	6,058	16,370	17,806	18,754	11,952	9,844
1993	12,460	6,036	15,779	17,872	18,414	12,215	9,587
1992	12,447	6,006	15,836	17,911	18,417	11,772	9,507
1991	12,537	6,220	15,515	18,101	17,621	11,850	9,800
1990	12,559	6,113	15,700	18,088	17,747	11,723	10,032
1989	12,651	6,229	16,078	18,147	17,277	12,045	10,063
1988	12,241	6,180	15,935	17,287	16,562	11,542	9,787
1987	11,902	6,325	15,753	17,211	16,161	10,820	9,895
1986	11,318	6,014	15,333	16,455	15,437	10,971	9,555
1985	10,933	5,743	14,965	15,565	14,572	10,866	9,563
1984	10,775	5,662	14,734	14,999	13,967	10,726	9,444
1983	10,341	5,658	13,916	14,500	13,428	10,030	9,163
1982	10,037	5,715	13,592	13,386	12,791	10,072	9,147
1981	9,874	3,611	13,746	13,326	12,718	9,724	8,514
1980	9,744	6,187	13,810	12,804	12,682	9,756	8,370
1979	9,586	6,218	13,987	12,967	12,326	9,661	8,284
1978	9,823	6,235	14,100	14,016	13,697	10,801	8,162
1977	10,164	5,904	15,222	14,283	14,624	11,691	7,988
1976	9,813	5,510	14,741	14,154	14,629	11,125	7,727
1975	9,818	5,464	14,653	13,646	14,693	11,311	7,828
1974	9,679	5,565	14,177	13,979	14,821	11,379	7,660
1973	9,656	–	14,304	14,193	14,860	11,849	7,318
1972	9,541	–	13,969	14,178	14,931	11,781	6,972
1971	9,107	–	13,407	13,736	14,821	11,652	6,452
1970	8,829	–	12,728	13,616	14,591	11,627	6,007

Percent change

	total	under 25	25 to 34	35 to 44	45 to 54	55 to 64	65 or older
1990 to 1998	14.9%	6.9%	16.3%	12.1%	21.6%	25.2%	4.7%
1970 to 1998	63.4	–	43.4	49.0	48.0	26.2	74.9

Note: (–) means data not available.
Source: Bureau of the Census, Internet web site <http://www.census.gov/hhes/income/histinc/p8.html>; calculations by New Strategist

Incomes Are Highest for Men and Women Aged 45 to 54

Incomes are lowest for the young and old.

In 1998, the median income of women with income stood at $14,430. The median income of women who worked full-time was a much higher $26,855. Thirty-five percent of women aged 15 or older work full-time. Among men, median income stood at $26,492, while those who worked full-time had a median income of $36,252. Fifty-four percent of men work full-time.

Incomes peak in the 45-to-54 age group for both men and women. Men's median income tops out at $38,922, while women's peaks at $21,588. Nearly 16 percent of men aged 45 to 54 have incomes of $75,000 or more versus fewer than 4 percent of their female counterparts. Seventy-eight percent of men aged 45 to 54 work full-time, as do 54 percent of women in the age group.

Young adults have lower incomes than older people because many are in college and many of those with jobs work only part-time. Men and women aged 65 or older have low incomes because most are retired and live on Social Security payments, pensions, and savings.

❖ As career-oriented baby-boom women entirely fill the 45-to-54 age group during the next few years, they will boost the median income of middle-aged women and narrow the income gap between the sexes.

Income Distribution of People by Age and Sex, 1998: Under Age 35

(number and percent distribution of total people and people under age 35 by income and sex, 1998; median income of people by work status and percent working full-time, year-round; people in thousands as of 1999)

	total		under age 25		aged 25 to 34	
	men	women	men	women	men	women
Total people	**102,048**	**109,628**	**19,131**	**18,791**	**18,923**	**19,551**
Without income	7,100	10,934	5,052	4,916	593	1,778
With income	94,948	98,694	14,079	13,875	18,330	17,773
Under $10,000	17,502	36,609	7,797	8,861	1,997	5,034
$10,000 to $14,999	9,548	14,113	2,057	1,944	1,639	2,384
$15,000 to $24,999	17,620	19,018	2,557	2,106	4,117	4,135
$25,000 to $34,999	14,718	12,504	971	686	3,955	3,137
$35,000 to $49,999	15,234	9,149	477	203	3,604	1,976
$50,000 to $74,999	11,763	5,094	160	49	2,085	844
$75,000 or more	8,562	2,208	61	27	931	263
Median income						
People with income	$26,492	$14,430	$8,190	$6,534	$28,117	$18,257
Full-time, year-round workers	36,252	26,855	19,510	17,348	31,600	26,301
Percent working full-time, year-round	**54.2%**	**35.4%**	**23.9%**	**16.9%**	**75.8%**	**49.4%**
Total people	**100.0%**	**100.0%**	**100.0%**	**100.0%**	**100.0%**	**100.0%**
Without income	7.0	10.0	26.4	26.2	3.1	9.1
With income	93.0	90.0	73.6	73.8	96.9	90.9
Under $10,000	17.2	33.4	40.8	47.2	10.6	25.7
$10,000 to $14,999	9.4	12.9	10.8	10.3	8.7	12.2
$15,000 to $24,999	17.3	17.3	13.4	11.2	21.8	21.1
$25,000 to $34,999	14.4	11.4	5.1	3.7	20.9	16.0
$35,000 to $49,999	14.9	8.3	2.5	1.1	19.0	10.1
$50,000 to $74,999	11.5	4.6	0.8	0.3	11.0	4.3
$75,000 or more	8.4	2.0	0.3	0.1	4.9	1.3

Source: Bureau of the Census, Money Income in the United States: 1998, *Current Population Reports, P20-206, 1999; calculations by New Strategist*

Income Distribution of People by Age and Sex, 1998: Aged 35 to 54

(number and percent distribution of total people and people aged 35 to 54 by income and sex, 1998; median income of people by work status and percent working full-time, year-round; people in thousands as of 1999)

	total		aged 35 to 44		aged 45 to 54	
	men	*women*	*men*	*women*	*men*	*women*
Total people	**102,048**	**109,628**	**22,156**	**22,588**	**17,144**	**18,088**
Without income	7,100	10,934	617	1,618	323	1,173
With income	94,948	98,694	21,539	20,970	16,821	16,915
Under $10,000	17,502	36,609	2,018	5,728	1,546	4,154
$10,000 to $14,999	9,548	14,113	1,245	2,594	995	1,948
$15,000 to $24,999	17,620	19,018	3,482	4,197	2,196	3,383
$25,000 to $34,999	14,718	12,504	3,944	3,378	2,648	2,834
$35,000 to $49,999	15,234	9,149	4,600	2,884	3,424	2,319
$50,000 to $74,999	11,763	5,094	3,668	1,517	3,341	1,622
$75,000 or more	8,562	2,208	2,582	671	2,671	653
Median income						
People with income	$26,492	$14,430	$35,177	$20,285	$38,922	$21,588
Full-time, year-round workers	36,252	26,855	39,226	28,585	43,482	30,027
Percent working full-time, year-round	**54.2%**	**35.4%**	**79.0%**	**51.3%**	**77.5%**	**53.5%**
Total people	**100.0%**	**100.0%**	**100.0%**	**100.0%**	**100.0%**	**100.0%**
Without income	7.0	10.0	2.8	7.2	1.9	6.5
With income	93.0	90.0	97.2	92.8	98.1	93.5
Under $10,000	17.2	33.4	9.1	25.4	9.0	23.0
$10,000 to $14,999	9.4	12.9	5.6	11.5	5.8	10.8
$15,000 to $24,999	17.3	17.3	15.7	18.6	12.8	18.7
$25,000 to $34,999	14.4	11.4	17.8	15.0	15.4	15.7
$35,000 to $49,999	14.9	8.3	20.8	12.8	20.0	12.8
$50,000 to $74,999	11.5	4.6	16.6	6.7	19.5	9.0
$75,000 or more	8.4	2.0	11.7	3.0	15.6	3.6

Source: Bureau of the Census, Money Income in the United States: 1998, *Current Population Reports, P20-206, 1999; calculations by New Strategist*

Income Distribution of People by Age and Sex, 1998: Aged 55 or Older

(number and percent distribution of total people and people aged 55 or older by income and sex, 1998; median income of people by work status and percent working full-time, year-round; people in thousands as of 1999)

	total		aged 55 to 64		aged 65 to 74		aged 75 or older	
	men	women	men	women	men	women	men	women
Total people	**102,048**	**109,628**	**10,967**	**11,943**	**8,027**	**9,816**	**5,700**	**8,851**
Without income	7,100	10,934	289	975	125	271	101	203
With income	94,948	98,694	10,678	10,968	7,902	9,545	5,599	8,648
Under $10,000	17,502	36,609	1,464	4,203	1,417	4,585	1,265	4,043
$10,000 to $14,999	9,548	14,113	913	1,367	1,464	1,750	1,235	2,126
$15,000 to $24,999	17,620	19,018	1,705	2,026	1,984	1,712	1,578	1,459
$25,000 to $34,999	14,718	12,504	1,510	1,331	1,070	698	620	440
$35,000 to $49,999	15,234	9,149	1,826	1,068	892	411	412	287
$50,000 to $74,999	11,763	5,094	1,678	617	558	257	273	186
$75,000 or more	8,562	2,208	1,583	355	518	131	216	107
Median income								
People with income	$26,492	$14,430	$32,776	$14,675	$19,734	$10,453	$16,479	$10,545
Full-time, year-round workers	36,252	26,855	44,095	27,783	43,060	27,438	43,750	33,716
Percent working full-time, year-round	**54.2%**	**35.4%**	**56.5%**	**34.5%**	**10.9%**	**5.0%**	**2.8%**	**1.1%**
Total people	**100.0%**	**100.0%**	**100.0%**	**100.0%**	**100.0%**	**100.0%**	**100.0%**	**100.0%**
Without income	7.0	10.0	2.6	8.2	1.6	2.8	1.8	2.3
With income	93.0	90.0	97.4	91.8	98.4	97.2	98.2	97.7
Under $10,000	17.2	33.4	13.3	35.2	17.7	46.7	22.2	45.7
$10,000 to $14,999	9.4	12.9	8.3	11.4	18.2	17.8	21.7	24.0
$15,000 to $24,999	17.3	17.3	15.5	17.0	24.7	17.4	27.7	16.5
$25,000 to $34,999	14.4	11.4	13.8	11.1	13.3	7.1	10.9	5.0
$35,000 to $49,999	14.9	8.3	16.6	8.9	11.1	4.2	7.2	3.2
$50,000 to $74,999	11.5	4.6	15.3	5.2	7.0	2.6	4.8	2.1
$75,000 or more	8.4	2.0	14.4	3.0	6.5	1.3	3.8	1.2

Source: Bureau of the Census, Money Income in the United States: 1998, *Current Population Reports, P20-206, 1999; calculations by New Strategist*

Income Gap Is Widest between White Men and Women

Gap is smallest between Hispanic men and women.

Men have higher incomes than women regardless of race or Hispanic origin. In part, men's incomes are higher because a much larger proportion work full-time, from a low of 47 percent among black men to a high of 57 percent among whites. The proportion of women who work full-time ranges from a low of 32 percent among Hispanics to a high of 39 percent among blacks.

Even among full-time workers, men make considerably more than women. The gap is widest between whites. The median income of white men who work full-time stood at $37,196 in 1998 versus $27,304 for their female counterparts. The gap in incomes is much narrower for blacks and Hispanics. Among full-time workers, black women make 87 percent as much as black men, while Hispanic women make 88 percent as much as their male counterparts. But the incomes of blacks and Hispanics are considerably lower than those of whites. The median income of white women who work full-time is just $168 less than that of black men with full-time jobs.

❖ White men have the highest incomes in part because they are much better educated than any other segment of the population. As white women gain on men in educational attainment, the income gap between whites will narrow.

Whites have the highest incomes

(median income of people aged 15 or older who work full-time, year-round, by sex, race, and Hispanic origin, 1998)

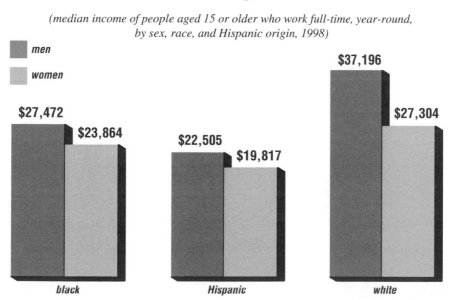

197

Income Distribution of People by Race, Hispanic Origin, and Sex, 1998

(number and percent distribution of people aged 15 or older by income, race, and Hispanic origin, 1998; median income of people by work status and percent working full-time, year-round; people in thousands as of 1999)

	black		Hispanic		white	
	men	*women*	*men*	*women*	*men*	*women*
Total people	**11,483**	**13,964**	**10,937**	**11,058**	**85,750**	**90,463**
Without income	1,707	1,692	1,320	2,653	4,854	8,400
With income	9,776	12,272	9,617	8,405	80,896	82,063
Under $10,000	2,880	4,934	2,343	3,900	13,660	30,027
$10,000 to $14,999	1,120	1,812	1,686	1,473	8,017	11,766
$15,000 to $24,999	2,022	2,444	2,436	1,534	14,744	15,698
$25,000 to $34,999	1,541	1,395	1,332	766	12,592	10,601
$35,000 to $49,999	1,219	1,075	952	464	13,434	7,700
$50,000 to $74,999	718	484	579	194	10,551	4,309
$75,000 or more	276	128	289	74	7,898	1,962
Median income						
People with income	$19,321	$13,137	$17,257	$10,862	$27,646	$14,617
Full-time, year-round workers	27,472	23,864	22,505	19,817	37,196	27,304
Percent working full-time, year-round	**47.0%**	**39.1%**	**56.2%**	**31.5%**	**57.0%**	**34.8%**
Total people	**100.0%**	**100.0%**	**100.0%**	**100.0%**	**100.0%**	**100.0%**
Without income	14.9	12.1	12.1	24.0	5.7	9.3
With income	85.1	87.9	87.9	76.0	94.3	90.7
Under $10,000	25.1	35.3	21.4	35.3	15.9	33.2
$10,000 to $14,999	9.8	13.0	15.4	13.3	9.3	13.0
$15,000 to $24,999	17.6	17.5	22.3	13.9	17.2	17.4
$25,000 to $34,999	13.4	10.0	12.2	6.9	14.7	11.7
$35,000 to $49,999	10.6	7.7	8.7	4.2	15.7	8.5
$50,000 to $74,999	6.3	3.5	5.3	1.8	12.3	4.8
$75,000 or more	2.4	0.9	2.6	0.7	9.2	2.2

Source: Bureau of the Census, Money Income in the United States: 1998, *Current Population Reports, P20-206, 1999; calculations by New Strategist*

Men's and Women's Incomes Rise with Education

The gap between men's and women's incomes does not vary much by education, however.

Incomes rise in lock step with education. This fact is behind the decades-long increase in college enrollment rates for men and women. The college educated have higher incomes than those with less education in part because they are more likely to work full-time. Among men, 74 percent of those with at least a bachelor's degree work full-time versus only 62 percent of those who went no further than high school. Among women, 51 percent of college graduates work full-time versus 37 percent of high school graduates.

Among full-time workers, education boosts income substantially. Men with a college degree who work full-time had a median income of $56,524 in 1998, versus a median of $37,906 for all men aged 25 or older with full-time jobs. Among women who work full-time, those with a college degree had a median income of $39,786 versus $27,956 for all women aged 25 or older.

Because the incomes of both men and women rise with years of schooling, the income gap between men and women varies little by education. Among full-time workers, women's incomes are 71 to 77 percent as high as men's regardless of educational level, with one exception. Women with professional degrees (doctors, lawyers, etc.) have incomes only 61 percent as high as men's. Behind this gap is the age difference between the average man and woman in this educational category. Men are far older than women and more likely to be in their peak earning years.

❖ The income gap between men and women with professional degrees will shrink dramatically in the next decade as the average age of women doctors and lawyers rises.

Income Distribution of People by Education and Sex, 1998: No College Degree

(number and percent distribution of people aged 25 or older who did not graduate from college by income and sex, 1998; median income of people by work status and percent working full-time, year-round; people in thousands as of 1999)

	total		not a high school graduate		high school graduate		some college or associate's degree	
	men	women	men	women	men	women	men	women
Total people	**82,917**	**90,837**	**13,726**	**15,115**	**26,368**	**31,566**	**20,042**	**23,134**
Without income	2,048	6,018	719	2,137	732	2,236	341	1,030
With income	80,869	84,819	13,007	12,978	25,636	29,330	19,701	22,104
Under $10,000	9,706	27,748	3,771	7,474	3,121	10,690	1,703	5,871
$10,000 to $14,999	7,491	12,169	2,637	2,746	2,637	5,078	1,456	2,939
$15,000 to $24,999	15,063	16,912	3,459	1,984	5,940	7,009	3,526	5,019
$25,000 to $34,999	13,747	11,818	1,664	457	5,540	3,700	3,850	3,910
$35,000 to $49,999	14,757	8,946	915	167	4,964	1,855	4,421	2,805
$50,000 to $74,999	11,603	5,045	400	101	2,585	752	3,311	1,153
$75,000 or more	8,501	2,181	162	50	848	246	1,433	407
Median income								
People with income	$30,654	$16,258	$15,328	$8,875	$26,542	$13,786	$32,890	$24,230
Full-time, year-round workers	37,906	27,956	22,397	15,873	31,477	22,780	37,699	28,253
Percent working full-time, year-round	**63.2%**	**39.2%**	**39.9%**	**17.8%**	**62.4%**	**36.8%**	**68.5%**	**45.8%**

(continued)

(continued from previous page)

Total people	total		not a high school graduate		high school graduate		some college or associate's degree	
	men	women	men	women	men	women	men	women
	100.0%	100.0%	100.0%	100.0%	100.0%	100.0%	100.0%	100.0%
Without income	2.5	6.6	5.2	14.1	2.8	7.1	1.7	4.5
With income	97.5	93.4	94.8	85.9	97.2	92.9	98.3	95.5
Under $10,000	11.7	30.5	27.5	49.4	11.8	33.9	8.5	25.4
$10,000 to $14,999	9.0	13.4	19.2	18.2	10.0	16.1	7.3	12.7
$15,000 to $24,999	18.2	18.6	25.2	13.1	22.5	22.2	17.6	21.7
$25,000 to $34,999	16.6	13.0	12.1	3.0	21.0	11.7	19.2	16.9
$35,000 to $49,999	17.8	9.8	6.7	1.1	18.8	5.9	22.1	12.1
$50,000 to $74,999	14.0	5.6	2.9	0.7	9.8	2.4	16.5	5.0
$75,000 or more	10.3	2.4	1.2	0.3	3.2	0.8	7.1	1.8

Source: Bureau of the Census, Money Income in the United States: 1998, Current Population Reports, P20-206, 1999; calculations by New Strategist

Income Distribution of People by Education and Sex, 1998: College Graduates

(number and percent distribution of people aged 25 or older who graduated from college by income and sex, 1998; median income of people by work status and percent working full-time, year-round; people in thousands as of 1999)

	bachelor's degree or more		bachelor's degree		master's degree		professional degree		doctoral degree	
	men	women	men	women	men	women	men	women	men	women
Total people	22,781	21,022	14,808	14,687	4,811	4,955	1,700	802	1,463	577
Without income	256	613	194	469	39	118	5	14	20	10
With income	22,525	20,409	14,614	14,218	4,772	4,837	1,695	788	1,443	567
Under $10,000	1,111	3,715	784	2,968	208	592	72	100	47	56
$10,000 to $14,999	762	1,406	522	1,113	157	227	35	48	49	17
$15,000 to $24,999	2,137	2,900	1,554	2,226	359	554	123	62	102	57
$25,000 to $34,999	2,693	3,751	2,046	2,782	439	830	114	82	94	57
$35,000 to $49,999	4,457	4,120	3,164	2,634	897	1,212	194	147	202	127
$50,000 to $74,999	5,306	3,038	3,392	1,693	1,291	1,024	292	180	331	141
$75,000 or more	6,058	1,479	3,153	803	1,421	396	866	168	618	111
Median income										
People with income	$50,272	$30,692	$45,749	$27,415	$55,784	$36,888	$76,362	$43,490	$65,319	$46,275
Full-time, year-round workers	56,524	39,786	51,405	36,559	62,244	45,283	94,737	57,565	75,078	57,796
Percent working full-time, year-round	73.5%	51.0%	74.7%	49.6%	71.0%	53.3%	74.4%	58.4%	68.2%	57.0%

(continued)

(continued from previous page)

	bachelor's degree or more		bachelor's degree		master's degree		professional degree		doctoral degree	
	men	*women*	*men*	*women*	*men*	*women*	*men*	*women*	*men*	*women*
Total people	100.0%	100.0%	100.0%	100.0%	100.0%	100.0%	100.0%	100.0%	100.0%	100.0%
Without income	1.1	2.9	1.3	3.2	0.8	2.4	0.3	1.7	1.4	1.7
With income	98.9	97.1	98.7	96.8	99.2	97.6	99.7	98.3	93.6	98.3
Under $10,000	4.9	17.7	5.3	20.2	4.3	11.9	4.2	12.5	3.2	9.7
$10,000 to $14,999	3.3	6.7	3.5	7.6	3.3	4.6	2.1	6.0	3.3	2.9
$15,000 to $24,999	9.4	13.8	10.5	15.2	7.5	11.2	7.2	7.7	7.0	9.9
$25,000 to $34,999	11.8	17.8	13.8	18.9	9.1	16.8	6.7	10.2	5.4	9.9
$35,000 to $49,999	19.6	19.6	21.4	17.9	18.6	24.5	11.4	18.3	13.8	22.0
$50,000 to $74,999	23.3	14.5	22.9	11.5	26.8	20.7	17.2	22.4	22.6	24.4
$75,000 or more	26.6	7.0	21.3	5.5	29.5	8.0	50.9	20.9	42.2	19.2

Source: Bureau of the Census, Money Income in the United States: 1998, Current Population Reports, P20-206, 1999; calculations by New Strategist

Gap in Earnings Is Greatest in Sales Occupations

Among sales workers, women earn only 60 percent as much as men.

Among full-time workers, women earned 73 percent as much as men in 1998, $25,862 versus $35,345. But the gap varies by occupation. Women make only 60 percent as much as men in sales occupations, but they make fully 84 percent as much as men in farming, forestry, and fishing occupations. Behind the earnings gap are the different career choices men and women make within occupations. Men, for example, are more likely to work in sales jobs that pay high commissions—such as car sales. Women are more likely to work as retail sales clerks earning only minimum wage.

Men and women in professional specialty occupations earn the most. Among men working full-time in these occupations, which include law and medicine, median earnings stood at $40,546 in 1998. Among women working full-time in these occupations, median earnings were $36,261, or 70 percent as much as men. Women who are full-time service workers in private households earned the least, a median of just $11,840. Men employed full-time in farming, forestry, and fishing occupations earned the least among men, just $18,855.

❖ The gap in earnings between men and women is greatest in occupations traditionally dominated by men. In those occupations, the average male worker is older than the average female worker. In time, this age difference will disappear and the income gap will narrow.

Median Earnings of People by Occupation and Sex, 1998

(median earnings of full-time workers by occupation of longest job and sex, and women's income as a percent of men's, 1998)

	men	women	women's income as a percent of men's
Total with earnings	**$35,345**	**$25,862**	**73.2%**
Executives, administrators, and managers	51,351	34,755	67.7
Professional specialty	51,654	36,261	70.2
Technical and related support	40,546	27,849	68.7
Sales	37,248	23,197	62.3
Administrative support, including clerical	31,153	23,835	76.5
Precision production, craft, and repair	31,631	23,907	75.6
Machine operators, assemblers, and inspectors	27,890	19,015	68.2
Transportation and material moving	30,422	21,449	70.5
Handlers, equipment cleaners, helpers, and laborers	21,871	16,550	75.7
Service workers	22,515	15,647	69.5
Private household	–	11,840	–
Other service workers	22,557	15,801	70.0
Farming, forestry, and fishing	18,855	15,865	84.1

Note: (–) means sample is too small to make a reliable estimate.
Source: Bureau of the Census, Money Income in the United States: 1998, *Current Population Reports, P20-206, 1999; calculations by New Strategist*

Pharmacists Receive the Highest Pay among Women

Among men, doctors have the highest wages.

Women pharmacists earned a median of $1,105 per week in 1999, putting them at the top of the pay scale among female workers. The wage of female pharmacists was 90 percent as high as that of their male counterparts. Other occupations in which women earn at least 90 percent as much as men are bookkeeper, cashier, mail carrier, mechanic and repairer, and registered nurse. Among all full-time wage and salary workers, women's median weekly earnings were 77 percent as high as men's.

Among men, physicians earned a median weekly wage of $1,364 in 1999, more than any other male workers. Female physicians earn a median of $852 a week, only 63 percent as high as the earnings of male physicians.

Child care workers in private households earn the least. Women in this profession earned a median of only $212 a week in 1999. Among men, the lowest-paid workers are cashiers, earning a median of $296 a week.

While many assume sex discrimination is the cause of the pay gap between men and women, a more important reason is that the average male worker is better educated and has more experience (i.e., has been on the job longer) than the average female worker. Typically, pay rises with education and experience.

❖ The earnings gap between men and women will narrow in the years ahead as well-educated career-oriented younger women gain job experience.

Median Weekly Earnings by Occupation and Sex, 1999

(median weekly earnings of full-time wage and salary workers aged 16 or older by selected occupation and sex, and women's earnings as a percent of men's, 1999)

	men	women	women's earnings as a percent of men's
Total	**$618**	**$473**	**76.5%**
Managerial and professional specialty	**952**	**681**	**71.5**
Executive, administrative, and managerial	967	652	67.4
Administrators and officials, public administration	1,007	725	72.0
Financial managers	1,154	703	60.9
Personnel and labor relations managers	1,014	742	73.2
Managers, marketing, adv., public relations	1,241	800	64.5
Administrators, education and related fields	1,076	819	76.1
Managers, medicine and health	1,006	714	71.0
Managers, food serving and lodging establishments	617	461	74.7
Managers, properties and real estate	679	578	85.1
Accountants and auditors	891	651	73.1
Professional specialty	939	707	75.3
Engineers	1,058	933	88.2
Computer systems analysts and scientists	1,079	907	84.1
Physicians	1,364	852	62.5
Registered nurses	791	747	94.4
Pharmacists	1,222	1,105	90.4
Therapists	793	707	89.2
Teachers, college and university	1,038	859	82.8
Teachers, prekindergarten and kindergarten	–	442	–
Teachers, elementary school	785	697	88.8
Teachers, secondary school	803	722	89.9
Librarians	–	684	–
Social workers	661	579	87.6
Clergy	676	–	–
Lawyers	1,340	974	72.7
Designers	757	512	67.6
Editors and reporters	803	709	88.3
Public relations specialists	881	684	77.6
Technical, sales, and administrative support	**626**	**431**	**68.8**
Technicians and related support	728	528	72.5
Licensed practical nurses	–	492	–
Computer programmers	935	788	84.3
Legal assistants	–	581	–
Sales occupations	666	399	59.9
Insurance sales	750	539	71.9

(continued)

(continued from previous page)

	men	women	women's earnings as a percent of men's
Real estate sales	$767	$585	76.3%
Securities and financial services sales	979	616	62.9
Advertising and related sales	892	626	70.2
Sales workers, retail and personal services	423	296	70.0
Cashiers	296	275	92.9
Administrative support, including clerical	539	427	79.2
Computer operators	612	485	79.2
Secretaries	–	443	–
Typists	–	455	–
Receptionists	–	373	–
File clerks	–	349	–
Bookkeepers	478	440	92.1
Telephone operators	–	365	–
Mail carriers, postal service	714	646	90.5
Bank tellers	–	343	–
Teachers' aides	–	314	–
Service occupations	**402**	**304**	**75.6**
Child care workers, private household	–	212	–
Cleaners and servants, private household	–	255	–
Police and detectives	766	574	74.9
Waiters, waitresses	325	294	90.5
Dental assistants	–	373	–
Nursing aides	367	318	86.6
Janitors and cleaners	351	293	83.5
Hairdressers and cosmetologists	–	323	–
Precision production, craft, and repair	**606**	**428**	**70.6**
Mechanics and repairers	622	592	95.2
Automobile mechanics	555	–	–
Construction trades	571	423	74.1
Carpenters	518	–	–
Electricians	651	–	–
Plumbers	596	–	–
Operators, fabricators, and laborers	**472**	**337**	**71.4**
Transportation and material moving occupations	522	394	75.5
Truck drivers	532	412	77.4
Bus drivers	498	384	77.1
Handlers, equipment cleaners, helpers, and laborers	377	314	83.3
Farming, forestry, and fishing	**341**	**283**	**83.0**
Farm workers	311	259	83.3
Groundskeepers and gardeners, except farm	322	–	–

Note: (–) means sample is too small to make a reliable estimate.
Source: Bureau of Labor Statistics, Employment and Earnings, *January 2000; calculations by New Strategist*

Middle-Aged Householders Have the Highest Incomes

Many middle-aged householders are dual-income couples.

Median household income peaks in the 45-to-54 age group because many householders of that age are dual-income married couples at the height of their careers. In 1998, those households had a median income of $54,148. Since 1970, householders aged 45 to 54 have seen their incomes rise 20 percent, after adjusting for inflation. In contrast, the median income of the average household rose only 13 percent.

A large proportion of householders aged 65 or older are women who live alone, which explains the relatively low median income of this household segment. The median income of householders aged 65 or older stood at $21,729 in 1998, lower than that of any other age group. Since 1970, however, the median income of elderly householders has grown 57 percent, faster than that of any other age group.

Households under age 35 are a mix of married couples, single parents, and nonfamily households. This explains the relatively low median household income of younger house-holders. Over the past few decades, as married couples made up a smaller share of households headed by the young, household income in the age group stagnated.

❖ The rising incomes of women have been the most important factor behind the gains in median household income over the past three decades.

Incomes peak in middle age

(median income of households by age of householder, 1998)

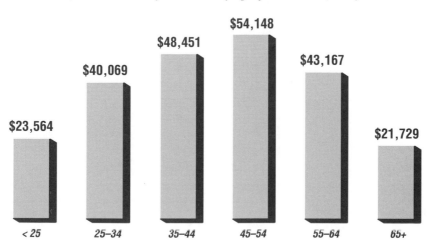

< 25	25–34	35–44	45–54	55–64	65+
$23,564	$40,069	$48,451	$54,148	$43,167	$21,729

Median Income of Households by Age of Householder, 1970 to 1998

(median income of households by age of householder, 1970 to 1998; percent change in income for selected years; in 1998 dollars)

	total	under 25	25 to 34	35 to 44	45 to 54	55 to 64	65 or older
1998	$38,885	$23,564	$40,069	$48,451	$54,148	$43,167	$21,729
1997	37,581	22,935	38,769	47,081	52,683	42,000	21,084
1996	36,872	22,271	37,283	46,147	52,434	41,363	20,204
1995	36,446	22,438	37,115	46,488	51,401	40,725	20,424
1994	35,486	21,271	36,462	45,828	51,981	38,750	19,902
1993	35,241	21,808	35,286	46,093	52,123	37,760	20,024
1992	35,593	20,521	36,293	46,301	51,626	39,493	19,907
1991	36,054	21,916	36,911	47,092	52,360	39,857	20,315
1990	37,343	22,451	37,862	48,091	52,282	40,363	21,020
1989	37,997	24,533	39,203	49,472	54,583	40,512	20,731
1988	37,512	23,479	39,142	50,366	52,652	39,824	20,562
1987	37,394	23,599	38,692	50,486	53,384	39,545	20,724
1986	37,027	22,769	38,516	48,762	53,034	39,822	20,591
1985	35,778	22,797	38,001	47,061	50,329	38,716	20,078
1984	35,165	22,007	37,236	46,726	49,443	37,799	20,079
1983	34,179	21,933	35,588	45,298	49,672	37,277	19,177
1982	34,392	23,557	36,285	44,961	47,715	37,638	18,825
1981	34,507	23,956	37,110	45,922	48,925	38,065	17,916
1980	35,076	25,175	38,298	46,795	49,754	38,714	17,391
1979	36,259	26,241	40,096	48,671	50,768	39,508	17,355
1978	36,377	26,597	39,849	48,122	51,148	38,705	17,099
1977	35,004	24,685	38,880	46,620	49,975	36,910	16,370
1976	34,812	24,318	38,404	45,884	48,472	36,804	16,360
1975	34,224	23,603	38,073	45,077	47,340	36,211	16,198
1974	35,166	25,477	39,013	46,752	48,281	36,023	16,620
1973	36,302	25,887	40,867	48,220	48,627	37,563	15,827
1972	35,599	25,922	39,931	46,580	48,184	36,837	15,305
1971	34,143	24,889	38,110	43,931	45,443	35,338	14,420
1970	34,471	26,321	38,244	43,931	45,044	35,150	13,806

Percent change

1990–1998	4.1%	5.0%	5.8%	0.7%	3.6%	6.9%	3.4%
1970 1998	12.8	−10.5	4.8	10.3	20.2	22.8	57.4

Source: Bureau of the Census, Internet web site <http://www.census.gov/hhes/income/histinc/h10.html>; calculations by New Strategist

Income Distribution of Households by Age of Householder, 1998

(number and percent distribution of households by income and age of householder, 1998; households in thousands as of 1999)

	total	under 25	25 to 34	35 to 44	45 to 54	55 to 64	65 to 74	75 or older
Total households	**103,874**	**5,770**	**18,819**	**23,968**	**20,158**	**13,571**	**11,373**	**10,216**
Under $10,000	10,705	1,075	1,506	1,494	1,288	1,507	1,712	2,125
$10,000 to $14,999	8,093	668	1,193	1,132	790	863	1,353	2,095
$15,000 to $24,999	14,587	1,325	2,521	2,426	1,831	1,590	2,400	2,493
$25,000 to $34,999	13,698	944	2,932	2,950	2,119	1,681	1,742	1,329
$35,000 to $49,999	16,660	932	3,502	4,387	3,123	2,086	1,645	986
$50,000 to $74,999	19,272	551	4,192	5,529	4,621	2,494	1,257	629
$75,000 to $99,999	9,934	151	1,713	3,002	2,724	1,515	587	243
$100,000 or more	10,926	123	1,260	3,049	3,663	1,835	678	317
Median income	**$38,885**	**$23,564**	**$40,069**	**$48,451**	**$54,148**	**$43,167**	**$26,112**	**$17,885**
Total households	**100.0%**	**100.0%**	**100.0%**	**100.0%**	**100.0%**	**100.0%**	**100.0%**	**100.0%**
Under $10,000	10.3	18.6	8.0	6.2	6.4	11.1	15.1	20.8
$10,000 to $14,999	7.8	11.6	6.3	4.7	3.9	6.4	11.9	20.5
$15,000 to $24,999	14.0	23.0	13.4	10.1	9.1	11.7	21.1	24.4
$25,000 to $34,999	13.2	16.4	15.6	12.3	10.5	12.4	15.3	13.0
$35,000 to $49,999	16.0	16.2	18.6	18.3	15.5	15.4	14.5	9.7
$50,000 to $74,999	18.6	9.5	22.3	23.1	22.9	18.4	11.1	6.2
$75,000 to $99,999	9.6	2.6	9.1	12.5	13.5	11.2	5.2	2.4
$100,000 or more	10.5	2.1	6.7	12.7	18.2	13.5	6.0	3.1

Source: Bureau of the Census, Money Income in the United States: 1998, *Current Population Reports, P20-206, 1999; calculations by New Strategist*

Women Living Alone Have Seen the Biggest Income Gain

Male-headed families have experienced the slowest income growth.

During the past two decades, the median income of women who live alone has grown a substantial 24 percent, after adjusting for inflation. Despite this gain, the median income of women who live alone is lower than that of any other household type—just $16,406 in 1998. Men who live alone saw their median income grow 14 percent between 1980 and 1998, to $26,021.

Married couples have the highest median income—$54,276 in 1998. The median income of couples was 18 percent higher in 1998 than in 1980, after adjusting for inflation.

The median income of female-headed families grew 14 percent between 1980 and 1998, while the median income of male-headed families was up just 6 percent. Nevertheless, male-headed families continue to have a much higher median income than female-headed families, $39,414 versus $24,393 in 1998.

❖ As women surged into the labor force during the past few decades, their economic power grew. This has boosted the incomes of married couples, female-headed families, and women who live alone.

Income growth varies by household type

(percent change in median income of households by household type, 1970 to 1998; in 1998 dollars)

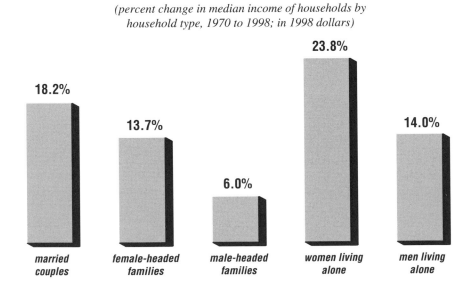

Median Income of Households by Type of Household, 1980 to 1998

(median income of households by household type, 1980 to 1998, percent change in income for selected years; in 1998 dollars)

| | total | family households | | | nonfamily households | | | |
| | | | female householder no spouse present | male householder no spouse present | female householder | | male householder | |
		married couples			total	living alone	total	living alone
1998	$38,885	$54,276	$24,393	$39,414	$18,615	$16,406	$30,414	$26,021
1997	37,581	52,486	23,399	37,205	17,887	15,772	28,022	24,243
1996	36,872	51,796	22,402	37,044	17,036	15,195	28,326	24,985
1995	36,446	50,407	22,833	35,866	16,997	15,328	27,833	24,157
1994	35,486	49,539	21,857	33,515	16,441	14,772	27,049	23,335
1993	35,241	48,651	20,919	33,671	16,788	14,659	27,894	24,108
1992	35,593	48,756	21,338	35,214	16,774	15,026	26,850	23,212
1991	36,055	49,157	21,500	37,112	17,146	15,359	27,552	24,245
1990	37,343	49,880	22,534	39,349	17,583	15,649	28,047	24,898
1989	37,997	50,824	22,850	39,877	18,081	16,024	29,475	25,787
1988	37,512	50,203	22,116	39,464	–	16,013	–	25,193
1987	37,394	50,153	22,212	38,318	–	15,379	–	24,384
1986	37,027	48,894	21,322	39,117	–	14,837	–	24,492
1985	35,778	47,205	21,687	36,893	–	14,806	–	24,711
1984	35,165	46,572	21,137	38,516	–	15,122	–	23,849
1983	34,179	44,725	20,030	37,447	–	14,960	–	23,108
1982	34,392	44,445	20,261	36,174	–	13,908	–	23,558
1981	34,507	45,419	20,698	37,163	–	13,396	–	23,223
1980	35,076	45,909	21,449	37,185	–	13,250	–	22,830

Percent change

1990–1998	4.1%	8.8%	8.2%	0.2%	5.9%	4.8%		4.5%
1980–1998	10.9	18.2	13.7	6.0	–	23.8	–	14.0

Note: (–) means data are not available.
Source: Bureau of the Census, Internet web site <http://www.census.gov/hhes/income/histinc/h09.html>; calculations by New Strategist

Income Distribution of Households by Type of Household, 1998

(number and percent distribution of households by income and type of household, 1998; households in thousands as of 1999)

		family households			nonfamily households			
			female house-holder	male house-holder	female householder		male householder	
	total	married couples	no spouse present	no spouse present	total	living alone	total	living alone
Total households	**103,874**	**54,770**	**12,789**	**3,976**	**17,971**	**15,640**	**14,368**	**10,966**
Under $10,000	10,705	1,541	2,412	236	4,435	4,313	2,084	1,925
$10,000 to $14,999	8,093	1,841	1,603	209	3,076	2,950	1,364	1,201
$15,000 to $24,999	14,587	5,488	2,511	640	3,473	3,155	2,475	2,118
$25,000 to $34,999	13,698	6,329	1,992	675	2,464	2,143	2,237	1,783
$35,000 to $49,999	16,660	9,454	1,979	759	2,053	1,638	2,415	1,768
$50,000 to $74,999	19,272	13,301	1,530	844	1,467	960	2,128	1,338
$75,000 to $99,999	9,934	7,739	433	320	595	295	849	425
$100,000 or more	10,926	9,077	333	293	408	186	816	408
Median income	**$38,885**	**$54,276**	**$24,393**	**$39,414**	**$18,615**	**$16,406**	**$30,414**	**$26,021**
Total households	**100.0%**	**100.0%**	**100.0%**	**100.0%**	**100.0%**	**100.0%**	**100.0%**	**100.0%**
Under $10,000	10.3	2.8	18.9	5.9	24.7	27.6	14.5	17.6
$10,000 to $14,999	7.8	3.4	12.5	5.3	17.1	18.9	9.5	11.0
$15,000 to $24,999	14.0	10.0	19.6	16.1	19.3	20.2	17.2	19.3
$25,000 to $34,999	13.2	11.6	15.6	17.0	13.7	13.7	15.6	16.3
$35,000 to $49,999	16.0	17.3	15.5	19.1	11.4	10.5	16.8	16.1
$50,000 to $74,999	18.6	24.3	12.0	21.3	8.2	6.1	14.8	12.2
$75,000 to $99,999	9.6	14.1	3.4	8.0	3.3	1.9	5.9	3.9
$100,000 or more	10.5	16.6	2.6	7.4	2.3	1.2	5.7	3.7

Source: Bureau of the Census, Money Income in the United States: 1998, *Current Population Reports, P20-206, 1999; calculations by New Strategist*

Married Men and Women Are the Nation's Income Elite

Middle-aged married couples make the most money.

Married couples headed by 45-to-54-year-olds have the highest median income, fully $69,824 in 1998. This figure was 80 percent greater than the median income of the average household. Behind the much higher incomes of married couples are two earners. Without the income provided by working wives, many couples would find it difficult to maintain a comfortable standard of living.

Most married couples have above-average incomes. Only those under age 25 and those aged 65 or older have incomes below the all-household median of $38,885.

Fully 26 percent of couples aged 45 to 54 have incomes of $100,000 or more. With the oldest members of the baby-boom generation now entirely filling the 45-to-54 age group and the youngest soon to follow, the nation's affluence will remain at record levels for years to come.

❖ While the two-earner lifestyle provides financial security, it creates extraordinary time pressures. Convenience is one of the most important benefits two-earner couples seek in the marketplace.

Income Distribution of Married Couples by Age, 1998

*(number and percent distribution of married couples by income and age of householder, 1998;
married couples in thousands as of 1999)*

	total	under 25	25 to 34	35 to 44	45 to 54	55 to 64	65 to 74	75 or older
Total couples	**54,770**	**1,484**	**9,375**	**14,141**	**12,152**	**8,091**	**5,975**	**3,552**
Under $10,000	1,541	107	263	230	215	293	243	189
$10,000 to $14,999	1,841	136	318	262	183	248	366	329
$15,000 to $24,999	5,488	332	828	846	585	710	1,184	1,003
$25,000 to $34,999	6,329	307	1,228	1,277	818	865	1,113	719
$35,000 to $49,999	9,455	341	1,900	2,540	1,682	1,324	1,124	544
$50,000 to $74,999	13,304	192	2,780	3,917	3,271	1,823	955	365
$75,000 to $99,999	7,739	48	1,181	2,434	2,224	1,236	446	170
$100,000 or more	9,077	22	877	2,635	3,172	1,595	545	230
Median income	$54,276	$30,221	$50,806	$61,186	$69,824	$56,758	$35,878	$27,719
Total couples	**100.0%**	**100.0%**	**100.0%**	**100.0%**	**100.0%**	**100.0%**	**100.0%**	**100.0%**
Under $10,000	2.8	7.2	2.8	1.6	1.8	3.6	4.1	5.3
$10,000 to $14,999	3.4	9.2	3.4	1.9	1.5	3.1	6.1	9.3
$15,000 to $24,999	10.0	22.4	8.8	6.0	4.8	8.8	19.8	28.2
$25,000 to $34,999	11.6	20.7	13.1	9.0	6.7	10.7	18.6	20.2
$35,000 to $49,999	17.3	23.0	20.3	18.0	13.8	16.4	18.8	15.3
$50,000 to $74,999	24.3	12.9	29.7	27.7	26.9	22.5	16.0	10.3
$75,000 to $99,999	14.1	3.2	12.6	17.2	18.3	15.3	7.5	4.8
$100,000 or more	16.6	1.5	9.4	18.6	26.1	19.7	9.1	6.5

*Source: Bureau of the Census, unpublished data from the 1999 Current Population Survey, Internet web site
<http://www.bls.census.gov/macro/o31999/hhinc/toc.htm>; calculations by New Strategist*

Male-Headed Families Have Above-Average Incomes

The incomes of female-headed families are below average.

The median income of male-headed families stood at $39,414 in 1998, slightly above the national median of $38,885. The youngest male family heads, those under age 25, have the lowest incomes—a median of $29,824. Those aged 45 to 54 have the highest incomes, a median of $45,716 in 1998.

The median income of female-headed families is below that of male-headed families at every age. Overall, female-headed families had a median income of $24,393 in 1998—just 63 percent of the national median. Those under age 35 are the poorest, most having incomes below $20,000. Female family heads aged 45 to 54 have the highest incomes, a median of $33,442 in 1998—still well below the national median.

Female- and male-headed families include both single parents raising children alone and men and women living with adult relatives such as grown children, siblings, or parents. Families headed by men and women under age 45 are likely to include children under age 18, while those headed by people aged 45 or older are likely to include related adults.

❖ Male and female family householders under age 45 are an important market for affordable children's products, while those aged 45 or older are a market for discretionary products and services such as entertainment and travel.

Income Distribution of Male-Headed Families by Age, 1998

(number and percent distribution of families headed by men with no spouse present by income and age of householder, 1998; families in thousands as of 1999)

	total	under 25	25 to 34	35 to 44	45 to 54	55 to 64	65 to 74	75 or older
Total male-headed families	**3,976**	**530**	**932**	**995**	**720**	**421**	**208**	**170**
Under $10,000	236	47	53	50	35	27	17	8
$10,000 to $14,999	209	44	60	47	29	11	11	8
$15,000 to $24,999	640	118	150	136	95	67	44	33
$25,000 to $34,999	675	101	157	166	94	80	39	40
$35,000 to $49,999	759	77	187	220	150	50	42	31
$50,000 to $74,999	844	80	202	250	160	102	26	26
$75,000 to $99,999	320	24	60	78	81	44	21	9
$100,000 or more	293	38	63	48	77	40	10	17
Median income	$39,414	$29,824	$40,077	$40,051	$45,716	$41,348	$33,933	$33,854
Total male-headed families	**100.0%**	**100.0%**	**100.0%**	**100.0%**	**100.0%**	**100.0%**	**100.0%**	**100.0%**
Under $10,000	5.9	8.9	5.7	5.0	4.9	6.4	8.2	4.7
$10,000 to $14,999	5.3	8.3	6.4	4.7	4.0	2.6	5.3	4.7
$15,000 to $24,999	16.1	22.3	16.1	13.7	13.2	15.9	21.2	19.4
$25,000 to $34,999	17.0	19.1	16.8	16.7	13.1	19.0	18.8	23.5
$35,000 to $49,999	19.1	14.5	20.1	22.1	20.8	11.9	20.2	18.2
$50,000 to $74,999	21.2	15.1	21.7	25.1	22.2	24.2	12.5	15.3
$75,000 to $99,999	8.0	4.5	6.4	7.8	11.3	10.5	10.1	5.3
$100,000 or more	7.4	7.2	6.8	4.8	10.7	9.5	4.8	10.0

Source: Bureau of the Census, unpublished data from the 1999 Current Population Survey, Internet web site <http://www.bls.census.gov/macro/o31999/hhinc/toc.htm>; calculations by New Strategist

Income Distribution of Female-Headed Families by Age, 1998

(number and percent distribution of families headed by women with no spouse present by income and age of householder, 1998; families in thousands as of 1999)

	total	under 25	25 to 34	35 to 44	45 to 54	55 to 64	65 to 74	75 or older
Total female-headed families	**12,789**	**1,229**	**2,911**	**3,683**	**2,251**	**1,122**	**868**	**725**
Under $10,000	2,412	456	745	657	263	133	99	58
$10,000 to $14,999	1,603	168	432	444	215	121	113	109
$15,000 to $24,999	2,511	262	660	722	356	186	152	174
$25,000 to $34,999	1,992	131	456	578	354	171	160	142
$35,000 to $49,999	1,979	119	323	612	411	202	185	128
$50,000 to $74,999	1,531	67	191	450	445	208	99	73
$75,000 to $99,999	433	13	55	144	99	64	36	20
$100,000 or more	333	13	49	76	111	38	27	20
Median income	$24,393	$14,692	$18,277	$25,274	$33,442	$32,054	$28,740	$26,217
Total female-headed families	**100.0%**	**100.0%**	**100.0%**	**100.0%**	**100.0%**	**100.0%**	**100.0%**	**100.0%**
Under $10,000	18.9	37.1	25.6	17.8	11.7	11.9	11.4	8.0
$10,000 to $14,999	12.5	13.7	14.8	12.1	9.6	10.8	13.0	15.0
$15,000 to $24,999	19.6	21.3	22.7	19.6	15.8	16.6	17.5	24.0
$25,000 to $34,999	15.6	10.7	15.7	15.7	15.7	15.2	18.4	19.6
$35,000 to $49,999	15.5	9.7	11.1	16.6	18.3	18.0	21.3	17.7
$50,000 to $74,999	12.0	5.5	6.6	12.2	19.8	18.5	11.4	10.1
$75,000 to $99,999	3.4	1.1	1.9	3.9	4.4	5.7	4.1	2.8
$100,000 or more	2.6	1.1	1.7	2.1	4.9	3.4	3.1	2.8

Source: Bureau of the Census, unpublished data from the 1999 Current Population Survey, Internet web site <http://www.bls.census.gov/macro/o31999/hhinc/toc.htm>; calculations by New Strategist

Low Incomes for Older Women Who Live Alone

Older men who live alone also have low incomes.

The median income of the 15.6 million women who live alone was just $16,406 in 1998. In contrast, the median income of the 11 million men who live alone is a much higher $26,021. Despite this large difference in overall medians, the incomes of men and women who live alone are fairly similar within age groups. The large gap in overall medians is due to the differing ages of men and women who live alone. Most women who live alone are older widows dependent on Social Security. Most men who live alone are of working age.

Among men who live alone, income peaks in the 35-to-44 age group at $31,611. Among women who live alone, income peaks in the same age group at a slightly lower $30,279. Among both men and women aged 65 or older who live alone, median income is well below $20,000.

❖ As career-oriented baby-boom women become widowed in the decades ahead, the incomes of older women who live alone will rise. Unlike today's older widows, most boomer women will collect their own pension and Social Security benefits in old age.

Income Distribution of Men Living Alone by Age, 1998

(number and percent distribution of men living alone by income and age of householder, 1998; men in thousands as of 1999)

	total	under 25	25 to 34	35 to 44	45 to 54	55 to 64	65 to 74	75 or older
Total men living alone	**10,966**	**645**	**2,166**	**2,521**	**2,108**	**1,272**	**1,127**	**1,127**
Under $10,000	1,925	165	217	295	364	328	319	235
$10,000 to $14,999	1,201	116	172	220	106	125	179	281
$15,000 to $24,999	2,118	184	392	420	335	221	233	334
$25,000 to $34,999	1,783	83	474	453	352	176	113	130
$35,000 to $49,999	1,768	68	462	499	386	172	108	71
$50,000 to $74,999	1,338	22	284	427	328	137	95	51
$75,000 to $99,999	425	3	99	123	106	46	39	12
$100,000 or more	408	2	65	83	133	69	42	15
Median income	$26,021	$16,707	$31,156	$31,611	$31,237	$23,155	$17,249	$16,167
Total men living alone	**100.0%**	**100.0%**	**100.0%**	**100.0%**	**100.0%**	**100.0%**	**100.0%**	**100.0%**
Under $10,000	17.6	25.6	10.0	11.7	17.3	25.8	28.3	20.9
$10,000 to $14,999	11.0	18.0	7.9	8.7	5.0	9.8	15.9	24.9
$15,000 to $24,999	19.3	28.5	18.1	16.7	15.9	17.4	20.7	29.6
$25,000 to $34,999	16.3	12.9	21.9	18.0	16.7	13.8	10.0	11.5
$35,000 to $49,999	16.1	10.5	21.3	19.8	18.3	13.5	9.6	6.3
$50,000 to $74,999	12.2	3.4	13.1	16.9	15.6	10.8	8.4	4.5
$75,000 to $99,999	3.9	0.5	4.6	4.9	5.0	3.6	3.5	1.1
$100,000 or more	3.7	0.3	3.0	3.3	6.3	5.4	3.7	1.3

Source: Bureau of the Census, unpublished data from the 1999 Current Population Survey, Internet web site <http://www.bls.census.gov/macro/o31999/hhinc/toc.htm>; calculations by New Strategist

Income Distribution of Women Living Alone by Age, 1998

(number and percent distribution of women living alone by income and age of householder, 1998; women in thousands as of 1999)

	total	under 25	25 to 34	35 to 44	45 to 54	55 to 64	65 to 74	75 or older
Total women living alone	**15,640**	**668**	**1,549**	**1,553**	**2,100**	**2,277**	**2,998**	**4,495**
Under $10,000	4,313	193	175	225	379	698	1,019	1,624
$10,000 to $14,999	2,950	133	130	127	209	332	670	1,350
$15,000 to $24,999	3,155	206	359	240	369	354	743	886
$25,000 to $34,999	2,143	88	385	351	411	341	283	283
$35,000 to $49,999	1,638	42	290	327	365	266	156	193
$50,000 to $74,999	960	8	167	197	251	162	74	102
$75,000 to $99,999	295	–	33	52	80	77	24	31
$100,000 or more	186	–	9	37	36	51	27	26
Median income	$16,406	$15,275	$27,035	$30,279	$26,878	$17,721	$13,410	$12,026
Total women living alone	**100.0%**	**100.0%**	**100.0%**	**100.0%**	**100.0%**	**100.0%**	**100.0%**	**100.0%**
Under $10,000	27.6	28.9	11.3	14.5	18.0	30.7	34.0	36.1
$10,000 to $14,999	18.9	19.9	8.4	8.2	10.0	14.6	22.3	30.0
$15,000 to $24,999	20.2	30.8	23.2	15.5	17.6	15.5	24.8	19.7
$25,000 to $34,999	13.7	13.2	24.9	22.6	19.6	15.0	9.4	6.3
$35,000 to $49,999	10.5	6.3	18.7	21.1	17.4	11.7	5.2	4.3
$50,000 to $74,999	6.1	1.2	10.8	12.7	12.0	7.1	2.5	2.3
$75,000 to $99,999	1.9	0.0	2.1	3.3	3.8	3.4	0.8	0.7
$100,000 or more	1.2	0.0	0.6	2.4	1.7	2.2	0.9	0.6

Note: (–) means sample is too small to make a reliable estimate.
Source: Bureau of the Census, unpublished data from the 1999 Current Population Survey, Internet web site <http://www.bls.census.gov/macro/o31999/hhinc/toc.htm>; calculations by New Strategist

Dual-Income Couples Have the Highest Incomes

Retirees have the lowest incomes.

In 60 percent of the nation's 55 million married couples, both husband and wife are in the labor force. The median income of these couples stood at $65,411 in 1998, 21 percent greater than the $54,180 median of all married couples. If both husband and wife work full-time, median income is $72,930, 35 percent greater than the median for all couples.

Only 16 percent of married couples are what was once regarded as the norm—a husband who works full-time and a wife who does not work. The median income of these couples stood at $48,514 in 1998, 10 percent below the median for all couples. Couples in which neither husband nor wife work, most of whom are retirees, have the lowest incomes—a median of just $25,657 in 1998.

There are nearly twice as many couples in which both husband and wife work full-time than couples in which only the husband works full-time. Among the nation's 16 million dual-income couples, median income is highest for those without children at home—$76,459 in 1998. Many of these couples are empty nesters in their peak earning years. One in four dual-income couples has an income of $100,000 or more.

❖ As men's incomes have stagnated and women's have grown, the income disparity between single-earner and dual-earner couples has grown.

Dual-income couples are more affluent

(median income of married couples by work status of husband and wife, 1998)

$72,930

husband and wife work full-time, year-round

$48,514

husband works full-time, year-round, wife doesn't work

223

Median Income of Married Couples by Work Status of Husband and Wife, 1998

(number, percent distribution, and median income of married couples by work status of husband and wife, and index of median compared to median of total couples, 1998; couples in thousands as of 1999)

	number	percent distribution	median income	index of median compared to median of total couples
Total couples	**54,778**	**100.0%**	**$54,180**	**100**
Husband worked	43,705	79.8	60,867	112
Wife worked	32,873	60.0	65,411	121
Wife worked full-time, year-round	19,132	34.9	70,918	131
Wife did not work	10,832	19.8	45,541	84
Husband worked full-time, year-round	36,285	66.2	63,750	118
Wife worked	27,799	50.7	68,075	126
Wife worked full-time, year-round	16,703	30.5	72,930	135
Wife did not work	8,486	15.5	48,514	90
Husband did not work	11,073	20.2	28,488	53
Wife worked	3,019	5.5	38,818	72
Wife worked full-time, year-round	1,666	3.0	43,080	80
Wife did not work	8,055	14.7	25,657	47

Note: The index is calculated by dividing the median income of each type of couple by the median income of total couples and multiplying by 100.
Source: Bureau of the Census, Money Income in the United States: 1998, *Current Population Reports, P20-206, 1999; calculations by New Strategist*

Income Distribution of Dual-Income Married Couples, 1998

(number and percent distribution of married couples in which both spouses work full-time, year-round by income and presence of children under age 18 at home, 1998; couples in thousands as of 1999)

	total	no children under age 18	with children under age 18
Total couples	**16,703**	**7,774**	**8,929**
Under $10,000	27	21	6
$10,000 to $14,999	53	26	27
$15,000 to $24,999	237	110	128
$25,000 to $34,999	805	318	487
$35,000 to $49,999	2,454	1,011	1,445
$50,000 to $74,999	5,154	2,295	2,859
$75,000 to $99,999	3,715	1,721	1,992
$100,000 or more	4,258	2,273	1,985
Median income	**$72,930**	**$76,459**	**$70,515**
Total couples	**100.0%**	**100.0%**	**100.0%**
Under $10,000	0.2	0.3	0.1
$10,000 to $14,999	0.3	0.3	0.3
$15,000 to $24,999	1.4	1.4	1.4
$25,000 to $34,999	4.8	4.1	5.5
$35,000 to $49,999	14.7	13.0	16.2
$50,000 to $74,999	30.9	29.5	32.0
$75,000 to $99,999	22.2	22.1	22.3
$100,000 or more	25.5	29.2	22.2

Source: Bureau of the Census, Money Income in the United States: 1998, *Current Population Reports, P20-206, 1999; calculations by New Strategist*

Many Wives Earn More Than Their Husbands

More than 7 million wives bring home more bacon.

The number of wives who earn more than their husbands has been climbing for many years. Seven million wives earned more than their husbands in 1998, an 82 percent increase over the 4 million who did so in 1981. The proportion of wives who earn more rose from 16 to 23 percent during those years.

One factor behind this long-term increase is the entry of career-oriented baby-boom women into the labor force. Another factor is the stagnation in the incomes of men, after adjusting for inflation. Because wives are better educated than husbands among today's young married couples, the proportion of women who earn more than their husbands should continue to climb in the years ahead.

❖ With millions of wives earning more than their husbands, marketers should abandon stereotypical thinking about who makes the spending decisions in the nation's households.

The rise of women breadwinners

(percent of married couples with earners in which wives earn more than husbands, 1981 to 1998)

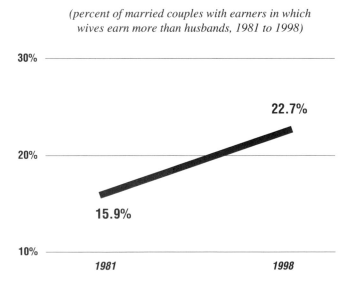

Wives Who Earn More Than Their Husbands, 1981 to 1998

(number of married couples in which both husband and wife have earnings, number in which wives earn more than husbands, and percent of wives earning more than husbands, 1981 to 1998; couples in thousands as of the following year)

	husbands and wives with earnings	wives earning more than husbands	percent of wives earning more than husbands
1998	32,783	7,435	22.7%
1997	32,745	7,446	22.7
1996	32,390	7,327	22.6
1995	32,030	7,028	21.9
1994	32,093	7,218	22.5
1993	31,267	6,960	22.3
1992	31,224	6,979	22.4
1991	31,003	6,499	21.0
1987	29,079	5,266	18.1
1983	26,120	4,800	18.4
1981	25,744	4,088	15.9

Source: Bureau of the Census, Internet web site <http://www.census.gov/hhes/income/histinc/t022.html>

Most of the Nation's Poor Are Female

The female share of the poor population has been stable for decades.

In 1998, females accounted for 57 percent of the population living in poverty, the same proportion as in 1970. The female poverty rate is also about the same today as it was nearly three decades ago. In 1970, 14.0 percent of females were poor, as compared with 14.3 percent in 1998. The female poverty rate peaked at 16.9 percent in 1993 and bottomed out at 12.5 percent in 1973.

The poverty rate among males was the same in 1998 as in 1970, standing at 11.1 percent. Since 1970, the poverty rate among males peaked at 13.5 percent in 1983 and bottomed out at 9.6 percent in 1973 and 1978.

❖ Although the poverty rate among males and females has changed little over the past three decades, today's poor are more likely to be children and less likely to be elderly than the poor of 1970.

Females are more likely to be poor than males

(poverty rate of people by sex, 1998)

11.1%

14.3%

males

females

People in Poverty by Sex, 1970 to 1998

(number and percent of people below poverty level by sex, and female share of poor, 1970 to 1998; people in thousands as of the following year)

	male		female		
	number	percent	number	percent	share of poor
1998	14,714	11.1%	19,764	14.3%	57.3%
1997	15,187	11.6	20,387	14.9	57.3
1996	15,611	12.0	20,918	15.4	57.3
1995	15,683	12.2	20,742	15.4	56.9
1994	16,316	12.8	21,744	16.3	57.1
1993	16,900	13.3	22,365	16.9	57.0
1992	16,222	12.9	21,792	16.6	57.3
1991	15,082	12.3	20,626	16.0	57.8
1990	14,211	11.7	19,373	15.2	57.7
1989	13,366	11.2	18,162	14.4	57.6
1988	13,599	11.5	18,146	14.5	57.2
1987	14,029	12.0	18,518	15.0	56.9
1986	13,721	11.8	18,649	15.2	57.6
1985	14,140	12.3	18,923	15.6	57.2
1984	14,537	12.8	19,163	15.9	56.9
1983	15,182	13.5	20,084	16.8	57.0
1982	14,842	13.4	19,556	16.5	56.9
1981	13,360	12.1	18,462	15.8	58.0
1980	12,207	11.2	17,065	14.7	58.3
1979	10,535	10.0	14,810	13.2	58.4
1978	10,017	9.6	14,480	13.0	59.1
1977	10,340	10.0	14,381	13.0	58.2
1976	10,373	10.1	14,603	13.4	58.5
1975	10,908	10.7	14,970	13.8	57.8
1974	10,313	10.2	13,881	12.9	57.4
1973	9,642	9.6	13,316	12.5	58.0
1972	10,190	10.2	14,258	13.4	58.3
1971	10,708	10.8	14,841	14.1	58.1
1970	10,879	11.1	14,632	14.0	57.4

Source: Bureau of the Census, Internet web site <http://wwwcensus.gov/hhes/poverty/histpov/hstpov7.html>; calculations by New Strategist

Female Share of Poor Varies Little by Race, Hispanic Origin

Females account for the majority of poor blacks, whites, and Hispanics.

Despite differences in poverty rates by race and Hispanic origin, females account for about the same share of the poor in each racial and ethnic group—from 55 percent among Hispanics to 59 percent among blacks. Females account for about one-half of poor children, but their share of the poor is much higher in the oldest age group. Among poor people aged 75 or older, the female share ranges from 69 percent among blacks to 78 percent among whites.

Females are more likely to be poor than males in nearly every age group, regardless of race or ethnicity. The biggest differences in poverty rates by sex are found among blacks. The poverty rate of black women aged 25 to 34 is nearly 13 percentage points greater than the poverty rate of their male counterparts, 27 versus 14 percent. Among blacks aged 55 to 59, however, men are slightly more likely to be poor than women. The differences in poverty rates between males and females are much smaller among Hispanics and whites. Nevertheless, females are more likely to be poor than males in every age group.

❖ Blacks and Hispanics are more likely to be poor than whites because they are much less likely to live in dual-earner married-couple families.

People in Poverty by Age and Sex, 1998: Total People

(number and percent of people below poverty level by age and sex, 1998; female share of poor and percentage point difference between male and female poverty rate; people in thousands as of 1999)

	male	female	female share of poor
NUMBER OF POOR			
Total poor people	**14,712**	**19,764**	**57.3%**
Under age 18	6,723	6,744	50.1
Aged 18 to 24	1,752	2,560	59.4
Aged 25 to 34	1,717	2,864	62.5
Aged 35 to 44	1,610	2,472	60.6
Aged 45 to 54	1,015	1,429	58.5
Aged 55 to 59	495	670	57.5
Aged 60 to 64	404	634	61.1
Aged 65 to 74	565	1,051	65.0
Aged 75 or older	430	1,340	75.7

	male	female	percentage point difference
POVERTY RATE			
Total people	**11.1%**	**14.3%**	**–3.2**
Under age 18	18.4	19.4	–1.0
Aged 18 to 24	13.5	19.6	–6.1
Aged 25 to 34	9.1	14.7	–5.6
Aged 35 to 44	7.3	10.9	–3.6
Aged 45 to 54	5.9	7.9	–2.0
Aged 55 to 59	8.2	10.2	–2.0
Aged 60 to 64	8.2	11.8	–3.6
Aged 65 to 74	7.0	10.7	–3.7
Aged 75 or older	7.5	15.1	–7.6

Source: Bureau of the Census, Poverty in the United States: 1998, *Current Population Reports, P60-207, 1999; calculations by New Strategist*

People in Poverty by Age and Sex, 1998: Blacks

(number and percent of blacks below poverty level by age and sex, 1998; female share of poor and percentage point difference between male and female poverty rate; people in thousands as of 1999)

	male	female	female share of poor
NUMBER OF POOR			
Total poor blacks	**3,741**	**5,350**	**58.8%**
Under age 18	2,081	2,070	49.9
Aged 18 to 24	387	656	62.9
Aged 25 to 34	336	777	69.8
Aged 35 to 44	306	691	69.3
Aged 45 to 54	208	343	62.3
Aged 55 to 59	120	146	54.9
Aged 60 to 64	81	170	67.7
Aged 65 to 74	128	283	68.9
Aged 75 or older	94	213	69.4

	male	female	percentage point difference
POVERTY RATE			
Total blacks	**23.0%**	**28.7%**	**–5.7**
Under age 18	36.0	37.3	–1.3
Aged 18 to 24	22.1	31.6	–9.5
Aged 25 to 34	14.2	26.9	–12.7
Aged 35 to 44	11.9	22.8	–10.9
Aged 45 to 54	12.0	16.2	–4.2
Aged 55 to 59	22.4	20.5	1.9
Aged 60 to 64	18.0	28.9	–10.9
Aged 65 to 74	19.3	30.0	–10.7
Aged 75 or older	22.5	30.4	–7.9

Source: Bureau of the Census, Poverty in the United States: 1998, *Current Population Reports, P60-207, 1999; calculations by New Strategist*

People in Poverty by Age and Sex, 1998: Hispanics

(number and percent of Hispanics below poverty level by age and sex, 1998; female share of poor and percentage point difference between male and female poverty rate; people in thousands as of 1999)

	male	female	female share of poor
NUMBER OF POOR			
Total poor Hispanics	**3,665**	**4,405**	**54.6%**
Under age 18	1,928	1,909	49.8
Aged 18 to 24	457	553	54.8
Aged 25 to 34	501	724	59.1
Aged 35 to 44	393	545	58.1
Aged 45 to 54	173	245	58.6
Aged 55 to 59	57	102	64.2
Aged 60 to 64	41	87	68.0
Aged 65 to 74	76	148	66.1
Aged 75 or older	40	93	69.9

	male	female	percentage point difference
POVERTY RATE			
Total Hispanics	**23.2%**	**28.0%**	**−4.8**
Under age 18	33.7	35.2	−1.5
Aged 18 to 24	22.4	29.1	−6.7
Aged 25 to 34	17.7	26.8	−9.1
Aged 35 to 44	17.1	23.4	−6.3
Aged 45 to 54	12.4	16.6	−4.2
Aged 55 to 59	13.0	18.6	−5.6
Aged 60 to 64	12.8	21.5	−8.7
Aged 65 to 74	15.3	24.8	−9.5
Aged 75 or older	16.0	26.0	−10.0

Source: Bureau of the Census, Poverty in the United States: 1998, *Current Population Reports, P60-207, 1999; calculations by New Strategist*

People in Poverty by Age and Sex, 1998: Whites

(number and percent of whites below poverty level by age and sex, 1998; female share of poor and percentage point difference between male and female poverty rate; people in thousands as of 1999)

	male	female	female share of poor
NUMBER OF POOR			
Total poor whites	**10,089**	**13,365**	**57.0%**
Under age 18	4,210	4,233	50.1
Aged 18 to 24	1,265	1,758	58.2
Aged 25 to 34	1,253	1,918	60.5
Aged 35 to 44	1,224	1,682	57.9
Aged 45 to 54	752	1,002	57.1
Aged 55 to 59	349	504	59.1
Aged 60 to 64	309	439	58.7
Aged 65 to 74	410	725	63.9
Aged 75 or older	317	1,103	77.7

	male	female	percentage point difference
POVERTY RATE			
Total whites	**9.2%**	**11.8%**	**−2.6**
Under age 18	14.7	15.5	−0.8
Aged 18 to 24	12.0	17.2	−5.2
Aged 25 to 34	8.1	12.4	−4.3
Aged 35 to 44	6.6	9.1	−2.5
Aged 45 to 54	5.1	6.7	−1.6
Aged 55 to 59	6.7	9.0	−2.3
Aged 60 to 64	7.2	9.5	−2.3
Aged 65 to 74	5.8	8.5	−2.7
Aged 75 or older	6.2	13.8	−7.6

Source: Bureau of the Census, Poverty in the United States: 1998, *Current Population Reports, P60-207, 1999; calculations by New Strategist*

Single Mothers Have the Highest Poverty Rate

But the poverty rate of single mothers is lower today than in 1980.

Female-headed families are much more likely to be poor than married couples or male-headed families. Thirty percent of female-headed families were poor in 1998 versus only 5 percent of married couples and 12 percent of male-headed families. The poverty rate of female-headed families was lower in 1998 than in 1980, however. The poverty rate of married couples also fell between 1980 and 1998, while the poverty rate of male-headed families rose slightly.

Families with children are more likely to be poor than those without children. Thirty-nine percent of single-parent families headed by women were poor in 1998, as were 7 percent of married couples with children and 17 percent of single-parent families headed by men. Since 1980, poverty rates for all three family types have declined, although the number of poor has increased.

❖ Families headed by women will continue to have a higher poverty rate than other family types. Unlike married couples, few female-headed families have two earners in the household. And because women are less likely to have full-time jobs than men, the average female-headed family will have a lower income than the average male-headed family.

Married couples are least likely to be poor

(poverty rate of families by family type, 1998)

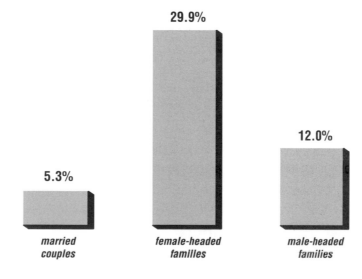

235

Families in Poverty by Family Type, 1980 to 1998

(total number of families, and number and percent below poverty level by type of family and presence of children under age 18 at home, 1980 to 1998; percent change in numbers and rates for selected years; families in thousands as of the following year)

	married couples			male householder, no spouse present			female householder, no spouse present		
		in poverty			*in poverty*			*in poverty*	
	total	*number*	*percent*	*total*	*number*	*percent*	*total*	*number*	*percent*
With and without children <18									
1998	54,778	2,879	5.3%	3,977	476	12.0%	12,796	3,831	29.9%
1997	54,321	2,821	5.2	3,911	508	13.0	12,652	3,995	31.6
1996	53,604	3,010	5.6	3,847	531	13.8	12,790	4,167	32.6
1995	53,570	2,982	5.6	3,513	493	14.0	12,514	4,057	32.4
1994	53,865	3,272	6.1	3,228	549	17.0	12,220	4,232	34.6
1993	53,181	3,481	6.5	2,914	488	16.8	12,411	4,424	35.6
1992	53,090	3,385	6.4	3,065	484	15.8	12,061	4,275	35.4
1991	52,457	3,158	6.0	3,025	392	13.0	11,693	4,161	35.6
1990	52,147	2,981	5.7	2,907	349	12.0	11,268	3,768	33.4
1989	52,137	2,931	5.6	2,884	348	12.1	10,890	3,504	32.2
1988	52,100	2,897	5.6	2,847	336	11.8	10,890	3,642	33.4
1987	51,675	3,011	5.8	2,833	340	12.0	10,696	3,654	34.2
1986	51,537	3,123	6.1	2,510	287	11.4	10,445	3,613	34.6
1985	50,933	3,438	6.7	2,414	311	12.9	10,211	3,474	34.0
1984	50,350	3,488	6.9	2,228	292	13.1	10,129	3,498	34.5
1983	50,081	3,815	7.6	2,038	268	13.2	9,896	3,564	36.0
1982	49,908	3,789	7.6	2,016	290	14.4	9,469	3,434	36.3
1981	49,630	3,394	6.8	1,986	205	10.3	9,403	3,252	34.6
1980	49,294	3,032	6.2	1,933	213	11.0	9,082	2,972	32.7
Percent change									
1990–1998	5.0%	−3.4%	−7.0%	36.8%	36.4%	0.0%	13.6%	1.7%	−10.5%
1980–1998	11.1	−5.0	−14.5	105.7	123.5	9.1	40.9	28.9	−8.6

(continued)

(continued from previous page)

	married couples			male householder, no spouse present			female householder, no spouse present		
		in poverty			*in poverty*			*in poverty*	
	total	*number*	*percent*	*total*	*number*	*percent*	*total*	*number*	*percent*
With children <18									
1998	26,226	1,822	6.9%	2,108	350	16.6%	8,934	3,456	38.7%
1997	26,430	1,863	7.1	2,175	407	18.7	8,822	3,614	41.0
1996	26,184	1,964	7.5	2,063	412	20.0	8,957	3,755	41.9
1995	26,034	1,961	7.5	1,934	381	19.7	8,751	3,634	41.5
1994	26,367	2,197	8.3	1,750	395	22.6	8,665	3,816	44.0
1993	26,121	2,363	9.0	1,577	354	22.5	8,758	4,034	46.1
1992	25,907	2,237	8.6	1,569	353	22.5	8,375	3,867	46.2
1991	25,357	2,106	8.3	1,513	297	19.6	7,991	3,767	47.1
1990	25,410	1,990	7.8	1,386	260	18.8	7,707	3,426	44.5
1989	25,476	1,872	7.3	1,358	246	18.1	7,445	3,190	42.8
1988	25,598	1,847	7.2	1,292	232	18.0	7,361	3,294	44.7
1987	25,464	1,963	7.7	1,316	221	16.8	7,216	3,281	45.5
1986	25,571	2,050	8.0	1,136	202	17.8	7,094	3,264	46.0
1985	25,496	2,258	8.9	1,147	197	17.1	6,892	3,131	45.4
1984	25,038	2,344	9.4	1,072	194	18.1	6,832	3,124	45.7
1983	25,216	2,557	10.1	949	192	20.2	6,622	3,122	47.1
1982	25,276	2,470	9.8	892	184	20.6	6,397	3,059	47.8
1981	25,278	2,199	8.7	822	115	14.0	6,488	2,877	44.3
1980	25,671	1,974	7.7	802	144	18.0	6,299	2,703	42.9
Percent change									
1990–1998	3.2%	−8.4%	−11.5%	52.1%	34.6%	−11.7%	15.9%	0.9%	−13.0%
1980–1998	2.2	−7.7	−10.4	162.8	143.1	−7.8	41.8	27.9	−9.8

Source: Bureau of the Census, Poverty in the United States: 1998, *Current Population Reports, P60–207, 1999; calculations by New Strategist*

5

Labor Force

❖ **Labor force rates of men and women are increasingly similar.**

Seventy-five percent of men and 60 percent of women aged 16 or older are in the labor force.

❖ **Working parents are the norm.**

Fully 95 percent of men and 72 percent of women who have children under age 18 at home are in the labor force.

❖ **Dual earners are in the majority.**

Fifty-six percent of married couples are dual earners, while only 21 percent are traditional—with only the husband in the labor force.

❖ **Pink or blue collars are still to be found in many occupations.**

Women are concentrated in administrative support jobs, while men dominate traditionally male occupations such as construction.

❖ **Job tenure has been stable for women.**

Between 1983 and 1998, job tenure changed little for women. It plummeted among older men.

❖ **More older men will be at work.**

Projections show an increase in the proportion of men aged 55 or older in the labor force as the early retirement trend reverses.

Labor Force Rates of Men and Women Are Increasingly Similar

In 1970, men were far more likely to work than women.

In 1999, 60 percent of women aged 16 or older were in the labor force, up from only 43 percent in 1970. Among men, 75 percent were in the labor force in 1999, down from 80 percent in 1970. As women's labor force participation has grown and men's has declined, the lifestyles of men and women have converged.

In 1970, the gap between the labor force participation rates between men and women was a substantial 37 percentage points (80 versus 43 percent). By 1999, the gap had shrunk to just 15 percentage points (75 versus 60 percent). The biggest change has occurred in the 25-to-34 age group. In 1970, the labor force participation rate of men aged 25 to 34 was 51 percentage points higher than that of women (96 versus 45 percent). By 1999, the gap had shrunk to just 17 percentage points (93 versus 76 percent) as working mothers became the norm.

The biggest drop in labor force participation has been among men aged 55 to 64. In 1970, 83 percent of men in that age group were in the labor force; by 1999, only 68 percent were. Behind the decline was the growing popularity of early retirement, a trend that has now come to a halt.

❖ As men's and women's lives have become more alike, marketers have had to adjust their products, services, and advertising messages to appeal to both sexes.

The gap is narrowing

(labor force participation rates by sex, 1970 and 1999)

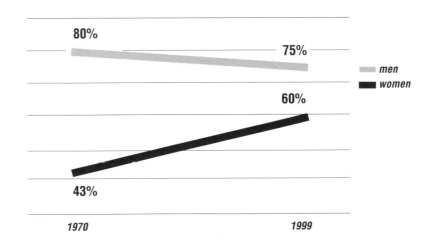

Labor Force Participation by Sex and Age, 1970 to 1999

(labor force participation rate of people aged 16 or older, by sex and age, 1970 to 1999; percentage point change, 1970–99)

	1999	*1990*	*1980*	*1970*	*percentage point change 1970–99*
Total men	**74.7%**	**76.1%**	**77.4%**	**79.7%**	**–5.0**
Aged 16 to 19	52.9	55.7	60.5	56.1	–3.2
Aged 20 to 24	81.9	84.3	85.9	83.3	–1.4
Aged 25 to 34	93.3	94.2	95.2	96.4	–3.1
Aged 35 to 44	92.8	94.4	95.5	96.9	–4.1
Aged 45 to 54	88.8	90.7	91.2	94.3	–5.5
Aged 55 to 64	67.9	67.7	72.1	83.0	–15.1
Aged 65 or older	16.9	16.4	19.0	26.8	–9.9
Total women	**60.0**	**57.5**	**51.5**	**43.3**	**16.7**
Aged 16 to 19	51.0	51.8	52.9	44.0	7.0
Aged 20 to 24	73.2	71.6	68.9	57.7	15.5
Aged 25 to 34	76.4	73.6	65.5	45.0	31.4
Aged 35 to 44	77.2	76.5	65.5	51.1	26.1
Aged 45 to 54	76.7	71.2	59.9	54.4	22.3
Aged 55 to 64	51.5	45.3	41.3	43.0	8.5
Aged 65 or older	8.9	8.7	8.1	9.7	–0.8

Note: The labor force includes both the employed and the unemployed.
Source: Bureau of Labor Statistics, Employment and Earnings, *January 2000 and January 1991; and* Handbook of Labor Statistics, *Bulletin 2340, 1989; calculations by New Strategist*

Unemployment Is Highest among the Young

Few middle-aged Americans are unemployed.

The nation is experiencing the lowest unemployment rate in decades. Nevertheless, the rate is still in the double-digits among teenagers. Fifteen percent of men and 13 percent of women aged 16 to 19 were unemployed in 1999. Unemployment was below 3 percent among the middle-aged.

Among men, the labor force participation rate peaks at 94 percent in the 30-to-34 age group. Among women it peaks at 79 percent in the 45-to-49 age group. Labor force participation falls sharply among both men and women aged 55 or older as early retirement lures them away from their jobs. Only 17 percent of men and 9 percent of women aged 65 or older are still in the labor force.

❖ The men and women most likely to be in the labor force are also the ones most likely to be raising children. They need convenient service, time-saving products, and innovative ways to simplify their lives.

Employment Status of Men by Age, 1999

(employment status of men aged 16 or older by age, 1999; numbers in thousands)

| | civilian noninstitutional population | civilian labor force | | | | |
		total	percent of population	employed	unemployed number	unemployed percent
Total men	**99,722**	**74,512**	**74.7%**	**71,446**	**3,066**	**4.1%**
Aged 16 to 19	8,167	4,318	52.9	3,685	633	14.7
Aged 16 to 17	4,143	1,732	41.8	1,437	295	17.0
Aged 18 to 19	4,024	2,587	64.3	2,249	338	13.1
Aged 20 to 24	8,899	7,291	81.9	6,729	562	7.7
Aged 25 to 34	18,565	17,318	93.3	16,694	624	3.6
Aged 25 to 29	8,931	8,283	92.7	7,949	334	4.0
Aged 30 to 34	9,634	9,035	93.8	8,745	290	3.2
Aged 35 to 44	21,969	20,382	92.8	19,811	571	2.8
Aged 35 to 39	11,026	10,287	93.3	9,999	288	2.8
Aged 40 to 44	10,942	10,095	92.3	9,811	283	2.8
Aged 45 to 54	17,335	15,394	88.6	14,991	403	2.6
Aged 45 to 49	9,444	8,532	90.3	8,302	229	2.7
Aged 50 to 54	7,892	6,862	87.0	6,689	173	2.5
Aged 55 to 64	11,008	7,477	67.9	7,274	203	2.7
Aged 55 to 59	6,123	4,799	78.4	4,671	128	2.7
Aged 60 to 64	4,885	2,678	54.8	2,603	75	2.8
Aged 65 or older	13,779	2,333	16.9	2,263	70	3.0
Aged 65 to 69	4,279	1,218	28.5	1,177	40	3.3
Aged 70 to 74	3,776	657	17.4	642	15	2.3
Aged 75 or older	5,724	458	8.0	444	14	3.1

Note: The civilian labor force includes both the employed and the unemployed. The civilian population includes both those in the labor force and those not in the labor force.
Source: Bureau of Labor Statistics, Employment and Earnings, *January 2000*

Employment Status of Women by Age, 1999

(employment status of women aged 16 or older by age, 1999; numbers in thousands)

| | civilian noninstitutional population | civilian labor force | | | | |
| | | total | percent of population | employed | unemployed | |
					number	percent
Total women	**108,031**	**64,855**	**60.0%**	**62,042**	**2,814**	**4.3%**
Aged 16 to 19	7,873	4,015	51.0	3,487	529	13.2
Aged 16 to 17	3,917	1,606	41.0	1,357	249	15.5
Aged 18 to 19	3,955	2,410	60.9	2,130	280	11.6
Aged 20 to 24	9,069	6,643	73.2	6,163	480	7.2
Aged 25 to 34	19,411	14,826	76.4	14,171	654	4.4
Aged 25 to 29	9,408	7,235	76.9	6,888	347	4.8
Aged 30 to 34	10,003	7,591	75.9	7,284	307	4.0
Aged 35 to 44	22,666	17,501	77.2	16,917	584	3.3
Aged 35 to 39	11,352	8,650	76.2	8,346	304	3.5
Aged 40 to 44	11,314	8,850	78.2	8,571	279	3.2
Aged 45 to 54	18,251	13,994	76.7	13,644	350	2.5
Aged 45 to 49	9,880	7,798	78.9	7,602	197	2.5
Aged 50 to 54	8,371	6,196	74.0	6,042	154	2.5
Aged 55 to 64	12,056	6,204	51.5	6,041	163	2.6
Aged 55 to 59	6,624	4,096	61.8	3,985	110	2.7
Aged 60 to 64	5,432	2,109	38.8	2,056	53	2.5
Aged 65 or older	18,705	1,673	8.9	1,619	54	3.2
Aged 65 to 69	5,002	920	18.4	888	32	3.5
Aged 70 to 74	4,764	459	9.6	446	13	2.9
Aged 75 or older	8,939	294	3.3	286	9	2.9

Note: The civilian labor force includes both the employed and the unemployed. The civilian population includes both those in the labor force and those not in the labor force.
Source: Bureau of Labor Statistics, Employment and Earnings, *January 2000*

Hispanic Men Are Most Likely to Be in the Labor Force

Hispanic women are least likely to work.

Eighty percent of Hispanic men aged 16 or older are in the labor force. This figure surpasses the 76 percent for their white counterparts, and it is far greater than the 69 percent among blacks. Hispanic men have a higher labor force participation rate than white men because they are younger, on average, and more likely to be in their prime working years.

Hispanic women have lower labor force participation rates than white or black women, with 56 percent of those aged 16 or older in the labor force in 1999. Black women have the highest labor force participation rate among women, at 64 percent. The participation rate of black women nearly matches that of black men. Among blacks aged 16 to 24, women are more likely to be in the labor force than men.

❖ Although labor force participation rates vary, the majorities of men and women are in the labor force regardless of race or ethnicity. For marketers the message is clear: convenience and simplicity are paramount for today's men and women.

Labor Force Participation by Race, Hispanic Origin, Age, and Sex, 1999

(labor force participation rate of people aged 16 or older by race, Hispanic origin, age, and sex; percentage point difference between men and women, 1999)

	men	women	percentage point difference
Total people	**74.7%**	**60.0%**	**14.7**
Aged 16 to 19	52.9	51.0	1.9
Aged 20 to 24	81.9	73.2	8.7
Aged 25 to 34	93.3	76.4	16.9
Aged 35 to 44	92.8	77.2	15.6
Aged 45 to 54	88.8	76.7	12.1
Aged 55 to 64	67.9	51.5	16.4
Aged 65 or older	16.9	8.9	8.0
Total blacks	**68.7**	**63.5**	**5.2**
Aged 16 to 19	38.6	38.8	–0.2
Aged 20 to 24	69.8	72.7	–2.9
Aged 25 to 34	89.2	82.1	7.1
Aged 35 to 44	86.0	80.4	5.6
Aged 45 to 54	78.5	74.6	3.9
Aged 55 to 64	55.5	48.4	7.1
Aged 65 or older	12.7	8.9	3.8
Total Hispanics	**79.8**	**55.9**	**23.9**
Aged 16 to 19	50.1	40.6	9.5
Aged 20 to 24	88.1	63.0	25.1
Aged 25 to 34	93.9	62.7	31.2
Aged 35 to 44	92.2	70.5	21.7
Aged 45 to 54	86.2	66.2	20.0
Aged 55 to 64	68.6	42.4	26.2
Aged 65 or older	18.2	6.5	11.7
Total whites	**75.6**	**59.6**	**16.0**
Aged 16 to 19	56.4	54.5	1.9
Aged 20 to 24	84.9	73.9	11.0
Aged 25 to 34	94.3	76.0	18.3
Aged 35 to 44	93.8	77.1	16.7
Aged 45 to 54	90.1	77.1	13.0
Aged 55 to 64	69.1	52.0	17.1
Aged 65 or older	17.2	8.9	8.3

Note: The labor force includes both the employed and the unemployed.
Source: Bureau of Labor Statistics, Employment and Earnings, *January 2000; calculations by New Strategist*

Most Women Work Full-Time

More than three-quarters of working women have full-time jobs.

The stereotype of the working woman has long been the wife who earns money for family extras at a part-time job. But this stereotype is wrong. Fully 75 percent of working women work full-time. Among working men, 90 percent have full-time jobs.

Those most likely to work part-time are teenagers. The majority of employed teens aged 16 to 19 have part-time jobs, including 62 percent of boys and 72 percent of girls. Part-time work continues to be important among young adults. Twenty percent of men and 32 percent of women aged 20 to 24 work only part-time. Many are in college.

Among men and women in their prime working years, the great majority are full-time workers. Only 4 percent of working men and 19 percent of working women aged 25 to 54 are part-time workers. Ninety-six percent of working men and 81 percent of working women in this age group have full-time jobs.

Part-time work is more important among workers aged 55 or older as many opt for more leisure time. Nineteen percent of working men and 33 percent of working women aged 55 or older have part-time jobs.

❖ If part-time work offered more of the benefits of full-time jobs—such as health insurance, vacations, and pension plans—more workers would opt to work part-time.

Full- and Part-time Workers by Age and Sex, 1999

(number and percent of people aged 16 or older employed full- or part-time by age and sex, and female share of workers, 1999; numbers in thousands)

	men		women		female share of workers
	number	percent of total male workers	number	percent of total female workers	
Total full-time workers	**63,930**	**89.5%**	**46,372**	**74.7%**	**42.0%**
Aged 16 to 19	1,416	38.4	969	27.8	40.6
Aged 20 to 24	5,371	79.8	4,196	68.1	43.9
Aged 25 to 54	49,428	96.0	36,101	80.7	42.2
Aged 55 or older	7,715	80.9	5,106	66.6	39.8
Total part-time workers	**7,516**	**10.5**	**15,670**	**25.3**	**67.6**
Aged 16 to 19	2,269	61.6	2,517	72.2	52.6
Aged 20 to 24	1,357	20.2	1,966	31.9	59.2
Aged 25 to 54	2,068	4.0	8,631	19.3	80.7
Aged 55 or older	1,822	19.1	2,555	33.4	58.4

Source: Bureau of Labor Statistics, Employment and Earnings, January 2000; calculations by New Strategist

Working Mothers and Fathers Are the Norm

Families with preschoolers are least likely to have working parents.

In 1998, 64 percent of married couples with children under age 18 were dual-income couples. The proportion stands at 69 percent among couples with school-aged children and at 58 percent among those with preschoolers.

Among single-parent families headed by women, 72 percent of mothers are employed. Among those headed by men, 85 percent of fathers are employed. Overall, all parents are employed in 67 percent of the nation's families with children.

❖ The children of working parents are often more independent than those with stay-at-home mothers. They are consumers in their own right, making purchasing decisions and influencing many family expenditures.

Most married couples with children are in the labor force

(percent distribution of married couples with children under age 18 at home by employment status of mother and father, 1998)

64%

29%

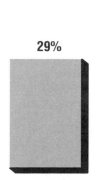

7%

mother and father employed   *only father employed*   *other*

Labor Force Status of Families with Children under Age 18, 1998

(number and percent distribution of families by employment status of parent and age of youngest own child under age 18 at home, by family type, 1998; numbers in thousands)

		with children under age 18	
	total	aged 6 to 17, none younger	under age 6
Married couples	**24,820**	**13,496**	**11,324**
One or both parents employed	24,088	13,065	11,023
Mother employed	16,911	9,991	6,920
Both parents employed	15,906	9,338	6,567
Mother employed not father	1,005	653	352
Father employed, not mother	7,178	3,074	4,103
Neither parent employed	731	431	301
Female-headed families	**7,573**	**4,638**	**2,936**
Mother employed	5,440	3,573	1,867
Mother not employed	2,133	1,065	1,068
Male-headed families	**1,839**	**1,075**	**763**
Father employed	1,572	913	660
Father not employed	266	162	104
Married couples	**100.0%**	**100.0%**	**100.0%**
One or both parents employed	97.1	96.8	97.3
Mother employed	68.1	74.0	61.1
Both parents employed	64.1	69.2	58.0
Mother employed not father	4.0	4.8	3.1
Father employed, not mother	28.9	22.8	36.2
Neither parent employed	2.9	3.2	2.7
Female-headed families	**100.0**	**100.0**	**100.0**
Mother employed	71.8	77.0	63.6
Mother not employed	28.2	23.0	36.4
Male-headed families	**100.0**	**100.0**	**100.0**
Father employed	85.5	84.9	86.5
Father not employed	14.5	15.1	13.6

Source: Bureau of Labor Statistics, Internet web site <http://www.bls.gov/news.release/famee.t04.htm>

Majority of Mothers Work Full-Time

Among women with infants, 36 percent work full-time.

Overall, 75 percent of men and and 60 percent of women aged 16 or older are in the labor force. Among people living with children under age 18, however, the labor force participation rate is much higher—95 percent for men and 72 percent for women.

Nine out of 10 men with children under age 18 at home work full-time. Few work part-time or not at all regardless of the age of their children. Fifty-seven percent of women with school-aged children at home work full-time, as do 42 percent of those with preschoolers. Among women with children under age 3, the proportion of those who work full-time slightly exceeds the proportion of those who do not work. Only among women with infants under age 1 does the proportion of those who do not work exceed the proportion of those who work full-time (42 versus 36 percent).

The labor force participation rate of men and women without children at home is much lower than that of parents because many are retirees. Thirty-three percent of men and 46 percent of women without children under age 18 at home do not work.

❖ As working parents have become the norm, lifestyles have changed. Second cars, take-out meals, and fast-paced schedules are typical of today's families.

Labor Force Status of People by Presence of Children at Home, 1998

(number and percent distribution of people aged 16 or older by sex, presence of children under age 18 at home, and labor force status, 1998; numbers in thousands)

	total		percent in labor force			not in
	number	*percent*	*total*	*full-time*	*part-time*	*labor force*
Total men	**96,885**	**100.0%**	**74.8%**	**63.8%**	**7.7%**	**25.2%**
No children under age 18	69,396	100.0	67.0	53.6	9.6	33.0
With children under age 18	27,489	100.0	94.6	89.4	2.8	5.4
With children 6 to 17 only	14,947	100.0	93.5	89.2	2.6	6.5
With children under age 6	12,543	100.0	96.1	90.3	3.0	3.9
Total women	**106,463**	**100.0**	**59.8**	**42.3**	**14.8**	**40.2**
No children under age 18	71,040	100.0	53.9	38.3	13.3	46.1
With children under age 18	35,423	100.0	71.8	50.3	17.9	28.2
With children 6 to 17 only	19,383	100.0	77.6	57.0	17.4	22.4
With children under age 6	16,040	100.0	64.9	42.2	18.5	35.1

Source: Bureau of Labor Statistics, Internet web site <http://www.bls.gov/news.release/famee.t05.htm>; calculations by New Strategist

Work Experience of Mothers with Children under Age 3, 1998

(number of women with children under age 3 by marital status and age of child, and percent distribution by labor force status, 1998; numbers in thousands)

	total		percent in labor force			not in
	number	percent	total	full-time	part-time	labor force
TOTAL MOTHERS						
With children under age 3	**9,333**	**100.0%**	**61.9%**	**38.9%**	**18.8%**	**38.1%**
Aged 2	2,772	100.0	64.4	41.5	18.9	35.6
Aged 1	3,213	100.0	64.0	39.9	19.8	36.0
Under age 1	3,348	100.0	57.9	35.7	17.9	42.1
MARRIED MOTHERS						
With children under age 3	**7,110**	**100.0**	**60.7**	**38.9**	**19.4**	**39.3**
Aged 2	2,073	100.0	62.3	40.1	19.9	37.7
Aged 1	2,493	100.0	62.6	39.7	20.4	37.4
Under age 1	2,544	100.0	57.6	37.1	18.0	42.4
NEVER MARRIED, DIVORCED, WIDOWED MOTHERS						
With children under age 3	**2,225**	**100.0**	**65.8**	**38.7**	**17.0**	**34.2**
Aged 2	700	100.0	70.7	45.4	15.9	29.3
Aged 1	721	100.0	68.7	40.5	17.9	31.3
Under age 1	804	100.0	58.8	31.1	17.3	41.2

Source: Bureau of Labor Statistics, Internet web site <http://www.bls.gov/news.release/famee.t06.htm>; calculations by New Strategist

The Majority of Couples Are Dual Earners

In 56 percent of the nation's married couples, both husband and wife are in the labor force.

Only 21 percent of the nation's married couples are traditional—that is, only the husband is in the labor force. In another 17 percent of couples—most of them retirees—neither husband nor wife is in the labor force. In 6 percent of couples only the wife works.

The dual-earner share hits 73 percent among couples aged 25 to 29, then falls slightly as couples have children and some wives stop working for a few years. The dual-earner share then rises again, peaking at 74 percent among couples aged 45 to 49. It drops steadily among couples aged 50 or older not only because many older women never worked, but also because of retirement.

The greatest diversity in labor force status occurs among couples aged 60 to 64, an age at which many experience the transition from work to retirement. One-third of couples in this age group are dual earners while 20 percent are traditional. In 18 percent of the couples, only the wife works (in most cases, her husband has retired), while neither husband nor wife work in 29 percent.

❖ With dual earners accounting for at least 70 percent of couples aged 25 to 49—most of whom also have children—time pressures are intense. Busy couples need ways to save time and simplify their lives.

Most married couples under age 60 are dual earners

(percent of married couples in which both husband and wife are in the labor force, by age, 1998)

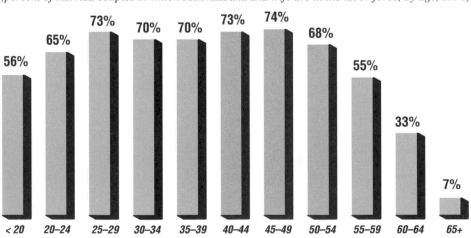

Married Couples by Labor Force Status of Husband and Wife, 1998

(number and percent distribution of married-couple households by age of householder and labor force status of husband and wife, 1999; numbers in thousands)

	total	husband and wife in labor force	husband only in labor force	wife only in labor force	husband and wife not in labor force
Total couples	**54,317**	**30,591**	**11,582**	**3,087**	**9,057**
Under age 20	86	48	37	–	–
Aged 20 to 24	1,287	841	392	24	30
Aged 25 to 29	3,967	2,880	992	62	33
Aged 30 to 34	5,919	4,118	1,593	142	65
Aged 35 to 39	6,941	4,861	1,822	161	98
Aged 40 to 44	7,239	5,250	1,600	255	134
Aged 45 to 49	6,239	4,619	1,251	252	117
Aged 50 to 54	5,495	3,749	1,201	303	242
Aged 55 to 59	4,192	2,312	1,045	427	408
Aged 60 to 64	3,744	1,248	746	680	1,072
Aged 65 or older	9,209	666	902	782	6,857
Median age	46.4	42.4	43.0	59.0	71.0
Total couples	**100.0%**	**56.3%**	**21.3%**	**5.7%**	**16.7%**
Under age 20	100.0	55.8	43.0	–	–
Aged 20 to 24	100.0	65.3	30.5	1.9	2.3
Aged 25 to 29	100.0	72.6	25.0	1.6	0.8
Aged 30 to 34	100.0	69.6	26.9	2.4	1.1
Aged 35 to 39	100.0	70.0	26.2	2.3	1.4
Aged 40 to 44	100.0	72.5	22.1	3.5	1.9
Aged 45 to 49	100.0	74.0	20.1	4.0	1.9
Aged 50 to 54	100.0	68.2	21.9	5.5	4.4
Aged 55 to 59	100.0	55.2	24.9	10.2	9.7
Aged 60 to 64	100.0	33.3	19.9	18.2	28.6
Aged 65 or older	100.0	7.2	9.8	8.5	74.5

Note: (–) means sample is too small to make a reliable estimate.
Source: Bureau of the Census, Household and Family Characteristics: March 1998 (Update), *Current Population Reports, P20-515, 1999; calculations by New Strategist*

Job Tenure Has Been Stable for Women

But tenure has fallen for older men.

Job tenure has changed little for women since 1983, while it has plummeted for older men, according to the Bureau of Labor Statistics. The number of years working women have been with their current employer has been stable because of women's increasing attachment to the labor force. As more women regard their work as a career rather than "just a job," they are remaining with their employers longer.

In contrast, job tenure for men of all ages has dropped. While the decline has been slight among younger men, it has been substantial for older men. In 1983, men aged 45 to 54 had been with their current employer a median of 12.8 years. By 1998 the figure had fallen to just 9.4 years. The median number of years men aged 55 to 64 have been with their current employer fell from 15.3 to 11.2 years.

❖ Job tenure declines when workers change jobs more frequently—either voluntarily or involuntarily. That job tenure has declined the most among older men points to involuntary layoffs as the biggest factor.

Job Tenure by Sex and Age, 1983 and 1998

(median number of years workers aged 16 or older have been with their current employer by sex and age, 1983 and 1998; change in years, 1983–98)

	1998	1983	change in years, 1983–98
Total employed men	**3.8**	**4.1**	**–0.3**
Aged 16 to 17	0.6	0.7	–0.1
Aged 18 to 19	0.7	0.8	–0.1
Aged 20 to 24	1.2	1.5	–0.3
Aged 25 to 34	2.8	3.2	–0.4
Aged 35 to 44	5.5	7.3	–1.8
Aged 45 to 54	9.4	12.8	–3.4
Aged 55 to 64	11.2	15.3	–4.1
Aged 65 or older	7.1	8.3	–1.2
Total employed women	**3.4**	**3.1**	**0.3**
Aged 16 to 17	0.7	0.7	0.0
Aged 18 to 19	0.7	0.8	–0.1
Aged 20 to 24	1.1	1.5	–0.4
Aged 25 to 34	2.5	2.8	–0.3
Aged 35 to 44	4.5	4.1	0.4
Aged 45 to 54	7.2	6.3	0.9
Aged 55 to 64	9.6	9.8	–0.2
Aged 65 or older	8.7	10.1	–1.4

Source: Bureau of Labor Statistics, Internet web site <http://www.bls.gov/news.release/tenure.t01.htm>; calculations by New Strategist

Some Occupations Are Dominated by Women, Others by Men

Traditional roles are still evident in the occupations of men and women.

Although working women are now the norm, many women still work in pink collar occupations. Men still dominate traditionally male occupations such as construction.

Twenty-three percent of women work in administrative support occupations. Among full-time workers, they account for 99 percent of secretaries and 96 percent of receptionists. Conversely, only 10 percent of engineers are women.

Men still dominate the skilled trades. Nineteen percent of men, but only 2 percent of women, work in precision production, craft, and repair occupations. Among full-time workers, 99 percent of automobile mechanics are men. Women account for only 1 to 2 percent of carpenters, electricians, and plumbers.

Women are making progress, however. They account for nearly one-half of managers and professionals. Among full-time workers, they are the majority of managers in finance, education, and health. Although women account for only 33 percent of lawyers today, the figure is rising as a growing share of young women opt to go into law rather than the traditionally female professions.

❖ The earnings gap between the sexes is due in part to the occupational choices men and women make. Many women choose low-paying support and service jobs while men are more likely to opt for jobs in the skilled trades or upper management.

Employment by Occupation and Sex, 1999

(number and percent distribution of employed people aged 16 or older by occupation and sex, and female share by occupation, 1999; numbers in thousands)

	men		women		female share of workers
	number	percent	number	percent	
TOTAL EMPLOYED	**71,446**	**100.0%**	**62,042**	**100.0%**	**46.5%**
Managerial and professional specialty	**20,446**	**28.6**	**20,021**	**32.3**	**49.5**
Executive, administrative, and managerial	10,744	15.0	8,840	14.2	45.1
Professional specialty	9,702	13.6	11,181	18.0	53.5
Technical, sales, and administrative support	**14,079**	**19.7**	**24,842**	**40.0**	**63.8**
Technicians and related support	2,094	2.9	2,261	3.6	51.9
Sales occupations	8,049	11.3	8,069	13.0	50.1
Administrative support, including clerical	3,936	5.5	14,512	23.4	78.7
Service occupations	**7,093**	**9.9**	**10,822**	**17.4**	**60.4**
Private household	40	0.1	791	1.3	95.2
Protective service	1,980	2.8	460	0.7	18.9
Service, except private household and protective	5,074	7.1	9,570	15.4	65.4
Precision production, craft, and repair	**13,286**	**18.6**	**1,307**	**2.1**	**9.0**
Operators, fabricators, and laborers	**13,793**	**19.3**	**4,374**	**7.1**	**24.1**
Handlers, equipment cleaners, helpers, and laborers	**4,188**	**5.9**	**1,077**	**1.7**	**20.5**
Farming, forestry, and fishing	**2,749**	**3.8**	**676**	**1.1**	**19.7**

Source: Bureau of Labor Statistics, Employment and Earnings, *January 2000; calculations by New Strategist*

Employment by Detailed Occupation and Sex, 1999

(number of full-time wage and salary workers aged 16 or older by selected detailed occupation and sex, and female share by occupation, 1999; numbers in thousands)

	men	women	female share of workers
TOTAL EMPLOYED	**55,181**	**42,444**	**43.5%**
Managerial and professional specialty	**15,537**	**15,167**	**49.4**
Executive, administrative, and managerial	7,981	6,992	46.7
Administrators and officials, public administration	300	310	50.8
Financial managers	344	353	50.6
Personnel and labor relations managers	74	108	59.3
Managers, marketing, adv., public relations	441	254	36.5
Administrators, education and related fields	282	420	59.8
Managers, medicine and health	139	462	76.9
Managers, food serving and lodging establishments	498	449	47.4
Managers, properties and real estate	149	189	55.9
Accountants and auditors	549	813	59.7
Professional specialty	7,556	8,175	52.0
Engineers	1,749	197	10.1
Computer systems analysts and scientists	959	390	28.9
Physicians	335	125	27.2
Registered nurses	141	1,443	91.1
Pharmacists	88	77	46.7
Therapists	101	256	71.7
Teachers, college and university	397	241	37.8
Teachers, prekindergarten and kindergarten	9	423	97.9
Teachers, elementary school	308	1,529	83.2
Teachers, secondary school	521	658	55.8
Librarians	32	151	82.5
Social workers	220	485	68.8
Clergy	256	38	12.9
Lawyers	386	191	33.1
Designers	233	220	48.6
Editors and reporters	113	98	46.4
Public relations specialists	58	97	62.6
Technical, sales, and administrative support	**10,525**	**16,863**	**61.6**
Technicians and related support	1,802	1,749	49.3
Licensed practical nurses	16	243	93.8
Computer programmers	405	159	28.2
Legal assistants	43	270	86.3
Sales occupations	5,402	4,326	44.5
Insurance sales	201	190	48.6

(continued)

(continued from previous page)

	men	women	female share of workers
Real estate sales	173	191	52.5%
Securities and financial services sales	276	123	30.8
Advertising and related sales	66	88	57.1
Sales workers, retail and personal services	1,475	1,849	55.6
Cashiers	301	989	76.7
Administrative support, including clerical	3,322	10,788	76.5
Computer operators	124	168	57.5
Secretaries	26	2,136	98.8
Typists	17	382	95.7
Receptionists	30	697	95.9
File clerks	43	162	79.0
Bookkeepers	107	977	90.1
Telephone operators	24	83	77.6
Mail carriers, postal service	218	82	27.3
Bank tellers	21	267	92.7
Teachers' aides	28	341	92.4
Service occupations	**5,209**	**5,632**	**52.0**
Child care workers, private household	1	156	99.4
Cleaners and servants, private household	15	205	93.2
Police and detectives	898	181	16.8
Waiters, waitresses	172	480	73.6
Dental assistants	5	123	96.1
Nursing aides	163	1,255	88.5
Janitors and cleaners	1,054	442	29.5
Hairdressers and cosmetologists	47	263	84.8
Precision production, craft, and repair	**10,861**	**1,066**	**8.9**
Mechanics and repairers	4,057	206	4.8
Automobile mechanics	628	7	1.1
Construction trades	4,059	85	2.1
Carpenters	950	12	1.2
Electricians	723	17	2.3
Plumbers	408	9	2.2
Operators, fabricators, and laborers	**11,685**	**3,498**	**23.0**
Transportation and material moving occupations	4,083	317	7.2
Truck drivers	2,409	85	3.4
Bus drivers	166	119	41.8
Handlers, equipment cleaners, helpers, and laborers	3,230	737	18.6
Farming, forestry, and fishing	**1,364**	**218**	**13.8**
Farm workers	463	68	12.8
Groundskeepers and gardeners, except farm	614	44	6.7

Source: Bureau of Labor Statistics, Employment and Earnings, *January 2000; calculations by New Strategist*

Women Dominate the Services Industries

Men dominate construction and mining.

While women account for nearly one-half of all workers, the statistics look very different on an industry-by-industry basis. In some sectors, workers are overwhelmingly female while in others they are overwhelmingly male.

Retail trade is one of the few industries in which workers are nearly evenly split, as 51 percent of them are female. Another such sector is finance, insurance, and real estate, which is 58 percent female. All other industries are lopsided. Only 10 percent of construction workers are female, for example, as are only 12 percent of workers in the mining industry. Fully 92 percent of private household workers are female.

Overall, 49 percent of women work in the service industries, which include everything from health and education to advertising and marketing. While the largest share of men also work in the service industries, the proportion is just 27 percent. Nineteen percent of men work in manufacturing versus only 10 percent of women. Women account for only 32 percent of manufacturing workers.

❖ The rise of the service industries over the past few decades has drawn women into the work force by the millions. It has also lured men out of traditionally male occupations such as agriculture, mining, and manufacturing.

Employment by Industry and Sex, 1999

(number and percent distribution of employed people aged 16 or older by industry and sex, and female share of total employed in industry, 1999; numbers in thousands)

	men		women		female share of workers
	number	percent	number	percent	
Total employed	**71,446**	**100.0%**	**62,042**	**100.0%**	**46.5%**
Agriculture	2,432	3.4	849	1.4	25.9
Mining	495	0.7	69	0.1	12.2
Construction	8,101	11.3	886	1.4	9.9
Manufacturing	13,647	19.1	6,423	10.4	32.0
Durable goods	8,894	12.4	3,389	5.5	27.6
Nondurable goods	4,753	6.7	3,034	4.9	39.0
Transportation and public utilities	6,815	9.5	2,740	4.4	28.7
Wholesale and retail trade	14,448	20.2	13,124	21.2	47.6
Wholesale trade	3,530	4.9	1,659	2.7	32.0
Retail trade	10,918	15.3	11,465	18.5	51.2
Finance, insurance, and real estate	3,699	5.2	5,115	8.2	58.0
Services	18,506	25.9	30,180	48.6	62.0
Private household	79	0.1	861	1.4	91.6
Other service industries	18,427	25.8	29,320	47.3	61.4
Professional services	9,808	13.7	22,562	36.4	69.7
Public Administration	3,303	4.6	2,655	4.3	44.6

Source: Bureau of Labor Statistics, Employment and Earnings, *January 2000; calculations by New Strategist*

Men Are More Likely to Be Self-Employed

Self-employment rises with age among both men and women.

Few Americans are self-employed. Among workers in nonagricultural industries, only 8.4 percent of men and 5.9 percent of women were self-employed in 1999, according to the Bureau of Labor Statistics. The bureau counts as self-employed only those whose longest job in the previous 12 months was self-employment. It does not include people who run their own business on the side.

The proportion of workers who are self-employed rises with age. Among those under age 25, fewer than 3 percent are self-employed. The share rises to 27 percent among working men aged 65 or older. Fifteen percent of working women aged 65 or older are self-employed.

Self-employment rises with age because older workers have the skills and experience necessary to sell themselves successfully in the marketplace. In addition, self-employment gives older workers the flexible schedules they want as they supplement their income in retirement.

❖ The self-employed, along with the many workers who earn extra money through a side business, create a vibrant market for home office equipment.

Self-Employment by Age and Sex, 1999

(number and percent of self employed workers aged 16 or older whose longest job was self-employment in nonagricultural industries, by age and sex, and female share of self-employed, 1999; numbers in thousands)

	men		women		female share of self-employed
	number	*percent*	*number*	*percent*	
Total self-employed	**5,366**	**8.4%**	**3,424**	**5.9%**	**39.0%**
Aged 16 to 19	35	1.0	24	0.7	40.7
Aged 20 to 24	155	2.5	109	1.8	41.3
Aged 25 to 34	848	5.5	633	4.7	42.7
Aged 35 to 44	1,551	8.8	1,038	6.6	40.1
Aged 45 to 54	1,462	11.1	919	7.3	38.6
Aged 55 to 64	883	14.5	495	9.1	35.9
Aged 65 or older	431	26.9	206	15.3	32.3

Source: Bureau of Labor Statistics, Employment and Earnings, *January 2000; calculations by New Strategist*

Men Are More Likely Than Women to Have Flexible Schedules

More than one in four workers has a flexible work schedule.

Although mothers, typically, take on greater childrearing responsibility than fathers, among full-time workers men are more likely than women to have flexible work schedules. Twenty-nine percent of men who work full-time are permitted to vary the time they begin or end work. Among their female counterparts, the proportion is a smaller 26 percent.

The proportion of working men who have flexible work schedules rises with age, from a low of 17 percent among those aged 16 to 19 to a high of 38 percent among men aged 65 or older. The proportion of women with flexible schedules does not vary much by age, ranging narrowly between the low of 21 percent among workers aged 65 or older and the high of 28 percent among those aged 25 to 34.

Among full-time workers aged 16 to 19, women are much more likely than men to have flexible schedules. The proportions are about equal among male and female workers aged 20 to 34. But after age 35, there is a growing gap between the proportions of men and women with flexible schedules.

❖ Older women are less likely to have flexible work schedules because many are "just a job" rather than "career" workers. As better-educated and career-oriented younger generations age, the proportion of older women with flexible work schedules will rise.

Workers with Flexible Schedules, 1997

(number of full-time wage and salary workers aged 16 or older, and number and percent with flexible work schedules, by age and sex, 1997; numbers in thousands)

	men			women		
		with flexible schedules			*with flexible schedules*	
	total	*number*	*percent*	*total*	*number*	*percent*
Total workers	**52,073**	**14,952**	**28.7%**	**38,476**	**10,079**	**26.2%**
Aged 16 to 19	1,050	177	16.9	590	161	27.4
Aged 20 to 24	4,968	1,111	22.4	3,494	812	23.2
Aged 25 to 34	14,721	4,231	28.7	10,486	2,931	27.9
Aged 35 to 44	15,434	4,730	30.6	11,321	3,051	26.9
Aged 45 to 54	10,806	3,118	28.9	8,790	2,237	25.4
Aged 55 to 64	4,431	1,334	30.1	3,347	796	23.8
Aged 65 or older	662	251	38.0	448	93	20.7

Note: Flexible schedules are those that allow employees to vary the time they begin or end work.
Source: Bureau of Labor Statistics, Internet web site <http://www.bls.gov/news.release/flex.t01.htm>

Men Are Less Likely to Work a Regular Daytime Schedule

Among men who work full-time, nearly one in five is a shift worker.

The average working man gets paid more than the average working woman. One reason for the disparity is that men are more likely than women to do shift work—which often pays a premium.

Overall, 86 percent of women who work full-time have a regular daytime schedule. Among men, the proportion is a smaller 81 percent. Nineteen percent of men, but only 14 percent of women are shift workers.

Men are more likely than women to work every type of shift, from evening, night, and rotating shifts to irregular schedules arranged by their employer. Among full-time workers, 5 percent of men and 4 percent of women work the evening shift. Four percent of men and 3 percent of women work the night shift.

❖ Many women—particularly single parents—are unable to accept shift work because of childrearing responsibilities and the difficulties of finding child care for the evening and night.

Shift Work by Sex, 1997

(number of full time wage and salary workers aged 16 or older, and percent distribution by shift work status, by sex, 1997; numbers in thousands)

	men	women
Total workers	52,073	38,476
Regular daytime schedule	80.5%	86.1%
Shift workers, total	19.1	13.7
Evening shift	5.0	4.1
Night shift	4.0	2.8
Rotating shift	3.5	2.2
Split shift	0.4	0.3
Employer-arranged irregular schedule	4.4	3.1
Other shift	1.7	1.0

Source: Bureau of Labor Statistics, Internet web site <http://www.bls.gov/news.release/flex.t01.htm>

Men and Women Are Equally Likely to Work at Home

Most are wage and salary workers who are not paid for working at home.

Seventeen percent of working men and 18 percent of working women perform at least some of their work at home. Those most likely to do so are married women with children under age 6. Twenty-four percent of working wives with preschoolers worked at home in 1997.

The majority of the nation's home workers are wage and salary workers who are not paid for the time they spend working at home. Many are simply catching up on office work after hours. Married women with preschoolers are the ones most likely to be paid for the work they do at home—25 percent of the home-based workers are wage and salary workers paid to work at home.

About one-third of men and slightly more than one-fourth of women who work at home are self-employed. Nineteen percent of men and women who work at home are operating their own business out of their home.

❖ The growing popularity of working at home has attracted women who once chose not to work—mothers with preschoolers—pulling them into the labor force and changing family life in the process.

People Who Work at Home, 1997

(number and percent of workers aged 16 or older employed in nonagricultural industries who work at home on their primary job by sex, marital status, and presence of own children under age 18 at home, and percent distribution of home workers by work status, 1997; numbers in thousands)

| | home-based workers | | percent distribution of home-based workers | | | | | |
| | | | | wage & salary | | self-employed | |
	number	percent of total workers	total	paid	unpaid	total	home-based
MEN							
Total men	**11,202**	**17.3%**	**100.0%**	**15.0%**	**50.1%**	**33.8%**	**19.3%**
Without children under age 18	6,259	15.4	100.0	16.0	47.1	35.8	21.3
With children under age 18	4,943	20.5	100.0	13.8	54.0	31.2	16.7
With children under age 6	2,118	18.8	100.0	14.2	55.5	28.7	16.3
Married Men	**8,385**	**21.1**	**100.0**	**14.8**	**50.8**	**33.4**	**18.3**
Without children under age 18	3,678	21.5	100.0	15.9	45.9	37.1	21.5
With children under age 18	4,707	20.8	100.0	13.9	54.6	30.5	15.9
With children under age 6	2,069	19.3	100.0	14.3	55.8	28.4	15.9
Single, divorced, widowed men	**2,817**	**11.2**	**100.0**	**15.8**	**48.1**	**34.8**	**22.0**
Without children under age 18	2,581	10.9	100.0	16.1	48.7	33.9	21.0
With children under age 18	236	16.1	100.0	12.8	41.4	44.9	33.3
WOMEN							
Total women	**10,275**	**18.3**	**100.0**	**19.1**	**53.1**	**26.2**	**19.2**
Without children under age 18	5,920	17.0	100.0	16.7	57.2	24.6	16.6
With children under age 18	4,356	20.4	100.0	22.4	47.4	28.3	22.7
With children under age 6	1,767	20.8	100.0	24.3	38.1	35.0	29.6
Married women	**6,790**	**22.3**	**100.0**	**19.6**	**49.2**	**29.3**	**21.5**
Without children under age 18	3,126	21.9	100.0	15.8	52.8	29.8	19.8
With children under age 18	3,664	22.6	100.0	22.9	46.2	28.9	23.0
With children under age 6	1,570	23.9	100.0	24.7	37.9	34.9	29.4
Single, divorced, widowed women	**3,485**	**13.6**	**100.0**	**18.0**	**60.5**	**20.0**	**14.6**
Without children under age 18	2,794	13.7	100.0	17.7	62.1	18.7	13.0
With children under age 18	691	13.4	100.0	19.4	54.2	25.1	20.9

Note: Percentages will not add to 100 because they exclude unpaid family workers, not shown separately. The self-employed include both the incorporated and the unincorporated.
Source: Bureau of Labor Statistics, Internet web site <http://www.bls.gov/news.release/homey.t02.htm>

Most Independent Contractors Are Men

Women are the majority of on-call and temporary-help workers.

Among the nation's workers, 11 percent of men and 8 percent of women are employed in what the Bureau of Labor Statistics terms "alternative" work arrangements. The bureau defines alternative workers as independent contractors, on-call workers, employees of temporary-help agencies, or workers provided by contract firms. These workers are considered alternative because they are not employees of the organization for whom they perform their services, nor do they necessarily work regular schedules.

Men are more likely than women to be alternative workers, especially in the older age groups. Fully 20 percent of working men aged 65 or older are independent contractors—freelancers, consultants, real estate agents, and others who obtain customers on their own for whom they provide a product or service. Many independent contractors are self-employed. Fourteen percent of working women aged 65 or older are independent contractors.

Women account for only 34 percent of independent contractors, but they are the majority of on-call workers (such as substitute teachers) and temps. Men account for the majority of workers provided by contract firms, such as security guards.

❖ As baby-boom men and women age, the number of independent contractors will surge.

Alternative Workers by Sex and Age, 1999

(number and percent distribution of employed people aged 16 or older by sex, age, and work arrangement; women's share of workers by age and arrangement, 1999; numbers in thousands)

	total employed	total in traditional arrangements	alternative workers				
			total	independent contractors	on-call workers	temporary help agency workers	workers provided by contract firms
NUMBER							
Total men	**70,040**	**62,464**	**7,495**	**5,459**	**993**	**501**	**542**
Aged 16 to 19	3,339	3,116	207	47	93	38	29
Aged 20 to 24	6,489	6,005	463	158	120	114	71
Aged 25 to 34	16,617	15,179	1,417	901	203	145	168
Aged 35 to 44	19,603	17,422	2,179	1,705	235	84	155
Aged 45 to 54	14,684	12,966	1,708	1,406	155	75	72
Aged 55 to 64	7,186	6,203	978	814	102	27	35
Aged 65 or older	2,122	1,575	541	427	84	18	12
Total women	**61,454**	**56,645**	**4,742**	**2,788**	**1,040**	**687**	**227**
Aged 16 to 19	3,323	3,149	153	29	86	30	8
Aged 20 to 24	5,973	5,632	324	93	81	134	16
Aged 25 to 34	14,351	13,231	1,114	578	266	203	67
Aged 35 to 44	16,812	15,538	1,266	786	272	147	61
Aged 45 to 54	13,459	12,367	1,088	772	149	107	60
Aged 55 to 64	5,876	5,302	562	397	103	50	12
Aged 65 or older	1,659	1,426	233	133	83	15	2
PERCENT DISTRIBUTION BY WORK ARRANGEMENT							
Total men	**100.0%**	**89.2%**	**10.7%**	**7.8%**	**1.4%**	**0.7%**	**0.8%**
Aged 16 to 19	100.0	93.3	6.2	1.4	2.8	1.1	0.9
Aged 20 to 24	100.0	92.5	7.1	2.4	1.8	1.8	1.1
Aged 25 to 34	100.0	91.3	8.5	5.4	1.2	0.9	1.0
Aged 35 to 44	100.0	88.9	11.1	8.7	1.2	0.4	0.8
Aged 45 to 54	100.0	88.3	11.6	9.6	1.1	0.5	0.5
Aged 55 to 64	100.0	86.3	13.6	11.3	1.4	0.4	0.5
Aged 65 or older	100.0	74.2	25.5	20.1	4.0	0.8	0.6

(continued)

(continued from previous page)

| | total employed | total in traditional arrange-ments | alternative workers | | | | |
			total	inde-pendent contractors	on-call workers	temporary help agency workers	workers provided by contract firms
Total women	**100.0%**	**92.2%**	**7.7%**	**4.5%**	**1.7%**	**1.1%**	**0.4%**
Aged 16 to 19	100.0	94.8	4.6	0.9	2.6	0.9	0.2
Aged 20 to 24	100.0	94.3	5.4	1.6	1.4	2.2	0.3
Aged 25 to 34	100.0	92.2	7.8	4.0	1.9	1.4	0.5
Aged 35 to 44	100.0	92.4	7.5	4.7	1.6	0.9	0.4
Aged 45 to 54	100.0	91.9	8.1	5.7	1.1	0.8	0.4
Aged 55 to 64	100.0	90.2	9.6	6.8	1.8	0.9	0.2
Aged 65 or older	100.0	86.0	14.0	8.0	5.0	0.9	0.1
WOMEN'S SHARE OF WORKERS							
Total workers	**46.7%**	**47.6%**	**38.8%**	**33.8%**	**51.2%**	**57.8%**	**29.5%**
Aged 16 to 19	49.9	50.3	42.5	38.2	48.0	44.1	21.6
Aged 20 to 24	47.9	48.4	41.2	37.1	40.3	54.0	18.4
Aged 25 to 34	46.3	46.6	44.0	39.1	56.7	58.3	28.5
Aged 35 to 44	46.2	47.1	36.7	31.6	53.6	63.6	28.2
Aged 45 to 54	47.8	48.8	38.9	35.4	49.0	58.8	45.5
Aged 55 to 64	45.0	46.1	36.5	32.8	50.2	64.9	25.5
Aged 65 or older	43.9	47.5	30.1	23.8	49.7	45.5	14.3

Note: Numbers may not add to total because the total employed includes day laborers, an alternative arrangement not shown separately, and a small number of workers were both on call and provided by contract firms. Independent contractors are workers who obtain customers on their own to provide a product or service, including the self-employed. On-call workers are in a pool of workers who are only called to work as needed, such as substitute teachers and construction workers supplied by a union hiring hall. Temporary help agency workers are those who said they are paid by a temporary help agency. Workers provided by contract firms are those employed by a company that provides employees or their services under contract, such as security, landscaping, and computer programming.
Source: Bureau of Labor Statistics, Internet web site <http://www.bls.gov/news.release/conemp.t05.htm>; calculations by New Strategist

Men Are More Likely to Belong to a Union

Union membership is most common among men aged 45 to 54.

Thirteen percent of women who are employed as wage and salary workers are represented by unions, while 11 percent are union members. Among men, 17 percent are represented by unions and 16 percent are union members. Union membership has been declining among both men and women in recent years.

Union representation and membership is most common among men and women aged 45 to 54. Among wage and salary workers aged 45 to 54, one in four employed men and one in five employed women are represented by a union. Workers aged 55 to 64 are more likely to be union members than those aged 35 to 44. Few workers under age 35 belong to a union.

❖ Women are less likely to be unionized than men because labor unions, historically, have concentrated their efforts in male-dominated industries.

Union Membership by Sex and Age, 1999

(number and percent of employed wage and salary workers aged 16 or older by sex, age, and union affiliation, 1999; numbers in thousands)

	total employed	represented by unions		members of unions	
		number	percent	number	percent
Total men	**61,914**	**10,758**	**17.4%**	**9,949**	**16.1%**
Aged 16 to 24	10,116	781	7.7	716	7 1
Aged 25 to 34	15,330	2,325	15.2	2,142	14.0
Aged 35 to 44	17,020	3,241	19.0	2,993	17.6
Aged 45 to 54	12,395	3,026	24.4	2,800	22.6
Aged 55 to 64	5,622	1,267	22.5	1,186	21.1
Aged 65 or older	1,431	118	8.2	111	7.7
Total women	**57,050**	**7,425**	**13.0**	**6,528**	**11.4**
Aged 16 to 24	9,489	458	4.8	393	4.1
Aged 25 to 34	13,327	1,460	11.0	1,273	9.6
Aged 35 to 44	15,418	2,187	14.2	1,924	12.5
Aged 45 to 54	12,270	2,351	19.2	2,081	17.0
Aged 55 to 64	5,258	839	16.0	746	14.2
Aged 65 or older	1,287	129	10.0	110	8.5

Note: Workers represented by unions are either members of a labor union or a similar employee association or workers who report no union affiliation but whose jobs are covered by a union or an employee association contract. Members of unions consist of union members and members of employee associations similar to unions.
Source: Bureau of Labor Statistics, Internet web site <http://www.bls.gov/news.release/union2.t01.htm>; calculations by New Strategist

Women Will Account for the Majority of New Workers

Men will account for most of those leaving the labor force.

Between 1998 and 2008, new entrants to the labor force will be almost evenly divided between men and women—with women having a slight edge. Men will leave the labor force in greater numbers than women during those years. Consequently, women will account for 47.5 percent of the labor force in 2008, up from 46.3 percent in 1998.

In 1998, the labor force numbered 138 million. By 2008 it will have grown to 155 million, a 12.0 percent gain. The number of men in the labor force will climb 9.7 percent between 1998 and 2008, while the number of working women will grow a larger 15.3 percent.

❖ With both men and women in the labor force, balancing work and family life has become a worker's issue rather than a woman's issue. Men and women need flexible schedules, health insurance coverage, and pension benefits.

The number of women in the labor force will grow faster than the number of men

(number of people aged 16 or older in the civilian labor force by sex, 1998 and 2008; numbers in millions)

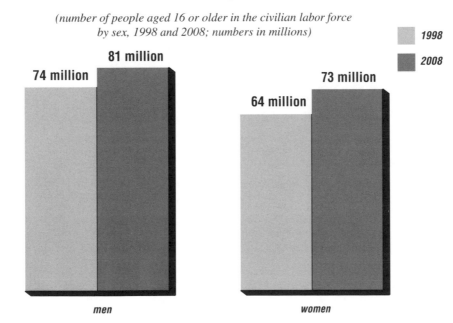

1998
2008

81 million
74 million
73 million
64 million

men
women

Workers Entering and Leaving the Labor Force by Sex, 1998 to 2008

(number and percent distribution of people aged 16 or older in the civilian labor force by sex, 1998 and 2008; projected entrants, leavers, and stayers by sex, 1998 to 2008; numbers in thousands)

| | total labor force, 1998 | 1998–2008 | | | total labor force, 2008 |
		entrants	leavers	stayers	
Total workers	**137,673**	**42,033**	**25,131**	**112,542**	**154,576**
Men	73,959	20,963	13,790	60,169	81,132
Women	63,714	21,070	11,341	52,373	73,444
Total workers	**100.0%**	**100.0%**	**100.0%**	**100.0%**	**100.0%**
Men	53.7	49.9	54.9	53.5	52.5
Women	46.3	50.1	45.1	46.5	47.5

Source: Bureau of Labor Statistics, Monthly Labor Review, *November 1999*

Older Men Will Be More Likely to Work

The labor force participation of older women will rise as well.

While men's overall labor force participation rate is projected to decline slightly between 1998 and 2008, from 74.9 to 73.7 percent, the decline will occur only among men under age 55. Among those approaching the age of retirement, labor force participation will rise slightly—up 1.3 percentage points among men aged 55 to 64 and 2.9 percentage points among men aged 65 to 74. Although many men will retire in their late fifties and early sixties, the rise in earlier retirement has ended.

Women's labor force participation rate is projected to rise from 59.8 percent in 1998 to 61.9 percent in 2008. In every age group, a larger share of women will be working in 2008 than in 1998. The biggest gain will occur among women aged 55 to 64 as the career-oriented baby-boom generation enters the age group and replaces women less inclined to work. The smallest increase in labor force participation will occur among women aged 16 to 24 because more in this age group will be going to college.

❖ As boomers enter their sixties, the labor force participation rate of older men will continue to rise.

Labor Force Participation Rates by Age and Sex, 1998 and 2008

(labor force participation rate for people aged 16 or older by age and sex, 1998 and 2008; percentage point change in rate, 1998 to 2008)

	men			women		
	1998	*2008*	*percentage point change*	*1998*	*2008*	*percentage point change*
Total people	**74.9%**	**73.7%**	**−1.2**	**59.8%**	**61.9%**	**2.1**
Aged 16 to 19	53.3	52.9	−0.4	52.3	52.4	0.1
Aged 20 to 24	82.0	81.4	−0.6	73.0	74.6	1.6
Aged 25 to 34	93.2	93.2	0.0	76.3	79.0	2.7
Aged 35 to 44	92.6	92.3	−0.3	77.1	80.0	2.9
Aged 45 to 54	89.2	88.8	−0.4	76.2	80.0	3.8
Aged 55 to 64	68.1	69.4	1.3	51.2	57.7	6.5
Aged 65 or older	16.5	17.8	1.3	8.6	9.1	0.5
Aged 65 to 74	22.6	25.5	2.9	13.7	14.8	1.1
Aged 75 or older	7.5	7.5	0.0	2.9	3.0	0.1

Source: Bureau of Labor Statistics, Monthly Labor Review, *November 1999; calculations by New Strategist*

Living Arrangements

❖ Men are more likely to be married than women.

The living arrangements of men and women are most alike in middle age, when the majorities of both are married. They diverge in old age as women become widows.

❖ The median age at first marriage is at a record high for women.

In 1998, half the women married before age 25 and half after that age. Among men, median age at first marriage stood at 26.7 in that year.

❖ Only 36 percent of black children live with both parents.

Among Hispanics, 64 percent of children live with both parents. Among whites, the figure is an even higher 74 percent.

❖ Most Americans who live alone are women.

Women account for the 58 percent majority of Americans who live alone. Among the elderly who live alone, about three-quarters are women.

❖ Most married couples have children living at home.

While only 47 percent of the nation's married couples have children under age 18 living under their roof, 58 percent have children of any age at home.

❖ Most women marry older men.

May–December romances are not common, however. Only 3 percent of husbands aged 75 or older are married to women under age 60.

Men Are More Likely to Be Married Than Women

Women are more likely to be widowed.

The living arrangements of men and women are most alike in middle age, when the majorities of both sexes are married. Among young adults, men are more likely to be single than women, and in old age women are more likely to be widowed than men.

Among people in their twenties, women are much more likely than men to be married. But among people aged 55 or older, men are much more likely to be married than women. In the 75-to-84 age group, fully 74 percent of men are married versus only 34 percent of their female counterparts. Among people aged 85 or older, half the men but only 13 percent of women are married.

Divorce is most common among people aged 45 to 54, and 18 percent of women and 14 percent of men that age are currently divorced. Many of the divorced have remarried, so these figures underestimate the proportion of people who have ever experienced divorce.

The proportion of women who are widowed rises steeply with age after age 55, reaching the majority among those aged 75 or older. In contrast, the proportion of men who are widowed peaks at 42 percent in the 85-plus age group. These differences exist because women tend to marry slightly older men and because men do not live as long as women, making widowhood the norm for women and the exception for men.

❖ As the baby-boom generation ages, the living arrangements of men and women will diverge, making it increasingly important to target women as individuals rather than as part of a couple.

Marital Status by Age and Sex, 1998: Total People

(number and percent of people aged 15 or older by marital status, age, and sex, and percentage point difference between men and women, 1998; numbers in thousands)

	men		women		percentage point difference
	number	percent	number	percent	
NEVER MARRIED					
Total people	**31,591**	**31.2%**	**26,713**	**24.7%**	**6.5**
Under age 20	9,778	98.6	9,235	96.8	1.8
Aged 20 to 24	7,360	83.4	6,178	70.3	13.1
Aged 25 to 29	4,822	51.0	3,689	38.6	12.4
Aged 30 to 34	2,939	29.2	2,219	21.6	7.6
Aged 35 to 39	2,444	21.6	1,626	14.3	7.3
Aged 40 to 44	1,676	15.6	1,095	9.9	5.7
Aged 45 to 54	1,481	8.9	1,263	7.2	1.7
Aged 55 to 64	572	5.4	538	4.6	0.8
Aged 65 to 74	328	4.1	425	4.3	−0.2
Aged 75 to 84	145	3.2	340	5.0	−1.8
Aged 85 or older	45	4.5	106	5.5	−1.0
MARRIED					
Total people	**58,633**	**58.0**	**59,333**	**54.8**	**3.2**
Under age 20	121	1.2	289	3.0	−1.8
Aged 20 to 24	1,332	15.1	2,372	27.0	−11.9
Aged 25 to 29	4,219	44.6	5,298	55.5	−10.9
Aged 30 to 34	6,345	63.0	7,044	68.6	−5.6
Aged 35 to 39	7,598	67.2	8,145	71.5	−4.3
Aged 40 to 44	7,633	71.0	8,016	72.8	−1.8
Aged 45 to 54	12,665	76.3	12,345	70.8	5.5
Aged 55 to 64	8,559	80.2	7,847	67.8	12.4
Aged 65 to 74	6,331	79.2	5,420	54.8	24.4
Aged 75 to 84	3,327	73.5	2,300	34.0	39.5
Aged 85 or older	502	49.9	258	13.4	36.5

(continued)

(continued from previous page)

	men		women		percentage point difference
	number	percent	number	percent	
DIVORCED					
Total people	**8,331**	**8.2%**	**11,093**	**10.3%**	**–2.1**
Under age 20	19	0.2	20	0.2	0.0
Aged 20 to 24	133	1.5	222	2.5	–1.0
Aged 25 to 29	398	4.2	525	5.5	–1.3
Aged 30 to 34	773	7.7	964	9.4	–1.7
Aged 35 to 39	1,213	10.7	1,484	13.0	–2.3
Aged 40 to 44	1,397	13.0	1,738	15.8	–2.8
Aged 45 to 54	2,303	13.9	3,154	18.1	–4.2
Aged 55 to 64	1,266	11.9	1,671	14.4	–2.5
Aged 65 to 74	626	7.8	882	8.9	–1.1
Aged 75 to 84	166	3.7	362	5.4	–1.7
Aged 85 or older	36	3.6	71	3.7	–0.1
WIDOWED					
Total people	**2,569**	**2.5**	**11,029**	**10.2**	**–7.7**
Under age 20	3	0.0	2	0.0	0.0
Aged 20 to 24	–	–	17	0.2	–
Aged 25 to 29	10	0.1	35	0.4	–0.3
Aged 30 to 34	20	0.2	55	0.5	–0.3
Aged 35 to 39	44	0.4	138	1.2	–0.8
Aged 40 to 44	50	0.5	166	1.5	–1.0
Aged 45 to 54	150	0.9	697	4.0	–3.1
Aged 55 to 64	275	2.6	1,526	13.2	–10.6
Aged 65 to 74	707	8.8	3,155	31.9	–23.1
Aged 75 to 84	888	19.6	3,752	55.6	–36.0
Aged 85 or older	423	42.0	1,487	77.4	–35.4

Note: (–) means sample is too small to make a reliable estimate.
Source: Bureau of the Census, Marital Status and Living Arrangements: March 1998 (Update), *Current Population Reports, P20-514, 1998; calculations by New Strategist*

Black Women Are Least Likely to Be Married

White men are most likely to have tied the knot.

Overall, only 36 percent of black women are married, with the proportion peaking at just 53 percent in the 40-to-44 age group. Among black men, the married share stands at 41 percent overall, but the proportion is above 50 percent at most ages. Sixty percent of white men are married, as are 58 percent of white women. Among Hispanics, more than half the men and women are married.

Nearly half the black men and women have never married—46 percent of men and 42 percent of women. Among whites, only 29 percent of men and 22 percent of women have not yet married.

Regardless of race or Hispanic origin, older women are far more likely to be widowed than older men. The proportion of widows reaches 83 percent among black women aged 85 or older. Widowhood is least common among Hispanics. Only 42 percent of Hispanic women and 14 percent of Hispanic men aged 85 or older are widowed.

❖ The dramatic differences in marital status by race and ethnicity create lifestyle differences affecting consumer behavior. These variances must be taken into account before targeting whites, blacks, or Hispanics.

Among women, whites are most likely to be married

(percent of women aged 15 or older who are currently married, by race and Hispanic origin, 1997)

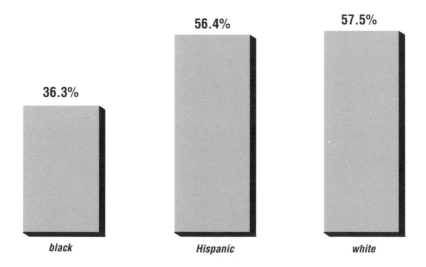

| black | Hispanic | white |
| 36.3% | 56.4% | 57.5% |

Marital Status by Age and Sex, 1998: Blacks

(number and percent of blacks aged 15 or older by marital status, age, and sex, and percentage point difference between men and women, 1998; numbers in thousands)

	men		women		percentage point difference
	number	percent	number	percent	
NEVER MARRIED					
Total blacks	**5,191**	**46.0%**	**5,689**	**41.5%**	**4.5**
Under age 20	1,496	98.3	1,516	98.7	−0.4
Aged 20 to 24	1,087	91.9	1,174	85.1	6.8
Aged 25 to 29	758	64.4	847	59.4	5.0
Aged 30 to 34	523	43.2	701	47.2	−4.0
Aged 35 to 39	519	39.7	530	34.3	5.4
Aged 40 to 44	391	32.3	365	25.4	6.9
Aged 45 to 54	254	15.5	308	15.2	0.3
Aged 55 to 64	104	10.8	136	10.8	0.0
Aged 65 to 74	36	5.4	63	6.6	−1.2
Aged 75 to 84	16	5.5	45	9.2	−3.7
Aged 85 or older	7	5.7	4	2.1	3.6
MARRIED					
Total blacks	**4,675**	**41.4**	**4,713**	**36.3**	**5.1**
Under age 20	20	1.3	19	1.2	0.1
Aged 20 to 24	96	8.2	189	13.8	−5.6
Aged 25 to 29	385	32.7	521	36.5	−3.8
Aged 30 to 34	574	47.3	652	43.9	3.4
Aged 35 to 39	671	51.4	732	47.4	4.0
Aged 40 to 44	639	52.7	755	52.6	0.1
Aged 45 to 54	1,045	63.9	1,056	52.1	11.8
Aged 55 to 64	640	66.1	580	46.2	19.9
Aged 65 to 74	420	63.8	344	35.9	27.9
Aged 75 to 84	157	53.2	118	23.8	29.4
Aged 85 or older	31	26.7	15	9.1	17.6

(continued)

(continued from previous page)

	men		women		percentage point difference
DIVORCED	*number*	*percent*	*number*	*percent*	
Total blacks	**1,035**	**9.2%**	**1,673**	**12.2%**	**–3.0**
Under age 20	6	0.4	2	0.1	0.3
Aged 20 to 24	–	–	14	1.0	–
Aged 25 to 29	35	2.9	55	3.9	–1.0
Aged 30 to 34	112	9.3	121	8.1	1.2
Aged 35 to 39	114	8.7	245	15.9	–7.2
Aged 40 to 44	172	14.2	273	19.0	–4.8
Aged 45 to 54	304	18.6	537	26.5	–7.9
Aged 55 to 64	154	15.9	275	21.9	–6.0
Aged 65 to 74	106	16.1	105	11.0	5.1
Aged 75 to 84	26	9.0	36	7.2	1.8
Aged 85 or older	7	5.7	10	5.5	0.2
WIDOWED					
Total blacks	**382**	**3.4**	**1,370**	**10.0**	**–6.6**
Under age 20	–	–	–	–	–
Aged 20 to 24	–	–	2	0.2	–
Aged 25 to 29	–	–	2	0.1	–
Aged 30 to 34	3	0.3	11	0.7	–0.4
Aged 35 to 39	3	0.2	37	2.4	–2.2
Aged 40 to 44	9	0.7	44	3.1	–2.4
Aged 45 to 54	34	2.1	127	6.2	–4.1
Aged 55 to 64	71	7.3	263	21	–13.7
Aged 65 to 74	97	14.7	444	46.4	–31.7
Aged 75 to 84	95	32.3	296	59.8	–27.5
Aged 85 or older	71	61.9	145	83.2	–21.3

Note: (–) means sample is too small to make a reliable estimate.
Source: Bureau of the Census, Marital Status and Living Arrangements: March 1998 (Update), *Current Population Reports, P20-514, 1998; calculations by New Strategist*

Marital Status by Age and Sex, 1998: Hispanics

(number and percent of Hispanics aged 15 or older by marital status, age, and sex, and percentage point difference between men and women, 1998; numbers in thousands)

	men		women		percentage point difference
	number	percent	number	percent	
NEVER MARRIED					
Total Hispanics	**4,370**	**39.9%**	**3,072**	**29.3%**	**10.6**
Under age 20	1,403	97.8	1,183	91.9	5.9
Aged 20 to 24	1,112	76.4	733	60.7	15.7
Aged 25 to 29	747	49.4	423	32.9	16.5
Aged 30 to 34	386	27.4	250	19.5	7.9
Aged 35 to 39	358	26.8	154	13.2	13.6
Aged 40 to 44	130	12.7	91	8.4	4.3
Aged 45 to 54	159	12.0	111	8.1	3.9
Aged 55 to 64	44	5.7	75	8.7	–3.0
Aged 65 or older	30	4.4	52	5.5	–1.1
MARRIED					
Total Hispanics	**5,797**	**52.9**	**5,911**	**56.4**	**–3.5**
Under age 20	28	2.0	100	7.8	–5.8
Aged 20 to 24	337	23.2	447	37.0	–13.8
Aged 25 to 29	733	48.6	810	63.0	–14.4
Aged 30 to 34	943	66.9	925	72.0	–5.1
Aged 35 to 39	854	63.7	862	73.9	–10.2
Aged 40 to 44	768	74.8	814	75.7	–0.9
Aged 45 to 54	1,003	75.8	987	71.6	4.2
Aged 55 to 64	629	81.9	565	65.4	16.5
Aged 65 or older	499	73.3	400	42.7	30.6

(continued)

(continued from previous page)

| | men | | women | | percentage |
	number	percent	number	percent	point difference
DIVORCED					
Total Hispanics	**647**	**5.9%**	**885**	**8.4%**	**–2.5**
Under age 20	3	0.2	3	0.2	0.0
Aged 20 to 24	6	0.4	23	1.9	–1.5
Aged 25 to 29	29	1.9	45	3.5	–1.6
Aged 30 to 34	79	5.6	97	7.5	–1.9
Aged 35 to 39	120	8.9	134	11.5	–2.6
Aged 40 to 44	126	12.3	153	14.2	–1.9
Aged 45 to 54	154	11.7	203	14.7	–3.0
Aged 55 to 64	77	10.1	133	15.4	–5.3
Aged 65 or older	53	7.8	94	10.0	–2.2
WIDOWED					
Total Hispanics	**131**	**1.2**	**617**	**5.9**	**–4.7**
Under age 20	–	–	2	0.2	–
Aged 20 to 24	–	–	5	0.4	–
Aged 25 to 29	2	0.1	7	0.6	–0.5
Aged 30 to 34	–	–	12	0.9	–
Aged 35 to 39	7	0.6	16	1.4	–0.8
Aged 40 to 44	2	0.2	17	1.6	–1.4
Aged 45 to 54	7	0.5	76	5.5	–5.0
Aged 55 to 64	18	2.3	91	10.6	–8.3
Aged 65 or older	95	14.0	390	41.6	–27.6

Note: (–) means sample is too small to make a reliable estimate.
Source: Bureau of the Census, Marital Status and Living Arrangements: March 1998 (Update), *Current Population Reports, P20-514, 1998; calculations by New Strategist*

Marital Status by Age and Sex, 1998: Whites

(number and percent of whites aged 15 or older by marital status, age, and sex, and percentage point difference between men and women, 1998; numbers in thousands)

	men		women		percentage point difference
	number	*percent*	*number*	*percent*	
NEVER MARRIED					
Total whites	**24,775**	**29.1%**	**19,614**	**21.9%**	**7.2**
Under age 20	7,832	98.6	7,239	96.3	2.3
Aged 20 to 24	5,887	81.6	4,662	67.0	14.6
Aged 25 to 29	3,697	47.7	2,591	34.3	13.4
Aged 30 to 34	2,214	26.8	1,402	17.0	9.8
Aged 35 to 39	1,807	19.1	1,011	10.9	8.2
Aged 40 to 44	1,238	13.7	684	7.6	6.1
Aged 45 to 54	1,199	8.4	895	6.1	2.3
Aged 55 to 64	451	4.9	387	3.9	1.0
Aged 65 to 74	285	4.0	351	4.1	−0.1
Aged 75 to 84	129	3.1	290	4.7	−1.6
Aged 85 or older	37	4.3	101	5.9	−1.6
MARRIED					
Total whites	**51,299**	**60.2**	**51,410**	**57.5**	**2.7**
Under age 20	100	1.3	259	3.4	−2.1
Aged 20 to 24	1,193	16.5	2,077	29.8	−13.3
Aged 25 to 29	3,688	47.6	4,478	59.3	−11.7
Aged 30 to 34	5,379	65.3	5,988	72.8	−7.5
Aged 35 to 39	6,551	69.4	6,966	75.2	−5.8
Aged 40 to 44	6,558	72.6	6,800	75.5	−2.9
Aged 45 to 54	11,035	77.2	10,633	72.9	4.3
Aged 55 to 64	7,559	81.6	6,927	70.1	11.5
Aged 65 to 74	5,730	80.6	4,920	56.9	23.7
Aged 75 to 84	3,060	74.6	2,127	34.8	39.8
Aged 85 or older	446	52.3	236	13.6	38.7

(continued)

(continued from previous page)

	men		women		percentage point difference
	number	percent	number	percent	
DIVORCED					
Total whites	**7,038**	**8.3%**	**9,115**	**10.2%**	**–1.9**
Under age 20	10	0.1	18	0.2	–0.1
Aged 20 to 24	131	1.8	206	3.0	–1.2
Aged 25 to 29	348	4.5	455	6.0	–1.5
Aged 30 to 34	639	7.7	800	9.7	–2.0
Aged 35 to 39	1,041	11.0	1,189	12.8	–1.8
Aged 40 to 44	1,194	13.2	1,412	15.7	–2.5
Aged 45 to 54	1,940	13.6	2,539	17.4	–3.8
Aged 55 to 64	1,060	11.4	1,362	13.8	–2.4
Aged 65 to 74	507	7.1	755	8.7	–1.6
Aged 75 to 84	138	3.4	318	5.2	–1.8
Aged 85 or older	29	3.4	62	3.6	–0.2
WIDOWED					
Total whites	**2,106**	**2.5**	**9,351**	**10.4**	**–7.9**
Under age 20	3	–	2	–	–
Aged 20 to 24	–	–	12	0.2	–
Aged 25 to 29	10	0.1	30	0.4	–0.3
Aged 30 to 34	16	0.2	42	0.5	–0.3
Aged 35 to 39	36	0.4	96	1.0	–0.6
Aged 40 to 44	41	0.5	112	1.2	–0.7
Aged 45 to 54	110	0.8	520	3.6	–2.8
Aged 55 to 64	189	2	1,206	12.2	–10.2
Aged 65 to 74	587	8.3	2,625	30.3	–22.0
Aged 75 to 84	775	18.9	3,373	55.2	–36.3
Aged 85 or older	340	39.9	1,332	77.0	–37.1

Note: (–) means sample is too small to make a reliable estimate.
Source: Bureau of the Census, Marital Status and Living Arrangements: March 1998 (Update), *Current Population Reports, P20-514, 1998; calculations by New Strategist*

A Return to Later Marriage

Median age at first marriage fell, then rose, during this century.

More than a century ago in 1890, one-half of women married for the first time at age 22 or older. The median age at first marriage for men was 26 in that year.

Age at first marriage fell during the first half of the 20th century. In the early 1950s, nearly half the women married while they were still in their teens. These are the women who gave birth to the baby-boom generation.

In 1963, median age at first marriage began to rise. As the baby-boom generation came of age, many boomers chose to postpone marriage while they went to college and started careers. In the late 1970s, median age at first marriage for women again reached age 22. By 1998, it was at a record high of 25. Also in that year, men's median age at first marrige of 26.7 was close to its record high of 26.9 reached in 1995.

❖ Like their counterparts a century ago, young adults are waiting to marry—but their reasons for doing so are different. Today's young adults are pursuing educations and careers before committing themselves to marriage and family, enjoying an independent lifestyle their great-grandparents could only dream about.

Age at first marriage is at a record high for women

(age at first marriage, by sex, 1890 to 1998)

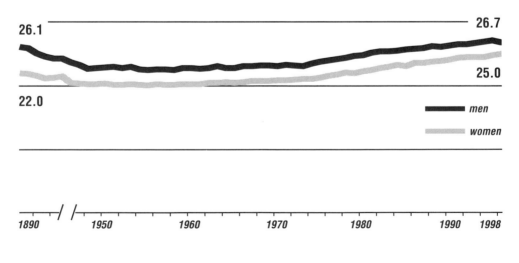

Median Age at First Marriage, 1890 to 1998

(median age at first marriage by sex, 1890–1998; in years)

	men	women
1998	26.7	25.0
1997	26.8	25.0
1996	27.1	24.8
1995	26.9	24.5
1994	26.7	24.5
1993	26.5	24.5
1992	26.5	24.4
1991	26.3	24.1
1990	26.1	23.9
1989	26.2	23.8
1988	25.9	23.6
1987	25.8	23.6
1986	25.7	23.1
1985	25.5	23.3
1984	25.4	23.0
1983	25.4	22.8
1982	25.2	22.5
1981	24.8	22.3
1980	24.7	22.0
1979	24.4	22.1
1978	24.2	21.8
1977	24.0	21.6
1976	23.8	21.3
1975	23.5	21.1
1974	23.1	21.1
1973	23.2	21.0
1972	23.3	20.9
1971	23.1	20.9
1970	23.2	20.8
1969	23.2	20.8
1968	23.1	20.8
1967	23.1	20.6
1966	22.8	20.5
1965	22.8	20.6

(continued)

(continued from previous page)

	men	women
1964	23.1	20.5
1963	22.8	20.5
1962	22.7	20.3
1961	22.8	20.3
1960	22.8	20.3
1959	22.5	20.2
1958	22.6	20.2
1957	22.6	20.3
1956	22.5	20.1
1955	22.6	20.2
1954	23.0	20.3
1953	22.8	20.2
1952	23.0	20.2
1951	22.9	20.4
1950	22.8	20.3
1949	22.7	20.3
1948	23.3	20.4
1947	23.7	20.5
1940	24.3	21.5
1930	24.3	21.3
1920	24.6	21.2
1910	25.1	21.6
1900	25.9	21.9
1890	26.1	22.0

Source: Bureau of the Census, Internet web site <http://www.census.gov/population/socdemo/ms-la/tabms-2 .txt>

Many Children Live with Only Their Mother

A minority of black children live with both parents.

The proportion of children who live with only one parent stood at 28 percent in 1998, and most of them lived with their mother. Overall, 23 percent of children live with only their mother, while just 4 percent live with only their father.

White children are most likely to live with both parents (74 percent). The majority of Hispanic children also live in two-parent homes (64 percent). Among black families, single parents are the norm. Fifty-five percent of black children live in single-parent families, almost all with their mother. Only 36 percent of black children live in two-parent homes. Black children are more likely than Hispanic or white children to live with other relatives, often a grandmother. Seven percent did so in 1998.

❖ Few men but many women are raising children on their own. Single-parent families headed by women have little free time or discretionary income, making them important customers of low-cost convenience.

Living Arrangements of Children by Race and Hispanic Origin, 1998

(number and percent distribution of children under age 18 by living arrangement, race, and Hispanic origin of child, 1998; numbers in thousands)

	total	black	Hispanic	white
Total children	**71,377**	**11,414**	**10,863**	**56,124**
Two parents	48,642	4,137	6,909	41,547
One parent	19,777	6,254	3,397	12,772
Mother only	16,634	5,830	2,915	10,210
Father only	3,143	424	482	2,562
Other relatives	2,126	843	380	1,164
Nonrelatives only	833	172	171	635
Total children	**100.0%**	**100.0%**	**100.0%**	**100.0%**
Two parents	68.1	36.2	63.6	74.0
One parent	27.7	54.8	31.3	22.8
Mother only	23.3	51.1	26.8	18.2
Father only	4.4	3.7	4.4	4.6
Other relatives	3.0	7.4	3.5	2.1
Nonrelatives only	1.2	1.5	1.6	1.1

Note: Numbers by race and Hispanic origin will not add to total because Hispanics may be of any race and because not all races are shown.
Source: Bureau of the Census, Internet web site <http://www.census.gov/population/socdemo/ms-la/tabch-2 .txt>

Men's and Women's Lifestyles Diverge with Age

Women are far more likely than men to live alone.

Most men and women aged 18 or older are married and heading their own households. The majorities of men and women adopt this lifestyle beginning in the 30-to-34 age group. The proportion peaks for men in the 65-to-74 age group at 76 percent. It peaks for women in the 40-to-44 age group at 67 percent. □After age 30, the married householder proportion among men falls below the majority only in the 85-or-older age group. Among women, the proportion falls below the majority in the 75-to-84 age group.

Among young adults, men are more likely to live alone than women. But among people aged 55 or older, women are far more likely than men to live alone. Most women aged 75 or older live alone, while among men the proportion never climbs above 33 percent.

In almost every age group, men are more likely than women to live with their parents. This is most pronounced among twentysomethings. Women aged 20 to 29 are more likely than men to be married and heading their own household, while men are more likely to live with mom and dad. At every age, women are more likely than men to head other types of families, and many of them are single parents.

❖ As the baby-boom generation ages, the older market will split into two important segments: couples and women who live alone.

Living Arrangements of Adults by Age and Sex, 1998

(number and percent distribution of people aged 18 or older by age, living arrangement, and sex; percentage point difference between men and women, 1998; numbers in thousands)

	men		women		percentage
	number	*percent*	*number*	*percent*	*point difference*
Total people	**95,009**	**100.0%**	**102,403**	**100.0%**	**–**
Married householder or spouse	54,310	57.2	54,272	53.0	4.2
Other family householder	3,845	4.0	12,609	12.3	–8.3
Child of householder	12,708	13.4	8,918	8.7	4.7
Living alone	11,000	11.6	15,312	15.0	–3.4
Other	13,146	13.8	11,292	11.0	2.8
Aged 18 to 19	**3,807**	**100.0**	**3,780**	**100.0**	**–**
Married householder or spouse	50	1.3	145	3.8	–2.5
Other family householder	102	2.7	109	2.9	–0.2
Child of householder	3,030	79.6	2,766	73.2	6.4
Living alone	63	1.7	60	1.6	0.1
Other	562	14.8	700	18.5	–3.8
Aged 20 to 24	**8,826**	**100.0**	**8,788**	**100.0**	**–**
Married householder or spouse	1,061	12.0	1,977	22.5	–10.5
Other family householder	384	4.4	943	10.7	–6.4
Child of householder	4,368	49.5	3,207	36.5	13.0
Living alone	649	7.4	463	5.3	2.1
Other	2,364	26.8	2,198	25.0	1.8
Aged 25 to 29	**9,450**	**100.0**	**9,546**	**100.0**	**–**
Married householder or spouse	3,742	39.6	4,753	49.8	–10.2
Other family householder	462	4.9	1,305	13.7	–8.8
Child of householder	1,848	19.6	1,165	12.2	7.4
Living alone	987	10.4	699	7.3	3.1
Other	2,411	25.5	1,624	17.0	8.5
Aged 30 to 34	**10,076**	**100.0**	**10,282**	**100.0**	**–**
Married householder or spouse	5,796	57.5	6,425	62.5	–5.0
Other family householder	404	4.0	1,582	15.4	–11.4
Child of householder	998	9.9	514	5.0	4.9
Living alone	1,235	12.3	757	7.4	4.9
Other	1,643	16.3	1,004	9.8	6.5
Aged 35 to 39	**11,299**	**100.0**	**11,392**	**100.0**	**–**
Married householder or spouse	6,968	61.7	7,427	65.2	–3.5
Other family householder	493	4.4	1,818	16.0	–11.6
Child of householder	1,073	9.5	458	4.0	5.5
Living alone	1,251	11.1	772	6.8	4.3
Other	1,514	13.4	917	8.0	5.3

(continued)

(continued from previous page)

	men		women		percentage point difference
	number	*percent*	*number*	*percent*	
Aged 40 to 44	**10,756**	**100.0%**	**11,015**	**100.0%**	–
Married householder or spouse	7,108	66.1	7,359	66.8	–0.7
Other family householder	562	5.2	1,819	16.5	–11.3
Child of householder	687	6.4	304	2.8	3.6
Living alone	1,304	12.1	727	6.6	5.5
Other	1,095	10.2	806	7.3	2.9
Aged 45 to 54	**16,598**	**100.0**	**17,459**	**100.0**	–
Married householder or spouse	11,872	71.5	11,383	65.2	6.3
Other family householder	700	4.2	2,260	12.9	–8.7
Child of householder	483	2.9	367	2.1	0.8
Living alone	2,011	12.1	2,109	12.1	0.0
Other	1,532	9.2	1,340	7.7	1.6
Aged 55 to 64	**10,673**	**100.0**	**11,582**	**100.0**	–
Married householder or spouse	8,027	75.2	7,348	63.4	11.8
Other family householder	352	3.3	1,099	9.5	–6.2
Child of householder	199	1.9	110	0.9	0.9
Living alone	1,153	10.8	2,148	18.5	–7.7
Other	942	8.8	877	7.6	1.3
Aged 65 to 74	**7,992**	**100.0**	**9,882**	**100.0**	–
Married householder or spouse	6,078	76.1	5,124	51.9	24.2
Other family householder	210	2.6	938	9.5	–6.9
Child of householder	22	0.3	21	0.2	0.1
Living alone	1,111	13.9	2,987	30.2	–16.3
Other	571	7.1	812	8.2	–1.1
Aged 75 to 84	**4,527**	**100.0**	**6,754**	**100.0**	–
Married householder or spouse	3,172	70.1	2,132	31.6	38.5
Other family householder	139	3.1	565	8.4	–5.3
Child of householder	–	–	3	0.0	–
Living alone	898	19.8	3,403	50.4	–30.5
Other	318	7.0	651	9.6	–2.6
Aged 85 or older	**1,006**	**100.0**	**1,923**	**100.0**	–
Married householder or spouse	436	43.3	200	10.4	32.9
Other family householder	37	3.7	173	9.0	–5.3
Child of householder	–	–	–	–	–
Living alone	336	33.4	1,187	61.7	–28.3
Other	197	19.6	363	18.9	0.7

Note: (–) means not applicable or sample is too small to make a reliable estimate.
Source: Bureau of the Census, Marital Status and Living Arrangements: March 1998 (Update), *Current Population Reports, P20-514, 1998; calculations by New Strategist*

The Majority of Americans Who Live Alone Are Women

At younger ages, men are more likely to live alone, however.

Twenty-six million Americans lived alone in 1998, 14 percent of women and 11 percent of men. Among men, the proportion of those who live alone tops 10 percent in the 25-to-29 age group and remains between 10 and 14 percent until old age. The figure peaks at 33 percent in the 85-or-older age group.

Among women, the proportion of those who live alone remains below 8 percent until the 45-to-54 age group, when it begins to climb steadily and rapidly. The share tops 50 percent in the 75-to-84 age group and peaks at 62 percent among women aged 85 or older.

The 58 percent majority of Americans who live alone are women. But among single-person households headed by people under age 45, men are the majority. The number of women who live alone surpasses the number of men who do so in the 45-to-54 age group. The proportion of single-person households headed by women peaks at 79 percent in the 75-to-84 age group.

❖ Single-person households represent two very different markets: younger men and older women. Because of the dramatic lifestyle differences between them, they should be targeted separately.

Most older women live alone

(percent of women who live alone, by age, 1998)

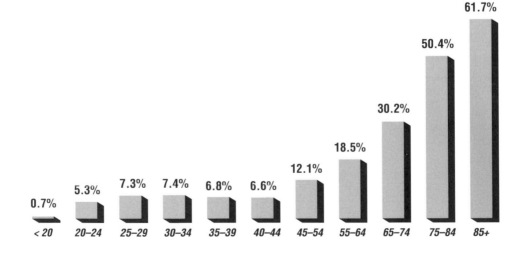

People Who Live Alone by Age and Sex, 1998

(number and percent of people who live alone by age and sex, and female share of total, 1998; numbers in thousands)

| | men | | women | | |
	number	percent	number	percent	share of total
Total people	**11,010**	**10.9%**	**15,317**	**14.2%**	**58.2%**
Under age 20	73	0.7	65	0.7	47.1
Aged 20 to 24	649	7.4	463	5.3	41.6
Aged 25 to 29	987	10.4	699	7.3	41.5
Aged 30 to 34	1,235	12.3	757	7.4	38.0
Aged 35 to 39	1,251	11.1	772	6.8	38.2
Aged 40 to 44	1,304	12.1	727	6.6	35.8
Aged 45 to 54	2,011	12.1	2,109	12.1	51.2
Aged 55 to 64	1,153	10.8	2,148	18.5	65.1
Aged 65 to 74	1,111	13.9	2,987	30.2	72.9
Aged 75 to 84	898	19.8	3,403	50.4	79.1
Aged 85 or older	336	33.4	1,187	61.7	77.9

Source: Bureau of the Census, Marital Status and Living Arrangements: March 1998 (Update), *Current Population Reports, P20-514, 1998; calculations by New Strategist*

Married Couples Are Losing Ground

Married couples accounted for just 53 percent of households in 1998.

A few decades ago, the overwhelming majority of American households were headed by married couples. In 1970, more than 70 percent of households were headed by couples, with the 40 percent plurality being married couples with children under age 18 at home. Fewer than one in five households was someone living alone or unrelated people living together (nonfamily households).

By 1998, American households were dramatically different. Married couples account for the bare majority of households anymore, and married couples with children are outnumbered by empty nesters (married couples without children at home) and by nonfamily households.

While the proportion of households headed by single parents grew between 1970 and 1998, those gains were dwarfed by the surge in nonfamily households. The nonfamily share of households rose from 19 to 31 percent between 1970 and 1998. One factor behind this increase was the growing number of women who live alone. Nonfamily households headed by women accounted for fully 17 percent of the nation's 102.5 million households in 1998.

❖ As lifestyles diversify, the use of traditional family imagery in advertising has less relevance to men and women in today's marketplace.

Households by Type, 1970 and 1998

(number and percent distribution of households by household type, 1970 and 1998; percent change in number and percentage point change in distribution, 1970–98; numbers in thousands)

	1998	*1970*	*percent change 1970–98*
TOTAL HOUSEHOLDS	**102,528**	**63,401**	**61.7%**
Family households	**70,880**	**51,456**	**37.7**
Married couples	54,317	44,728	21.4
With children under 18	25,269	25,541	−1.1
Without children under 18	29,048	19,187	51.4
Female householder, no spouse present	12,652	5,500	130.0
With children under 18	7,693	2,971	158.9
Without children under 18	4,959	2,529	96.1
Male householder, no spouse present	3,911	1,228	218.5
With children under 18	1,798	345	421.2
Without children under 18	2,113	883	139.3
Nonfamily households	**31,648**	**11,945**	**164.9**
Female householder	17,516	7,882	122.2
Male householder	14,133	4,063	247.8

	1998	*1970*	*percentage point change, 1970–98*
TOTAL HOUSEHOLDS	**100.0%**	**100.0%**	**–**
Family households	**69.1**	**81.2**	**−12.0**
Married couples	53.0	70.5	−17.6
With children under 18	24.6	40.3	−15.6
Without children under 18	28.3	30.3	−1.9
Female householder, no spouse present	12.3	8.7	3.7
With children under 18	7.5	4.7	2.8
Without children under 18	4.8	4.0	0.8
Male householder, no spouse present	3.8	1.9	1.9
With children under 18	1.8	0.5	1.2
Without children under 18	2.1	1.4	0.7
Nonfamily households	**30.9**	**18.8**	**12.0**
Female householder	17.1	12.4	4.7
Male householder	13.8	6.4	7.4

Source: Bureau of the Census, Household and Family Characteristics: March 1998 (Update), *Current Population Reports, P20-515, 1999; calculations by New Strategist*

Married Couples Head the Majority of Households in Middle Age

Sixty percent of householders aged 45 to 64 are married couples.

Slightly more than one-half (53 percent) of American households were headed by married couples in 1998. Couples account for just 25 percent of households headed by people under age 25, but become the majority in the 25-to-34 age group. The married-couple share of households remains above 50 percent until the 75-or-older age groups.

Households headed by people under age 25 are the most diverse as young men and women make the transition from living with their parents to living on their own. One-fifth of the youngest householders are women heading families without a spouse, while another one-fifth are women heading nonfamily households. Household diversity is also great among householders aged 65 to 84 as men and (primarily) women make the transition from living as a married couple to living by themselves following the death of the spouse.

❖ Because of the increasing diversity of households, businesses must look beyond married couples when marketing products and services. Even among the most-likely-to-be-married householders, those aged 45 to 64, a substantial 40 percent are not married couples.

Households by Type and Age of Householder, 1998

(number and percent distribution of households by household type and age of householder, 1998; numbers in thousands)

	total	under 25	25 to 34	35 to 44	45 to 54	55 to 64	65 to 74	75 to 84	85 or older
TOTAL HOUSEHOLDS	102,528	5,435	19,033	23,943	19,547	13,072	11,272	8,090	2,135
Family households	70,880	3,019	13,639	18,872	14,694	9,387	6,989	3,707	575
Married couples	54,317	1,373	9,886	14,180	11,734	7,936	5,841	5,003	365
With children under 18	25,269	811	7,237	11,592	4,935	591	82	20	–
Without children under 18	29,048	562	2,649	2,588	6,799	7,345	5,759	2,981	365
Female householder, no spouse present	12,652	1,095	2,887	3,637	2,260	1,099	938	563	173
With children under 18	7,693	866	2,693	3,041	966	104	20	2	–
Without children under 18	4,959	229	194	596	1,294	995	918	563	173
Male householder, no spouse present	3,911	551	866	1,055	700	352	210	135	37
With children under 18	1,798	186	489	694	349	65	10	2	2
Without children under 18	2,113	365	377	361	351	287	200	135	35
Nonfamily households	31,648	2,417	5,394	5,072	4,853	3,685	4,283	4,384	1,560
Female householder	17,516	1,080	2,070	1,863	2,421	2,337	3,080	3,460	1,204
Living alone	15,317	528	1456	1,499	2109	2,148	2,987	3,403	1,187
Male householder	14,133	1,336	3,325	3,208	2,432	1,348	1,203	923	356
Living alone	11,010	722	2,222	2,555	2,011	1,153	1,111	893	336

(continued)

AMERICAN MEN AND WOMEN

(continued from previous page)

	total	under 25	25 to 34	35 to 44	45 to 54	55 to 64	65 to 74	75 to 84	85 or older
TOTAL HOUSEHOLDS	100.0%	100.0%	100.0%	100.0%	100.0%	100.0%	100.0%	100.0%	100.0%
Family households	69.1	55.5	71.7	78.8	75.2	71.8	62.0	45.8	26.9
Married couples	53.0	25.3	51.9	59.2	60.0	60.7	51.8	37.1	17.1
With children under 18	24.6	14.9	38.0	48.4	25.2	4.5	0.7	0.3	–
Without children under 18	28.3	10.3	13.9	10.8	34.8	56.2	51.1	36.8	17.1
Female householder, no spouse present	12.3	20.1	15.2	15.2	11.6	8.4	8.3	7.0	8.1
With children under 18	7.5	15.9	14.1	12.7	4.9	0.8	0.2	0.0	–
Without children under 18	4.8	4.2	1.0	2.5	6.6	7.6	8.1	7.0	8.1
Male householder, no spouse present	3.8	10.1	4.5	4.4	3.6	2.7	1.9	1.7	1.7
With children under 18	1.8	3.4	2.6	2.9	1.8	0.5	0.1	0.0	0.1
Without children under 18	2.1	6.7	2.0	1.5	1.8	2.2	1.8	1.7	1.6
Nonfamily households	30.9	44.5	28.3	21.2	24.8	28.2	38.0	54.2	73.1
Female householder	17.1	19.9	10.9	7.8	12.4	17.9	27.3	42.8	56.4
Living alone	14.9	9.7	7.6	6.3	10.8	16.4	26.5	42.1	55.6
Male householder	13.8	24.6	17.5	13.4	12.4	10.3	10.7	11.4	16.7
Living alone	10.7	13.3	11.7	10.7	10.3	8.8	9.9	11.1	15.7

Note: (–) means sample is too small to make a reliable estimate.
Source: Bureau of the Census, Household and Family Characteristics: March 1998 (Update), Current Population Reports, P20-5i5, 1999; and Marital Status and Living Arrangements: March 1998 (Update), Current Population Reports, P20-514, 1998; calculations by New Strategist

Households Vary Sharply by Race and Ethnicity

Black households are more diverse than white or Hispanic households.

Fewer than one-third of black households are headed by married couples, while an almost equal proportion are female-headed families. In contrast, more one-than half of white and Hispanic households are headed by married couples.

Hispanic households are more likely to be nuclear families (husband, wife, and children) than both white and black households. In 1998, 36 percent of Hispanic households were married couples with children under age 18 at home, as compared with only 25 percent of white and 17 percent of black households. Although blacks are still the largest minority in the U.S., Hispanic married couples with children outnumber their black counterparts by more than 1 million.

Single-parent families headed by women account for only 6 percent of white households, but for 13 percent of Hispanic and 21 percent of black households. Blacks account for one-third of all female-headed single-parent families.

Women living alone account for much larger shares of black and white households than of Hispanic households. Between 15 and 16 percent of black and white householders are women living alone, versus only 7 percent of Hispanic householders.

❖ The diversity of household types by race and ethnicity means that white, black, and Hispanic consumers often have different needs.

Households by Type, Race, and Hispanic Origin of Householder, 1998

(number and percent distribution of households by household type, race, and Hispanic origin of householder, 1998; numbers in thousands)

	white	black	Hispanic
TOTAL HOUSEHOLDS	**86,106**	**12,474**	**8,590**
Family households	**59,511**	**8,408**	**6,961**
Married couples	48,066	3,921	4,804
With children under 18	21,910	2,055	3,121
Without children under 18	26,156	1,866	1,683
Female householder, no spouse present	8,308	3,926	1,612
With children under 18	4,912	2,569	1,121
Without children under 18	3,396	1,357	491
Male householder, no spouse present	3,137	562	545
With children under 18	1,514	223	233
Without children under 18	1,623	339	312
Nonfamily households	**26,596**	**4,066**	**1,630**
Female householders	14,871	2,190	754
Living alone	12,980	1,982	617
Male householders	11,725	1,876	875
Living alone	9,018	1,594	623
TOTAL HOUSEHOLDS	**100.0%**	**100.0%**	**100.0%**
Family households	**69.1**	**67.4**	**81.0**
Married couples	55.8	31.4	55.9
With children under 18	25.4	16.5	36.3
Without children under 18	30.4	15.0	19.6
Female householder, no spouse present	9.6	31.5	18.8
With children under 18	5.7	20.6	13.1
Without children under 18	3.9	10.9	5.7
Male householder, no spouse present	3.6	4.5	6.3
With children under 18	1.8	1.8	2.7
Without children under 18	1.9	2.7	3.6
Nonfamily households	**30.9**	**32.6**	**19.0**
Female householders	17.3	17.6	8.8
Living alone	15.1	15.9	7.2
Male householders	13.6	15.0	10.2
Living alone	10.5	12.8	7.3

Source: Bureau of the Census, Household and Family Characteristics: March 1998 (Update), *Current Population Reports, P20-515, 1999; and* Marital Status and Living Arrangements: March 1998 (Update), *Current Population Reports, P20-514, 1998; calculations by New Strategist*

Only One-Third of Households Include Children under Age 18

The proportion peaks at 67 percent in households headed by 35-to-39-year-olds.

Just 34 percent of American households include children under age 18, a proportion that has fallen with family size over the past few decades. Even among married couples, only a 47 percent minority have children under age 18 at home. Between the ages of 20 and 44, however, most married couples have children at home.

Fully 61 percent of female-headed families have children under age 18 at home. The proportion surpasses 90 percent among female householders aged 25 to 39. Female-headed families without children under age 18 at home are women living with adult children or other relatives, such as siblings. Only 46 percent of all male-headed families include children under age 18, but the majority of those aged 25 to 44 have dependent children at home.

❖ Men and women can be divided into two consumer groups—with and without dependent children. Most consumers under age 45 are harried parents. Most consumers aged 45 or older have more time and money to spend on themselves.

Most female-headed families include children

(percent of households with own children under age 18 by household type, 1998)

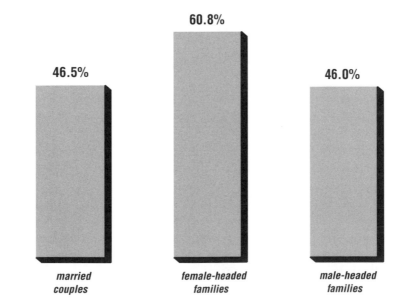

Households with Children by Type of Household, 1998

(number and percent of households with own children under age 18, by age of householder and type of household, 1998; numbers in thousands)

	total households		married-couple families		female-headed families		male-headed families	
	total	with children	total	with children	total	with children	total	with children
Total households	**102,528**	**34,760**	**54,317**	**25,269**	**12,652**	**7,693**	**3,911**	**1,798**
Under age 20	705	150	86	56	152	76	167	18
Aged 20 to 24	4,730	1,712	1,287	755	943	790	384	168
Aged 25 to 29	8,463	3,990	3,967	2,535	1,305	1,204	462	251
Aged 30 to 34	10,570	6,429	5,919	4,702	1,582	1,489	404	238
Aged 35 to 39	11,838	7,984	6,941	5,967	1,818	1,684	493	332
Aged 40 to 44	12,105	7,345	7,239	5,625	1,819	1,357	562	362
Aged 45 to 54	19,547	6,249	11,734	4,935	2,260	966	700	349
Aged 55 to 64	13,072	760	7,936	591	1,099	104	352	65
Aged 65 or older	21,497	139	9,209	104	1,676	22	386	14
Total households	**100.0%**	**33.9%**	**100.0%**	**46.5%**	**100.0%**	**60.8%**	**100.0%**	**46.0%**
Under age 20	100.0	21.3	100.0	65.1	100.0	50.0	100.0	10.8
Aged 20 to 24	100.0	36.2	100.0	58.7	100.0	83.8	100.0	43.8
Aged 25 to 29	100.0	47.1	100.0	63.9	100.0	92.3	100.0	54.3
Aged 30 to 34	100.0	60.8	100.0	79.4	100.0	94.1	100.0	58.9
Aged 35 to 39	100.0	67.4	100.0	86.0	100.0	92.6	100.0	67.3
Aged 40 to 44	100.0	60.7	100.0	77.7	100.0	74.6	100.0	64.4
Aged 45 to 54	100.0	32.0	100.0	42.1	100.0	42.7	100.0	49.9
Aged 55 to 64	100.0	5.8	100.0	7.4	100.0	9.5	100.0	18.5
Aged 65 or older	100.0	0.6	100.0	1.1	100.0	1.3	100.0	3.6

Source: Bureau of the Census, Household and Family Characteristics: March 1998 (Update), *Current Population Reports, P20-515, 1999; calculations by New Strategist*

Most Families Find Nest Slow to Empty

Many older married couples still have children living at home.

Although only 47 percent of married couples have children under age 18 at home, the 58 percent majority have children of any age at home because many children choose to live with their parents well into adulthood. Fully 88 percent of female-headed families have children of any age at home, as do 64 percent of male-headed families.

Among married couples, about one-fifth have teens, one-fifth have children aged 6 to 11, and one-fifth have preschoolers in the home. Those most likely to have teens at home are couples aged 40 to 44, at 50 percent. Those most likely to have preschoolers at home are 30-to-34-year-olds, at 60 percent. Among female-headed families, the proportions peak at a slightly younger age. Sixty percent of female family householders aged 35 to 39 have teens at home, and 76 percent of those aged 20 to 24 have preschoolers at home.

Among older married couples, a substantial percentage still have children at home. The proportion does not fall below the majority until the 55-to-64 age group. It never drops below 10 percent. Among female-headed families, more than 70 percent of the oldest householders have children living with them. Among male-headed families, at least two-thirds of the oldest householders have children at home.

❖ Until age 55, most family householders have children living under their roof. Even if those children are adults, parents continue to feel responsible for their well-being.

Married Couples with Children by Age of Children, 1998

(number and percent distribution of total married couples and couples with own children at home, by age of householder and age of children, 1998; numbers in thousands)

	total	with children at home				
		of any age	under age 18	aged 12 to 17	aged 6 to 11	under age 6
Total couples	**54,317**	**31,288**	**25,269**	**11,406**	**12,285**	**11,773**
Under age 20	86	56	56	1	–	55
Aged 20 to 24	1,287	760	755	12	99	731
Aged 25 to 29	3,967	2,543	2,535	104	984	2,227
Aged 30 to 34	5,919	4,712	4,702	873	2,376	3,566
Aged 35 to 39	6,941	6,047	5,967	2,436	3,670	3,045
Aged 40 to 44	7,239	6,098	5,625	3,636	3,093	1,477
Aged 45 to 54	11,734	7,550	4,935	3,819	1,872	593
Aged 55 to 64	7,936	2,332	591	468	153	55
Aged 65 to 74	5,841	859	82	40	33	18
Aged 75 or older	3,368	332	22	16	5	5
Total couples	**100.0%**	**57.6%**	**46.5%**	**21.0%**	**22.6%**	**21.7%**
Under age 20	100.0	65.1	65.1	1.2	–	64.0
Aged 20 to 24	100.0	59.1	58.7	0.9	7.7	56.8
Aged 25 to 29	100.0	64.1	63.9	2.6	24.8	56.1
Aged 30 to 34	100.0	79.6	79.4	14.7	40.1	60.2
Aged 35 to 39	100.0	87.1	86.0	35.1	52.9	43.9
Aged 40 to 44	100.0	84.2	77.7	50.2	42.7	20.4
Aged 45 to 54	100.0	64.3	42.1	32.5	16.0	5.1
Aged 55 to 64	100.0	29.4	7.4	5.9	1.9	0.7
Aged 65 to 74	100.0	14.7	1.4	0.7	0.6	0.3
Aged 75 or older	100.0	9.9	0.7	0.5	0.1	0.1

Note: Numbers will not add to total because households may contain children in more than one age group.
(–) means sample is too small to make a reliable estimate.
Source: Bureau of the Census, Household and Family Characteristics: March 1998 (Update), *Current Population Reports, P20-515, 1999; calculations by New Strategist*

Female-Headed Families with Children by Age of Children, 1998

(number and percent distribution of total female headed families and of those with own children at home, by age of householder and age of children, 1998; numbers in thousands)

	total	of any age	under age 18	aged 12 to 17	aged 6 to 11	under age 6
		with children at home				
Total female-headed families	**12,652**	**11,175**	**7,693**	**3,741**	**3,740**	**3,000**
Under age 20	152	76	76	5	2	72
Aged 20 to 24	943	793	790	6	183	718
Aged 25 to 29	1,305	1,210	1,204	73	764	819
Aged 30 to 34	1,582	1,492	1,489	679	1,078	632
Aged 35 to 39	1,818	1,761	1,684	1,082	899	497
Aged 40 to 44	1,819	1,720	1,357	1,014	563	185
Aged 45 to 54	2,260	2,013	966	794	217	64
Aged 55 to 64	1,099	894	104	77	22	9
Aged 65 to 74	938	689	20	10	11	4
Aged 75 or older	738	527	2	2	–	–
Total female-headed families	**100.0%**	**88.3%**	**60.8%**	**29.6%**	**29.6%**	**23.7%**
Under age 20	100.0	50.0	50.0	3.3	1.3	47.4
Aged 20 to 24	100.0	84.1	83.8	0.6	19.4	76.1
Aged 25 to 29	100.0	92.7	92.3	5.6	58.5	62.8
Aged 30 to 34	100.0	94.3	94.1	42.9	68.1	39.9
Aged 35 to 39	100.0	96.9	92.6	59.5	49.4	27.3
Aged 40 to 44	100.0	94.6	74.6	55.7	31.0	10.2
Aged 45 to 54	100.0	89.1	42.7	35.1	9.6	2.8
Aged 55 to 64	100.0	81.3	9.5	7.0	2.0	0.8
Aged 65 to 74	100.0	73.5	2.1	1.1	1.2	0.4
Aged 75 or older	100.0	71.4	0.3	0.3	–	–

Note: Numbers will not add to total because households may contain children in more than one age group.
(–) means sample is too small to make a reliable estimate.
Source: Bureau of the Census, Household and Family Characteristics: March 1998 (Update), *Current Population Reports, P20-515, 1999; calculations by New Strategist*

Male-headed Families with Children by Age of Children, 1998

(number and percent distribution of total male-headed families and of those with own children at home, by age of householder and age of children, 1998; numbers in thousands)

	total	with children at home				
		of any age	*under age 18*	*aged 12 to 17*	*aged 6 to 11*	*under age 6*
Total male-headed families	**3,911**	**2,516**	**1,798**	**764**	**653**	**759**
Under age 20	167	18	18	5	3	13
Aged 20 to 24	384	177	168	7	14	163
Aged 25 to 29	462	257	251	4	57	220
Aged 30 to 34	404	239	238	39	134	146
Aged 35 to 39	493	345	332	155	171	101
Aged 40 to 44	562	438	362	242	147	69
Aged 45 to 54	700	525	349	256	111	40
Aged 55 to 64	352	244	65	47	10	8
Aged 65 to 74	210	138	10	7	5	–
Aged 75 or older	176	135	4	2	2	–
Total male-headed families	**100.0%**	**64.3%**	**46.0%**	**19.5%**	**16.7%**	**19.4%**
Under age 20	100.0	10.8	10.8	3.0	1.8	7.8
Aged 20 to 24	100.0	46.1	43.8	1.8	3.6	42.4
Aged 25 to 29	100.0	55.6	54.3	0.9	12.3	47.6
Aged 30 to 34	100.0	59.2	58.9	9.7	33.2	36.1
Aged 35 to 39	100.0	70.0	67.3	31.4	34.7	20.5
Aged 40 to 44	100.0	77.9	64.4	43.1	26.2	12.3
Aged 45 to 54	100.0	75.0	49.9	36.6	15.9	5.7
Aged 55 to 64	100.0	69.3	18.5	13.4	2.8	2.3
Aged 65 to 74	100.0	65.7	4.8	3.3	2.4	–
Aged 75 or older	100.0	76.7	2.3	1.1	1.1	–

Note: Numbers will not add to total because households may contain children in more than one age group.
(–) means sample is too small to make a reliable estimate.
Source: Bureau of the Census, Household and Family Characteristics: March 1998 (Update), *Current Population Reports, P20-515, 1999; calculations by New Strategist*

Married Couples Are Much Better Educated Than Single Parents

Most couples with children at home have at least some college experience.

Fully 58 percent of married couples with children under age 18 at home have at least some college experience, and 30 percent are college graduates. They are by far the best educated family heads. Only 50 percent of married couples without children at home have college experience. Their educational level is lower because so many of them are older, and older Americans are less educated than younger adults.

Single parents are far less educated than married couples. The proportion of single parents who are college graduates is less than half the proportion among couples. Forty-four percent of women who head single-parent families have at least some college experience. This compares with only 37 percent of their male counterparts.

❖ Because of their greater educational level, married parents are more sophisticated and demanding consumers than single parents and a tougher sell for marketers.

Many women who head single-parent families have been to college

(percent of householders with children under age 18 at home who have at least some college experience, by type of household, 1998)

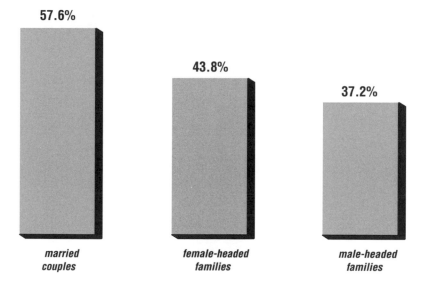

57.6%
43.8%
37.2%

married couples

female-headed families

male-headed families

Families by Educational Attainment of Householder and Presence of Children, 1998

(number and percent distribution of families by educational attainment of householder, family type, and presence of own children under age 18 at home, 1998; numbers in thousands)

	married couples		female-headed families		male-headed families	
	with children	without children	with children	without children	with children	without children
Total families	**25,269**	**29,048**	**7,693**	**4,959**	**1,798**	**2,113**
Not a high school graduate	3,007	5,072	1,563	1,492	375	561
High school graduate or more	22,262	23,976	6,131	3,467	1,423	1,552
Some college	6,996	6,635	2,430	1,118	437	563
Bachelor's degree or more	7,557	7,814	938	620	232	299
Total families	**100.0%**	**100.0%**	**100.0%**	**100.0%**	**100.0%**	**100.0%**
Not a high school graduate	11.9	17.5	20.3	30.1	20.9	26.5
High school graduate or more	88.1	82.5	79.7	69.9	79.1	73.5
Some college	27.7	22.8	31.6	22.5	24.3	26.6
Bachelor's degree or more	29.9	26.9	12.2	12.5	12.9	14.2

Source: Bureau of the Census, Marital Status and Living Arrangements: March 1998 (Update)*, Current Population Reports, P20-514, 1998; calculations by New Strategist*

Most Women Marry Older Men

By marrying older, most women face eventual widowhood.

It is evident in the statistics on the next page that women usually marry older men. Among husbands aged 45 to 54, for example, 62 percent are married to a woman in the same age group, while 33 percent are married to a younger woman and just 4 percent to an older woman. Among women aged 45 to 54, 65 percent are married to a man in the same age group, while 26 percent are married to an older man and just 9 percent to a younger man. The same pattern occurs in every age group.

The tendency of women to marry older men makes widowhood and lone living the norm for older women. In contrast, many older men who are widowed remarry, aided by the abundance of single older women. Many of them marry younger women. Among women aged 75 or older, 88 percent are married to men in the same age group. But among men aged 75 or older, only 57 percent are married to women of comparable age. Forty-three percent are married to younger women. May–December romances are not common, however. Only 3 percent of husbands aged 75 or older are married to women under age 60.

❖ Despite the fact that women tend to marry slightly older men, most husbands and wives are not far apart in age.

Married Couples by Age of Husband and Age of Wife, 1998

(number and percent distribution of married couples by age of husband and age of wife; numbers in thousands)

	total wives	< 25	25 to 34	35 to 44	45 to 54	55 to 59	60 to 61	62 to 64	65 to 69	70 to 74	75 or older
Total husbands	55,305	2,366	11,428	14,950	11,549	4,124	1,455	1,873	2,799	2,382	2,380
Under age 25	1,246	982	223	24	12	–	–	–	2	–	3
Aged 25 to 34	9,840	1,270	7,497	1,000	55	7	2	–	6	–	2
Aged 35 to 44	14,230	80	3,377	9,741	982	34	2	5	4	–	4
Aged 45 to 54	12,014	20	258	3,737	7,487	405	38	22	32	5	8
Aged 55 to 59	4,364	2	36	293	2,091	1,680	144	64	45	5	5
Aged 60 to 61	1,582	3	4	38	306	769	288	99	59	11	4
Aged 62 to 64	2,208	5	17	52	271	642	518	515	137	39	12
Aged 65 to 69	3,417	3	9	35	235	422	353	899	1,211	198	51
Aged 70 to 74	2,730	–	–	9	68	108	80	208	996	1,062	199
Aged 75 or older	3,674	–	7	20	42	57	30	60	307	1,061	2,092

(continued)

(continued from previous page)

Percent distribution by age of wife

	total wives	< 25	25 to 34	35 to 44	45 to 54	55 to 59	60 to 61	62 to 64	65 to 69	70 to 74	75 or older
Total husbands	100.0%	4.3%	20.7%	27.0%	20.9%	7.5%	2.6%	3.4%	5.1%	4.3%	4.3%
Under age 25	100.0	78.8	17.9	1.9	1.0	–	–	–	0.2	–	0.2
Aged 25 to 34	100.0	12.9	76.2	10.2	0.6	0.1	0.0	–	0.1	–	0.0
Aged 35 to 44	100.0	0.6	23.7	68.5	6.9	0.2	0.0	0.0	0.0	–	0.0
Aged 45 to 54	100.0	0.2	2.1	31.1	62.3	3.4	0.3	0.2	0.3	0.0	0.1
Aged 55 to 59	100.0	0.0	0.8	6.7	47.9	38.5	3.3	1.5	1.0	0.1	0.1
Aged 60 to 61	100.0	0.2	0.3	2.4	19.3	48.6	18.2	6.3	3.7	0.7	0.3
Aged 62 to 64	100.0	0.2	0.8	2.4	12.3	29.1	23.5	23.3	6.2	1.8	0.5
Aged 65 to 69	100.0	0.1	0.3	1.0	6.9	12.4	10.3	26.3	35.4	5.8	1.5
Aged 70 to 74	100.0	–	–	0.3	2.5	4.0	2.9	7.6	36.5	38.9	7.3
Aged 75 or older	100.0	–	0.2	0.5	1.1	1.6	0.8	1.6	8.4	28.9	56.9

Percent distribution by age of husband

	total husbands	< 25	25 to 34	35 to 44	45 to 54	55 to 59	60 to 61	62 to 64	65 to 69	70 to 74	75 or older
Total husbands	100.0%	100.0%	100.0%	100.0%	100.0%	100.0%	100.0%	100.0%	100.0%	100.0%	100.0%
Under age 25	2.3	41.5	2.0	0.2	0.1	–	–	–	0.1	–	0.1
Aged 25 to 34	17.8	53.7	65.6	6.7	0.5	0.2	0.1	–	0.2	–	0.1
Aged 35 to 44	25.7	3.4	29.6	65.2	8.5	0.8	0.1	0.3	0.1	–	0.2
Aged 45 to 54	21.7	0.8	2.3	25.0	64.8	9.8	2.6	1.2	1.1	0.2	0.3
Aged 55 to 59	7.9	0.1	0.3	2.0	18.1	40.7	9.9	3.4	1.6	0.2	0.2
Aged 60 to 61	2.9	0.1	0.0	0.3	2.6	18.6	19.8	5.3	2.1	0.5	0.2
Aged 62 to 64	4.0	0.2	0.1	0.3	2.3	15.6	35.6	27.5	4.9	1.6	0.5
Aged 65 to 69	6.2	0.1	0.1	0.2	2.0	10.2	24.3	48.0	43.3	8.3	2.1
Aged 70 to 74	4.9	–	–	0.1	0.6	2.6	5.5	11.1	35.6	44.6	8.4
Aged 75 or older	6.6	–	0.1	0.1	0.4	1.4	2.1	3.2	11.0	44.5	87.9

Note: (–) means sample is too small to make a reliable estimate.
Source: Bureau of the Census, Household and Family Characteristics: March 1998 (Update), Current Population Reports, P20-515, 1999; calculations by New Strategist

Cohabiting Couples Number Nearly 6 Million

The largest share is headed by 25-to-34-year-olds.

The number of households consisting of two unrelated adults has increased substantially over the past few decades as growing numbers of men and women opted for living together before marriage. In addition, more of the divorced are choosing to live with a partner rather than remarry. Finally, the growing acceptance of homosexuality has encouraged more same-sex couples to live together.

In 1998, there were 5.9 million cohabiting couples in the United States. The majority of cohabiting householders are under age 35, while fewer than one-fourth are aged 45 or older. Twenty-seven percent of male cohabiting householders and 30 percent of female cohabiting householders have partners of the same sex.

Despite the rise in the number of cohabiting couples, they remain a tiny proportion of the nation's total households. With marriage regaining some of its luster in recent years, cohabitation is likely to remain little more than a lifestage among young adults.

❖ The number of older cohabiting couples will increase substantially as the baby-boom generation ages and is slow to remarry following divorce or the death of the spouse.

Cohabiting Couples by Age and Sex, 1998

(number and percent distribution of households with two unrelated adults by age of householder and sex of householder and partner, 1998; numbers in thousands)

	male householder			female householder		
	total	partner of		total	partner of	
		opposite sex	same sex		opposite sex	same sex
Total households	**3,217**	**2,352**	**865**	**2,694**	**1,885**	**810**
Under age 25	612	408	204	571	369	203
Aged 25 to 34	1,200	891	309	989	727	262
Aged 35 to 44	695	514	181	501	343	158
Aged 45 to 64	580	441	140	479	356	123
Aged 65 or older	129	98	31	154	90	64
Percent distribution by age						
Total households	**100.0%**	**100.0%**	**100.0%**	**100.0%**	**100.0%**	**100.0%**
Under age 25	19.0	17.3	23.6	21.2	19.6	25.1
Aged 25 to 34	37.3	37.9	35.7	36.7	38.6	32.3
Aged 35 to 44	21.6	21.9	20.9	18.6	18.2	19.5
Aged 45 to 64	18.0	18.8	16.2	17.8	18.9	15.2
Aged 65 or older	4.0	4.2	3.6	5.7	4.8	7.9
Percent distribution by sex of partner						
Total households	**100.0%**	**73.1%**	**26.9%**	**100.0%**	**70.0%**	**30.1%**
Under age 25	100.0	66.7	33.3	100.0	64.6	35.6
Aged 25 to 34	100.0	74.3	25.8	100.0	73.5	26.5
Aged 35 to 44	100.0	74.0	26.0	100.0	68.5	31.5
Aged 45 to 64	100.0	76.0	24.1	100.0	74.3	25.7
Aged 65 or older	100.0	76.0	24.0	100.0	58.4	41.6

Source: Bureau of the Census, Marital Status and Living Arrangements: March 1998 (Update), *Current Population Reports, P20-514, 1998; calculations by New Strategist*

7

Population

❖ **Women outnumber men by a growing margin with age.**

Fifty-eight percent of people aged 65 or older are women, as are 82 percent of centenarians.

❖ **Rapid growth in sixtysomethings during the next decade.**

The number of men and women aged 60 to 64 will expand more than 50 percent between 2000 and 2010 as baby boomers fill the age group.

❖ **The number of elderly will grow rapidly in many states.**

Several western states will see a doubling in the number of men and women aged 65 or older between 2000 and 2025.

❖ **Men and women are about equally likely to move.**

Women account for the slight majority of movers in most age groups.

❖ **Females account for the majority of legal immigrants.**

Females account for 58 percent of immigrants from Mexico but for only 42 percent of those from Cuba.

❖ **Most voters are women.**

Fifty-three percent of voters in the 1996 presidential election were women.

More Women Than Men

At older ages, women outnumber men by a wide margin.

There are more females than males in America, even though in any given year more boys are born than girls. Males continue to outnumber females until they are in their mid-twenties, when parity is reached. After that age, women begin to outnumber men by a growing margin. Fifty-one percent of all Americans are female. But the proportion ranges from a low of 49 percent among people under age 25 to a high of 82 percent among Americans aged 100 or older.

The reason for the numerical superiority of women lies in the differing death rates of males and females. Simply put, women outlive men. This continues to be true despite medical advances and lifestyle changes that might, in theory, bring greater equality to life expectancy. Females, it appears, are biologically sturdier than males.

❖ With 6 million more females than males in the United States, women account for the majority of consumers—especially in the older age groups.

With age, females outnumber males by a growing margin

(female share of population by age, 2000)

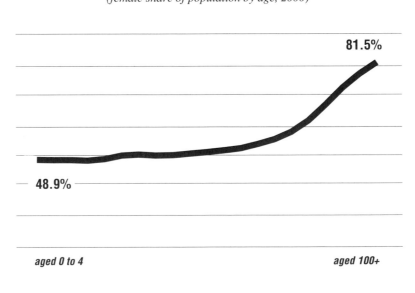

81.5%

48.9%

aged 0 to 4   *aged 100+*

Population by Age and Sex, 2000

(number of people by age and sex and percent female, 2000; numbers in thousands)

	total	males	females number	females percent
Total people	**275,306**	**134,554**	**140,752**	**51.1%**
Aged 0 to 4	18,865	9,639	9,227	48.9
Aged 5 to 9	19,781	10,122	9,659	48.8
Aged 10 to 14	19,908	10,196	9,712	48.8
Aged 15 to 19	19,897	10,227	9,670	48.6
Aged 20 to 24	18,518	9,433	9,085	49.1
Aged 25 to 29	17,861	8,876	8,984	50.3
Aged 30 to 34	19,580	9,682	9,898	50.6
Aged 35 to 39	22,276	11,071	11,205	50.3
Aged 40 to 44	22,618	11,218	11,400	50.4
Aged 45 to 49	19,901	9,776	10,125	50.9
Aged 50 to 54	17,265	8,398	8,867	51.4
Aged 55 to 59	13,324	6,397	6,927	52.0
Aged 60 to 64	10,677	5,046	5,631	52.7
Aged 65 to 69	9,436	4,334	5,102	54.1
Aged 70 to 74	8,753	3,876	4,877	55.7
Aged 75 to 79	7,422	3,103	4,319	58.2
Aged 80 to 84	4,913	1,866	3,047	62.0
Aged 85 to 89	2,705	883	1,821	67.3
Aged 90 to 94	1,179	319	861	73.0
Aged 95 to 99	364	81	283	77.7
Aged 100 or older	65	12	53	81.5
Aged 18 to 24	26,596	13,572	13,023	49.0
Aged 18 or older	204,932	98,509	106,423	51.9
Aged 21 or older	192,760	92,273	100,487	52.1
Aged 65 or older	34,835	14,473	20,362	58.5

Source: Bureau of the Census, Projections of the Resident Population by Age, Sex, Race, and Hispanic Origin: 1999 to 2100, *Internet web site <http://www.census.gov/population/www/projections/natproj.html>; calculations by New Strategist*

Sixtysomethings to Grow Rapidly in the Coming Decade

A 50 percent increase in the number of 60-to-64-year-olds is projected.

The patterns of growth projected for the male and female populations of the United States for the next decade are similar. Analysts project the greatest growth for the oldest Americans. The number of men aged 100 or older should more than double between 2000 and 2010, while the number of women in the age group will grow 94 percent. Despite this rapid growth, centenarians will number only 129,000 in 10 years.

The most significant growth the Census Bureau forecasts for the coming decade is among 60-to-64-year-olds. The numbers of men and women aged 60 to 64 will climb more than 50 percent as the oldest boomers enter the age group. In contrast, the number of people in the 35-to-39 age group will decline as the small Generation X enters its late thirties.

The aging of the large baby-boom generation greatly influences the nation's mindset. When boomers were teens and young adults, youth issues commanded attention. Now that boomers are middle-aged, menopause, grandchildren, and retirement planning are taking center stage.

❖ As the shares of older men and women in the population expand, businesses that have long targeted the young will have to rethink their products, services, and marketing messages to appeal to fifty- and sixtysomething consumers.

Males by Age, 2000 and 2010

(number and percent distribution of males by age, 2000 and 2010; percent change in number, 2000–10; numbers in thousands)

	2000		2010		percent change 2000–10
	number	percent	number	percent	
Total males	**134,554**	**100.0%**	**146,679**	**100.0%**	**9.0%**
Under age 5	9,639	7.2	10,272	7.0	6.6
Aged 5 to 9	10,122	7.5	9,936	6.8	−1.8
Aged 10 to 14	10,196	7.6	10,183	6.9	−0.1
Aged 15 to 19	10,227	7.6	11,132	7.6	8.8
Aged 20 to 24	9,433	7.0	10,776	7.3	14.2
Aged 25 to 29	8,876	6.6	9,901	6.8	11.5
Aged 30 to 34	9,682	7.2	9,385	6.4	−3.1
Aged 35 to 39	11,071	8.2	9,380	6.4	−15.3
Aged 40 to 44	11,218	8.3	10,069	6.9	−10.2
Aged 45 to 49	9,776	7.3	10,967	7.5	12.2
Aged 50 to 54	8,398	6.2	10,739	7.3	27.9
Aged 55 to 59	6,397	4.8	9,248	6.3	44.6
Aged 60 to 64	5,046	3.8	7,725	5.3	53.1
Aged 65 to 69	4,334	3.2	5,640	3.8	30.1
Aged 70 to 74	3,876	2.9	4,066	2.8	4.9
Aged 75 to 79	3,103	2.3	3,110	2.1	0.2
Aged 80 to 84	1,866	1.4	2,247	1.5	20.4
Aged 85 to 89	883	0.7	1,242	0.8	40.7
Aged 90 to 94	319	0.2	497	0.3	55.8
Aged 95 to 99	81	0.1	139	0.1	71.6
Aged 100 or older	12	0.0	26	0.0	116.7
Aged 18 to 24	13,572	10.1	15,388	10.5	13.4
Aged 18 or older	98,509	73.2	109,768	74.8	11.4
Aged 21 or older	92,273	68.6	102,806	70.1	11.4
Aged 65 or older	14,473	10.8	16,966	11.6	17.2

Source: Bureau of the Census, Projections of the Resident Population by Age, Sex, Race, and Hispanic Origin: 1999 to 2100, *Internet web site <http://www.census.gov/population/www/projections/natproj.html>; calculations by New Strategist*

Females by Age, 2000 and 2010

(number and percent distribution of females by age, 2000 and 2010; percent change in number, 2000–10; numbers in thousands)

	2000		2010		percent change 2000–10
	number	*percent*	*number*	*percent*	
Total females	**140,752**	**100.0%**	**153,183**	**100.0%**	**8.8%**
Under age 5	9,227	6.6	9,827	6.4	6.5
Aged 5 to 9	9,659	6.9	9,502	6.2	−1.6
Aged 10 to 14	9,712	6.9	9,724	6.3	0.1
Aged 15 to 19	9,670	6.9	10,536	6.9	9.0
Aged 20 to 24	9,085	6.5	10,375	6.8	14.2
Aged 25 to 29	8,984	6.4	9,948	6.5	10.7
Aged 30 to 34	9,898	7.0	9,617	6.3	−2.8
Aged 35 to 39	11,205	8.0	9,659	6.3	−13.8
Aged 40 to 44	11,400	8.1	10,334	6.7	−9.4
Aged 45 to 49	10,125	7.2	11,260	7.4	11.2
Aged 50 to 54	8,867	6.3	11,195	7.3	26.3
Aged 55 to 59	6,927	4.9	9,929	6.5	43.3
Aged 60 to 64	5,631	4.0	8,528	5.6	51.4
Aged 65 to 69	5,102	3.6	6,520	4.3	27.8
Aged 70 to 74	4,877	3.5	4,929	3.2	1.1
Aged 75 to 79	4,319	3.1	4,065	2.7	−5.9
Aged 80 to 84	3,047	2.2	3,353	2.2	10.0
Aged 85 to 89	1,821	1.3	2,234	1.5	22.7
Aged 90 to 94	861	0.6	1,128	0.7	31.0
Aged 95 to 99	283	0.2	417	0.3	47.3
Aged 100 or older	53	0.0	103	0.1	94.3
Aged 18 to 24	13,023	9.3	14,775	9.6	13.5
Aged 18 or older	106,423	75.6	117,993	77.0	10.9
Aged 21 or older	100,487	71.4	111,355	72.7	10.8
Aged 65 or older	20,362	14.5	22,749	14.9	11.7

Source: Bureau of the Census, Projections of the Resident Population by Age, Sex, Race, and Hispanic Origin: 1999 to 2100, *Internet web site <http://www.census.gov/population/www/projections/natproj.html>; calculations by New Strategist*

Females Outnumber Males in Nearly Every Racial and Ethnic Group

Among Hispanics, however, males slightly outnumber females.

Among all Americans, females outnumber males by a considerable margin. This is also true for most racial and ethnic groups. Females account for 52 percent of Asian Americans, for example. They account for 53 percent of blacks. Among Hispanics, however, females are a slight minority. One reason why males outnumber females among Hispanics is the youthfulness of the Hispanic population, since males outnumber females among children and young adults regardless of race or ethnicity.

With age, women come to outnumber men. Regardless of race or ethnicity, at least 58 percent of Americans aged 65 or older are women. Among the oldest blacks and whites—those aged 90 or older—women account for more than 70 percent of the population.

❖ Women account for the majority of voters in every racial and ethnic group, a fact that should be of some importance to the nation's politicians.

Population by Age and Sex, 2000: Asians

(number of Asians by age and sex and percent female, 2000; numbers in thousands)

	total	males	females number	females percent
Total Asians	**11,275**	**5,397**	**5,878**	**52.1%**
Aged 0 to 4	930	471	459	49.4
Aged 5 to 9	908	467	440	48.5
Aged 10 to 14	855	440	415	48.5
Aged 15 to 19	848	429	419	49.4
Aged 20 to 24	797	393	405	50.8
Aged 25 to 29	909	418	491	54.0
Aged 30 to 34	988	455	533	53.9
Aged 35 to 39	983	468	515	52.4
Aged 40 to 44	934	442	492	52.7
Aged 45 to 49	802	375	427	53.2
Aged 50 to 54	648	299	349	53.9
Aged 55 to 59	457	213	244	53.4
Aged 60 to 64	362	168	194	53.6
Aged 65 to 69	289	125	164	56.7
Aged 70 to 74	231	95	135	58.4
Aged 75 to 79	166	70	96	57.8
Aged 80 to 84	93	39	54	58.1
Aged 85 to 89	47	19	28	59.6
Aged 90 to 94	20	8	12	60.0
Aged 95 to 99	7	3	4	57.1
Aged 100 or older	1	–	1	–
Aged 18 to 24	1,129	559	570	50.5
Aged 18 or older	8,066	3,757	4,309	53.4
Aged 21 or older	7,568	3,507	4,061	53.7
Aged 65 or older	853	360	494	57.9

Note: (–) means fewer than 500 people or not applicable.
Source: Bureau of the Census, Projections of the Resident Population by Age, Sex, Race, and Hispanic Origin: 1999 to 2100, *Internet web site <http://www.census.gov/population/www/projections/natproj.html>; calculations by New Strategist*

Population by Age and Sex, 2000: Blacks

(number of blacks by age and sex and percent female, 2000; numbers in thousands)

	total	males	females number	females percent
Total blacks	**35,332**	**16,781**	**18,551**	**52.5%**
Aged 0 to 4	2,784	1,413	1,371	49.2
Aged 5 to 9	3,087	1,568	1,519	49.2
Aged 10 to 14	3,173	1,613	1,560	49.2
Aged 15 to 19	3,056	1,555	1,500	49.1
Aged 20 to 24	2,787	1,379	1,408	50.5
Aged 25 to 29	2,592	1,240	1,352	52.2
Aged 30 to 34	2,659	1,249	1,411	53.1
Aged 35 to 39	2,900	1,364	1,536	53.0
Aged 40 to 44	2,816	1,322	1,494	53.1
Aged 45 to 49	2,326	1,068	1,258	54.1
Aged 50 to 54	1,810	813	997	55.1
Aged 55 to 59	1,331	582	749	56.3
Aged 60 to 64	1,086	463	622	57.3
Aged 65 to 69	940	401	539	57.3
Aged 70 to 74	758	314	444	58.6
Aged 75 to 79	564	221	343	60.8
Aged 80 to 84	342	122	221	64.6
Aged 85 to 89	185	58	126	68.1
Aged 90 to 94	92	26	66	71.7
Aged 95 to 99	37	9	28	75.7
Aged 100 or older	9	2	7	77.8
Aged 18 to 24	4,026	2,004	2,022	50.2
Aged 18 or older	24,472	11,258	13,215	54.0
Aged 21 or older	22,601	10,315	12,286	54.4
Aged 65 or older	2,927	1,153	1,774	60.6

Source: Bureau of the Census, Projections of the Resident Population by Age, Sex, Race, and Hispanic Origin: 1999 to 2100, *Internet web site <http://www.census.gov/population/www/projections/natproj.html>; calculations by New Strategist*

Population by Age and Sex, 2000: Hispanics

(number of Hispanics by age and sex and percent female, 2000; numbers in thousands)

	total	males	females number	females percent
Total Hispanics	**32,479**	**16,312**	**16,167**	**49.8%**
Aged 0 to 4	3,549	1,811	1,738	49.0
Aged 5 to 9	3,347	1,709	1,638	48.9
Aged 10 to 14	2,874	1,469	1,405	48.9
Aged 15 to 19	2,848	1,479	1,369	48.1
Aged 20 to 24	2,801	1,454	1,347	48.1
Aged 25 to 29	2,624	1,337	1,287	49.0
Aged 30 to 34	2,692	1,385	1,307	48.6
Aged 35 to 39	2,668	1,370	1,298	48.7
Aged 40 to 44	2,274	1,150	1,124	49.4
Aged 45 to 49	1,760	870	889	50.5
Aged 50 to 54	1,344	647	697	51.9
Aged 55 to 59	985	461	524	53.2
Aged 60 to 64	775	353	422	54.5
Aged 65 to 69	635	282	352	55.4
Aged 70 to 74	513	224	289	56.3
Aged 75 to 79	372	159	213	57.3
Aged 80 to 84	216	84	132	61.1
Aged 85 to 89	124	43	80	64.5
Aged 90 to 94	56	18	38	67.9
Aged 95 to 99	19	6	13	68.4
Aged 100 or older	3	2	5	166.7
Aged 18 to 24	3,978	2,067	1,911	48.0
Aged 18 or older	21,037	10,457	10,580	50.3
Aged 21 or older	19,259	9,530	9,729	50.5
Aged 65 or older	1,938	817	1,121	57.8

Source: Bureau of the Census, Projections of the Resident Population by Age, Sex, Race, and Hispanic Origin: 1999 to 2100, *Internet web site <http://www.census.gov/population/www/projections/natproj.html>; calculations by New Strategist*

Population by Age and Sex, 2000: Native Americans

(number of Native Americans by age and sex and percent female, 2000; numbers in thousands)

	total	males	females number	females percent
Total Native Americans	**2,433**	**1,204**	**1,230**	**50.6%**
Aged 0 to 4	203	103	101	49.8
Aged 5 to 9	212	108	104	49.1
Aged 10 to 14	254	129	125	49.2
Aged 15 to 19	238	120	119	50.0
Aged 20 to 24	202	101	101	50.0
Aged 25 to 29	192	98	94	49.0
Aged 30 to 34	184	94	89	48.4
Aged 35 to 39	185	93	92	49.7
Aged 40 to 44	177	87	90	50.8
Aged 45 to 49	148	72	76	51.4
Aged 50 to 54	118	57	61	51.7
Aged 55 to 59	86	41	46	53.5
Aged 60 to 64	66	31	36	54.5
Aged 65 to 69	51	23	28	54.9
Aged 70 to 74	41	18	23	56.1
Aged 75 to 79	33	14	19	57.6
Aged 80 to 84	20	8	12	60.0
Aged 85 to 89	12	4	8	66.7
Aged 90 to 94	6	2	4	66.7
Aged 95 to 99	3	1	2	66.7
Aged 100 or older	1	–	1	–
Aged 18 to 24	292	146	146	50.0
Aged 18 or older	1,616	790	827	51.2
Aged 21 or older	1,481	722	760	51.3
Aged 65 or older	167	70	96	57.5

Note: (–) means fewer than 500 people or not applicable.
Source: Bureau of the Census, Projections of the Resident Population by Age, Sex, Race, and Hispanic Origin: 1999 to 2100, Internet web site <http://www.census.gov/population/www/projections/natproj.html>; calculations by New Strategist

Population by Age and Sex, 2000: Whites

(number of whites by age and sex and percent female, 2000; numbers in thousands)

	total	males	females number	females percent
Total whites	**226,266**	**111,172**	**115,094**	**50.9%**
Aged 0 to 4	14,948	7,653	7,295	48.8
Aged 5 to 9	15,575	7,979	7,596	48.8
Aged 10 to 14	15,626	8,014	7,612	48.7
Aged 15 to 19	15,755	8,123	7,632	48.4
Aged 20 to 24	14,732	7,560	7,171	48.7
Aged 25 to 29	14,166	7,120	7,046	49.7
Aged 30 to 34	15,749	7,884	7,865	49.9
Aged 35 to 39	18,209	9,147	9,062	49.8
Aged 40 to 44	18,691	9,367	9,324	49.9
Aged 45 to 49	16,625	8,262	8,364	50.3
Aged 50 to 54	14,689	7,228	7,460	50.8
Aged 55 to 59	11,450	5,561	5,888	51.4
Aged 60 to 64	9,163	4,384	4,779	52.2
Aged 65 to 69	8,156	3,785	4,371	53.6
Aged 70 to 74	7,723	3,448	4,275	55.4
Aged 75 to 79	6,658	2,797	3,861	58.0
Aged 80 to 84	4,458	1,697	2,761	61.9
Aged 85 to 89	2,461	802	1,659	67.4
Aged 90 to 94	1,061	283	778	73.3
Aged 95 to 99	317	68	249	78.5
Aged 100 or older	54	9	45	83.3
Aged 18 to 24	21,148	10,862	10,285	48.6
Aged 18 or older	170,778	82,705	88,073	51.6
Aged 21 or older	161,110	77,727	83,382	51.8
Aged 65 or older	30,888	12,890	17,998	58.3

Source: Bureau of the Census, Projections of the Resident Population by Age, Sex, Race, and Hispanic Origin: 1999 to 2100, *Internet web site <http://www.census.gov/population/www/projections/natproj.html>; calculations by New Strategist*

Population by Age and Sex, 2000: Non-Hispanic Whites

(number of non Hispanic whites by age and sex and percent female, 2000; numbers in thousands)

	total	*males*	females *number*	*percent*
Total non-Hispanic whites	**196,670**	**96,299**	**100,371**	**51.0%**
Aged 0 to 4	11,699	5,996	5,704	48.8
Aged 5 to 9	12,520	6,421	6,100	48.7
Aged 10 to 14	13,030	6,688	6,342	48.7
Aged 15 to 19	13,165	6,776	6,388	48.5
Aged 20 to 24	12,167	6,226	5,942	48.8
Aged 25 to 29	11,769	5,895	5,874	49.9
Aged 30 to 34	13,304	6,624	6,680	50.2
Aged 35 to 39	15,786	7,902	7,884	49.9
Aged 40 to 44	16,631	8,324	8,306	49.9
Aged 45 to 49	15,030	7,473	7,557	50.3
Aged 50 to 54	13,466	6,639	6,826	50.7
Aged 55 to 59	10,551	5,140	5,411	51.3
Aged 60 to 64	8,455	4,060	4,394	52.0
Aged 65 to 69	7,574	3,526	4,048	53.4
Aged 70 to 74	7,250	3,241	4,009	55.3
Aged 75 to 79	6,313	2,649	3,663	58.0
Aged 80 to 84	4,257	1,619	2,638	62.0
Aged 85 to 89	2,345	761	1,584	67.5
Aged 90 to 94	1,008	266	742	73.6
Aged 95 to 99	299	63	236	78.9
Aged 100 or older	51	8	42	82.4
Aged 18 to 24	17,510	8,969	8,542	48.8
Aged 18 or older	151,599	73,161	78,438	51.7
Aged 21 or older	143,555	69,030	74,522	51.9
Aged 65 or older	29,097	12,134	16,963	58.3

Source: Bureau of the Census, Projections of the Resident Population by Age, Sex, Race, and Hispanic Origin: 1999 to 2100, *Internet web site <http://www.census.gov/population/www/projections/natproj.html>; calculations by New Strategist*

Diversity of Males and Females Is Greatest among the Young

Non-Hispanic whites are a much larger share of older Americans.

Only 62 percent of the nation's preschoolers—boys and girls under age 5—are non-Hispanic white. In contrast, non-Hispanic whites account for 83 to 84 percent of men and women aged 65 or older. The diversity gap between young and old, combined with the generation gap, creates populations with very different wants and needs.

Because the Hispanic population is growing much faster than the black population, Hispanics will soon be the largest minority in the United States. Among males, Hispanics already outnumber non-Hispanic blacks. Hispanics account for 12.1 percent of the nation's males, non-Hispanic blacks for 11.8 percent. Among females, non-Hispanic blacks continue to hold a slight edge—12.5 percent of females are non-Hispanic black while 11.5 percent are Hispanic. Asians trail far behind, accounting for slightly fewer than 4 percent of males and females. Native Americans represent less than 1 percent of the population.

Hispanics may be of any race, but more than 90 percent are white. Slightly fewer than 6 percent of Hispanics are black, with 1 to 2 percent of Hispanics being Asian or Native American.

❖ As the diverse younger generations age, the wants and needs of minorities will gain much greater influence in the consumer marketplace.

Males of Non-Hispanic Origin by Age and Race, 2000

(number and percent distribution of males of non-Hispanic origin by age and race, 2000; numbers in thousands)

| | | non-Hispanic | | | | | | | non-Hispanic | | | | | |
	total	total	white	black	Native American	Asian	Hispanic	total	total	white	black	Native American	Asian	Hispanic
Total males	**134,554**	**118,242**	**96,299**	**15,863**	**1,006**	**5,074**	**16,312**	**100.0%**	**87.9%**	**71.6%**	**11.8%**	**0.7%**	**3.8%**	**12.1%**
Under age 5	9,639	7,828	5,996	1,312	83	437	1,811	100.0	81.2	62.2	13.6	0.9	4.5	18.8
Aged 5 to 9	10,122	8,413	6,421	1,471	89	433	1,709	100.0	83.1	63.4	14.5	0.9	4.3	16.9
Aged 10 to 14	10,196	8,727	6,688	1,524	107	407	1,469	100.0	85.6	65.6	14.9	1.0	4.0	14.4
Aged 15 to 19	10,227	8,748	6,776	1,474	99	399	1,479	100.0	85.5	66.3	14.4	1.0	3.9	14.5
Aged 20 to 24	9,433	7,979	6,226	1,304	83	366	1,454	100.0	84.6	66.0	13.8	0.9	3.9	15.4
Aged 25 to 29	8,876	7,539	5,895	1,173	80	391	1,337	100.0	84.9	66.4	13.2	0.9	4.4	15.1
Aged 30 to 34	9,682	8,297	6,624	1,171	76	427	1,385	100.0	85.7	68.4	12.1	0.8	4.4	14.3
Aged 35 to 39	11,071	9,701	7,902	1,282	77	441	1,370	100.0	87.6	71.4	11.6	0.7	4.0	12.4
Aged 40 to 44	11,218	10,068	8,324	1,251	73	418	1,150	100.0	89.7	74.2	11.2	0.7	3.7	10.3
Aged 45 to 49	9,776	8,906	7,473	1,015	61	357	870	100.0	91.1	76.4	10.4	0.6	3.7	8.9
Aged 50 to 54	8,398	7,751	6,639	776	50	286	647	100.0	92.3	79.1	9.2	0.6	3.4	7.7
Aged 55 to 59	6,397	5,936	5,140	556	36	204	461	100.0	92.8	80.4	8.7	0.6	3.2	7.2
Aged 60 to 64	5,046	4,693	4,060	443	27	161	353	100.0	93.0	80.5	8.8	0.5	3.2	7.0
Aged 65 to 69	4,334	4,052	3,526	385	21	120	282	100.0	93.5	81.4	8.9	0.5	2.8	6.5

(continued)

(continued from previous page)

	total	non-Hispanic				Asian	Hispanic	total	non-Hispanic				Asian	Hispanic
		total	white	black	Native American				total	white	black	Native American		
Aged 70 to 74	3,876	3,652	3,241	303	17	92	224	100.0%	94.2%	83.6%	7.8%	0.4%	2.4%	5.8%
Aged 75 to 79	3,103	2,944	2,649	214	13	68	159	100.0	94.9	85.4	6.9	0.4	2.2	5.1
Aged 80 to 84	1,866	1,782	1,619	118	7	38	84	100.0	95.5	86.8	6.3	0.4	2.0	4.5
Aged 85 or older	1,295	1,226	1,098	93	7	28	69	100.0	94.7	84.8	7.2	0.5	2.2	5.3
Aged 18 to 24	13,572	11,505	8,969	1,896	120	521	2,067	100.0	84.8	66.1	14.0	0.9	3.8	15.2
Aged 18 or older	98,509	88,052	73,161	10,674	665	3,552	10,457	100.0	89.4	74.3	10.8	0.7	3.6	10.6
Aged 21 or older	92,273	82,743	69,029	9,783	610	3,319	9,530	100.0	89.7	74.8	10.6	0.7	3.6	10.3
Aged 65 or older	14,473	13,656	12,134	1,112	64	347	817	100.0	94.4	83.8	7.7	0.4	2.4	5.6

Source: Bureau of the Census, Projections of the Resident Population by Age, Sex, Race, and Hispanic Origin: 1999 to 2100, Internet web site <http://www.census.gov /population/www/projections/natproj.html>; calculations by New Strategist

Females of Non-Hispanic Origin by Age and Race, 2000

(number and percent distribution of females of non-Hispanic origin by age and race, 2000; numbers in thousands)

	total	non-Hispanic					total	non-Hispanic					
		total	white	black	Native American	Asian		total	white	black	Native American	Asian	Hispanic
													Hispanic
Total females	**140,752**	**124,585**	**100,371**	**17,627**	**1,042**	**5,546**	**16,167**	**100.0%**	**88.5%**	**71.3%**	**12.5%**	**0.7%**	**3.9%**	**11.5%**
Under age 5	9,227	7,489	5,704	1,276	82	427	1,738	100.0	81.2	61.8	13.8	0.9	4.6	18.8
Aged 5 to 9	9,659	8,021	6,100	1,427	87	407	1,638	100.0	83.0	63.2	14.8	0.9	4.2	17.0
Aged 10 to 14	9,712	8,307	6,342	1,478	104	384	1,405	100.0	85.5	65.3	15.2	1.1	4.0	14.5
Aged 15 to 19	9,670	8,301	6,388	1,424	99	390	1,369	100.0	85.8	66.1	14.7	1.0	4.0	14.2
Aged 20 to 24	9,085	7,738	5,942	1,334	83	379	1,347	100.0	85.2	65.4	14.7	0.9	4.2	14.8
Aged 25 to 29	8,984	7,697	5,874	1,281	78	465	1,287	100.0	85.7	65.4	14.3	0.9	5.2	14.3
Aged 30 to 34	9,898	8,591	6,680	1,333	74	504	1,307	100.0	86.8	67.5	13.5	0.7	5.1	13.2
Aged 35 to 39	11,205	9,907	7,884	1,457	77	488	1,298	100.0	88.4	70.4	13.0	0.7	4.4	11.6
Aged 40 to 44	11,400	10,276	8,306	1,426	77	468	1,124	100.0	90.1	72.9	12.5	0.7	4.1	9.9
Aged 45 to 49	10,125	9,236	7,557	1,205	66	407	889	100.0	91.2	74.6	11.9	0.7	4.0	8.8
Aged 50 to 54	8,867	8,170	6,826	956	54	334	697	100.0	92.1	77.0	10.8	0.6	3.8	7.9
Aged 55 to 59	6,927	6,403	5,411	719	41	233	524	100.0	92.4	78.1	10.4	0.6	3.4	7.6
Aged 60 to 64	5,631	5,209	4,394	597	32	186	422	100.0	92.5	78.0	10.6	0.6	3.3	7.5
Aged 65 to 69	5,102	4,750	4,048	518	25	158	352	100.0	93.1	79.3	10.2	0.5	3.1	6.9

(continued)

(continued from previous page)

		non-Hispanic								non-Hispanic				
	total	total	white	black	Native American	Asian	Hispanic	total	total	white	black	Native American	Asian	Hispanic
Aged 70 to 74	4,877	4,588	4,009	428	20	130	289	100.0%	94.1%	82.2%	8.8%	0.4%	2.7%	5.9%
Aged 75 to 79	4,319	4,106	3,663	332	17	93	213	100.0	95.1	84.8	7.7	0.4	2.2	4.9
Aged 80 to 84	3,047	2,915	2,638	215	11	52	132	100.0	95.7	86.6	7.1	0.4	1.7	4.3
Aged 85 or older	3,018	2,883	2,604	222	14	43	136	100.0	95.5	86.3	7.4	0.5	1.4	4.5
Aged 18 to 24	13,023	11,112	8,542	1,917	120	533	1,911	100.0	85.3	65.6	14.7	0.9	4.1	14.7
Aged 18 or older	106,423	95,843	78,438	12,605	708	4,091	10,580	100.0	90.1	73.7	11.8	0.7	3.8	9.9
Aged 21 or older	100,488	90,759	74,522	11,724	651	3,862	9,729	100.0	90.3	74.2	11.7	0.6	3.8	9.7
Aged 65 or older	20,362	19,241	16,963	1,715	88	475	1,121	100.0	94.5	83.3	8.4	0.4	2.3	5.5

Source: Bureau of the Census, Projections of the Resident Population by Age, Sex, Race, and Hispanic Origin: 1999 to 2100, Internet web site <http://www.census.gov /population/www/projections/natproj.html>; calculations by New Strategist

Males of Hispanic Origin by Age and Race, 2000

(number and percent distribution of males of Hispanic origin by age and race, 2000; numbers in thousands)

	Hispanic					Hispanic				
	total	white	black	Native American	Asian	total	white	black	Native American	Asian
Total males	16,312	14,873	918	198	323	100.0%	91.2%	5.6%	1.2%	2.0%
Under age 5	1,811	1,657	101	20	34	100.0	91.5	5.6	1.1	1.9
Aged 5 to 9	1,709	1,558	97	19	34	100.0	91.2	5.7	1.1	2.0
Aged 10 to 14	1,469	1,326	89	22	33	100.0	90.3	6.1	1.5	2.2
Aged 15 to 19	1,479	1,347	81	21	30	100.0	91.1	5.5	1.4	2.0
Aged 20 to 24	1,454	1,334	75	18	27	100.0	91.7	5.2	1.2	1.9
Aged 25 to 29	1,337	1,225	67	18	27	100.0	91.6	5.0	1.3	2.0
Aged 30 to 34	1,385	1,260	78	18	28	100.0	91.0	5.6	1.3	2.0
Aged 35 to 39	1,370	1,245	82	16	27	100.0	90.9	6.0	1.2	2.0
Aged 40 to 44	1,150	1,043	71	14	24	100.0	90.7	6.2	1.2	2.1
Aged 45 to 49	870	789	53	11	18	100.0	90.7	6.1	1.3	2.1
Aged 50 to 54	647	589	37	7	13	100.0	91.0	5.7	1.1	2.0
Aged 55 to 59	461	421	26	5	9	100.0	91.3	5.6	1.1	2.0
Aged 60 to 64	353	324	20	4	7	100.0	91.8	5.7	1.1	2.0
Aged 65 to 69	282	259	16	2	5	100.0	91.8	5.7	0.7	1.8

(continued)

(continued from previous page)

| | Hispanic | | | | | Hispanic | | | |
	total	white	black	Native American	Asian	total	white	black	Native American	Asian
Aged 70 to 74	224	207	11	1	3	100.0%	92.4%	4.9%	0.4%	1.3%
Aged 75 to 79	159	148	7	1	2	100.0	93.1	4.4	0.6	1.3
Aged 80 to 84	84	78	4	1	1	100.0	92.9	4.8	1.2	1.2
Aged 85 or older	69	64	2	–	2	100.0	92.8	2.9	–	2.9
Aged 18 to 24	2,067	1,893	108	26	38	100.0	91.6	5.2	1.3	1.8
Aged 18 or older	10,457	9,544	584	125	204	100.0	91.3	5.6	1.2	2.0
Aged 21 or older	9,530	8,698	532	112	188	100.0	90.6	5.5	1.2	2.0
Aged 65 or older	817	756	41	6	13	100.0	92.5	5.0	0.7	1.6

Note: (–) means fewer than 500 people.
Source: Bureau of the Census, Projections of the Resident Population by Age, Sex, Race, and Hispanic Origin: 1999 to 2100, Internet web site <http://www.census.gov /population/www/projections/natproj.html>; calculations by New Strategist

Females of Hispanic Origin by Age and Race, 2000

(number and percent distribution of females of Hispanic origin by age and race, 2000; numbers in thousands)

	total	white	black	Native American	Asian	total	white	black	Native American	Asian
			Hispanic					Hispanic		
Total females	16,167	14,723	924	188	332	100.0%	91.1%	5.7%	1.2%	2.1%
Under age 5	1,738	1,591	95	19	32	100.0	91.5	5.5	1.1	1.8
Aged 5 to 9	1,638	1,496	92	17	33	100.0	91.3	5.6	1.0	2.0
Aged 10 to 14	1,405	1,270	82	21	31	100.0	90.4	5.8	1.5	2.2
Aged 15 to 19	1,369	1,244	76	20	29	100.0	90.9	5.6	1.5	2.1
Aged 20 to 24	1,347	1,229	74	18	26	100.0	91.2	5.5	1.3	1.9
Aged 25 to 29	1,287	1,172	71	16	26	100.0	91.1	5.5	1.2	2.0
Aged 30 to 34	1,307	1,185	78	15	29	100.0	90.7	6.0	1.1	2.2
Aged 35 to 39	1,298	1,178	79	15	27	100.0	90.8	6.1	1.2	2.1
Aged 40 to 44	1,124	1,018	68	13	24	100.0	90.6	6.0	1.2	2.1
Aged 45 to 49	889	807	53	10	20	100.0	90.8	6.0	1.1	2.2
Aged 50 to 54	697	634	41	7	15	100.0	91.0	5.9	1.0	2.2
Aged 55 to 59	524	477	30	5	11	100.0	91.0	5.7	1.0	2.1
Aged 60 to 64	422	385	25	4	8	100.0	91.2	5.9	0.9	1.9
Aged 65 to 69	352	323	21	3	6	100.0	91.8	6.0	0.9	1.7

(continued)

(continued from previous page)

	total	white	Hispanic black	Native American	Asian	total	white	Hispanic black	Native American	Asian
Aged 70 to 74	289	266	16	3	5	100.0%	92.0%	5.5%	1.0%	1.7%
Aged 75 to 79	213	198	11	2	3	100.0	93.0	5.2	0.9	1.4
Aged 80 to 84	132	123	6	1	2	100.0	93.2	4.5	0.8	1.5
Aged 85 or older	136	127	5	1	2	100.0	93.4	3.7	0.7	1.5
Aged 18 to 24	1,911	1,743	105	26	37	100.0	91.2	5.5	1.4	1.9
Aged 18 or older	10,580	9,635	610	119	218	100.0	91.1	5.8	1.1	2.1
Aged 21 or older	9,730	8,860	562	109	199	100.0	91.1	5.8	1.1	2.0
Aged 65 or older	1,121	1,035	59	8	19	100.0	92.3	5.3	0.7	1.7

Source: Bureau of the Census, Projections of the Resident Population by Age, Sex, Race, and Hispanic Origin: 1999 to 2100, Internet web site <http://www.census.gov /population/www/projections/natproj.html>; calculations by New Strategist

Diversity Is Greatest in the South and West

Minorities are already the majority in a handful of states.

The West is the most diverse region. Only 61 percent of Americans living in the region are non-Hispanic white. Hispanics are the largest minority in the West, accounting for 23 and 24 percent, respectively, of the females and males living there. In the South, non-Hispanic whites account for only 68 and 69 percent of the female and male populations. Nineteen percent of males and 20 percent of females living in the South are black.

Among both males and females, non-Hispanic whites are a minority in California, the District of Columbia, Hawaii, and New Mexico. Non-Hispanic whites account for only 56 percent of the population of Texas. In contrast, non-Hispanic whites are fully 94 percent of the population of Iowa, 95 percent of West Virginia's population, and 97 percent of the populations of New Hampshire and Vermont.

❖ Regional and state differences in diversity make marketing to men and women a complex task, requiring a different strategy in California than in South Carolina, for example.

Males by Region, Race, and Hispanic Origin, 2000

(number and percent distribution of males by region, race, and Hispanic origin, 2000; numbers in thousands)

	total	black	Native American	Asian	white	Hispanic	non-Hispanic white
Total males	**134,174**	**16,804**	**1,184**	**5,388**	**110,798**	**15,796**	**96,437**
Northeast	25,181	3,087	72	1,018	21,004	2,457	19,064
Midwest	30,968	3,093	201	586	27,088	1,250	25,943
South	47,455	8,953	329	906	37,267	4,785	32,794
West	30,570	1,671	582	2,878	25,439	7,304	18,636

Percent distribution by race and Hispanic origin

	total	black	Native American	Asian	white	Hispanic	non-Hispanic white
Total males	**100.0%**	**12.5%**	**0.9%**	**4.0%**	**82.6%**	**11.8%**	**71.9%**
Northeast	100.0	12.3	0.3	4.0	83.4	9.8	75.7
Midwest	100.0	10.0	0.6	1.9	87.5	4.0	83.8
South	100.0	18.9	0.7	1.9	78.5	10.1	69.1
West	100.0	5.5	1.9	9.4	83.2	23.9	61.0

Percent distribution by region

	total	black	Native American	Asian	white	Hispanic	non-Hispanic white
Total males	**100.0%**	**100.0%**	**100.0%**	**100.0%**	**100.0%**	**100.0%**	**100.0%**
Northeast	18.8	18.4	6.1	18.9	19.0	15.6	19.8
Midwest	23.1	18.4	17.0	10.9	24.4	7.9	26.9
South	35.4	53.3	27.8	16.8	33.6	30.3	34.0
West	22.8	9.9	49.2	53.4	23.0	46.2	19.3

Note: The U.S. totals by race in this table are slightly different from the U.S. totals shown in the national tables because the state figures are from an earlier projection series. Numbers will not add to total because Hispanics may be of any race.
Source: Bureau of the Census, Internet web site <http://www.census.gov/population/projections/state/stpjrace .txt>; calculations by New Strategist

Females by Region, Race, and Hispanic Origin, 2000

(number and percent distribution of females by region, race, and Hispanic origin, 2000; numbers in thousands)

	total	black	Native American	Asian	white	Hispanic	non-Hispanic white
Total females	**140,447**	**18,637**	**1,217**	**5,857**	**114,736**	**15,564**	**100,625**
Northeast	26,923	3,486	75	1,086	22,276	2,558	20,263
Midwest	32,532	3,458	205	629	28,240	1,189	27,153
South	50,145	10,024	335	996	38,790	4,814	34,286
West	30,847	1,669	602	3,146	25,430	7,003	18,923
Percent distribution by race and Hispanic origin							
Total females	**100.0%**	**13.3%**	**0.9%**	**4.2%**	**81.7%**	**11.1%**	**71.6%**
Northeast	100.0	12.9	0.3	4.0	82.7	9.5	75.3
Midwest	100.0	10.6	0.6	1.9	86.8	3.7	83.5
South	100.0	20.0	0.7	2.0	77.4	9.6	68.4
West	100.0	5.4	2.0	10.2	82.4	22.7	61.3
Percent distribution by region							
Total females	**100.0%**	**100.0%**	**100.0%**	**100.0%**	**100.0%**	**100.0%**	**100.0%**
Northeast	19.2	18.7	6.2	18.5	19.4	16.4	20.1
Midwest	23.2	18.6	16.8	10.7	24.6	7.6	27.0
South	35.7	53.8	27.5	17.0	33.8	30.9	34.1
West	22.0	9.0	49.5	53.7	22.2	45.0	18.8

Note: The U.S. totals by race in this table are slightly different from the U.S. totals shown in the national tables because the state figures are from an earlier projection series. Numbers will not add to total because Hispanics may be of any race.

Source: Bureau of the Census, Internet web site <http://www.census.gov/population/projections/state/stpjrace .txt>; calculations by New Strategist

Males by State, Race, and Hispanic Origin, 2000

(number and percent distribution of males by state, race, and Hispanic origin, 2000; numbers in thousands)

	total	black	Native American	Asian	white	Hispanic	non-Hispanic white	total	black	Native American	Asian	white	Hispanic	non-Hispanic white
Total males	**134,174**	**16,804**	**1,184**	**5,388**	**110,798**	**15,796**	**96,437**	**100.0%**	**12.5%**	**0.9%**	**4.0%**	**82.6%**	**11.8%**	**71.9%**
Alabama	2,140	527	9	16	1,588	19	1,572	100.0	24.6	0.4	0.7	74.2	0.9	73.5
Alaska	340	16	46	22	256	16	243	100.0	4.7	13.5	6.5	75.3	4.7	71.5
Arizona	2,368	90	127	51	2,100	537	1,600	100.0	3.8	5.4	2.2	88.7	22.7	67.6
Arkansas	1,269	190	7	9	1,063	17	1,047	100.0	15.0	0.6	0.7	83.8	1.3	82.5
California	16,216	1,198	145	2,052	12,821	5,452	7,717	100.0	7.4	0.9	12.7	79.1	33.6	47.6
Colorado	2,067	99	21	51	1,896	298	1,618	100.0	4.8	1.0	2.5	91.7	14.4	78.3
Connecticut	1,596	154	4	39	1,399	142	1,275	100.0	9.6	0.3	2.4	87.7	8.9	79.9
Delaware	374	70	1	7	296	13	285	100.0	18.7	0.3	1.9	79.1	3.5	76.2
District of Columbia	245	146	–	7	92	20	76	100.0	59.6	–	2.9	37.6	8.2	31.0
Florida	7,367	1,111	26	123	6,107	1,167	5,041	100.0	15.1	0.4	1.7	82.9	15.8	68.4
Georgia	3,831	1,071	9	68	2,683	101	2,594	100.0	28.0	0.2	1.8	70.0	2.6	67.7
Hawaii	632	19	3	383	227	54	196	100.0	3.0	0.5	60.6	35.9	8.5	31.0
Idaho	671	4	11	8	648	51	601	100.0	0.6	1.6	1.2	96.6	7.6	89.6
Illinois	5,877	875	13	204	4,785	657	4,170	100.0	14.9	0.2	3.5	81.4	11.2	71.0
Indiana	2,944	238	8	29	2,669	70	2,605	100.0	8.1	0.3	1.0	90.7	2.4	88.5
Iowa	1,414	31	5	21	1,357	28	1,332	100.0	2.2	0.4	1.5	96.0	2.0	94.2

(continued)

(continued from previous page)

	total	black	Native American	Asian	white	Hispanic	non-Hispanic white	total	black	Native American	Asian	white	Hispanic	non-Hispanic white
Kansas	1,314	86	13	24	1,191	71	1,126	100.0%	6.5%	1.0%	1.8%	90.6%	5.4%	85.7%
Kentucky	1,939	136	3	14	1,786	17	1,771	100.0	7.0	0.2	0.7	92.1	0.9	91.3
Louisiana	2,131	677	10	30	1,414	59	1,363	100.0	31.8	0.5	1.4	66.4	2.8	64.0
Maine	614	3	3	4	604	4	600	100.0	0.5	0.5	0.7	98.4	0.7	97.7
Maryland	2,562	702	8	106	1,746	107	1,658	100.0	27.4	0.3	4.1	68.1	4.2	64.7
Massachusetts	3,001	201	7	119	2,674	216	2,504	100.0	6.7	0.2	4.0	89.1	7.2	83.4
Michigan	4,714	672	30	78	3,934	131	3,818	100.0	14.3	0.6	1.7	83.5	2.8	81.0
Minnesota	2,379	80	32	67	2,200	49	2,158	100.0	3.4	1.3	2.8	92.5	2.1	90.7
Mississippi	1,350	471	4	9	866	11	856	100.0	34.9	0.3	0.7	64.1	0.8	63.4
Missouri	2,685	294	12	30	2,349	45	2,309	100.0	10.9	0.4	1.1	87.5	1.7	86.0
Montana	471	2	30	3	436	10	427	100.0	0.4	6.4	0.6	92.6	2.1	90.7
Nebraska	835	35	8	11	781	31	753	100.0	4.2	1.0	1.3	93.5	3.7	90.2
Nevada	943	69	15	40	819	144	687	100.0	7.3	1.6	4.2	86.9	15.3	72.9
New Hampshire	603	5	1	7	590	9	582	100.0	0.8	0.2	1.2	97.8	1.5	96.5
New Jersey	3,962	586	10	228	3,138	518	2,699	100.0	14.8	0.3	5.8	79.2	13.1	68.1
New Mexico	918	25	82	13	798	364	450	100.0	2.7	8.9	1.4	86.9	39.7	49.0
New York	8,741	1,537	35	498	6,671	1,360	5,649	100.0	17.6	0.4	5.7	76.3	15.6	64.6
North Carolina	3,777	814	46	46	2,871	54	2,816	100.0	21.6	1.2	1.2	76.0	1.7	74.6
North Dakota	328	3	16	3	306	3	303	100.0	0.9	4.9	0.9	93.3	0.9	92.4
Ohio	5,479	620	11	68	4,780	91	4,699	100.0	11.3	0.2	1.2	87.2	1.7	85.8
Oklahoma	1,648	137	137	25	1,349	54	1,294	100.0	8.3	8.3	1.5	81.9	3.9	78.5

(continued)

(continued from previous page)

	total	black	Native American	Asian	white	Hispanic	non-Hispanic white	total	black	Native American	Asian	white	Hispanic	non-Hispanic white
Oregon	1,674	33	25	55	1,561	103	1,467	100.0%	2.0%	1.5%	3.3%	93.2%	6.2%	87.6%
Pennsylvania	5,879	573	9	106	5,191	167	5,051	100.0	9.7	0.2	1.8	88.3	2.8	85.9
Rhode Island	482	27	2	14	439	38	409	100.0	5.6	0.4	2.9	91.1	7.9	84.9
South Carolina	1,862	538	4	15	1,305	22	1,286	100.0	28.9	0.2	0.8	70.1	1.2	69.1
South Dakota	382	3	29	2	348	4	344	100.0	0.8	7.6	0.5	91.1	1.0	90.1
Tennessee	2,733	434	6	27	2,266	29	2,240	100.0	15.9	0.2	1.0	82.9	1.1	82.0
Texas	9,909	1,227	48	272	8,362	2,932	5,547	100.0	12.4	0.5	2.7	84.4	29.6	56.0
Utah	1,099	12	18	30	1,039	70	975	100.0	1.1	1.6	2.7	94.5	6.4	88.7
Vermont	303	1	1	3	298	3	295	100.0	0.3	0.3	1.0	98.3	1.0	97.4
Virginia	3,433	675	10	127	2,621	138	2,501	100.0	19.7	0.3	3.7	76.3	4.0	72.9
Washington	2,909	101	53	168	2,587	188	2,420	100.0	3.5	1.8	5.8	88.9	6.5	83.2
West Virginia	885	27	1	5	852	5	847	100.0	3.1	0.1	0.6	96.3	0.6	95.7
Wisconsin	2,617	156	24	49	2,388	70	2,326	100.0	6.0	0.9	1.9	91.2	2.7	88.9
Wyoming	262	3	6	2	251	17	235	100.0	1.1	2.3	0.8	95.8	6.5	89.7

Note: The U.S. totals by race in this table are slightly different from the U.S. totals shown in the national tables because the state figures are from an earlier projection series. Numbers will not add to total because Hispanics may be of any race.

Source: Bureau of the Census, Internet web site <http://www.census.gov/population/projections/state/stpjrace.txt>; calculations by New Strategist

Females by State, Race, and Hispanic Origin, 2000

(number and percent distribution of females by state, race, and Hispanic origin, 2000; numbers in thousands)

	total	black	Native American	Asian	white	Hispanic	non-Hispanic white	total	black	Native American	Asian	white	Hispanic	non-Hispanic white
Total females	**140,447**	**18,637**	**1,217**	**5,857**	**114,736**	**15,564**	**100,625**	**100.0%**	**13.3%**	**0.9%**	**4.2%**	**81.7%**	**11.1%**	**71.6%**
Alabama	2,311	610	9	18	1,674	18	1,659	100.0	26.4	0.4	0.8	72.4	0.8	71.8
Alaska	314	13	47	24	230	15	218	100.0	4.1	15.0	7.6	73.2	4.8	69.4
Arizona	2,430	87	135	56	2,152	534	1,654	100.0	3.6	5.6	2.3	88.6	22.0	68.1
Arkansas	1,360	219	8	10	1,123	16	1,108	100.0	16.1	0.6	0.7	82.6	1.2	81.5
California	16,307	1,227	147	2,237	12,696	5,195	7,845	100.0	7.5	0.9	13.7	77.9	31.9	48.1
Colorado	2,101	97	20	57	1,927	296	1,650	100.0	4.6	1.0	2.7	91.7	14.1	78.5
Connecticut	1,689	170	4	41	1,474	146	1,347	100.0	10.1	0.2	2.4	87.3	3.6	79.8
Delaware	393	77	1	8	307	12	297	100.0	19.6	0.3	2.0	78.1	3.1	75.6
District of Columbia	275	175	–	8	92	20	76	100.0	63.6	–	2.9	33.5	7.3	27.6
Florida	7,865	1,215	25	144	6,481	1,223	5,364	100.0	15.4	0.3	1.8	82.4	15.5	68.2
Georgia	4,043	1,208	8	74	2,753	88	2,676	100.0	29.9	0.2	1.8	68.1	2.2	66.2
Hawaii	624	12	3	413	196	53	167	100.0	1.9	0.5	66.2	31.4	8.5	26.8
Idaho	675	4	10	9	652	45	610	100.0	0.6	1.5	1.3	96.6	6.7	90.4
Illinois	6,173	990	13	219	4,951	610	4,383	100.0	16.0	0.2	3.5	80.2	9.9	71.0
Indiana	3,100	264	8	31	2,797	70	2,733	100.0	8.5	0.3	1.0	90.2	2.3	88.2
Iowa	1,486	31	4	22	1,429	26	1,405	100.0	2.1	0.3	1.5	96.2	1.7	94.5

(continued)

(continued from previous page)

	total	black	Native American	Asian	white	Hispanic	non-Hispanic white	total	black	Native American	Asian	white	Hispanic	non-Hispanic white
Kansas	1,355	87	14	26	1,228	67	1,167	100.0%	6.4%	1.0%	1.9%	90.6%	4.9%	86.1%
Kentucky	2,054	151	3	15	1,885	15	1,872	100.0	7.4	0.1	0.7	91.8	0.7	91.1
Louisiana	2,294	771	10	32	1,481	60	1,429	100.0	33.6	0.4	1.4	64.6	2.6	62.3
Maine	644	2	3	5	634	4	630	100.0	0.3	0.5	0.8	98.4	0.6	97.8
Maryland	2,712	787	8	117	1,800	107	1,713	100.0	29.0	0.3	4.3	66.4	3.9	63.2
Massachusetts	3,199	216	7	127	2,849	221	2,678	100.0	6.8	0.2	4.0	89.1	6.9	83.7
Michigan	4,966	763	31	85	4,087	130	3,972	100.0	15.4	0.6	1.7	82.3	2.6	80.0
Minnesota	2,451	78	32	72	2,269	46	2,229	100.0	3.2	1.3	2.9	92.6	1.9	90.9
Mississippi	1,463	541	4	10	908	10	899	100.0	37.0	0.3	0.7	62.1	0.7	61.4
Misscuri	2,855	334	12	33	2,476	45	2,436	100.0	11.7	0.4	1.2	86.7	1.6	85.3
Montana	479	1	31	4	443	10	434	100.0	0.2	6.5	0.8	92.5	2.1	90.6
Nebraska	871	37	8	12	814	30	787	100.0	4.2	0.9	1.4	93.5	3.4	90.4
Nevada	930	69	16	45	800	133	679	100.0	7.4	1.7	4.8	86.0	14.3	73.0
New Hampshire	621	4	1	7	609	8	602	100.0	0.6	0.2	1.1	98.1	1.3	96.9
New Jersey	4,214	653	10	247	3,304	526	2,859	100.0	15.5	0.2	5.9	78.4	12.5	67.8
New Mexico	943	23	87	16	817	372	462	100.0	2.4	9.2	1.7	86.6	39.4	49.0
New York	9,406	1,762	38	530	7,076	1,445	5,991	100.0	18.7	0.4	5.6	75.2	15.4	63.7
North Carolina	4,002	924	48	50	2,980	57	2,932	100.0	23.1	1.2	1.2	74.5	1.4	73.3
North Dakota	332	2	16	3	311	3	308	100.0	0.6	4.8	0.9	93.7	0.9	92.8
Ohio	5,838	700	11	72	5,055	92	4,973	100.0	12.0	0.2	1.2	86.6	1.6	85.2
Oklahoma	1,725	145	144	26	1,410	60	1,359	100.0	8.4	8.3	1.5	81.7	3.5	78.8

(continued)

(continued from previous page)

	total	black	Native American	Asian	white	Hispanic	non-Hispanic white	total	black	Native American	Asian	white	Hispanic	non-Hispanic white
Oregon	1,725	32	26	61	1,606	92	1,523	100.0%	1.9%	1.5%	3.5%	93.1%	5.3%	88.3%
Pennsylvania	6,322	651	9	112	5,550	167	5,409	100.0	10.3	0.1	1.8	87.8	2.6	85.6
Rhode Island	515	27	2	14	472	38	442	100.0	5.2	0.4	2.7	91.7	7.4	85.8
South Carolina	1,995	618	4	18	1,355	20	1,338	100.0	31.0	0.2	0.9	67.9	1.0	67.1
South Dakota	394	2	31	3	358	4	354	100.0	0.5	7.9	0.8	90.9	1.0	89.8
Tennessee	2,923	495	6	30	2,392	28	2,367	100.0	16.9	0.2	1.0	81.8	1.0	81.0
Texas	10,211	1,316	47	290	8,558	2,943	5,726	100.0	12.9	0.5	2.8	83.8	23.8	56.1
Utah	1,109	10	19	32	1,048	68	986	100.0	0.9	1.7	2.9	94.5	5.1	88.9
Vermont	313	1	1	3	308	3	305	100.0	0.3	0.3	1.0	98.4	1.0	97.4
Virginia	3,564	741	9	140	2,674	131	2,560	100.0	20.8	0.3	3.9	75.0	3.7	71.8
Washington	2,948	91	54	190	2,613	172	2,461	100.0	3.1	1.8	6.4	88.6	5.8	83.5
West Virginia	955	31	1	6	917	6	911	100.0	3.2	0.1	0.6	96.0	0.6	95.4
Wisconsin	2,711	170	25	51	2,465	66	2,406	100.0	6.3	0.9	1.9	90.9	2.4	88.7
Wyoming	262	3	7	2	250	18	234	100.0	1.1	2.7	0.8	95.4	6.9	89.3

Note: The U.S. totals by race in this table are slightly different from the U.S. totals shown in the national tables because the state figures are from an earlier projection series. Numbers will not add to total because Hispanics may be of any race.

Source: Bureau of the Census, Internet web site <http://www.census.gov/population/projections/state/stpjrace.txt>; calculations by New Strategist

Rapid Growth in 65-or-Older Population by State

The number of older men will grow faster than the number of older women.

Women account for the 59 percent majority of Americans aged 65 or older today. This figure is projected to decline to 55 percent by 2025 as the baby-boom generation enters the age group and death rates for men continue their decline. While older women will still outnumber older men in every state, the margin will shrink. The number of men aged 65 or older will rise 96 percent while the number of women will grow 66 percent.

Many states will see dramatic growth in the numbers of elderly men and women between 2000 and 2025. In some states—particularly those in the West—the number of elderly men and women is projected to more than double. The greatest growth in elderly men is projected for Idaho, up 156 percent between 2000 and 2025. For elderly women, the fastest growth is projected for Alaska, with a 140 percent gain.

The number of elderly Americans will grow much more slowly in some states, such as Pennsylvania. There, the number of men aged 65 or older is projected to grow 56 percent between 2000 and 2025, while the number of elderly women will grow only 29 percent.

❖ Businesses targeting older Americans should pay close attention to their distribution by state, especially as boomers move to retirement areas beginning in a few years.

The number of older men will grow faster than the number of older women

(percent change in number of men and women aged 65 or older, 2000 to 2025)

96%

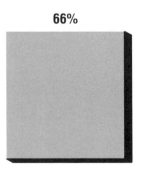

66%

men

women

People Aged 65 or Older by State and Sex, 2000 and 2025

(number of people aged 65 or older by state and sex, and percent female by state, 2000 and 2025; percent change in numbers of males and females, 2000–25; numbers in thousands)

| | 2000 | | | 2025 | | | percent change, 2000 to 2025 | |
| | | women | | | women | | | |
	men	number	percent	men	number	percent	men	women
Total people	**14,344**	**20,363**	**58.7%**	**28,093**	**33,861**	**54.7%**	**95.9%**	**66.3%**
Alabama	233	349	60.0	469	600	56.1	101.3	71.9
Alaska	18	20	52.6	44	48	52.2	144.4	140.0
Arizona	276	359	56.5	641	727	53.1	132.2	102.5
Arkansas	155	222	58.9	327	404	55.3	111.0	82.0
California	1,436	1,951	57.6	2,943	3,481	54.2	104.9	78.4
Colorado	193	259	57.3	492	552	52.9	154.9	113.1
Connecticut	189	272	59.0	305	366	54.5	61.4	34.6
Delaware	41	56	57.7	76	89	53.9	85.4	58.9
District of Columbia	27	42	60.9	37	55	59.8	37.0	31.0
Florida	1,173	1,582	57.4	2,499	2,954	54.2	113.0	86.7
Georgia	309	470	60.3	737	931	55.8	138.5	98.1
Hawaii	70	87	55.4	128	161	55.7	82.9	85.1
Idaho	70	87	55.4	179	195	52.1	155.7	124.1
Illinois	603	881	59.4	996	1,238	55.4	65.2	40.5
Indiana	310	453	59.4	571	689	54.7	84.2	52.1
Iowa	181	261	59.0	313	373	54.4	72.9	42.9
Kansas	148	211	58.8	279	326	53.9	88.5	54.5
Kentucky	206	303	59.5	408	509	55.5	98.1	68.0
Louisiana	212	311	59.5	413	532	56.3	94.8	71.1
Maine	71	101	58.7	141	163	53.6	98.6	61.4
Maryland	242	347	58.9	462	567	55.1	90.9	63.4
Massachusetts	337	506	60.0	565	687	54.9	67.7	35.8
Michigan	498	699	58.4	829	992	54.5	66.5	41.9
Minnesota	249	347	58.2	512	587	53.4	105.6	69.2
Mississippi	135	209	60.8	264	351	57.1	95.6	67.9
Missouri	307	448	59.3	565	693	55.1	84.0	54.7
Montana	55	73	57.0	130	144	52.6	136.4	97.3
Nebraska	99	140	58.6	185	220	54.3	86.9	57.1
Nevada	100	119	54.3	231	255	52.5	131.0	114.3
New Hampshire	59	83	58.5	128	145	53.1	116.9	74.7

(continued)

(continued from previous page)

	2000			2025			percent change, 2000 to 2025	
	men	women		men	women		men	women
		number	percent		number	percent		
New Jersey	446	644	59.1%	740	914	55.3%	65.9%	41.9%
New Mexico	90	116	56.3	204	237	53.7	126.7	104.3
New York	951	1,407	59.7	1,442	1,821	55.8	51.6	29.4
North Carolina	399	592	59.7	888	1,116	55.7	122.6	88.5
North Dakota	42	57	57.6	76	90	54.2	81.0	57.9
Ohio	623	902	59.1	1,036	1,269	55.1	66.3	40.7
Oklahoma	195	277	58.7	402	486	54.7	106.2	75.5
Oregon	202	269	57.1	498	556	52.8	146.5	106.7
Pennsylvania	764	1,135	59.8	1,195	1,464	55.1	56.4	29.0
Rhode Island	59	89	60.1	96	118	55.1	62.7	32.6
South Carolina	193	285	59.6	426	537	55.8	120.7	88.4
South Dakota	47	63	57.3	87	101	53.7	85.1	60.3
Tennessee	283	424	60.0	597	758	55.9	111.0	78.8
Texas	875	1,226	58.4	1,971	2,393	54.8	125.3	95.2
Utah	89	113	55.9	240	255	51.5	169.7	125.7
Vermont	30	43	58.9	64	74	53.6	113.3	72.1
Virginia	322	466	59.1	683	832	54.9	112.1	78.5
Washington	294	391	57.1	749	831	52.6	154.8	112.5
West Virginia	116	171	59.6	206	254	55.2	77.6	48.5
Wisconsin	294	411	58.3	555	645	53.8	88.8	56.9
Wyoming	28	34	54.8	69	76	52.4	146.4	123.5

Note: The U.S. totals in this table are slightly different from the U.S. totals shown in the national tables because the state figures are from an earlier projection series.
Source: Bureau of the Census, Internet web site <http://www.census.gov/population/projections/state/stpjage .txt>; calculations by New Strategist

Sixteen Percent of Males and Females Move Each Year

Women account for the majority of movers aged 65 or older.

Sixteen percent of Americans aged 1 or older moved between March 1997 and March 1998, according to the Census Bureau. Young adults are most likely to move. Among females, the mobility rate peaks at 36 percent in the 20-to-24 age group—that is, 36 percent of women in the age group were living in a different house in March 1998 than in March 1997. Among men, mobility peaks at 33 percent in the 20-to-24 age group.

The mobility rate falls with age as people buy homes and establish roots in a community. The lowest mobility rate prevails among people aged 50 or older, fewer than 10 percent of whom move each year. At retirement ages, 60 to 64, mobility continues to slide for men, but rises slightly for women. Although many older people move in retirement, their numbers are not large enough to significantly boost mobility rates.

❖ Americans are less likely to move today than in the 1950s and 1960s. One reason for the decline in mobility is the increasing number of two-income couples. When both husband and wife have jobs, moving to a new city or state becomes much more difficult.

Geographical Mobility by Age and Sex, 1997–98

(number and percent of people aged 1 or older who moved between March 1997 and March 1998, by age and sex, and female share of movers; numbers in thousands)

	male		female		
	number	*percent*	*number*	*percent*	*share of movers*
Total, aged 1 or older	**21,154**	**16.3%**	**21,354**	**15.8%**	**50.2%**
Under age 5	1,940	23.9	1,769	23.0	47.7
Aged 5 to 9	1,860	17.9	1,797	17.9	49.1
Aged 10 to 14	1,406	14.0	1,485	15.5	51.4
Aged 15 to 17	761	12.4	807	14.0	51.5
Aged 18 to 19	704	18.5	823	21.8	53.9
Aged 20 to 24	2,889	32.7	3,142	35.8	52.1
Aged 25 to 29	3,022	32.0	2,858	29.9	48.6
Aged 30 to 34	2,246	22.3	2,252	21.9	50.1
Aged 35 to 39	1,904	16.9	1,844	16.2	49.2
Aged 40 to 44	1,405	13.1	1,302	11.8	48.1
Aged 45 to 49	963	10.6	929	9.8	49.1
Aged 50 to 54	633	8.5	694	8.7	52.3
Aged 55 to 59	501	8.5	487	7.7	49.3
Aged 60 to 61	131	6.6	124	5.6	48.6
Aged 62 to 64	153	5.4	187	6.1	54.8
Aged 65 to 69	198	4.6	256	5.0	56.3
Aged 70 to 74	206	5.6	217	4.5	51.4
Aged 75 to 79	106	3.7	180	4.5	62.9
Aged 80 to 84	68	4.2	121	4.4	63.7
Aged 85 or older	56	5.6	80	4.2	59.3

Source: Bureau of the Census, Internet web site <http://www.census.gov/population/socdemo/migration/p20-520/tab01.txt>; calculations by New Strategist

Most of the Nation's Foreign-Born Are Female

Females account for the majority of immigrants as well.

The nation's foreign-born numbered more than 25 million in 1998, and females account for the 52 percent majority of this population. Among the foreign-born under age 45, males outnumber females in most age groups, in part because more men than women come to the U.S. to work. But among those aged 45 or older, women outnumber men by a growing margin. Women account for two out of three of the foreign-born aged 80 or older, in part because women live longer than men.

In 1997, fully 798,378 legal immigrants were admitted to the United States. Females outnumbered males by about 67,000, accounted for 54 percent of the total. The female share of immigrants varies little by country of birth, with a few exceptions. Only 42 percent of immigrants from Cuba are female versus 58 percent of immigrants from China, Colombia, and Mexico.

❖ Both the male and female populations of the United States are becoming increasingly multicultural thanks to immigration and the growing ranks of the foreign-born.

Among immigrants, females outnumber males

(number of legal immigrants admitted to the U.S., by sex, 1997)

432,699

365,484

males *females*

Foreign-Born by Age and Sex, 1998

(number of foreign-born people by age and sex and percent female, 1998; numbers in thousands)

	total	male	female number	female percent
Total foreign born	**25,208**	**12,182**	**13,026**	**51.7%**
Under age 5	175	83	93	53.1
Aged 5 to 9	477	239	238	49.9
Aged 10 to 14	899	462	437	48.6
Aged 15 to 19	1,415	748	666	47.1
Aged 20 to 24	1,919	989	930	48.5
Aged 25 to 29	2,388	1,189	1,200	50.3
Aged 30 to 34	2,891	1,462	1,430	49.5
Aged 35 to 39	2,912	1,486	1,427	49.0
Aged 40 to 44	2,604	1,307	1,297	49.8
Aged 45 to 49	2,134	1,041	1,094	51.3
Aged 50 to 54	1,733	819	914	52.7
Aged 55 to 59	1,371	620	751	54.8
Aged 60 to 64	1,145	503	643	56.2
Aged 65 to 69	942	399	543	57.6
Aged 70 to 74	782	312	470	60.1
Aged 75 to 79	597	242	355	59.5
Aged 80 or older	823	284	539	65.5

Source: Bureau of the Census, Internet web site <http://www.census.gov/population/estimates/nation/nativity/fbtab002.txt>; calculations by New Strategist

Immigrants by Age and Sex, 1997

(number of immigrants admitted for permanent residence by age and sex, and percent female, fiscal year 1997)

	total	male	female number	female percent
Total immigrants	**798,378**	**365,484**	**432,699**	**54.2%**
Under age 5	36,439	16,960	19,476	53.4
Aged 5 to 9	49,458	25,269	24,170	48.9
Aged 10 to 14	71,192	36,777	34,404	48.3
Aged 15 to 19	79,841	40,327	39,504	49.5
Aged 20 to 24	76,214	33,440	42,758	56.1
Aged 25 to 29	108,128	47,075	61,016	56.4
Aged 30 to 34	95,184	43,758	51,399	54.0
Aged 35 to 39	66,981	29,914	37,048	55.3
Aged 40 to 44	50,772	21,893	28,864	56.9
Aged 45 to 49	39,971	17,447	22,515	56.3
Aged 50 to 54	31,390	13,241	18,141	57.8
Aged 55 to 59	28,809	11,658	17,144	59.5
Aged 60 to 64	24,753	10,339	14,408	58.2
Aged 65 to 69	18,885	8,466	10,415	55.1
Aged 70 to 74	11,101	5,001	6,100	55.0
Aged 75 to 79	5,275	2,374	2,901	55.0
Aged 80 or older	3,809	1,460	2,349	61.7

Note: Numbers will not add to total because immigrants of unknown age and sex are not shown.
Source: Immigration and Naturalization Service, Statistical Yearbook of the Immigration and Naturalization Service, 1997, *1999; calculations by New Strategist*

Immigrants by Country of Birth and Sex, 1997

(number of immigrants admitted to the U.S. by selected country of birth and sex, and percent female, 1997)

	total	male	female number	female percent
Total immigrants	**798,378**	**365,484**	**432,699**	**54.2%**
Bangladesh	8,681	4,365	4,315	49.7
Canada	11,609	5,544	6,048	52.1
China, People's Republic	41,147	17,226	23,900	58.1
Colombia	13,004	5,424	7,574	58.2
Cuba	33,587	19,519	14,059	41.9
Dominican Republic	27,053	12,657	14,395	53.2
Ecuador	7,780	3,682	4,098	52.7
El Salvador	17,969	7,722	10,247	57.0
Guatemala	7,785	3,688	4,096	52.6
Guyana	7,257	3,366	3,890	53.6
Haiti	15,057	6,935	8,122	53.9
Honduras	7,616	3,270	4,346	57.1
India	38,071	18,503	19,560	51.4
Iran	9,642	4,271	5,371	55.7
Jamaica	17,840	8,085	9,755	54.7
Korea	14,239	6,439	7,796	54.8
Mexico	146,865	61,498	85,351	58.1
Nigeria	7,038	3,389	3,648	51.8
Pakistan	12,967	6,446	6,518	50.3

Note: Numbers will not add to total because immigrants of unknown sex are not shown.
Source: Immigration and Naturalization Service, Statistical Yearbook of the Immigration and Naturalization Service, 1997, 1999; calculations by New Strategist

Women Are the Majority of Voters

At most ages, women are more likely to vote than men.

Women account for 53 percent of voters. In the 1996 presidential election, 56 million women and 49 million men went to the polls. Women accounted for the majority of voters in every age group.

Women are more likely than men to go to the polls in all but the oldest age group. Among women, the proportion of those who vote ranges from 34 percent of 18-to-20-year-olds to 65 percent of 45-to-64-year-olds. Among men, the proportion ranges more widely, from just 28 percent of 18-to-20-year-olds to 71 percent of those aged 65 or older. Only 64 percent of women aged 65 or older voted in 1996, considerably below the share of men who voted. Nevertheless, among voters aged 65 or older, women outnumbered men by more than 2 million because there are more older women than older men.

❖ As the baby-boom generation ages, the support of older women will become increasingly important to politicians.

Among voters, women outnumber men

(number of people voting in the 1996 presidential election, by sex)

56.1 million

48.9 million

men   women

Voters by Age and Sex, 1996

(number and percent of people voting in the 1996 presidential election by age and sex, and women's share of voters; numbers in thousands)

	men		women		
	voters	percent voting	voters	percent voting	share of voters
Total voters	**48,909**	**52.8%**	**56,108**	**55.5%**	**53.4%**
Aged 18 to 20	1,521	28.3	1,845	34.1	54.8
Aged 20 to 24	2,140	31.0	2,490	35.8	53.8
Aged 25 to 44	19,211	46.8	21,840	51.5	53.2
Aged 45 to 64	16,530	63.7	18,085	65.1	52.2
Aged 65 or older	9,507	70.9	11,849	64.1	55.5

Source: Bureau of the Census, Voting and Registration in the Election of November 1996, *Current Population Reports, P20-504, 1997; calculations by New Strategist*

8

Spending

❖ **Married couples with children spend the most.**

They spent an average of $48,771 in 1998—or 37 percent more than average. In contrast, single parents spent an average of only $26,567.

❖ **Married couples without children spend big on many items.**

These couples, many of whom are empty-nesters, spend much more than average on public transportation, a category that includes cruises and air travel. They also spend big on household furnishings and alcoholic beverages.

❖ **Men who live alone spend more than married couples on some items.**

They spend more on alcoholic beverages than any other household type, an annual average of $430 in 1997–98.

❖ **Among women who live alone, spending peaks in the 35-to-44 age group.**

Women aged 35 to 44 who live alone spend more on clothes than any other household type, an annual average of $1,107 in 1997–98.

Married Couples with Children Are the Biggest Spenders

Single parents spend much less, with some exceptions.

Married couples spent $44,974 in 1998, 27 percent more than the $35,535 spent by the average household. But married couples with children spent even more, an average of $48,771—or 37 percent more than average.

Spending by households headed by single parents was only 75 percent of the average ($26,567), primarily because they have less money to spend. Single parents spend more than they make—which means these families are borrowing money or depending on gifts to make ends meet.

The Bureau of Labor Statistics collects spending data for households, not for individuals. Therefore, it does not provide spending data by sex—except for single-person households, which are shown later in this chapter. The data on spending by household type reveals how men and women in families spend their money. Together, married-couple, single-parent, and single-person households (shown in the tables in this chapter) account for about 87 percent of the nation's households.

Married couples spend more than average

(average annual spending of consumer units by type, 1998)

$35,535

$39,900

$48,771

$26,567

| average consumer unit | husband and wife only | husband and wife with children at home | single parent with children under 18 at home |

The average spending table that follows shows how much married couples and single parents spent in 1998. The indexed spending table following it compares the spending of each type of household to the spending of the average household. An index of 100 means the household type spends an average amount on an item. An index above 100 means the household type spends more than average on an item, while an index below 100 signifies below-average spending.

A look at the table reveals that spending of single-parent households is well below average, although they spend close to the average on most foods. Single-parent households spend twice the average (with an index of 205) on personal services, most of which is daycare. They spend 78 percent more than the average household on boys' clothes, more than twice the average on girls' clothes (224), and 43 percent more than average on footwear.

Married couples with children at home spend more than average on most items. They, too, are big spenders on household personal services (daycare), with an index of 227. They spend well above average on children's clothes, entertainment, and education. They spend less than average on alcoholic beverages, with an index of 94.

Married couples without children at home (many of them empty nesters) spend 23 percent more than the average household on alcoholic beverages. They are big spenders on public transportation, a category that includes cruises and air travel. They spend the most on cash contributions, health care, household furnishings, and gifts.

❖ Because women handle the checkbook and make the majority of day-to-day spending decisions for most married couples, knowing how to reach women with a compelling message is vital to consumer marketers.

Spending of Married Couples and Single Parents, 1998

(number, selected characteristics, and average annual spending of total, married-couple, and single-parent consumer units (cu) by spending category, 1998)

		married couples						single parents with children < 18 at home
				couples with children of any age at home				
	average consumer unit	total	husband and wife only	total	oldest child < 6	oldest child 6 to 17	oldest child 18+	
Number of consumer units (in thousands)	107,182	56,655	23,302	29,193	5,471	15,994	7,728	6,546
Income before taxes	$41,622	$55,345	$49,395	$59,653	$55,800	$58,775	$64,243	$24,530
Average number of persons in cu	2.5	3.2	2.0	4.0	3.4	4.2	3.9	2.9
Average number of earners in cu	1.3	1.7	1.2	2.0	1.7	1.9	2.6	1.1
Average number of vehicles owned by cu	2.0	2.6	2.4	2.7	2.2	2.6	3.4	1.1
Percent homeowners	64%	81%	83%	79%	67%	79%	88%	36%
With mortgage	39	53	40	64	58	67	60	29
Without mortgage	26	28	43	16	9	12	28	7
Percent renters	36	19	17	21	33	21	12	64
Percent black	12	8	5	9	8	9	10	34
Average annual expenditures	$35,535	$44,974	$39,900	$48,771	$43,601	$48,829	$52,370	$26,567
FOOD	**$4,810**	**$6,100**	**$4,974**	**$6,854**	**$5,699**	**$6,969**	**$7,466**	**$4,133**
Food at home	2,780	3,545	2,809	3,964	3,399	4,052	4,203	2,589
Cereals/bakery products	425	541	413	626	503	663	640	407
Cereals/cereal products	146	186	129	225	167	249	217	152
Bakery products	278	355	285	401	335	414	423	254
Meats, poultry, fish, eggs	723	937	740	1,012	791	1,014	1,175	682
Beef	218	294	234	313	220	305	400	186
Pork	146	185	151	192	149	192	222	150
Other meats	92	120	94	131	101	135	143	82
Poultry	137	176	129	203	160	208	225	140
Fish and seafood	98	123	100	132	128	130	138	95
Eggs	32	39	31	42	33	42	47	28
Dairy products	301	386	294	450	384	479	437	284
Fresh milk and cream	120	155	108	185	158	200	172	114
Other dairy products	181	231	186	265	226	279	265	169

(continued)

(continued from previous page)

	average consumer unit	married couples						single parents with children < 18 at home
				couples with children of any age at home				
		total	husband and wife only	total	oldest child < 6	oldest child 6 to 17	oldest child 18+	
Fruits and vegetables	$472	$599	$513	$646	$604	$639	$692	$419
Fresh fruits	149	187	165	201	180	207	205	129
Fresh vegetables	145	185	163	192	181	184	219	116
Processed fruits	101	126	101	141	151	132	154	101
Processed vegetables	76	100	83	111	92	117	114	74
Other food at home	858	1,082	850	1,230	1,117	1,257	1,258	798
Sugar/other sweets	109	137	114	152	112	169	147	101
Fats and oils	77	98	80	103	88	105	110	70
Miscellaneous foods	388	489	360	580	611	584	548	373
Nonalcoholic beverages	231	289	228	323	253	330	360	229
Food prepared by cu on out-of-town trips	53	70	68	73	52	70	94	25
Food away from home	**2,030**	**2,555**	**2,165**	**2,890**	**2,300**	**2,917**	**3,263**	**1,543**
ALCOHOLIC BEVERAGES	**$309**	**$328**	**$379**	**$291**	**$338**	**$266**	**$308**	**$191**
HOUSING	**$11,713**	**$14,319**	**$12,908**	**$15,368**	**$15,945**	**$15,583**	**$14,520**	**$9,869**
Shelter	**6,680**	**7,998**	**7,020**	**8,775**	**9,085**	**9,013**	**8,064**	**5,574**
Owned dwellings*	4,245	5,987	5,053	6,785	6,620	7,040	6,372	2,450
Mortgage interest and charges	2,455	3,565	2,521	4,415	4,753	4,645	3,699	1,600
Property taxes	1,015	1,390	1,356	1,424	1,100	1,424	1,653	535
Maintenance, repairs, insurance, etc.	775	1,032	1,177	946	768	971	1,021	315
Rented dwellings	1,978	1,374	1,241	1,418	2,188	1,398	914	2,980
Other lodging	458	637	726	573	276	575	777	144
Utilities, fuels, and public services	**2,405**	**2,899**	**2,629**	**3,048**	**2,571**	**3,062**	**3,354**	**2,231**
Natural gas	284	336	302	357	295	363	388	277
Electricity	921	1,127	1,033	1,170	941	1,191	1,288	859
Fuel oil and other fuels	85	107	110	107	83	99	141	55
Telephone	830	954	850	1,013	937	1,005	1,083	829
Water/other public svcs.	285	375	333	401	315	404	455	211
Household services	**546**	**705**	**423**	**913**	**1,832**	**865**	**360**	**713**
Personal services	260	349	37	591	1,523	523	71	532
Other household services	286	355	386	322	309	343	289	181

(continued)

(continued from previous page)

| | average consumer unit | married couples | | | | | | single parents with children < 18 at home |
| | | total | husband and wife only | couples with children of any age at home | | | | |
				total	oldest child < 6	oldest child 6 to 17	oldest child 18+	
Housekeeping supplies	$482	$646	$671	$623	$519	$639	$668	$267
Laundry/cleaning supplies	118	156	137	161	120	162	192	85
Other household products	232	324	372	298	249	313	302	115
Postage and stationery	132	166	162	164	150	164	175	66
Household furnishings and equipment	1,601	2,071	2,165	2,009	1,938	2,003	2,074	1,084
Household textiles	105	134	133	131	110	140	127	63
Furniture	377	504	502	508	692	479	439	311
Floor coverings	144	189	292	131	67	150	138	40
Major appliances	164	196	189	200	184	184	241	172
Small appliances, misc. housewares	80	105	104	105	72	103	135	45
Misc. household equip.	729	944	945	934	813	947	993	452
APPAREL	$1,674	$2,057	$1,559	$2,432	$2,081	$2,522	$2,503	$1,789
Men and boys	399	538	388	644	426	691	709	245
Men, aged 16 or older	314	416	367	451	311	419	622	94
Boys, aged 2 to 15	85	122	21	193	115	271	87	151
Women and girls	651	768	621	897	662	953	956	869
Women, aged 16 or older	548	624	592	661	549	608	855	637
Girls, aged 2 to 15	103	144	28	236	112	345	101	231
Children under age 2	73	105	37	151	457	94	39	77
Footwear	281	332	230	404	234	458	421	401
Other apparel products and services	270	315	282	336	303	326	379	198
TRANSPORTATION	$6,616	$8,799	$7,275	$9,946	$8,079	$9,538	$12,113	$4,166
Vehicle purchases	2,964	4,065	3,081	4,857	3,701	4,661	6,081	1,727
Cars and trucks, new	1,383	2,026	1,613	2,391	1,796	2,170	3,268	432
Cars and trucks, used	1,532	1,999	1,448	2,415	1,768	2,457	2,785	1,258
Other vehicles	49	40	21	51	137	33	28	37
Gasoline and motor oil	1,017	1,326	1,125	1,454	1,190	1,418	1,714	703
Other vehicle expenses	2,206	2,874	2,434	3,170	2,819	3,010	3,750	1,511
Vehicle finance charges	319	441	326	520	512	491	585	190
Maintenance and repairs	641	784	705	829	644	845	927	556

(continued)

(continued from previous page)

	average consumer unit	married couples						single parents with children < 18 at home
				couples with children of any age at home				
		total	husband and wife only	total	oldest child < 6	oldest child 6 to 17	oldest child 18₁	
Vehicle insurance	$739	$952	$824	$1,037	$822	$911	$1,452	$466
Vehicle rentals, leases, licenses, other charges	507	697	579	784	842	764	785	298
Public transportation	**429**	**535**	**635**	**466**	**369**	**450**	**568**	**225**
HEALTH CARE	**$1,903**	**$2,469**	**$2,881**	**$2,152**	**$1,685**	**$2,110**	**$2,569**	**$1,027**
Health insurance	913	1,192	1,376	1,036	905	984	1,237	492
Medical services	542	717	768	698	520	713	793	303
Drugs	346	425	586	291	187	280	390	178
Medical supplies	102	135	151	126	74	133	150	54
ENTERTAINMENT	**$1,746**	**$2,239**	**$1,986**	**$2,429**	**$1,976**	**$2,622**	**$2,360**	**$1,199**
Fees and admissions	449	595	560	646	445	730	614	250
Television, radios, sound equipment	535	648	577	678	515	724	698	501
Pets, toys, and playground equipment	329	438	393	477	455	539	367	251
Other entertainment products and services	433	559	457	629	560	628	681	197
PERSONAL CARE PRODUCTS AND SERVICES	**$401**	**$483**	**$464**	**$501**	**$425**	**$491**	**$578**	**$402**
READING	**$161**	**$200**	**$220**	**$189**	**$164**	**$192**	**$200**	**$87**
EDUCATION	**$580**	**$738**	**$448**	**$997**	**$372**	**$931**	**$1,576**	**$367**
TOBACCO PRODUCTS/ SMOKING SUPPLIES	**$273**	**$293**	**$247**	**$308**	**$198**	**$316**	**$369**	**$222**
MISCELLANEOUS	**$860**	**$981**	**$940**	**$964**	**$810**	**$958**	**$1,086**	**$763**
CASH CONTRIBUTIONS	**$1,109**	**$1,337**	**$1,629**	**$1,112**	**$962**	**$1,060**	**$1,325**	**$527**
PERSONAL INSURANCE AND PENSIONS	**$3,381**	**$4,632**	**$3,991**	**$5,229**	**$4,867**	**$5,271**	**$5,397**	**$1,825**
Life and other personal insurance	398	595	632	567	444	604	577	182
Pensions/Social Security	2,982	4,038	3,359	4,662	4,423	4,667	4,820	1,643
PERSONAL TAXES	**$3,264**	**$4,359**	**$4,068**	**$4,703**	**$4,921**	**$4,390**	**$5,200**	**$1,381**
Federal income taxes	2,472	3,316	3,081	3,598	3,790	3,335	4,011	1,016

(continued)

(continued from previous page)

	average consumer unit	married couples		couples with children of any age at home				single parents with children < 18 at home
		total	husband and wife only	total	oldest child < 6	oldest child 6 to 17	oldest child 18+	
State/local income taxes	$630	$821	$752	$900	$964	$868	$923	$288
Other taxes	162	223	235	204	168	187	266	77
GIFTS**	**$1,068**	**$1,334**	**$1,544**	**$1,193**	**$834**	**$1,148**	**$1,541**	**$595**
Food	**84**	**116**	**138**	**110**	**35**	**121**	**141**	**32**
Housing	**314**	**402**	**432**	**381**	**369**	**335**	**487**	**198**
Housekeeping supplies	41	53	55	53	45	54	55	23
Household textiles	16	23	25	20	14	14	35	1
Appliances and misc. housewares	30	40	46	36	18	31	62	21
Major appliances	7	9	11	7	3	7	10	15
Small appliances and misc. housewares	22	31	35	29	15	23	52	5
Misc. household equip.	71	89	103	72	72	58	101	29
Other housing	156	197	202	200	220	177	234	125
Apparel	**225**	**254**	**256**	**246**	**262**	**198**	**332**	**160**
Males, aged 2 and older	60	70	76	58	54	43	92	19
Females, aged 2 and older	80	100	108	99	98	87	124	49
Children under age 2	32	42	29	52	84	49	35	30
Other apparel products and services	52	42	43	37	26	20	82	63
Jewelry and watches	25	16	19	14	12	8	29	18
All other apparel products and services	27	26	24	23	14	12	53	44
Transportation	**49**	**63**	**85**	**50**	**20**	**64**	**40**	**26**
Health care	**38**	**25**	**34**	**17**	**5**	**15**	**31**	**24**
Entertainment	**85**	**112**	**147**	**75**	**59**	**75**	**85**	**37**
Toys, games, hobbies, and tricycles	30	37	52	22	33	18	25	13
Other entertainment	55	75	94	52	26	58	60	24
Education	**154**	**225**	**286**	**201**	**27**	**216**	**293**	**46**
All other gifts	**119**	**136**	**167**	**113**	**56**	**124**	**133**	**71**

* This figure does not include the amount paid for mortgage principle, which is considered an asset.
** Expenditures on gifts are also included in the preceding product and service categories.
Note: The Bureau of Labor Statistics uses consumer units rather than households as the sampling unit in the Consumer Expenditure survey. For the definition of consumer unit, see Glossary.
Source: Bureau of Labor Statistics, Internet web site, <http://www.bls.gov/pub/special.requests/ce/standard/1998/cucomp.txt>

Indexed Spending of Married Couples and Single Parents, 1998

(indexed spending of married-couple and single-parent consumer units (cu) by category of spending, 1998)

	average consumer unit	total	husband and wife only	total	oldest child < 6	oldest child 6 to 17	oldest child 18+	single parents with children < 18 at home
					married couples			
				couples with children of any age at home				
Average annual expenditures	**100**	**127**	**112**	**137**	**123**	**137**	**147**	**75**
FOOD	**100**	**127**	**103**	**142**	**118**	**145**	**155**	**86**
Food at home	**100**	**128**	**101**	**143**	**122**	**146**	**151**	**93**
Cereals/bakery products	100	127	97	147	118	156	151	96
Cereals/cereal products	100	127	88	154	114	171	149	104
Bakery products	100	128	103	144	121	149	152	91
Meats, poultry, fish, eggs	100	130	102	140	109	140	163	94
Beef	100	135	107	144	101	140	183	85
Pork	100	127	103	132	102	132	152	103
Other meats	100	130	102	142	110	147	155	89
Poultry	100	128	94	148	117	152	164	102
Fish and seafood	100	126	102	135	131	133	141	97
Eggs	100	122	97	131	103	131	147	88
Dairy products	100	128	98	150	128	159	145	94
Fresh milk and cream	100	129	90	154	132	167	143	95
Other dairy products	100	128	103	146	125	154	146	93
Fruits and vegetables	100	127	109	137	128	135	147	89
Fresh fruits	100	126	111	135	121	139	138	87
Fresh vegetables	100	128	112	132	125	127	151	80
Processed fruits	100	125	100	140	150	131	152	100
Processed vegetables	100	132	109	146	121	154	150	97
Other food at home	100	126	99	143	130	147	147	93
Sugar and other sweets	100	126	105	139	103	155	135	93
Fats and oils	100	127	104	134	114	136	143	91
Miscellaneous foods	100	126	93	149	157	151	141	96
Nonalcoholic beverages	100	125	99	140	110	143	156	99
Food prepared by cu on out-of-town trips	100	132	128	138	98	132	177	47
Food away from home	**100**	**126**	**107**	**142**	**113**	**144**	**161**	**76**

(continued)

(continued from previous page)

	average consumer unit	married couples						single parents with children < 18 at home
				couples with children of any age at home				
		total	husband and wife only	total	oldest child < 6	oldest child 6 to 17	oldest child 18+	
ALCOHOLIC BEVERAGES	**100**	**106**	**123**	**94**	**109**	**86**	**100**	**62**
HOUSING	**100**	**122**	**110**	**131**	**136**	**133**	**124**	**84**
Shelter	**100**	**120**	**105**	**131**	**136**	**135**	**121**	**83**
Owned dwellings	100	141	119	160	156	166	150	58
Mortgage interest and charges	100	145	103	180	194	189	151	65
Property taxes	100	137	134	140	108	140	163	53
Maintenance, repairs, insurance, etc.	100	133	152	122	99	125	132	41
Rented dwellings	100	69	63	72	111	71	46	151
Other lodging	100	139	159	125	60	126	170	31
Utilities, fuels, and public services	**100**	**121**	**109**	**127**	**107**	**127**	**139**	**93**
Natural gas	100	118	106	126	104	128	137	98
Electricity	100	122	112	127	102	129	140	93
Fuel oil and other fuels	100	126	129	126	98	116	166	65
Telephone	100	115	102	122	113	121	130	100
Water/other public svcs.	100	132	117	141	111	142	160	74
Household services	**100**	**129**	**77**	**167**	**336**	**158**	**66**	**131**
Personal services	100	134	14	227	586	201	27	205
Other household services	100	124	135	113	108	120	101	63
Housekeeping supplies	**100**	**134**	**139**	**129**	**108**	**133**	**139**	**55**
Laundry/cleaning supplies	100	132	116	136	102	137	163	72
Other household products	100	140	160	128	107	135	130	50
Postage and stationery	100	126	123	124	114	124	133	50
Household furnishings and equipment	**100**	**129**	**135**	**125**	**121**	**125**	**130**	**68**
Household textiles	100	128	127	125	105	133	121	60
Furniture	100	134	133	135	184	127	116	82
Floor coverings	100	131	203	91	47	104	96	28
Major appliances	100	120	115	122	112	112	147	105
Small appliances, misc. housewares	100	131	130	131	90	129	169	56
Misc. household equip.	100	129	130	128	112	130	136	62

(continued)

(continued from previous page)

| | average consumer unit | married couples | | | | | | single parents with children < 18 at home |
| | | total | husband and wife only | couples with children of any age at home | | | | |
				total	oldest child < 6	oldest child 6 to 17	oldest child 18+	
APPAREL	100	123	93	145	124	151	150	107
Men and boys	100	135	97	161	107	173	178	61
Men, aged 16 or older	100	132	117	144	99	133	198	30
Boys, aged 2 to 15	100	144	25	227	135	319	102	178
Women and girls	100	118	95	138	102	146	147	133
Women, aged 16 or older	100	114	108	121	100	111	156	116
Girls, aged 2 to 15	100	140	27	229	109	335	98	224
Children under age 2	100	144	51	207	626	129	53	105
Footwear	100	118	82	144	83	163	150	143
Other apparel products and services	100	117	104	124	112	121	140	73
TRANSPORTATION	100	133	110	150	122	144	183	63
Vehicle purchases	100	137	104	164	125	157	205	58
Cars and trucks, new	100	146	117	173	130	157	236	31
Cars and trucks, used	100	130	95	158	115	160	182	82
Other vehicles	100	82	43	104	280	67	57	76
Gasoline and motor oil	100	130	111	143	117	139	169	69
Other vehicle expenses	100	130	110	144	128	136	170	68
Vehicle finance charges	100	138	102	163	161	154	183	60
Maintenance and repairs	100	122	110	129	100	132	145	87
Vehicle insurance	100	129	112	140	111	123	196	63
Vehicle rentals, leases, licenses, other charges	100	137	114	155	166	151	155	59
Public transportation	100	125	148	109	86	105	132	52
HEALTH CARE	100	130	151	113	89	111	135	54
Health insurance	100	131	151	113	99	108	135	54
Medical services	100	132	142	129	96	132	146	56
Drugs	100	123	169	84	54	81	113	51
Medical supplies	100	132	148	124	73	130	147	53
ENTERTAINMENT	100	128	114	139	113	150	135	69
Fees and admissions	100	133	125	144	99	163	137	56

(continued)

(continued from previous page)

	average consumer unit	married couples						single parents with children < 18 at home
		total	husband and wife only	couples with children of any age at home				
				total	oldest child < 6	oldest child 6 to 17	oldest child 18+	
Television, radios, sound equipment	100	121	108	127	96	135	130	94
Pets, toys, and playground equipment	100	133	119	145	138	164	112	76
Other entertainment products and services	100	129	106	145	129	145	157	45
PERSONAL CARE PRODUCTS AND SERVICES	**100**	**120**	**116**	**125**	**106**	**122**	**144**	**100**
READING	**100**	**124**	**137**	**117**	**102**	**119**	**124**	**54**
EDUCATION	**100**	**127**	**77**	**172**	**64**	**161**	**272**	**63**
TOBACCO PRODUCTS/ SMOKING SUPPLIES	**100**	**107**	**90**	**113**	**73**	**116**	**135**	**81**
MISCELLANEOUS	**100**	**114**	**109**	**112**	**94**	**111**	**126**	**89**
CASH CONTRIBUTIONS	**100**	**121**	**147**	**100**	**87**	**96**	**119**	**48**
PERSONAL INSURANCE AND PENSIONS	**100**	**137**	**118**	**155**	**144**	**156**	**160**	**54**
Life and other personal insurance	100	149	159	142	112	152	145	46
Pensions/Social Security	100	135	113	156	148	157	162	55
PERSONAL TAXES	**100**	**134**	**125**	**144**	**151**	**134**	**159**	**42**
Federal income taxes	100	134	125	146	153	135	162	41
State/local income taxes	100	130	119	143	153	138	147	46
Other taxes	100	138	145	126	104	115	164	48
GIFTS	**100**	**125**	**145**	**112**	**78**	**107**	**144**	**56**
Food	**100**	**138**	**164**	**131**	**42**	**144**	**168**	**38**
Housing	**100**	**128**	**138**	**121**	**118**	**107**	**155**	**63**
Housekeeping supplies	100	129	134	129	110	132	134	56
Household textiles	100	144	156	125	88	88	219	6
Appliances and misc. housewares	100	133	153	120	60	103	207	70
Major appliances	100	129	157	100	43	100	143	214
Small appliances and misc. housewares	100	141	159	132	68	105	236	23

(continued)

(continued from previous page)

	average consumer unit	married couples		couples with children of any age at home				single parents with children < 18 at home
		total	husband and wife only	total	oldest child < 6	oldest child 6 to 17	oldest child 18+	
Misc. household equip.	100	125	145	101	101	82	142	41
Other housing	100	126	129	128	141	113	150	80
Apparel	**100**	**113**	**114**	**109**	**116**	**88**	**148**	**71**
Males, aged 2 and older	100	117	127	97	90	72	153	32
Females, aged 2 and older	100	125	135	124	123	109	155	61
Children under age 2	100	131	91	163	263	153	109	94
Other apparel products and services	100	81	83	71	50	38	158	121
Jewelry and watches	100	64	76	56	48	32	116	72
All other apparel products and services	100	96	89	85	52	44	196	163
Transportation	**100**	**129**	**173**	**102**	**41**	**131**	**82**	**53**
Health care	**100**	**66**	**89**	**45**	**13**	**39**	**82**	**63**
Entertainment	**100**	**132**	**173**	**88**	**69**	**88**	**100**	**44**
Toys, games, hobbies, and tricycles	100	123	173	73	110	60	83	43
Other entertainment	100	136	171	95	47	105	109	44
Education	**100**	**146**	**186**	**131**	**18**	**140**	**190**	**30**
All other gifts	**100**	**114**	**140**	**95**	**47**	**104**	**112**	**60**

Note: The index compares the spending of each type of consumer unit with the spending of the average consumer unit, which corresponds to an index of 100. An index of 132 means spending is 32 percent above average, while an index of 75 means spending is 25 percent below average. The Bureau of Labor Statistics uses consumer units rather than households as the sampling unit in the Consumer Expenditure Survey. For the definition of consumer unit, see Glossary.

Source: Calculations by New Strategist based on the Bureau of Labor Statistics' Consumer Expenditure Survey, Internet web site, <http://www.bls.gov/pub/special.requests/ce/standard/1998/cucomp.txt>

Among Men Who Live Alone, Spending Peaks in 45-to-54 Age Group

Men who live alone are big spenders on food away from home.

Men who live alone spent an annual average of $23,389 in 1997–98. Those aged 45 to 54 spent the most, an average of $29,508, while those under age 25 spent the least—just $14,628. Most men who live alone are under age 45, and only 17 percent are aged 65 or older.

The average spending table shows how much men who live alone spent annually in 1997–98, by age group. The indexed spending table compares the spending of men who live alone with the spending of the average man who lives alone. An index of 100 means men in the age group spend an average amount on an item. An index above 100 means men in the age group spend more than average on an item, while an index below 100 signifies below-average spending.

Among men who live alone, those under age 25 spend much more than average on education, with an index of 331. They spent $1,470 on food away from home, another $1,018 on entertainment, and $396 on alcoholic beverages. Men who live alone spend more on alcoholic beverages than any other household type.

The oldest and youngest spend the least

(average annual spending of single-person consumer units headed by men, by age, 1997–98)

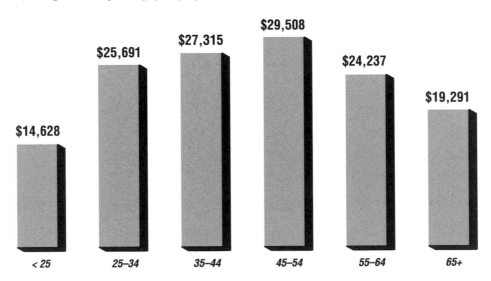

< 25	25–34	35–44	45–54	55–64	65+
$14,628	$25,691	$27,315	$29,508	$24,237	$19,291

Men aged 25 to 64 have much higher incomes than those younger or older. Consequently, they spend considerably more than the average man who lives alone on most items, including food away from home, alcoholic beverages, entertainment, and transportation.

Spending peaks among men aged 45 to 54. This age group spends 61 percent more than average on gifts, 80 percent more on furniture, 87 percent more on new cars and trucks, and 96 percent more on cash contributions.

The income of men aged 65 or older who live alone is relatively low. Consequently, they spend less than their middle-aged counterparts. Many men aged 65 or older who live alone are widowers. They spend more than the average man who lives alone on many grocery items, personal household services (such as cleaning), and health care.

❖ As the baby-boom generation ages, the number of men who live alone is likely to remain stable or even decline, while the number of women who live alone will rise substantially. Consequently, the buying decisions of women will increasingly dominate the spending of single-person households.

Spending of Men Who Live Alone by Age, 1997–98

(number, selected characteristics, and average annual spending of single-person consumer units (cu) headed by men, by spending category and age, 1997–98)

	average man living alone	under 25	25 to 34	35 to 44	45 to 54	55 to 64	65+
Number of consumer units (in thousands)	**12,923**	**2,340**	**2,940**	**2,499**	**1,897**	**1,066**	**2,181**
Income before taxes	**$27,400**	**$11,605**	**$30,230**	**$35,398**	**$40,867**	**$28,801**	**$18,750**
Percent homeowners	**38%**	**4%**	**23%**	**44%**	**56%**	**55%**	**65%**
With mortgage	**20**	**2**	**20**	**32**	**37**	**25**	**10**
Without mortgage	**18**	**2**	**3**	**12**	**19**	**30**	**55**
Percent renters	**62**	**96**	**77**	**56**	**44**	**45**	**35**
Percent black	**10**	**6**	**9**	**11**	**13**	**9**	**9**
Average annual expenditures	**$23,389**	**$14,628**	**$25,691**	**$27,315**	**$29,508**	**$24,237**	**$19,291**
FOOD	**$2,996**	**$2,133**	**$3,287**	**$3,247**	**$3,054**	**$3,370**	**$2,843**
Food at home	**1,344**	**663**	**1,340**	**1,397**	**1,398**	**1,671**	**1,665**
Cereals and bakery products	212	109	242	211	193	236	264
Cereals and cereal products	75	44	92	72	66	83	86
Bakery products	137	66	150	139	126	153	178
Meats, poultry, fish, and eggs	335	132	297	342	381	448	451
Beef	98	37	92	102	105	143	126
Pork	67	21	48	59	72	94	119
Other meats	51	26	46	59	51	66	62
Poultry	60	25	64	62	89	66	58
Fish and seafood	41	12	32	44	49	55	62
Eggs	17	10	15	16	14	24	24
Dairy products	143	72	129	157	141	184	184
Fresh milk and cream	58	33	56	59	57	73	75
Other dairy products	85	40	73	98	84	112	109
Fruits and vegetables	215	94	192	197	261	270	305
Fresh fruits	70	30	62	65	84	79	108
Fresh vegetables	60	21	53	60	75	78	82
Processed fruits	53	32	52	44	60	69	71
Processed vegetables	31	12	25	28	42	44	44
Other food at home	440	255	478	490	423	533	462
Sugar and other sweets	49	26	48	45	40	80	63
Fats and oils	32	17	29	28	37	46	42
Miscellaneous foods	209	103	230	243	208	228	227

(continued)

(continued from previous page)

	average man living alone	under 25	25 to 34	35 to 44	45 to 54	55 to 64	65+
Nonalcoholic beverages	$119	$81	$131	$141	$108	$134	$115
Food prepared by cu on out-of-town trips	31	29	40	32	30	45	15
Food away from home	**1,652**	**1,470**	**1,948**	**1,850**	**1,656**	**1,699**	**1,178**
ALCOHOLIC BEVERAGES	**$430**	**$396**	**$622**	**$431**	**$467**	**$335**	**$253**
HOUSING	**$7,837**	**$4,264**	**$8,797**	**$9,359**	**$9,502**	**$8,545**	**$6,781**
Shelter	**5,131**	**2,968**	**6,052**	**6,299**	**6,194**	**5,486**	**3,774**
Owned dwellings*	2,026	129	1,630	3,019	3,430	2,730	1,890
Mortgage interest and charges	1,099	80	1,078	1,859	2,006	1,371	430
Property taxes	521	38	319	677	860	792	708
Maintenance, repairs, insurance, etc.	405	12	234	482	564	567	752
Rented dwellings	2,789	2,396	4,174	3,077	2,346	2,346	1,616
Other lodging	316	442	247	203	418	410	269
Utilities, fuels, public services	**1,475**	**707**	**1,486**	**1,670**	**1,801**	**1,683**	**1,674**
Natural gas	170	48	159	187	209	194	249
Electricity	537	219	483	606	680	670	685
Fuel oil and other fuels	53	7	22	74	43	83	115
Telephone	578	400	711	661	673	563	417
Water and other public services	137	33	111	141	196	174	208
Household services	**189**	**45**	**145**	**190**	**223**	**200**	**368**
Personal services	38	5	28	36	31	–	116
Other household services	151	40	117	155	192	200	252
Housekeeping supplies	**192**	**75**	**159**	**203**	**226**	**176**	**304**
Laundry and cleaning supplies	42	10	55	47	41	40	52
Other household products	90	50	64	69	132	54	168
Postage and stationery	60	15	39	86	54	82	84
Household furnishings and equipment	**850**	**468**	**956**	**996**	**1,058**	**1,000**	**661**
Household textiles	34	16	42	25	34	68	35
Furniture	189	99	236	238	341	104	77
Floor coverings	50	1	75	63	45	102	28
Major appliances	85	31	85	158	85	69	67
Small appliances, misc. housewares	35	28	31	52	33	33	29
Miscellaneous household equipment	456	294	487	460	521	625	424

(continued)

(continued from previous page)

	average man living alone	under 25	25 to 34	35 to 44	45 to 54	55 to 64	65+
APPAREL	$821	$658	$1,192	$862	$859	$809	$458
Men and boys	391	326	591	416	334	382	233
Men, aged 16 and older	382	325	578	401	322	367	233
Boys, aged 2 to 15	9	1	13	15	12	15	1
Women and girls	47	45	34	65	60	40	40
Women, aged 16 and older	36	45	21	50	53	23	26
Girls, aged 2 to 15	11	–	12	16	6	18	14
Children under age 2	8	5	21	4	–	6	5
Footwear	150	123	196	175	188	157	66
Other apparel products/services	225	159	350	202	276	223	113
TRANSPORTATION	$3,974	$2,932	$4,559	$4,443	$5,519	$3,557	$2,621
Vehicle purchases	1,652	1,348	1,721	1,851	2710	1079	1,019
Cars and trucks, new	680	608	651	568	1,270	688	407
Cars and trucks, used	899	665	1,049	1,250	1,415	380	353
Other vehicles	73	75	22	33	25	10	259
Gasoline and motor oil	693	539	781	812	782	727	509
Other vehicle expenses	1,320	777	1,653	1,511	1,661	1,367	909
Vehicle finance charges	140	69	232	192	155	72	51
Maintenance and repairs	459	320	504	503	574	530	357
Vehicle insurance	438	243	540	496	504	481	364
Vehicle rentals, leases, licenses, other charges	283	144	376	320	428	284	137
Public transportation	308	269	404	268	366	384	183
HEALTH CARE	$961	$175	$583	$744	$912	$1,195	$2,477
Health insurance	446	72	304	381	442	467	1,108
Medical services	324	61	168	234	281	458	891
Drugs	142	23	74	87	130	187	403
Medical supplies	48	18	37	43	59	82	76
ENTERTAINMENT	$1,268	$1,018	$1,563	$1,502	$1,438	$1,440	$663
Fees and admissions	348	337	471	333	388	303	204
Television, radios, sound equipment	421	411	507	437	516	303	272
Pets, toys, playground equipment	160	77	156	181	226	227	131
Other entertainment products and services	339	193	428	551	307	608	56

(continued)

(continued from previous page)

	average man living alone	under 25	25 to 34	35 to 44	45 to 54	55 to 64	65+
PERSONAL CARE PRODUCTS AND SERVICES	$150	$71	$203	$110	$126	$113	$125
READING	$115	$62	$129	$127	$131	$140	$111
EDUCATION	$537	$1,779	$567	$158	$316	$65	$23
TOBACCO PRODUCTS AND SMOKING SUPPLIES	$253	$151	$226	$332	$325	$378	$186
MISCELLANEOUS	$842	$224	$724	$1,092	$1,273	$1,511	$661
CASH CONTRIBUTIONS	$1,073	$60	$652	$1,598	$2,098	$494	$1,520
PERSONAL INSURANCE AND PENSIONS	$2,151	$703	$2,587	$3,302	$3,489	$2,286	$570
Life and other personal insurance	179	41	122	214	221	257	289
Pensions and Social Security	1,972	662	2,466	3,089	3,268	2,028	281
PERSONAL TAXES	$2,699	$676	$3,207	$3,887	$4,749	$2,507	$1,114
Federal income taxes	2,092	544	2,504	2,988	3,803	1,788	814
State and local income taxes	533	130	683	828	838	567	141
Other taxes	74	2	20	71	108	152	158
GIFTS **	$919	$657	$833	$891	$1,478	$887	$900

* This figure does not include the amount paid for mortgage principle, which is considered an asset.
** Expenditures on gifts are also included in the preceding product and service categories.
Note: The Bureau of Labor Statistics uses consumer units rather than households as the sampling unit in the Consumer Expenditure survey. For the definition of consumer unit, see Glossary. (–) means sample is too small to make a reliable estimate.
Source: Bureau of Labor Statistics, Internet web site, <http://www.bls.gov/pub/special.requests/ce/CrossTabs/y9798/SEXbyAGE/malesage.TXT>

Indexed Spending of Men Who Live Alone by Age, 1997–98

(indexed spending of single-person consumer units (cu) headed by men, by spending category and age, 1997–98)

Average annual expenditures	average man living alone 100	under 25 63	25 to 34 110	35 to 44 117	45 to 54 126	55 to 64 104	65+ 82
FOOD	**100**	**71**	**110**	**108**	**102**	**112**	**95**
Food at home	**100**	**49**	**100**	**104**	**104**	**124**	**124**
Cereals and bakery products	100	51	114	100	91	111	125
Cereals and cereal products	100	59	123	96	88	111	115
Bakery products	100	48	109	101	92	112	130
Meats, poultry, fish, and eggs	100	39	89	102	114	134	135
Beef	100	38	94	104	107	146	129
Pork	100	31	72	88	107	140	178
Other meats	100	51	90	116	100	129	122
Poultry	100	42	107	103	148	110	97
Fish and seafood	100	29	78	107	120	134	151
Eggs	100	59	88	94	82	141	141
Dairy products	100	50	90	110	99	129	129
Fresh milk and cream	100	57	97	102	98	126	129
Other dairy products	100	47	86	115	99	132	128
Fruits and vegetables	100	44	89	92	121	126	142
Fresh fruits	100	43	89	93	120	113	154
Fresh vegetables	100	35	88	100	125	130	137
Processed fruits	100	60	98	83	113	130	134
Processed vegetables	100	39	81	90	135	142	142
Other food at home	100	58	109	111	96	121	105
Sugar and other sweets	100	53	98	92	82	163	129
Fats and oils	100	53	91	88	116	144	131
Miscellaneous foods	100	49	110	116	100	109	109
Nonalcoholic beverages	100	68	110	118	91	113	97
Food prepared by cu on out-of-town trips	100	94	129	103	97	145	48
Food away from home	**100**	**89**	**118**	**112**	**100**	**103**	**71**
ALCOHOLIC BEVERAGES	**100**	**92**	**145**	**100**	**109**	**78**	**59**

(continued)

(continued from previous page)

	average man living alone	under 25	25 to 34	35 to 44	45 to 54	55 to 64	65+
HOUSING	**100**	**54**	**112**	**119**	**121**	**109**	**87**
Shelter	**100**	**58**	**118**	**123**	**121**	**107**	**74**
Owned dwellings	100	6	80	149	169	135	93
Mortgage interest and charges	100	7	98	169	183	125	39
Property taxes	100	7	61	130	165	152	136
Maintenance, repairs, insurance, etc.	100	3	58	119	139	140	186
Rented dwellings	100	86	150	110	84	84	58
Other lodging	100	140	78	64	132	130	85
Utilities, fuels, public services	**100**	**48**	**101**	**113**	**122**	**114**	**113**
Natural gas	100	28	94	110	123	114	146
Electricity	100	41	90	113	127	125	128
Fuel oil and other fuels	100	13	42	140	81	157	217
Telephone	100	69	123	114	116	97	72
Water and other public services	100	24	81	103	143	127	152
Household services	**100**	**24**	**77**	**101**	**118**	**106**	**195**
Personal services	100	13	74	95	82	–	305
Other household services	100	26	77	103	127	132	167
Housekeeping supplies	**100**	**39**	**83**	**106**	**118**	**92**	**158**
Laundry and cleaning supplies	100	24	131	112	98	95	124
Other household products	100	56	71	77	147	60	187
Postage and stationery	100	25	65	143	90	137	140
Household furnishings and equipment	**100**	**55**	**112**	**117**	**124**	**118**	**78**
Household textiles	100	47	124	74	100	200	103
Furniture	100	52	125	126	180	55	41
Floor coverings	100	2	150	126	90	204	56
Major appliances	100	36	100	186	100	81	79
Small appliances, misc. housewares	100	80	89	149	94	94	83
Miscellaneous household equipment	100	64	107	101	114	137	93
APPAREL	**100**	**80**	**145**	**105**	**105**	**99**	**56**
Men and boys	**100**	**83**	**151**	**106**	**85**	**98**	**60**
Men, aged 16 and older	100	85	151	105	84	96	61
Boys, aged 2 to 15	100	11	144	167	133	167	11
Women and girls	**100**	**96**	**72**	**138**	**128**	**85**	**85**
Women, aged 16 and older	100	125	58	139	147	64	72

(continued)

(continued from previous page)

	average man living alone	under 25	25 to 34	35 to 44	45 to 54	55 to 64	65+
Girls, aged 2 to 15	100	–	109	145	55	164	127
Children under age 2	**100**	**63**	**263**	**50**	**–**	**75**	**63**
Footwear	**100**	**82**	**131**	**117**	**125**	**105**	**44**
Other apparel products/services	**100**	**71**	**156**	**90**	**123**	**99**	**50**
TRANSPORTATION	**100**	**74**	**115**	**112**	**139**	**90**	**66**
Vehicle purchases	**100**	**82**	**104**	**112**	**164**	**65**	**62**
Cars and trucks, new	100	89	96	84	187	101	60
Cars and trucks, used	100	74	117	139	157	42	39
Other vehicles	100	103	30	45	34	14	355
Gasoline and motor oil	**100**	**78**	**113**	**117**	**113**	**105**	**73**
Other vehicle expenses	**100**	**59**	**125**	**114**	**126**	**104**	**69**
Vehicle finance charges	100	49	166	137	111	51	36
Maintenance and repairs	100	70	110	110	125	115	78
Vehicle insurance	100	55	123	113	115	110	83
Vehicle rentals, leases, licenses, other charges	100	51	133	113	151	100	48
Public transportation	**100**	**87**	**131**	**87**	**119**	**125**	**59**
HEALTH CARE	**100**	**18**	**61**	**77**	**95**	**124**	**258**
Health insurance	100	16	68	85	99	105	248
Medical services	100	19	52	72	87	141	275
Drugs	100	16	52	61	92	132	284
Medical supplies	100	38	77	90	123	171	158
ENTERTAINMENT	**100**	**80**	**123**	**118**	**113**	**114**	**52**
Fees and admissions	100	97	135	96	111	87	59
Television, radios, sound equipment	100	98	120	104	123	72	65
Pets, toys, playground equipment	100	48	98	113	141	142	82
Other entertainment products and services	100	57	126	163	91	179	17
PERSONAL CARE PRODUCTS AND SERVICES	**100**	**55**	**156**	**91**	**97**	**87**	**96**
READING	**100**	**54**	**112**	**110**	**114**	**122**	**97**
EDUCATION	**100**	**331**	**106**	**29**	**59**	**12**	**4**
TOBACCO PRODUCTS AND SMOKING SUPPLIES	**100**	**60**	**89**	**131**	**128**	**149**	**74**

(continued)

(continued from previous page)

	average man living alone	under 25	25 to 34	35 to 44	45 to 54	55 to 64	65+
MISCELLANEOUS	100	27	86	130	151	179	79
CASH CONTRIBUTIONS	100	6	61	149	196	46	142
PERSONAL INSURANCE AND PENSIONS	100	33	120	154	162	106	26
Life and other personal insurance	100	23	68	120	123	144	161
Pensions and Social Security	100	34	125	157	166	103	14
PERSONAL TAXES	100	25	119	144	176	93	41
Federal income taxes	100	26	120	143	182	85	39
State and local income taxes	100	24	128	155	157	106	26
Other taxes	100	3	27	96	146	205	214
GIFTS	100	71	91	97	161	97	98

Note: The index compares the spending of men living alone in each age group with the spending of the average man who lives alone, which corresponds to an index of 100. An index of 132 means spending is 32 percent above average, while an index of 75 means spending is 25 percent below average. The Bureau of Labor Statistics uses consumer units rather than households as the sampling unit in the Consumer Expenditure Survey. For the definition of consumer unit, see Glossary. (–) means sample is too small to make a reliable estimate.
Source: Calculations by New Strategist based on the Bureau of Labor Statistics' Consumer Expenditure Survey, Internet web site, <http://www.bls.gov/pub/special.requests/ce/CrossTabs/y9798/SEXbyAGE/malesage.TXT>

Among Women Who Live Alone, Spending Peaks in 35-to-44 Age Group

The biggest spenders on health care, however, are the oldest women.

Women who live alone spent an annual average of $19,546 in 1997–98. Those aged 35 to 44 spent the most, an average of $27,514, while those under age 25 spent the least—just $12,117. Most women who live alone are aged 55 or older, and 43 percent are aged 65 or older.

The average spending table shows how much women who live alone spent annually in 1997–98, by age group. The indexed spending table compares the spending of women who live alone with the spending of the average woman who lives alone. An index of 100 means women in the age group spend an average amount on an item. An index above 100 means women in the age group spend more than average on an item, while an index below 100 signifies below-average spending.

Among women who live alone, those under age 25 spend much more than average on education, with an index of 351. Many of these young women are in college. Women in the

Spending peaks in middle age

(average annual spending of single-person consumer units headed by women, by age, 1997–98)

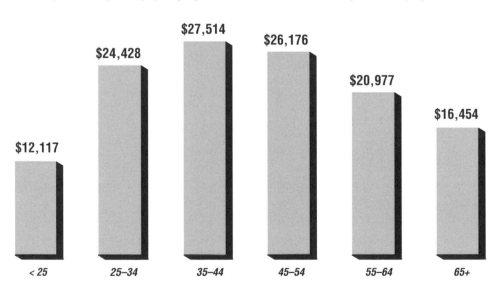

age group spent 25 percent more on footwear (with an index of 125), 20 percent more than average on food away from home, and 18 percent more on alcoholic beverages.

Women aged 25 to 54 have much higher incomes than those younger or older. Consequently, they spend considerably more than the average woman who lives alone. They spend more on food away from home, alcoholic beverages, entertainment, and clothes. Health care is one of the few categories in which their spending is below average.

Spending peaks among women aged 35 to 44. This age group spends twice the average on alcoholic beverages (with an index of 209), 81 percent more than average on clothes, 60 percent more than average on food away from home, 55 percent more than average on personal care products and services, and 46 percent more than average on entertainment. In fact, women aged 35 to 44 who live alone spend more on clothes than any other household type. They spend more on alcoholic beverages than married couples with children.

The incomes of women aged 55 or older who live alone are relatively low. Consequently, their spending is lower than that of middle-aged women. Many women aged 65 or older who live alone are widows. They spend more than the average woman who lives alone on many grocery items, health care, and cash contributions.

❖ As baby-boom women become widows and live alone, their unique tastes will change the spending patterns of older women. Businesses should prepare for these sophisticated and demanding older consumers.

Spending of Women Who Live Alone by Age, 1997–98

(number, selected characteristics, and average annual spending of single-person consumer units (cu) headed by women, by spending category and age, 1997–98)

	average woman living alone	under 25	25 to 34	35 to 44	45 to 54	55 to 64	65+
Number of consumer units (in thousands)	**17,584**	**2,259**	**1,844**	**1,765**	**2,144**	**2,009**	**7,563**
Income before taxes	**$18,997**	**$9,354**	**$28,132**	**$31,193**	**$28,142**	**$19,538**	**$13,944**
Percent homeowners	**50%**	**3%**	**21%**	**42%**	**58%**	**58%**	**68%**
With mortgage	**18**	**1**	**19**	**34**	**41**	**26**	**10**
Without mortgage	**32**	**1**	**2**	**9**	**17**	**33**	**59**
Percent renters	**50**	**97**	**79**	**58**	**42**	**42**	**32**
Percent black	**13**	**8**	**12**	**16**	**21**	**16**	**10**
Average annual expenditures	**$19,546**	**$12,117**	**$24,428**	**$27,514**	**$26,176**	**$20,977**	**$16,454**
FOOD	**$2,288**	**$1,825**	**$2,527**	**$2,939**	**$2,678**	**$2,610**	**$2,015**
Food at home	**1,407**	**770**	**1,166**	**1,533**	**1,687**	**1,748**	**1,438**
Cereals and bakery products	219	132	192	209	242	255	234
Cereals and cereal products	69	44	66	72	79	72	73
Bakery products	149	88	126	137	163	182	162
Meats, poultry, fish, and eggs	311	121	191	354	383	414	332
Beef	81	24	48	84	111	109	87
Pork	62	16	22	77	73	99	66
Other meats	38	20	26	37	35	51	43
Poultry	64	30	53	76	77	79	64
Fish and seafood	50	23	32	65	67	56	52
Eggs	17	8	11	16	19	20	19
Dairy products	158	104	138	163	178	184	164
Fresh milk and cream	59	33	48	56	66	67	66
Other dairy products	99	71	90	107	112	118	98
Fruits and vegetables	278	154	245	268	327	326	294
Fresh fruits	95	49	80	88	117	109	102
Fresh vegetables	85	44	70	96	106	97	88
Processed fruits	61	43	63	55	58	71	64
Processed vegetables	37	18	32	29	46	49	40
Other food at home	442	258	400	539	558	568	413
Sugar and other sweets	63	32	57	67	91	69	64
Fats and oils	42	16	26	40	51	60	46
Miscellaneous foods	191	117	171	238	244	247	174

(continued)

(continued from previous page)

	average woman living alone	under 25	25 to 34	35 to 44	45 to 54	55 to 64	65+
Nonalcoholic beverages	$119	$73	$108	$158	$142	$152	$110
Food prepared by cu							
on out-of-town trips	27	19	39	35	31	40	20
Food away from home	**881**	**1,056**	**1,360**	**1,406**	**991**	**862**	**577**
ALCOHOLIC BEVERAGES	**$162**	**$191**	**$284**	**$338**	**$212**	**$154**	**$74**
HOUSING	**$7,626**	**$4,034**	**$9,203**	**$10,410**	**$10,134**	**$8,053**	**$6,832**
Shelter	**4,521**	**2,700**	**6,156**	**6,964**	**6,162**	**4,509**	**3,634**
Owned dwellings*	2,048	109	1,484	3,078	3,480	2,458	2,009
Mortgage interest and charges	877	65	1,049	1,995	2,189	1,120	379
Property taxes	580	32	226	603	665	689	773
Maintenance, repairs,							
insurance, etc.	591	12	209	480	626	649	857
Rented dwellings	2,273	2,355	4,478	3,613	2,444	1,822	1,468
Other lodging	201	236	194	273	237	229	157
Utilities, fuels, public services	**1,604**	**721**	**1,627**	**1,780**	**1,912**	**1,785**	**1,685**
Natural gas	203	51	164	205	213	191	257
Electricity	581	193	497	601	711	699	645
Fuel oil and other fuels	65	4	36	44	43	83	98
Telephone	585	449	854	771	737	620	465
Water and other public services	169	24	76	159	208	192	220
Household services	**321**	**35**	**121**	**270**	**321**	**269**	**479**
Personal services	71	–	5	20	55	11	142
Other household services	249	35	116	251	266	258	337
Housekeeping supplies	**282**	**127**	**232**	**280**	**384**	**406**	**276**
Laundry and cleaning supplies	58	19	51	62	66	86	59
Other household products	121	43	87	124	159	184	122
Postage and stationery	103	65	94	94	159	136	95
Household furnishings							
and equipment	**898**	**451**	**1,067**	**1,116**	**1,355**	**1,085**	**757**
Household textiles	79	25	58	86	66	127	87
Furniture	228	123	439	312	297	210	173
Floor coverings	72	17	10	40	16	67	125
Major appliances	100	34	70	88	257	119	84
Small appliances, misc. housewares	61	42	79	99	87	68	46
Miscellaneous household equipment	358	209	411	490	633	494	243

(continued)

(continued from previous page)

	average woman living alone	under 25	25 to 34	35 to 44	45 to 54	55 to 64	65+
APPAREL	$1,025	$1,019	$1,377	$1,738	$1,197	$1,149	$701
Men and boys	57	27	81	54	90	63	50
Men, aged 16 and older	40	25	35	34	63	44	40
Boys, aged 2 to 15	17	2	46	20	26	20	10
Women and girls	629	635	839	1,135	756	674	417
Women, aged 16 and older	611	629	829	1,107	694	650	409
Girls, aged 2 to 15	18	6	10	28	62	24	9
Children under age 2	13	9	11	9	27	35	7
Footwear	168	210	181	246	109	229	133
Other apparel products/services	158	138	265	294	215	148	92
TRANSPORTATION	$2,780	$1,764	$4,646	$4,590	$4,606	$2,758	$1,697
Vehicle purchases	1,048	635	2,083	2,023	1,911	748	525
Cars and trucks, new	576	297	832	1,382	1,109	384	308
Cars and trucks, used	466	338	1,197	642	803	364	217
Other vehicles	6	–	54	–	–	–	–
Gasoline and motor oil	441	400	608	650	604	528	295
Other vehicle expenses	1,018	526	1,555	1,520	1,761	1,115	681
Vehicle finance charges	84	67	215	149	151	81	24
Maintenance and repairs	343	202	340	478	611	413	260
Vehicle insurance	381	155	579	597	548	426	290
Vehicle rentals, leases, licenses, other charges	210	103	421	295	451	195	107
Public transportation	274	204	401	397	329	368	196
HEALTH CARE	$1,434	$267	$815	$1,173	$1,319	$1,507	$2,006
Health insurance	658	80	264	367	515	570	1,058
Medical services	385	93	397	544	444	526	379
Drugs	315	61	97	199	263	340	476
Medical supplies	76	32	57	63	98	71	92
ENTERTAINMENT	$788	$659	$1,078	$1,152	$1,071	$799	$589
Fees and admissions	229	231	333	322	274	255	163
Television, radios, sound equipment	309	251	416	441	346	258	270
Pets, toys, playground equipment	165	83	213	243	239	234	122
Other entertainment products and services	85	95	116	146	211	52	34

(continued)

(continued from previous page)

	average woman living alone	under 25	25 to 34	35 to 44	45 to 54	55 to 64	65+
PERSONAL CARE PRODUCTS AND SERVICES	$343	$230	$423	$530	$427	$411	$272
READING	$128	$61	$132	$155	$178	$135	$125
EDUCATION	$339	$1,191	$711	$282	$238	$138	$90
TOBACCO PRODUCTS AND SMOKING SUPPLIES	$113	$80	$98	$188	$200	$181	$66
MISCELLANEOUS	$569	$194	$465	$746	$731	$1,005	$502
CASH CONTRIBUTIONS	$716	$111	$287	$484	$401	$462	$1,214
PERSONAL INSURANCE AND PENSIONS	$1,234	$488	$2,382	$2,788	$2,784	$1,615	$274
Life and other personal insurance	148	12	74	164	245	200	162
Pensions and Social Security	1,086	477	2,308	2,625	2,539	1,415	111
PERSONAL TAXES	$1,528	$413	$3,013	$3,552	$2,748	$1,634	$640
Federal income taxes	1,139	310	2,282	2,696	2,108	1,267	427
State and local income taxes	302	102	712	796	537	271	85
Other taxes	88	1	19	61	103	96	129
GIFTS**	$767	$521	$625	$786	$1,064	$1,005	$724

* This figure does not include the amount paid for mortgage principle, which is considered an asset.
** Expenditures on gifts are also included in the preceding product and service categories.
Note: The Bureau of Labor Statistics uses consumer units rather than households as the sampling unit in the Consumer Expenditure survey. For the definition of consumer unit, see Glossary. (–) means sample is too small to make a reliable estimate.
Source: Bureau of Labor Statistics, Internet web site, http://www.bls.gov/pub/special.requests/ce/CrossTabs/y9798/SEXbyAGE/femalage.TXT>

Indexed Spending of Women Who Live Alone by Age, 1997–98

(indexed spending of single-person consumer units (cu) headed by women by spending category and age, 1997–98)

Average annual expenditures	average woman living alone 100	under 25 62	25 to 34 125	35 to 44 141	45 to 54 134	55 to 64 107	65+ 84
FOOD	**100**	**80**	**110**	**128**	**117**	**114**	**88**
Food at home	**100**	**55**	**83**	**109**	**120**	**124**	**102**
Cereals and bakery products	100	60	88	95	111	116	107
Cereals and cereal products	100	64	96	104	114	104	106
Bakery products	100	59	85	92	109	122	109
Meats, poultry, fish, and eggs	100	39	61	114	123	133	107
Beef	100	30	59	104	137	135	107
Pork	100	26	35	124	118	160	106
Other meats	100	53	68	97	92	134	113
Poultry	100	47	83	119	120	123	100
Fish and seafood	100	46	64	130	134	112	104
Eggs	100	47	65	94	112	118	112
Dairy products	100	66	87	103	113	116	104
Fresh milk and cream	100	56	81	95	112	114	112
Other dairy products	100	72	91	108	113	119	99
Fruits and vegetables	100	55	88	96	118	117	106
Fresh fruits	100	52	84	93	123	115	107
Fresh vegetables	100	52	82	113	125	114	104
Processed fruits	100	70	103	90	95	116	105
Processed vegetables	100	49	86	78	124	132	108
Other food at home	100	58	90	122	126	129	93
Sugar and other sweets	100	51	90	106	144	110	102
Fats and oils	100	38	62	95	121	143	110
Miscellaneous foods	100	61	90	125	128	129	91
Nonalcoholic beverages	100	61	91	133	119	128	92
Food prepared by cu on out-of-town trips	100	70	144	130	115	148	74
Food away from home	**100**	**120**	**154**	**160**	**112**	**98**	**65**
ALCOHOLIC BEVERAGES	**100**	**118**	**175**	**209**	**131**	**95**	**46**

(continued)

(continued from previous page)

	average woman living alone	under 25	25 to 34	35 to 44	45 to 54	55 to 64	65+
HOUSING	100	53	121	137	133	106	90
Shelter	100	60	136	154	136	100	80
Owned dwellings	100	5	72	150	170	120	98
Mortgage interest and charges	100	7	120	227	250	128	43
Property taxes	100	6	39	104	115	119	133
Maintenance, repairs, insurance, etc.	100	2	35	81	106	110	145
Rented dwellings	100	104	197	159	108	80	65
Other lodging	100	117	97	136	118	114	78
Utilities, fuels, public services	100	45	101	111	119	111	105
Natural gas	100	25	81	101	105	94	127
Electricity	100	33	86	103	122	120	111
Fuel oil and other fuels	100	6	55	68	66	128	151
Telephone	100	77	146	132	126	106	79
Water and other public services	100	14	45	94	123	114	130
Household services	100	11	38	84	100	84	149
Personal services	100	–	7	28	77	15	200
Other household services	100	14	47	101	107	104	135
Housekeeping supplies	100	45	82	99	136	144	98
Laundry and cleaning supplies	100	33	88	107	114	148	102
Other household products	100	36	72	102	131	152	101
Postage and stationery	100	63	91	91	154	132	92
Household furnishings and equipment	100	50	119	124	151	121	84
Household textiles	100	32	73	109	84	161	110
Furniture	100	54	193	137	130	92	76
Floor coverings	100	24	14	56	22	93	174
Major appliances	100	34	70	88	257	119	84
Small appliances, misc. housewares	100	69	130	162	143	111	75
Miscellaneous household equipment	100	58	115	137	177	138	68
APPAREL	100	99	134	170	117	112	68
Men and boys	100	47	142	95	158	111	88
Men, aged 16 and older	100	63	88	85	158	110	100
Boys, aged 2 to 15	100	12	271	118	153	118	59
Women and girls	100	101	133	180	120	107	66
Women, aged 16 and older	100	103	136	181	114	106	67

(continued)

(continued from previous page)

	average woman living alone	under 25	25 to 34	35 to 44	45 to 54	55 to 64	65+
Girls, aged 2 to 15	100	33	56	156	344	133	50
Children under age 2	100	69	85	69	208	269	54
Footwear	100	125	108	146	65	136	79
Other apparel products/services	100	87	168	186	136	94	58
TRANSPORTATION	100	63	167	165	166	99	61
Vehicle purchases	100	61	199	193	182	71	50
Cars and trucks, new	100	52	144	240	193	67	53
Cars and trucks, used	100	73	257	138	172	78	47
Other vehicles	100	–	900	–	–	–	–
Gasoline and motor oil	100	91	138	147	137	120	67
Other vehicle expenses	100	52	153	149	173	110	67
Vehicle finance charges	100	80	256	177	180	96	29
Maintenance and repairs	100	59	99	139	178	120	76
Vehicle insurance	100	41	152	157	144	112	76
Vehicle rentals, leases, licenses, other charges	100	49	200	140	215	93	51
Public transportation	100	74	146	145	120	134	72
HEALTH CARE	100	19	57	82	92	105	140
Health insurance	100	12	40	56	78	87	161
Medical services	100	24	103	141	115	137	98
Drugs	100	19	31	63	83	108	151
Medical supplies	100	42	75	83	129	93	121
ENTERTAINMENT	100	84	137	146	136	101	75
Fees and admissions	100	101	145	141	120	111	71
Television, radios, sound equipment	100	81	135	143	112	83	87
Pets, toys, playground equipment	100	50	129	147	145	142	74
Other entertainment products and services	100	112	136	172	248	61	40
PERSONAL CARE PRODUCTS AND SERVICES	100	67	123	155	124	120	79
READING	100	48	103	121	139	105	98
EDUCATION	100	351	210	83	70	41	27
TOBACCO PRODUCTS AND SMOKING SUPPLIES	100	71	87	166	177	160	58

(continued)

(continued from previous page)

	average woman living alone	under 25	25 to 34	35 to 44	45 to 54	55 to 64	65+
MISCELLANEOUS	**100**	**34**	**82**	**131**	**128**	**177**	**88**
CASH CONTRIBUTIONS	**100**	**16**	**40**	**68**	**56**	**65**	**170**
PERSONAL INSURANCE AND PENSIONS	**100**	**40**	**193**	**226**	**226**	**131**	**22**
Life and other personal insurance	100	8	50	111	166	135	109
Pensions and Social Security	100	44	213	242	234	130	10
PERSONAL TAXES	**100**	**27**	**197**	**232**	**180**	**107**	**42**
Federal income taxes	100	27	200	237	185	111	37
State and local income taxes	100	34	236	264	178	90	28
Other taxes	100	1	22	69	117	109	147
GIFTS	**100**	**68**	**81**	**102**	**139**	**131**	**94**

Note: The index compares the spending of women living alone in each age group with the spending of the average woman who lives alone, which corresponds to an index of 100. An index of 132 means spending is 32 percent above average, while an index of 75 means spending is 25 percent below average. The Bureau of Labor Statistics uses consumer units rather than households as the sampling unit in the Consumer Expenditure Survey. For the definition of consumer unit, see Glossary. (–) means sample is too small for a reliable estimate.
Source: Calculations by New Strategist based on the Bureau of Labor Statistics' Consumer Expenditure Survey, Internet web site, <http://www.bls.gov/pub/special.requests/ce/CrossTabs/y9798/SEXbyAGE/femalage.TXT>

Wealth

❖ **The net worth of men and women peaks in the older age groups.**

Householders aged 65 to 74 had the highest net worth, a median of $146,500 in 1998.

❖ **Financial assets have grown rapidly during the late 1990s.**

The median value of the financial assets of the average household grew 36 percent between 1995 and 1998, thanks to the booming stock market.

❖ **The home is the most valuable asset of most Americans.**

The median value of the primary residence stood at $100,000 in 1998.

❖ **More than 80 percent of married couples are homeowners.**

The majority of women who live alone are homeowners as well.

❖ **Household debt soared in the late 1990s.**

The median amount of money owed by the average household climbed 42 percent between 1995 and 1998, after adjusting for inflation.

❖ **Working men and women are about equally likely to have pension coverage.**

Among workers, 44 percent of men and 40 percent of women have pension coverage.

Net Worth Rises with Age

Householders aged 65 to 74 have the largest net worth.

The median net worth (assets minus liabilities) of American households stood at $71,600 in 1998, according to the Federal Reserve Board's 1998 Survey of Consumer Finances. This amount was 20 percent greater than the $59,700 median net worth of households in 1989, after adjusting for inflation. Most of the gains in net worth have occurred since 1995 as the economy boomed.

Net worth rises to a peak in older age as people accumulate assets and pay off debts. The net worth of older householders has grown rapidly in the past decade as a more affluent generation entered the older age groups and as the wealth of older Americans grew due to rising housing values and stock market gains. In 1998, net worth peaked in the 65-to-74 age group at $146,500. The net worth of this age group grew 51 percent between 1989 and 1998, after adjusting for inflation. The net worth of householders aged 75 or older grew 36 percent between 1989 and 1998. Householders aged 35 to 54 have experienced a decline in net worth since 1989, although they have regained some ground since 1995. The youngest householders have seen their net worth fall sharply.

❖ With the net worth of older householders rising rapidly, women are gaining more control of the nation's wealth.

Net worth peaks in older age groups

(median net worth of households, by age of householder, 1998)

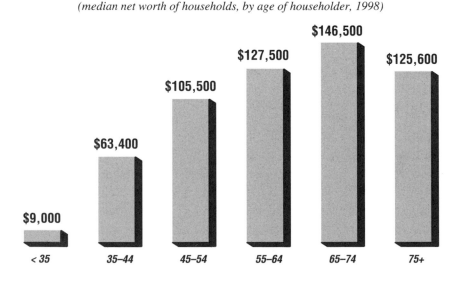

$9,000 — < 35
$63,400 — 35–44
$105,500 — 45–54
$127,500 — 55–64
$146,500 — 65–74
$125,600 — 75+

Net Worth of Households, 1989 to 1998

(median net worth of households by household income and age of householder, 1989, 1995, and 1998, and percent change, 1989–98 and 1995–98; in 1998 dollars; numbers in thousands)

	1998	1995	1989	percent change 1995–98	percent change 1989–98
Total households	$71,600	$60,900	$59,700	17.6%	19.9%
Household income					
Under $10,000	3,600	4,800	1,900	−25.0	89.5
$10,000 to $24,999	24,800	31,000	22,800	−20.0	8.8
$25,000 to $49,999	60,300	56,700	58,100	6.3	3.8
$50,000 to $99,999	152,000	126,600	131,400	20.1	15.7
$100,000 or more	510,800	511,400	542,100	−0.1	−5.8
Age of householder					
Under age 35	9,000	12,700	9,900	−29.1	−9.1
Aged 35 to 44	63,400	54,900	71,800	15.5	−11.7
Aged 45 to 54	105,500	100,800	125,700	4.7	−16.1
Aged 55 to 64	127,500	122,400	124,600	4.2	2.3
Aged 65 to 74	146,500	117,900	97,100	24.3	50.9
Aged 75 or older	125,600	98,800	92,200	27.1	36.2

Source: Federal Reserve Board, Recent Changes in U.S. Family Finances: Results from the 1998 Survey of Consumer Finances, *Federal Reserve Bulletin, January 2000; calculations by New Strategist*

Financial Assets Are Growing

The median value of the financial assets the average household owns stood at $22,400 in 1998.

The financial assets of households have grown sharply in the past few years as Americans poured money into the booming stock market. Financial assets accounted for 41 percent of all household assets in 1998, up from 30 percent in 1989. During those years, the percentage of households owning stock directly and indirectly (through mutual funds and retirement accounts) grew from 32 to 49 percent.

The percentage of households owning financial assets crept up slightly between 1995 and 1998, to 93.9 percent. The value of those financial assets soared a hefty 36 percent during the three-year period, to $22,400. Only the youngest householders, and those with incomes below $25,000, did not see a gain in financial assets between 1995 and 1998.

The most commonly held financial asset is a transaction account, such as a checking account, owned by more than 90 percent of households. Forty-nine percent of households own a retirement account, the median value being just $24,000. The median value of such accounts peaks at $46,800 among householders aged 55 to 64.

❖ The huge gains in financial assets over the past few years should benefit baby-boom men and women in retirement—unless their new-found wealth disappears in a stock market downturn.

Financial Assets of Households, 1995 and 1998

(percentage of households owning financial assets and median value of assets for owners, by household income and age of householder, 1995 and 1998; percentage point change in ownership and percent change in value of asset, 1995–98; in 1998 dollars)

	percent owning any financial asset			median value of financial assets		
	1998	1995	percentage point change 1995–98	1998	1995	percent change 1995–98
Total households	**92.9%**	**91.0%**	**1.9**	**$22,400**	**$16,500**	**35.8%**
Household income						
Under $10,000	70.6	67.4	3.2	1,100	1,400	−21.4
$10,000 to $24,999	89.9	87.8	2.1	4,800	5,900	−18.6
$25,000 to $49,999	97.3	97.0	0.3	17,600	13,300	32.3
$50,000 to $99,999	99.8	99.5	0.3	57,200	44,000	30.0
$100,000 or more	100.0	100.0	0.0	244,300	218,500	11.8
Age of householder						
Under age 35	88.6	86.9	1.7	4,500	5,700	−21.1
Aged 35 to 44	93.3	91.8	1.5	22,900	14,600	56.8
Aged 45 to 54	94.9	92.8	2.1	37,800	29,700	27.3
Aged 55 to 64	95.6	90.8	4.8	45,600	34,800	31.0
Aged 65 to 74	95.6	92.6	3.0	45,800	22,500	103.6
Aged 75 or older	92.1	94.2	−2.1	36,600	24,300	50.6

Source: Federal Reserve Board, Recent Changes in U.S. Family Finances: Results from the 1998 Survey of Consumer Finances, *Federal Reserve Bulletin, January 2000; calculations by New Strategist*

Financial Assets of Households, 1998

(percentage of households owning financial assets and median value of assets for owners, by household income, age of householder, and type of asset, 1998)

	any financial asset	transaction accounts	CDs	savings bonds	bonds	stocks	mutual funds	retirement accounts	life insurance	other managed	other financial
Percent owning, total households	92.9%	90.5%	15.3%	19.3%	3.0%	19.2%	16.5%	48.8%	29.6%	5.9%	9.4%
Household income											
Under $10,000	70.6	61.9	7.7	3.5	–	3.8	1.9	6.4	15.7	–	8.0
$10,000 to $24,999	89.9	86.5	16.8	10.2	1.3	7.2	7.6	25.4	20.9	4.9	8.2
$25,000 to $49,999	97.3	95.8	15.9	20.4	2.4	17.7	14.0	54.2	28.1	3.9	10.2
$50,000 to $99,999	99.8	99.3	16.4	30.6	3.3	27.7	25.8	73.5	39.8	8.0	9.1
$100,000 or more	100.0	100.0	16.8	32.3	12.2	56.6	44.8	88.6	50.1	15.8	12.7
Age of householder											
Under age 35	88.6	84.6	6.2	17.2	1.0	13.1	12.2	39.8	18.0	1.9	10.1
Aged 35 to 44	93.3	90.5	9.4	24.9	1.5	18.9	16.0	59.5	29.0	3.9	11.8
Aged 45 to 54	94.9	93.5	11.8	21.8	2.8	22.6	23.0	59.2	32.9	6.5	9.1
Aged 55 to 64	95.6	93.9	18.6	18.1	3.5	25.0	15.2	58.3	35.8	6.5	8.4
Aged 65 to 74	95.6	94.1	29.9	16.1	7.2	21.0	18.0	46.1	39.1	11.8	7.3
Aged 75 or older	92.1	89.7	35.9	12.0	5.9	18.0	15.1	16.7	32.6	11.6	6.4

(continued)

(continued from previous page)

	any financial asset	transaction accounts	CDs	savings bonds	bonds	stocks	mutual funds	retirement accounts	life insurance	other managed	other financial
Median value, total households	$22,400	$3,100	$15,000	$1,000	$44,800	$17,500	$25,000	$24,000	$7,300	$31,500	$3,000
Household income											
Under $10,000	$1,100	$500	$7,000	$1,800	–	$14,000	$6,000	$7,500	$3,000	–	$500
$10,000 to $24,999	4,800	1,300	20,000	1,000	$8,400	10,000	26,000	8,000	5,000	$30,000	1,100
$25,000 to $49,999	17,600	2,500	14,500	600	25,000	8,000	11,000	13,000	5,000	15,000	2,000
$50,000 to $99,999	57,200	6,000	13,300	1,000	19,000	15,000	25,000	31,000	9,500	32,000	5,000
$100,000 or more	244,300	19,000	22,000	1,500	108,000	55,000	65,000	93,000	18,000	100,000	25,000
Age of householder											
Under age 35	4,500	1,500	2,500	500	3,000	500	7,000	7,000	2,700	19,400	1,000
Aged 35 to 44	22,900	2,800	8,000	700	55,300	12,000	14,000	21,000	8,500	25,000	2,500
Aged 45 to 54	37,800	4,500	11,500	1,000	31,700	24,000	30,000	34,000	10,000	39,300	6,000
Aged 55 to 64	45,600	4,100	17,000	1,500	100,000	21,000	58,000	46,800	9,500	65,000	10,000
Aged 65 to 74	45,800	5,600	20,000	2,000	52,000	50,000	60,000	38,000	8,500	41,300	6,000
Aged 75 or older	36,600	6,100	30,000	5,000	18,800	50,000	59,000	30,000	5,000	30,000	8,200

Note: (–) means sample is too small to make a reliable estimate.
Source: Federal Reserve Board, Recent Changes in U.S. Family Finances: Results from the 1998 Survey of Consumer Finances, Federal Reserve Bulletin, January 2000

For Most Americans, the Home Is the Most Valuable Asset

The median value of the primary residence stood at $100,000 in 1998.

Although more households own a vehicle (83 percent) than own a home (66 percent), the median value of vehicles was just $10,800 in 1998. For homeowners, the value of their house is greater than the value of any other single asset they own.

The value of Americans' nonfinancial assets depends largely on housing prices. Between 1995 and 1998, the median value of the average household's nonfinancial assets rose 11 percent, after adjusting for inflation, thanks to gains in housing values. All but the youngest age group saw their nonfinancial assets grow.

Not surprisingly, the value of owned homes rises with income. The median value reaches $240,000 among households with incomes of $100,000 or more. By age, housing values peak in the 45-to-54 age group at $120,000. Householders aged 45 to 64 have more nonfinancial assets than those younger or older.

❖ The rising homeownership rate of the 1990s means greater wealth for American men and women.

Nonfinancial Assets of Households, 1995 and 1998

(percentage of households owning nonfinancial assets and median value of assets for owners, by household income and age of householder, 1995 and 1998; percentage point change in ownership and percent change in value of asset, 1995–98; in 1998 dollars)

	percent owning any nonfinancial asset			median value of nonfinancial assets		
	1998	1995	percentage point change 1995–98	1998	1995	percent change 1995–98
Total households	**89.9%**	**90.9%**	**–1.0**	**$97,800**	**$88,100**	**11.0%**
Household income						
Under $10,000	62.7	66.8	–4.1	16,300	14,200	14.8
$10,000 to $24,999	85.9	89.4	–3.5	43,700	45,700	–4.4
$25,000 to $49,999	95.6	96.4	–0.8	83,500	84,000	–0.6
$50,000 to $99,999	98.0	98.8	–0.8	156,300	146,700	6.5
$100,000 or more	98.9	99.5	–0.6	380,000	314,700	20.7
Age of householder						
Under age 35	83.3	87.1	–3.8	22,700	23,200	–2.2
Aged 35 to 44	92.0	90.6	1.4	103,500	102,200	1.3
Aged 45 to 54	92.9	93.6	–0.7	126,800	120,000	5.7
Aged 55 to 64	93.8	93.9	–0.1	126,900	114,700	10.6
Aged 65 to 74	92.0	92.6	–0.6	109,900	100,700	9.1
Aged 75 or older	87.2	89.9	–2.7	96,100	83,900	14.5

Source: Federal Reserve Board, Recent Changes in U.S. Family Finances: Results from the 1998 Survey of Consumer Finances, *Federal Reserve Bulletin, January 2000; calculations by New Strategist*

Nonfinancial Assets of Households, 1998

(percentage of households owning nonfinancial assets, and median value of assets for owners, by household income, age of householder, and type of asset, 1998; numbers in thousands)

	any nonfinancial asset	vehicles	primary residence	other residential property	equity non-residential property	business	other non-financial
Percent owning, total households	**89.9%**	**82.8%**	**66.2%**	**12.8%**	**8.6%**	**11.5%**	**8.5%**
Household income							
Under $10,000	62.7	51.3	34.5	–	–	3.8	2.6
$10,000 to $24,999	85.9	78.0	51.7	5.8	5.0	5.0	5.6
$25,000 to $49,999	95.6	89.6	68.2	11.4	7.6	10.3	9.4
$50,000 to $99,999	98.0	93.6	85.0	19.0	12.0	15.0	10.2
$100,000 or more	98.9	88.7	93.3	37.3	22.6	34.7	17.1
Age of householder							
Under age 35	83.3	78.3	38.9	3.5	2.7	7.2	7.3
Aged 35 to 44	92.0	85.8	67.1	12.2	7.5	14.7	8.8
Aged 45 to 54	92.9	87.5	74.4	16.2	12.2	16.2	9.2
Aged 55 to 64	93.8	88.7	80.3	20.4	10.4	14.3	8.5
Aged 65 to 74	92.0	83.4	81.5	18.4	15.3	10.1	10.3
Aged 75 or older	87.2	69.8	77.0	13.6	8.1	2.7	7.0
Median value, total households	**$97,800**	**$10,800**	**$100,000**	**$65,000**	**$38,000**	**$60,000**	**$10,000**
Household income							
Under $10,000	16,300	4,000	51,000	–	–	37,500	$5,000
$10,000 to $24,999	43,700	5,700	71,900	70,000	25,000	31,100	5,000
$25,000 to $49,999	83,500	10,200	85,000	50,000	28,000	37,500	6,000
$50,000 to $99,999	156,300	16,600	130,000	60,000	30,000	56,000	12,000
$100,000 or more	380,000	26,800	240,000	132,000	114,100	230,000	36,000
Age of householder							
Under age 35	22,700	8,900	84,000	42,500	25,000	34,000	5,000
Aged 35 to 44	103,500	11,400	101,000	45,000	20,000	62,500	8,000
Aged 45 to 54	126,800	12,800	120,000	74,000	45,000	100,000	14,000
Aged 55 to 64	126,900	13,500	110,000	70,000	54,000	62,500	28,000
Aged 65 to 74	109,900	10,800	95,000	75,000	45,000	61,100	10,000
Aged 75 or older	96,100	7,000	85,000	103,000	54,000	40,000	10,000

Note: (–) means sample is too small to make a reliable estimate.
Source: Federal Reserve Board, Recent Changes in U.S. Family Finances: Results from the 1998 Survey of Consumer Finances, *Federal Reserve Bulletin, January 2000*

More Debt for the Average Household

Householders of all ages are taking on more debt.

Americans are much deeper in debt in 1998 than they were in 1995. The median amount owed by the average debtor household stood at $33,300 in 1998, up from $23,400 in 1995 after adjusting for inflation. Thanks to even greater growth in financial and nonfinancial assets during those years, however, households have made gains in net worth.

The percentage of households in debt barely changed between 1995 and 1998, but householders in every age group have taken on more debt. Credit card debt is most common, and 44 percent of households owed a median of $1,700 on their credit cards in 1998. Another 44 percent of households have installment loans (primarily car loans), owing a median of $8,700. Forty-three percent of households have mortgages, owing a median of $62,000.

The percentage of households with debt rises with income. But debt levels decline with age after peaking in the 35-to-54 age group. The expenses of buying a home and raising children explain why 87 to 88 percent of 35-to-54-year-olds are in debt. Householders aged 75 or older are the sole group of which only a minority (just 25 percent) is in debt.

❖ With baby boomers filling the most debt-prone age group, 35 to 54, debt is a fact of life for millions of households. As boomer men and women get older and pay off their debts, they will have more money to spend on entertainment, travel, and other pleasures.

Debt of Households, 1995 and 1998

(percentage of households with debts and median amount of debt for debtors, by household income and age of householder, 1995 and 1998; percentage point change in debt and percent change in amount of debt, 1995–98; in 1998 dollars)

	percent with debt			median amount of debt		
	1998	1995	percentage point change 1995–98	1998	1995	percent change 1995–98
Total households	**74.1%**	**74.5%**	**–0.4**	**$33,300**	**$23,400**	**42.3%**
Household income						
Under $10,000	41.7	47.2	–5.5	4,100	2,200	86.4
$10,000 to $24,999	63.7	65.8	–2.1	8,000	8,400	–4.8
$25,000 to $49,999	79.6	82.2	–2.6	27,100	21,600	25.5
$50,000 to $99,999	89.4	89.4	0.0	75,000	64,100	17.0
$100,000 or more	87.8	85.3	2.5	135,400	114,800	17.9
Age of householder						
Under age 35	81.2	83.5	–2.3	19,200	16,100	19.3
Aged 35 to 44	87.6	86.9	0.7	55,700	40,000	39.3
Aged 45 to 54	87.0	86.3	0.7	48,400	42,400	14.2
Aged 55 to 64	76.4	73.7	2.7	34,600	22,400	54.5
Aged 65 to 74	51.4	53.4	–2.0	11,900	7,400	60.8
Aged 75 or older	24.6	28.4	–3.8	8,000	2,000	300.0

Source: Federal Reserve Board, Recent Changes in U.S. Family Finances: Results from the 1998 Survey of Consumer Finances, *Federal Reserve Bulletin, January 2000; calculations by New Strategist*

Households with Debt, 1998

(percentage of households with debt, and median value of debt for debtors, by household income, age of householder, and type of debt, 1998; numbers in thousands)

	any debt	home secured	other residential property	installment loans	other lines of credit	credit card balances	other debt
Percent with debt, total households	**74.1%**	**43.1%**	**5.1%**	**43.7%**	**2.3%**	**44.1%**	**8.8%**
Household income							
Under $10,000	41.7	8.3	–	25.7	–	20.6	3.6
$10,000 to $24,999	63.7	21.3	1.8	34.4	1.2	37.9	7.0
$25,000 to $49,999	79.6	43.7	4.1	50.0	2.9	49.9	7.7
$50,000 to $99,999	89.4	71.0	7.7	55.0	3.3	56.7	12.2
$100,000 or more	87.8	73.4	16.4	43.2	2.6	40.4	14.8
Age of householder							
Under age 35	81.2	33.2	2.0	60.0	2.4	50.7	9.6
Aged 35 to 44	87.6	58.7	6.7	53.3	3.6	51.3	11.4
Aged 45 to 54	87.0	58.8	6.7	51.2	3.6	52.5	11.1
Aged 55 to 64	76.4	49.4	7.8	37.9	1.6	45.7	8.3
Aged 65 to 74	51.4	26.0	5.1	20.2	–	29.2	4.1
Aged 75 or older	24.6	11.5	1.8	4.2	–	11.2	2.0
Median amount owed, total households	**$33,300**	**$62,000**	**$40,000**	**$8,700**	**$2,500**	**$1,700**	**$3,000**
Household income							
Under $10,000	4,100	16,000	–	4,000	–	1,100	600
$10,000 to $24,999	8,000	34,200	34,000	6,000	1,100	1,000	1,300
$25,000 to $49,999	27,100	47,000	20,000	8,000	3,000	1,900	2,200
$50,000 to $99,999	75,000	75,000	42,000	11,300	2,800	2,400	3,800
$100,000 or more	135,400	123,800	60,000	15,400	5,000	3,200	10,000
Age of householder							
Under age 35	19,200	71,000	55,000	9,100	1,000	1,500	1,700
Aged 35 to 44	55,700	70,000	40,000	7,700	1,400	2,000	3,000
Aged 45 to 54	48,400	68,800	40,000	10,000	3,000	1,800	5,000
Aged 55 to 64	34,600	49,400	41,000	8,300	4,900	2,000	5,000
Aged 65 to 74	11,900	29,000	56,000	6,500	–	1,100	4,500
Aged 75 or older	8,000	21,200	29,800	8,900	–	700	1,700

Note: (–) means sample is too small to make a reliable estimate.
Source: Federal Reserve Board, Recent Changes in U.S. Family Finances: Results from the 1998 Survey of Consumer Finances, *Federal Reserve Bulletin, January 2000*

Homeownership Rate Rises across the Board

All household types and age groups have gained ground.

Americans were more likely to be homeowners in 1998 than in 1990, with the percentage of households owning their home rising from 63.9 to 66.3 percent during those years. The homeownership rate rose for every household type. Among married couples, the homeownership rate rose 3.4 percentage points to 81.5 percent—the highest rate among all household types. The homeownership rate of women who head families rose 3.0 percentage points, while that for men who head families was up only 0.5 percentage points.

The homeownership rate of nonfamily households, which includes people who live alone and those who live with nonrelatives, also rose between 1990 and 1998. The homeownership rate of men and women who live alone rose 3.3 percentage points. The rate for men and women who live with nonrelatives climbed even more steeply.

The homeownership rate increased in every age group between 1990 and 1998, the biggest gains coming among the oldest Americans. While few householders under age 30 own a home, the rate climbs above 50 percent in the 30-to-34 age group. The homeownership rate peaks at 82 percent among householders aged 60 to 74.

❖ The homeownership rate has reached a record high thanks to the economic boom of the past few years. The rate should continue to rise as the large baby-boom generation enters the peak homeowning age groups.

Homeownership rate is highest for married couples

(percent of households that own their home, by type of household, 1998)

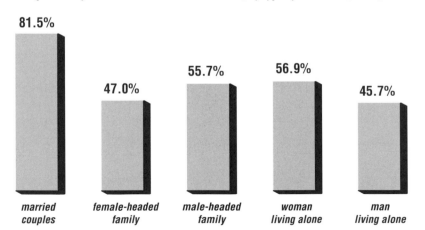

married couples	female-headed family	male-headed family	woman living alone	man living alone
81.5%	47.0%	55.7%	56.9%	45.7%

Homeownership by Type of Household, 1990 and 1998

(percent of householders who own their home by household type, 1990 and 1998; percentage point change 1990–98)

	1998	1990	percentage point change, 1990–98
Total households	66.3%	63.9%	2.4
Family households			
Married couples	81.5	78.1	3.4
Female householder, no spouse present	47.0	44.0	3.0
Male householder, no spouse present	55.7	55.2	0.5
Nonfamily households			
Woman living alone	56.9	53.6	3.3
Man living alone	45.7	42.4	3.3
Other female-headed nonfamily household	40.3	32.5	7.8
Other male-headed nonfamily household	38.2	31.7	6.5

Source: Bureau of the Census, Internet web site <http://www.census.gov/hhes/www/housing/hvs/annual98/ann98t15.html>; calculations by New Strategist

Homeownership by Age of Householder, 1990 and 1998

(percent of householders who own their home by age of householder, 1990 and 1998; percentage point change 1990–98)

	1998	1990	percentage point change, 1990–98
Total households	**66.3%**	**63.9%**	**2.4**
Under age 25	18.2	15.7	2.5
Aged 25 to 29	36.2	35.2	1.0
Aged 30 to 34	53.6	51.8	1.8
Aged 35 to 39	63.7	63.0	0.7
Aged 40 to 44	70.0	69.8	0.2
Aged 45 to 49	73.9	73.9	0.0
Aged 50 to 54	77.8	76.8	1.0
Aged 55 to 59	79.8	78.8	1.0
Aged 60 to 64	82.1	79.8	2.3
Aged 65 to 69	81.9	80.0	1.9
Aged 70 to 74	82.2	78.4	3.8
Aged 75 or older	76.2	72.3	3.9

Source: Bureau of the Census, Internet web site <http://www.census.gov/hhes/www/housing/hvs/annual98/ann98t15.html>; calculations by New Strategist

Men Are More Likely to Have Pension Coverage

The gender gap in pension coverage is greatest in middle age.

Among workers under age 65 with earnings in 1997, 45 percent of men and 40 percent of women were covered by pensions. Pension coverage peaks among workers aged 45 to 64, at 56 percent of men and 51 percent of women.

Among young-adult workers, men and women are about equally likely to be covered by pensions, but coverage in the age group is extremely low—13 percent of men and 11 percent of women. Pension coverage approaches 50 percent for both male and female workers in the 25-to-44 age group. It reaches the majority in the 45-to-64 age group. The gap in pension coverage between the sexes is greatest among workers aged 45 to 64, at 5.4 percentage points. Behind this gap is the fact that many older women are "just a job" workers, who are less likely to have pension coverage than those with careers. As the career-oriented baby-boom women fill the older age groups, the gap in pension coverage between men and women should shrink.

❖ Millions of baby-boom women will have pension coverage in old age because of their propensity to work. Consequently, many of today's dual-income couples will be dual-pension couples in retirement.

Pension Coverage by Age and Sex, 1998

(number and percent of workers with earnings in 1997 who are covered by pensions by age and sex, and percentage point difference between men and women, 1998; numbers in thousands)

	men		women		percentage point difference
	number	*percent*	*number*	*percent*	
Total with coverage	**33,689**	**43.9%**	**27,022**	**39.8%**	**4.1**
Under age 65	33,028	44.6	26,532	40.4	4.2
Aged 15 to 24	1,571	12.6	1,319	11.3	1.3
Aged 25 to 44	18,591	48.0	14,869	44.1	3.9
Aged 45 to 64	12,866	56.3	10,344	50.9	5.4
Aged 65 or older	661	24.2	490	22.3	1.9

Source: Bureau of the Census, Statistical Abstract of the United States, 1999; *calculations by New Strategist*

For More Information

The federal government is a rich source of accurate and reliable data about almost every aspect of American life. Below are the web site addresses of the agencies collecting the data analyzed in this book as well as the phone numbers of agencies and subject specialists, organized alphabetically by topic. Also here is a list of State Data Centers and Small Business Development Centers where researchers can go for help in tracking down demographic and economic information.

Web site addresses

Bureau of the Census .... <http://www.census.gov>

Bureau of Labor Statistics .... <http://www.bls.gov>

Current Population Survey .... <http://www.bls.census.gov/cps>

Consumer Expenditure Survey .... <http://www.bls.gov/csxhome.htm>

Federal Reserve Board .... <http://www.bog.frb.fed.us>

Immigration and Naturalization Service .... <http://www.usdoj.gov/ins>

National Center for Education Statistics .... <http://nces.ed.gov/>

National Center for Health Statistics .... <http://www.cdc.gov/nchswww/>

National Opinion Research Center .... <http://www.norc.uchicago.edu>

Subject Specialists

Absences from work, Staff 202-691-6378

Aging population, Staff 301-457-2422

Ancestry, Staff 301-457-2403

Apportionment, Ed Byerly 301-457-2381

Census, 1990 tabulations, Staff 301-457-2422

Census, 2000

• Address list, Joel Sobel 301-457-1106

• Advertising 301-457-3622

• Aging population, Staff 301-457-2378

• American Community Survey, Larry McGinn 301-457-8050

• American Indian & Alaska Native Program, Sydnee Chattin-Reynolds 301-457-2032

- Annexations/boundary changes, Joe Marinucci 301-457-1099
- Apportionment/redistricting, Marshall Turner, Jr. 301-457-4039
- Armed forces, Staff 301-457-2422
- Census history, William Micarelli 301-457-1167
- Census in the schools, Kim Crews 301-457-3626
- Census methodology, Rajendra Singh 301-457-4199
- Citizenship, Dianne Schmidley 301-457-2403
- Commuting, means of trans., place of work, Gloria Swieczkowski 301-457-2454
- Confidentiality & privacy, Jerry Gates 301-457-2515
- Count review, Paul Campbell 301-457-2390
- Data dissemination, Marian Brady 301-457-4102
- Disability, John McNeil 301-457-3225
- Dress rehearsal, Paulette Lichtman-Panzer 301-457-3961
- Education, Staff 301-457-2464
- Emigration, Staff 301-457-2438
- Employment/unemployment, Staff 301-457-3242
- Field maps, Beverly Davis 301-457-1116
- Foreign born, Dianne Schmidley 301-457-2403
- Geographic entities, Staff 301-457-1099
- Group quarters population, Denise Smith 301-457-2378
- Housing (general information), Staff 301-457-3242
- Hispanic origin/ethnicity/ancestry, Kevin Deardorff 301-457-2403
- Immigration, Dianne Schmidley 301-457-2403
- Income, Kirby Posey 301-457-3243
- Labor force status/work experience, Thomas Palumbo 301-457-3220
- Language spoken in home, Wendy Bruno 301-457-2464
- Living arrangements, Staff 301-457-2465
- Media relations, Neil Tillman 301-457-3691
- Metropolitan areas, concepts & standards, Michael Ratcliffe 301-457-2419
- Microdata files, Amanda Shields 301-457-1326
- Migration, Kris Hansen 301-457-2454
- Occupation/industry, Staff 301-457-3210
- Outlying areas, Idabelle Hovland 301-457-4041
- Partnerships, Brenda August 301-457-1646
- Census 2000 plans, Andrew McNansky 301-457-8567
- Population (general information), Staff 301-457-2422

- Promotion, Jennifer Marks 301-457-3135
- Questionnaire content, Louisa Miller 301-457-2073
- Race, Staff 301-457-2402
- Recruiting, Clifton Taylor, Jr. 301-457-3662
- Residence rules, Karen Mills 301-457-2390
- Sampling, Rajendra Singh 301-457-4199
- Special places/group quarters, Denise Smith 301-457-2378
- Special population, Staff 301-457-2378
- Special tabulations, Marie Pees 301-457-2447
- Undercount, Rajendra Singh 301-457-4199
- Demographic, Greg Robinson 301-457-2103
- Urban/rural, Ryan Short 301-457-1099
- User maps, Staff 301-457-1101
- U.S. citizens abroad, Staff 301-457-2422
- Veteran status, Thomas Palumbo 301-457-3220
- Voting districts, Doug Geverdt 301-457-2464
- Women, Staff 301-457-2378
- ZIP codes, Staff 301-457-2422

Census Bureau Customer Services 301-457-4100

Child care, Martin O'Connell/Kristin Smith 301-457-2465

Children, Staff 301-457-2465

Citizenship, Staff 301-457-2403

College graduate job outlook, Tiny Shelley 202-691-5726

Commuting, Phil Salopek/Celia Boertlein 301-457-2454

Consumer Expenditure Survey, Staff 202-691-6900

Contingent workers, Sharon Cohany 202-691-6378

County population, Staff 301-457-2422

Crime, Marilyn Monahan 301-457-3925

Current Population Survey (general information), Staff 301-457-2408

Demographic surveys, Staff 301-457-2422

Disability, Jack McNeil 301-457-3225

Discouraged workers, Staff 202-691-6378

Displaced workers, Steve Hipple 202-691-6378

Economic Census, 1997

- Accommodations, Fay Dorsett 301-457-2687
- Commodity Flow Survey, Jim Fowler 301-457-2108

Homeless, Audrian Gray 301-457-3977

Household wealth, Staff 301-457-3242

Households and families, Staff 301-457-2465

Housing

- Affordability, Peter Fronczek 301-457-3199
- American Housing Survey, Jane Kneessi 301-457-3235
- Census, Staff 301-457-3237
- Homeownership and vacancy data, Linda Cavanaugh 301-457-3199
- Market absorption, Alan Friedman 301-457-3199
- Residential finance, Howard Savage 301-457-3199

Immigration, (general information), Staff 301-457-2422

Immigration, illegal, Staff 301-457-2438

Income statistics, Staff 301-457-3242

Industry

- Business expenditures, Sheldon Ziman 301-457-3315
- Business investment, Charles Funk 301-457-3324
- Characteristics of business owners, Valerie Strang 301-457-3316
- County business patterns, Paul Hanczaryk 301-457-2580
- Economic studies, Arnold Reznek 301-457-1856
- Enterprise statistics, Eddie Salyers 301-457-3318
- Industry and commodity classification, James Kristoff 301-457-4631
- Mineral industries, Pat Horning 301-457-4680
- Minority/women-owned businesses, Valerie Strang 301-457-3316
- North American Industry Class. Sys., Bruce Goldhirsch 301-457-2559
- Puerto Rico and outlying areas, Irma Harahush 301-457-3314
- Quarterly Financial Report, Ronald Lee 301-457-3343
- Statistics of U.S. Businesses, Melvin Cole 301-457-8641

International statistics

- Africa, Asia, Latin Am., North Am., Oceania, Patricia Rowe 301-457-1358
- Aging population, Victoria Velkoff 301-457-1371
- China, People's Republic, Loraine West 301-457-1363
- Europe, former Soviet Union, Marc Rubin 301-457-1362
- Health, Karen Stanecki 301-457-1406
- International database, Pat Dickerson 301-457-1403
- Technical assistance & training, Diana Lopez-Meisel 301-457-1444
- Women in development, Victoria Velkoff 301-457-1371

Race (concepts and interpretation), Staff 301-457-2402

Reapportionment and redistricting, Marshall Turner, Jr. 301-457-4015

Sampling methods, Census, Rajendra Singh 301-457-4199

School Districts, 1990 Census, NCES 202-219-1627

School Enrollment, Staff 301-457-2464

Seasonal adjustment methodology, Robert McIntire 202-691-6345

Special censuses, Josephine Ruffin 301-457-1429

Special surveys, Sarah Higgins 301-457-3801

Special tabulations, Marie Pees 301-457-2447

State population and projections, Staff 301-457-2422

Survey of Income & Program Participation (SIPP), Staff 301-457-3242

Undercount, demographic analysis, Gregg Robinson 301-457-2103

Union membership, Staff 202-691-6378

Urban/rural, Michael Ratcliff/Rodger Johnson 301-457-2419

Veterans in the labor force, Staff 202-691-6378

Veterans' status, Staff 301-457-3242

Voters, characteristics, Lynne Casper 301-457-2445

Voting age population, Staff 301-457-2465

Weekly earnings, Staff 202-691-6378

Women, Staff 301-457-2378

Women in the labor force, Staff 202-691-6378

Work experience, Staff 202-691-6378

Working poor, Staff 202-691-6378

Youth, students, and dropouts, Staff 202-691-6378

Census Regional Offices

Atlanta, GA 404-730-3833

Boston, MA 617-424-0510

Charlotte, NC 704-344-6144

Chicago, IL 312-353-9747

Dallas, TX 214-655-3050

Denver, CO 303-969-7750

Detroit, MI 313-259-1875

Kansas City, KS 913-551-6711

Los Angeles, CA 818-904-6339

New York, NY 212-264-4730

Philadelphia, PA 215-656-7578

Seattle, WA 206-553-5837

State Data Centers and Business/Industry Data Centers

Below are listed the State Data Center and Business/Industry Data Center (BIDC) lead agency contacts only. Lead data centers are usually state government agencies, universities, or libraries that head up a network of affiliate centers. Every state has a State Data Center. The asterisks (*) identify states that also have a Business/Industry Data Center. In some states, one agency serves as the lead for both the State Data Center and the Business/Industry Data Center. The Business/Industry Data Center is listed separately if there is a separate agency serving as the lead.

Alabama, Annette Watters, University of Alabama 205-348-6191

Alaska, Kathryn Lizik, Department of Labor 907-465-2437

*Arizona, Betty Jeffries, Department of Econ. Security 602-542-5984

Arkansas, Sarah Breshears, University of Arkansas-Little Rock 501-569-8530

California, Linda Gage, Department of Finance 916-323-4086

Colorado, Rebecca Picaso, Department of Local Affairs 303-866-2156

Connecticut, Bill Kraynak, Office of Policy & Management 860-418-6230

*Delaware, Rob Skomorucha, Econ. Development Office 302-739-4271

District of Columbia, Herb Bixhorn, Mayor's Office of Planning 202-442-7603

*Florida, Pam Schenker, Dept. of Labor & Employment Security 850-488-1048

Georgia, Robert Giacomini, Office of Planning & Budget 404-656-0911

Hawaii, Jan Nakamoto, Dept. of Business, Econ. Dev., & Tourism 808-586-2493

Idaho, Alan Porter, Department of Commerce 208-334-2470

Illinois, Suzanne Ebetsch, Bureau of the Budget 217-782-1381

*Indiana, Roberta Brooken, State Library 317-232-3733

Indiana BIDC, Carol Rogers, Business Research Center 317-274-2205

Iowa, Beth Henning, State Library 515-281-4350

Kansas, Marc Galbraith, State Library 913-296-3296

*Kentucky, Ron Crouch, University of Louisville 502-852-7990

Louisiana, Karen Paterson, Office of Planning & Budget 504-342-7410

*Maine, Eric Vonmagnus, State Planning Office 207-287-1476

*Maryland, Jane Traynham, Office of Planning 410-767-4450

*Massachusetts, John Gaviglio, Institute. for Social and Econ. Res. 413-545-3460

Michigan, Carolyn Lauer, Dept. of Management & Budget 517-373-7910

*Minnesota, David Birkholz, State Demographer's Office 651-296-2557

Minnesota BIDC, Barbara Ronningen, State Dem. Office 651-297-3255

*Mississippi, Rachael McNeely, University of Mississippi 601-232-7288

Mississippi BIDC, Deloise Tate, Dept. of Econ. & Comm. Dev. 601-359-3593

*Missouri, Debra Pitts, State Library 573-526-7648

Missouri BIDC, Fred Goss, Small Business Dev. Centers 573-341-4559

*Montana, Jan Clark, Department of Commerce 406-444-4393

Nebraska, Jerome Deichert, University of Nebraska-Omaha ,,,,,,,,,,,,,,,,,,,,, 402-554-2134

Nevada, Susan Kendall, State Library & Archives 775-684-3303

New Hampshire, Thomas Duffy, Office of State Planning 603-271-2155

*New Jersey, David Joye, Department of Labor 609-984-2595

*New Mexico, Kevin Kargacin, University of New Mexico 505-277-6626

*New York, Staff, Department of Economic Development 518-292-5300

*North Carolina, Staff, State Library 919-733-3270

North Dakota, Richard Rathge, State University 701-231-8621

*Ohio, Barry Bennett, Department of Development 614-466-2115

*Oklahoma, Jeff Wallace, Department of Commerce 405-815-5184

Oregon, George Hough, Portland State Univ 503-725-5159

*Pennsylvania, Diane Shoop, Penn. State Univ.-Harrisburg 717-948-6336

Puerto Rico, Lillian Torres Aguirre, Planning Bd. 787-728-4430

Rhode Island, Mark Brown, Department of Administration 401-222-6183

South Carolina, Mike MacFarlane, Budget & Control Board 803-734-3780

South Dakota, Nancy Craig, Univ. of South Dakota 605-677-5287

Tennessee, Becky Vickers, State Planning Office 423-974-6080

Texas, Steve Murdock, Texas A&M University 409-845-5115

*Utah, David Abel, Office of Planning & Budget 801-538-1036

Vermont, Sharon Whitaker, Univ. of Vermont 802-656-3021

*Virginia, Don Lillywhite, Virginia Employment Commission 804-786-8026

*Washington, Yi Zhao, Office of Financial Management 360-586-2504

*West Virginia, Delphine Coffey, Office of Comm. & Industrial Dev. 304-558-4010

West Virginia BIDC, Brian Lego, Center for Econ. Research 304-293-7836

*Wisconsin, Robert Naylor, Department of Administration 608-266-1927

Wisconsin BIDC, Dan Veroff, Univ. of Wisconsin 608-265-9545

Wyoming, Wenlin Liu, Dept. of Administration & Information 307-777-7504

Glossary

adjusted for inflation Income or a change in income that has been adjusted for the rise in the cost of living, or the consumer price index (CPI-U-XI).

Asian In this book, the term "Asian" includes both Asians and Pacific Islanders.

baby boom Americans born between 1946 and 1964. Baby boomers were aged 36 to 54 in 2000.

baby bust Americans born between 1965 and 1976, also known as Generation X. In 2000, baby busters were aged 24 to 35.

central cities The largest city in a metropolitan area is called the central city. The balance of the metropolitan area outside the central city is regarded as the "suburbs."

Consumer Expenditure Survey The Consumer Expenditure Survey (CEX) is an ongoing study of the day-to-day spending of American households administered by the Bureau of Labor Statistics. The survey is used to update prices for the Consumer Price Index. The CEX includes an interview survey and a diary survey. The average spending figures shown in this book are the integrated data from both the diary and interview components of the survey. Two separate, nationally representative samples are used for the interview and diary surveys. For the interview survey, about 5,000 consumer units are interviewed on a rotating panel basis each quarter for five consecutive quarters. For the diary survey, 5,000 consumer units keep weekly diaries of spending for two consecutive weeks.

consumer unit *(on spending tables only)* For convenience, the terms consumer unit and household are used interchangeably in the spending section of this book, although consumer units are somewhat different from the Census Bureau's households. Consumer units are all related members of a household, or financially independent members of a household. A household may include more than one consumer unit.

Current Population Survey A nationally representative survey of the civilian noninstitutional population aged 15 or older. It is taken monthly by the Census Bureau, collecting information from 50,000 households on employment and unemployment. In March of each year, the survey includes a demographic supplement that is the source of most national data on the characteristics of Americans, such as their educational attainment, living arrangements, and incomes.

dual-earner couple A married couple in which both husband and wife are in the labor force.

earnings One type of income. *See also* Income.

employed All civilians who did any work as a paid employee or farmer/self-employed worker, or who worked 15 hours or more as an unpaid farm worker or in a family-owned business, during the reference period. All those who have jobs but who are temporarily absent from their jobs due to illness, bad weather, vacation, labor management dispute, or personal reasons are considered employed.

expenditure The transaction cost including excise and sales taxes of goods and services acquired during the survey period. The full cost of each purchase is recorded even though full payment may not have been made at the date of purchase. Average expenditure figures may be artificially low for infrequently purchased items such as cars because figures are calculated using all consumer units within a demographic segment rather than just purchasers. Expenditure estimates include money spent on gifts for others.

family A group of two or more people (one of whom is the householder) related by birth, marriage, or adoption and living in the same household.

family household A household maintained by a householder who lives with one or more people related to him or her by blood, marriage, or adoption.

female/male householder A woman or man who maintains a household without a spouse present. May head family or nonfamily households.

full-time employment Full-time is 35 or more hours of work per week during a majority of the weeks worked during the preceding calendar year.

full-time, year-round Indicates 50 or more weeks of full-time employment during the preceding calendar year.

General Social Survey The General Social Survey (GSS) is a biennial survey of the attitudes of Americans taken by the University of Chicago's National Opinion Research Center (NORC). NORC is the oldest nonprofit, university-affiliated national survey research facility in the nation. It conducts the GSS through face-to-face interviews with an independently drawn, representative sample of 1,500 to 3,000 noninstitutionalized English-speaking people aged 18 or older who live in the United States.

Generation X Americans born between 1965 and 1976, also known as the baby bust generation. In 2000, Generation Xers were aged 24 to 35.

geographic regions The four major regions and nine census divisions of the United States are the state groupings as shown below:

Northeast:
—New England: Connecticut, Maine, Massachusetts, New Hampshire, Rhode Island, and Vermont
—Middle Atlantic: New Jersey, New York, and Pennsylvania

Midwest:
—East North Central: Illinois, Indiana, Michigan, Ohio, and Wisconsin
—West North Central: Iowa, Kansas, Minnesota, Missouri, Nebraska, North Dakota, and South Dakota

South:
—South Atlantic: Delaware, District of Columbia, Florida, Georgia, Maryland, North Carolina, South Carolina, Virginia, and West Virginia

—East South Central: Alabama, Kentucky, Mississippi, and Tennessee
—West South Central: Arkansas, Louisiana, Oklahoma, and Texas

West:
—Mountain: Arizona, Colorado, Idaho, Montana, Nevada, New Mexico, Utah, and Wyoming
—Pacific: Alaska, California, Hawaii, Oregon, and Washington

Hispanic People or householders who identify their origin as Mexican, Puerto Rican, Central or South American, or some other Hispanic origin.

People of Hispanic origin may be of any race. In other words, there are black Hispanics, white Hispanics, Asian Hispanics, and Native American Hispanics.

household All the people who occupy a housing unit. A household includes the related family members and all unrelated people, if any, such as lodgers, foster children, wards, or employees who share the housing unit. A person living alone is counted as a household. A group of unrelated people who share a housing unit as roommates or unmarried partners is also counted as a household. Households do not include group quarters such as college dormitories, prisons, or nursing homes.

household, race/ethnicity of Households are categorized according to the race or ethnicity of the householder only.

householder The householder is the person (or one of the persons) in whose name the housing unit is owned or rented or, if there is no such person, any adult member. With married couples, the householder may be either the husband or wife. The householder is the reference person for the household.

householder, age of The age of the householder is used to categorize households into age groups such as those used in this book. Married couples, for example, are classified according to the age of either the husband or wife, depending on which one identified him or herself as the householder.

income Money received in the preceding calendar year by each person aged 15 or older from each of the following sources: (1) earnings from longest job (or self-employment); (2) earnings from jobs other than longest job; (3) unemployment compensation; (4) workers' compensation; (5) Social Security; (6) Supplemental Security income; (7) public assistance; (8) veterans' pay-

ments; (9) survivor benefits; (10) disability benefits; (11) retirement pensions; (12) interest; (13) dividends; (14) rents and royalties or estates and trusts; (15) educational assistance; (16) alimony; (17) child support; (18) financial assistance from outside the household, and other periodic income. Income is reported in several ways in this book. Household income is the combined income of all household members. Income of persons is all income accruing to a person from all sources. Earnings is the amount of money a person receives from his or her job.

industry Refers to the industry in which a person worked longest in the preceding calendar year.

job tenure The length of time a worker has been employed continuously by the same employer.

labor force The labor force tables in this book show the civilian labor force only. The labor force includes both the employed and the unemployed (people who are looking for work). People are counted as in the labor force if they were working or looking for work during the reference week in which the Census Bureau fields the Current Population Survey.

labor force participation rate The percent of the civilian noninstitutional population that is in the civilian labor force, which includes both the employed and the unemployed.

married couples with or without children under age 18 Refers to married couples with or without own children under age 18 living in the same household. Couples without children under age 18 may be parents of grown children who live elsewhere, or they could be childless couples.

median The median is the amount that divides the population or households into two equal portions: one below and one above the median.

Medians can be calculated for income, age, and many other characteristics.

median income The amount that divides the income distribution into two equal groups, half having incomes above the median, half having incomes below the median. The medians for households or families are based on all households or families. The median for people are based on all people aged 15 or older with income.

metropolitan area An area qualifies for recognition as a metropolitan area if: (1) it includes a city of at least 50,000 population, or (2) it includes a Census Bureau-defined urbanized area of at least 50,000 with a total metropolitan population of at least 100,000 (75,000 in New England). In addition to the county containing the main city or urbanized area, a metropolitan area may include other counties having strong commuting ties to the central county.

millennial generation Americans born between 1977 and 1994. Millennials were aged 6 to 23 in 2000.

nonfamily household A household maintained by a householder who lives alone or who lives with people to whom he or she is not related.

nonfamily householder A householder who lives alone or with nonrelatives.

non-Hispanic People who do not identify themselves as Hispanic are classified as non-Hispanic. Non-Hispanics may be of any race.

nonmetropolitan area Counties that are not classified as metropolitan areas.

occupation Occupational classification is based on the kind of work a person did at his or her job during the previous calendar year. If a person changed jobs during the year, the data refer to the occupation of the job held the longest during that year.

outside central city The portion of a metropolitan county or counties that falls outside of the central city or cities; generally regarded as the suburbs.

own children Own children are sons and daughters, including stepchildren and adopted children, of the householder. The totals include never-married children living away from home in college dormitories.

owner occupied A housing unit is owner occupied if the owner lives in the unit, even if it is mortgaged or not fully paid for. A cooperative or condominium unit is owner occupied only if the owner lives in it. All other occupied units are classified as renter occupied.

part-time employment Part-time is less than 35 hours of work per week in a majority of the weeks worked during the year.

percent change The change (either positive or negative) in a measure that is expressed as a proportion of the starting measure. When median income changes from $20,000 to $25,000, for example, this is a 25 percent increase.

percentage point change The change (either positive or negative) in a value which is already expressed as a percentage. When a labor force participation rate changes from 70 percent of 75 percent, for example, this is a 5 percentage point increase.

poverty level The official income threshold below which families and persons are classified as living in poverty. The threshold rises each year with inflation and varies depending on family size and age of householder. In 1998, the poverty threshold for a family of four was $16,660.

proportion or share The value of a part expressed as a percentage of the whole. If there are 4 million people aged 25 and 3 million of them are white, then the white proportion is 75 percent.

race Race is self-reported and appears in four categories in this book: white, black, Native American, and Asian. A household is assigned the race of the householder.

rounding Percentages are rounded to the nearest tenth of a percent; therefore, the percentages in a distribution do not always add exactly to 100.0 percent. The totals, however, are always shown as 100.0. Moreover, individual figures are rounded to the nearest thousand without being adjusted to group totals, which are independently rounded; percentages are based on the unrounded numbers.

self-employment A person is categorized as self-employed if he or she was self-employed in the job held longest during the reference period. People who report self-employment from a second job are excluded, but those who report wage-and-salary income from a second job are included. Unpaid workers in family businesses are excluded. Self-employment statistics include only nonagricultural workers and exclude people who work for themselves in incorporated businesses.

sex ratio The number of men per 100 women.

suburbs *See* Outside central city.

Survey of Consumer Finances The Survey of Consumer Finances is a triennial survey taken by the Federal Reserve Board. It collects data on the assets, debts, and net worth of American households. For the 1998 survey, the Federal Reserve Board interviewed a random sample of 2,813 households and a supplemental sample of 1,496 wealthy households based on tax-return data.

unemployed Unemployed people are those who, during the survey period, had no employment but were available and looking for work. Those who were laid off from their jobs and were waiting to be recalled are also classified as unemployed.

work experience Work experience is based on work for pay or work without pay on a family-operated farm or business at any time during the previous year, on a part-time or full-time basis.

Bibliography

Bureau of the Census

    Internet web site <http://www.censu.gov>

    —1999 Current Population Survey, unpublished data

    —*Educational Attainment in the United States: March 1998*, detailed tables from Current Population Reports, P20-513, 1998

    —*Geographic Mobility: March 1997 to March 1998*, Current Population Reports, P20-520, 2000

    —*Household and Family Characteristics: March 1998*, detailed tables from Current Population Reports, P20-515, 1998

    —Housing Vacancy Surveys, unpublished data

    —*Marital Status and Living Arrangements: March 1998*, Current Population Reports, P20-514, 1999

    —*Money Income in the United States: 1998*, Current Population Reports, P60-206, 1999

    —*Preliminary Estimates on Caregiving from Wave 7 of the 1996 Survey of Income and Program Participation*, John M. McNeil, No. 231, Survey of Income and Program Participation, 1999

    —*Projections of the Resident Population of the United States by Age, Sex, Race, and Hispanic Origin: 1999 to 2100*, 2000

    —*Poverty in the United States: 1998*, Current Population Reports, P60-207, 1999

    —*Projections of the Total Population of States: 1995 to 2025*, PPL-47, 1996

    —*School Enrollment—Social and Economic Characteristics of Students: October 1998*, Current Population Reports, P20-521, 1999

    —*Statistical Abstract of the United States: 1999* (119th edition) Washington, D.C. 1999

    —*Voting and Registration in the Election of November 1996*, Current Population Reports, P20-504, 1998

Bureau of Labor Statistics

    Internet web site <http://www.bls.gov>

    —1998 Consumer Expenditure Survey, unpublished data

    —*Contingent and Alternative Employment Arrangements*, 1999

    —*Employment and Earnings*, January 1991 and January 2000

    —*Handbook of Labor Statistics*, Bulletin 2340, 1989

    —*Monthly Labor Review*, November 1999

    —*Work at Home in 1997*, USDL 98-93

Federal Reserve Board

Internet web site <http://www.bog.frb.fed.us>

—*Recent Changes in U.S. Family Finances: Results from the 1998 Survey of Consumer Finances*, Federal Reserve Bulletin, January 2000

Higher Education Research Institute, University of California at Los Angeles

Internet web site <http://www.gseis.ucla.edu/heri>

—*The American Freshman: National Norms for Fall 1998*, 1999

Immigration and Naturalization Service

Internet web site <http://www.usdoj.gov/ins>

—*Statistical Yearbook of the Immigration and Naturalization Service 1997*, 1999

National Center for Education Statistics

Internet web site <http://nces.ed.gov>

—*Degrees and Other Awards Conferred by Title IV Eligible Degree-granting Institutions, 1996–97*, NCES 2000–174, 1999

—*Digest of Education Statistics 1998*, NCES 1999036, 1999

—*Projections of Education Statistics to 2009*, NCES 1999038, 1999

National Center for Health Statistics

Internet web site <http://www.cdc.gov/nchswww>

—*1997 Summary: National Hospital Discharge Survey*, Advance Data, No. 308, 1999

—*Adoption, Adoption Seeking, and Relinquishment for Adoption in the United States*, Advance Data, No. 306, 1999

—*Births: Final Data for 1997*, National Vital Statistics Report, Vol. 47, No. 18, 1999

—*Births and Deaths: Preliminary Data for 1998*, National Vital Statistics Report, Vol. 47, No. 25, 1999

—*Current Estimates from the National Health Interview Survey, 1996*, Series 10, No. 200, 1999

—*Deaths: Final Data for 1997*, National Vital Statistics Report, Vol. 47, No. 19, 1999

—*Health United States*, 1998 and 1999

National Opinion Research Center

Internet web site <http://www.norc.uchicago.edu>

—1994, 1996, and 1998 General Social Surveys, unpublished data

U.S. Department of Agriculture

Internet web site <http://www.barc.usda.gov

—ARS Food Surveys Research Group, Data Tables: Results from USDA's 1994–96 Diet and Health Knowledge Survey, 1999

—ARS Food Surveys Research Group, Supplementary Data Tables: USDA's 1994–96 Continuing Survey of Food Intakes by Individuals, 1999

Index